W9-BSV-906

Over 600 Super-Quick Recipes and Hints!

EVERY BUSY COOK needs time-saving strategies for putting wholesome, delicious, family-pleasing food on the table. And you get *hundreds* of them in this 11th edition of our ever-popular cookbook series.

2009 Quick Cooking Annual Recipes features every single fast-to-fix dish that appeared in *Simple & Delicious* magazine during 2008...plus dozens of the magazine's helpful hints. That adds up to more than 600 recipes and hints—all here at your fingertips!

With hundreds of gorgeous, full-color photos showing the prepared recipes, this can't-miss collection makes it as easy as ever for you to serve home-cooked, scrumptious meals every day of the week.

Here's what else you'll find inside:

Chapters That Meet Your Needs. We divided the recipes in this book into 21 chapters that make sense for busy cooks. Just turn to whatever chapter fits your needs, and you'll enjoy plenty of mouth-watering options. (See page 3 for a complete list of chapters.)

For example, when you have only 10 minutes to spare in the kitchen, try Simple Shrimp Scampi, Parmesan-Coated Brie, Baked Beans with Ham, White Chili, Smooth Chocolate Fondue or any of the 14 other super-quick dishes in the "10 Minutes to the Table" chapter.

Or, on hectic weekdays when your family is hungry for dinner and the clock is ticking, see the "30 Minutes to Mealtime" chapter for 26 complete menus that are table-ready in half an hour or less.

Six-Week Menu Planner. The experts in our Test Kitchen put together 6 full weeks of Monday-through-Friday dinners, complete with a shopping list for each week. Just follow these handy meal plans to enjoy weeks of stress-free suppers. (This chapter starts on page 108.)

Contest-Winning Dishes. You get all of the standout specialties that earned honors in the six national recipe contests held last year: Warm and Welcoming Casseroles, It's All About the Dough, All Fired Up, Easy Freezer Desserts, Halloween Spooktacular and Greatest Gift Recipe. Turn to page 4 to "meet" the Grand Prize winners and see where each contest-winning recipe is located in the book.

Special Sections Built for You. In the "On-the-Go Odds 'n' Ends" chapter, you'll find recipes grouped by theme—grilling, cooking with leftovers and stovetop suppers. Plus, you'll see an all-new "Cooking for 2" section filled with smaller-yield recipes sized right for small households.

Reader-Friendly Indexes. We've listed every recipe in two handy indexes. (See page 316.) The general index lists each recipe by category and/or major ingredient. The alphabetical listing is great when you're looking for a specific dish. In both indexes, you'll find a red checkmark (✓) next to recipes that include Nutrition Facts and Diabetic Exchanges.

Every rapid recipe and kitchen tip in this collection was specially selected with time-crunched cooks in mind. So no matter how full your schedule is, you and your loved ones will be able to enjoy this indispensable treasury right away—and for many years to come!

2009 Quick Cooking Annual Recipes

Editor: Michelle Bretl
Art Director: Gretchen Trautman
Vice President/Books: Heidi Reuter Lloyd
Senior Editor/Books: Mark Hagen
Layout Designers: Nancy Novak (lead), Emma Acevedo, Kathy Crawford, Catherine Fletcher
Proofreader: Linne Bruskewitz
Editorial Assistant: Barb Czysz
Indexer: Jean Duerst

Taste of Home Books
©2009 Reiman Media Group, Inc.
5400 S. 60th St., Greendale WI 53129

International Standard Book Number (10): 0-89821-712-1
International Standard Book Number (13): 978-0-89821-712-4
International Standard Serial Number: 1522-6603

PICTURED ON THE FRONT COVER: Chocolate Silk Pie (p. 210), Country Fried Chicken (p. 310), Mashed Potatoes Supreme (p. 132) and Lemon-Pepper Green Beans (p. 23). Cover photography by Lori Foy. Food styled by Tamara Kaufman. Set styled by Jenny Bradley Vent.

PICTURED ON THE BACK COVER: Minty Cream Cheese Bars (p. 211), Sausage & Beans with Rice (p. 247) and Hearty Short Ribs (p. 164).

For other *Taste of Home* books and products, visit ***www.ShopTasteofHome.com***.

taste of home simple & delicious

Editor: Mary Spencer
Managing Editor: Mary C. Hanson
Art Director: Nicholas Mork
Food Editor: Amy Welk-Thieding RD
Recipe Asset Management System: Coleen Martin (Manager), Sue A. Jurack (Specialist)
Recipe Editors: Mary King, Christine Rukavena
Associate Editors: John McMillan, Elizabeth Russell
Copy Editor: S.K. Enk
Layout Designer: Kristen Johnson
Editorial Assistant: Marilyn Iczkowski
Executive Assistant: Marie Brannon
Test Kitchen Manager: Karen Scales
Associate Food Editors: Alicia Bozewicz RD, Tina Johnson, Marie Parker, Annie Rundle
Test Kitchen Coordinator: Kristy Martin
Test Kitchen Associates: Megan Taylor, Laura Scharnott
Test Kitchen Assistants: Rita Krajcir, Sue Megonigle
Photographers: Rob Hagen (Senior), Dan Roberts, Jim Wieland, Lori Foy
Set Stylists: Jenny Bradley Vent (Senior), Stephanie Marchese (Senior), Dee Dee Jacq, Melissa Haberman
Food Stylists: Sarah Thompson (Senior), Tamara Kaufman, Kaitlyn Besasie
Assistant Food Stylists: Alynna Malson, Shannon Roum, Leah Rekau
Photo Studio Coordinator: Kathy Swaney

...

Senior Vice President/Editor in Chief: Catherine Cassidy
Chief Marketing Officer: Lisa Karpinski
Creative Director: Ardyth Cope
Food Director: Diane Werner RD

...

President and Chief Executive Officer: Mary G. Berner
President, RDA Food & Entertaining: Suzanne M. Grimes

Contents

Recipe Contests Yield Quick Winning Dishes....4
See a list of all the contest-winning recipes from the past year—and meet the Grand Prize cooks.

Chapter 1: Readers' Favorite Fast Meals ...6
These on-the-go moms share the fast-to-fix dinners and shortcut ideas they regularly rely on.

Chapter 2: Holiday and Seasonal Pleasers....20
Celebrate special occasions throughout the year with these festive meals, sweets and more.

Chapter 3: 30 Minutes to Mealtime 42
Each of the 26 complete menus in this big chapter can be prepared in just 30 minutes or less.

Chapter 4: Fun Foods For Kids.................70
These playful yet wholesome dishes will make kids smile—and clean their plates, too.

Chapter 5: Give Me 5 or Fewer 80
Although these rapid recipes have a mere five ingredients or fewer, they're all big on flavor.

Chapter 6: 10 Minutes to the Table 98
Next time you're "down to the wire," turn here.

Chapter 7: Shop Once...Eat All Week 108
Enjoy 6 weeks of Monday-through-Friday dinners and complete shopping lists.

Chapter 8: Speedy Sides and Salads......128
Rounding out family meals is a cinch with these easy but pleasing accompaniments.

Chapter 9: Breads in a Jiffy 146
Quick breads and bread machines give you home-baked goodness with minimal kitchen time.

Chapter 10: Slow-Cooked Sensations....156
Take advantage of your slow cooker to prepare effortless, flavorful meals.

Chapter 11: Breakfast & Brunch Favorites................................168
You don't need to scramble in order to serve your family a rise-and-shine breakfast.

Chapter 12: Snappy Soups & Sandwiches 178
This popular duo is a classic mealtime mainstay you can serve your family in a snap.

Chapter 13: Easy Half-Hour Entrees 190
It takes just 30 minutes—or less—to get each of these delicious main dishes on the dinner table.

Chapter 14: Delectable Desserts............208
Before you know it, you'll have a tempting selection of treats to share—with time to spare!

Chapter 15: Make-Ahead Marvels 228
Take a few moments to make these do-ahead delights now and reap the rewards later.

Chapter 16: Casseroles and Oven Suppers.................................238
Comforting casseroles and other hot-from-the-oven dishes always satisfy.

Chapter 17: Fast, Delicious...and Nutritious..252
If you're trying to reduce fat, sugar or salt in your diet, these lightened-up foods will fit right in.

Chapter 18: Plan an Instant Party 262
Revel in these fun-filled but fast party recipes your family and friends will love.

Chapter 19: Swift Snacks & Easy Appetizers.................................272
When you want taste-tempting munchies, these quick bites will satisfy your appetite.

Chapter 20: Test Kitchen Secrets...........284
Our expert home economists share clever tips and techniques to speed up your cooking.

Chapter 21: On-the-Go Odds & Ends....302
Here's a collection of reliable theme-related recipes that are tops for taste.

General Recipe Index 316
Every recipe in the book is listed according to food category, major ingredient and/or cooking method.

Alphabetical Index................................332
Every recipe in the book is listed alphabetically.

Recipe Contests Yield Quick Winning Dishes

FOR THE SIX national recipe contests held by *Simple & Delicious* magazine during the past year, busy cooks from across the country submitted their very best time-saving recipes.

Wondering which delicious, fast-to-finish dishes were deemed tops in those contests? You can find out by checking the special section here.

On these two pages, we've featured the six talented cooks who took home the Grand Prize in a 2008 contest. We've also let you know where to find their first-place recipes in this book, so you can turn to those celebrated dishes right away...and even prepare them for your family tonight!

Plus, we've added the 11 other recipes that were honored in each contest. You get a complete listing of dishes—all 72 of them—that our panel of judges selected as contest winners during the past year.

Because we've included the page numbers for all of the runners-up, too, you'll easily be able to locate each prize-winning recipe in this book. Dozens of top-honor dishes are right at your fingertips!

From Backyard Grills to Halloween Thrills

The contest topics during the past year yielded a wide range of reader recipes. But all of those dishes have one thing in common—they're quick-to-fix foods that suit busy cooks' lifestyles.

In the "Warm and Welcoming Casseroles" contest, readers relied on the oven to get comforting family suppers on the table fast. And "It's All About the Dough" put convenient refrigerated bread dough to especially yummy uses.

Love to get out that grill? Choose from the fresh-air foods highlighted in the "All Fired Up" contest. And on those warm summer days, you'll want to see "Easy Freezer Desserts" for cool make-ahead treats you just take out, serve and enjoy.

When you're planning for October parties, look to "Halloween Spooktacular" for easy goodies that create chills and thrills. You can get started on Christmas, too, with the guaranteed-to-please edible presents in "Greatest Gift Recipe."

Just pick your favorites from this exciting array of prize-winning recipes...or go ahead and try each one. Either way, you'll have standout sensations you and your family are sure to love.

Winning Recipe Was Fresh from the Oven

TO THOSE who know her well, it comes as no surprise that Susan Davis won the "Warm and Welcoming Casseroles" recipe contest. This German teacher likes to cook for friends and family, and her Grand Prize-winning Zucchini Crescent Pie is a popular request.

"The recipe came from my mother," Susan relates from Ann Arbor, Michigan. "Everyone I serve it to loves the fact that it's both delicious and full of wholesome ingredients. Plus, it's nice any time of day."

Warm and Welcoming Casseroles Contest Winners

Zucchini Crescent Pie *(Grand Prize)*....p. 241
Baked Apple French Toast *(2nd Place)*....p. 174
Mashed Potatoes Supreme *(3rd Place)*....p. 132
Tortilla Lasagna *(4th Place)*....p. 245
Chicken Lasagna *(Runner-Up)*....p. 247
Sweet Potato Sausage Casserole *(Runner-Up)*....p. 241
Chicken Penne Casserole *(Runner-Up)*....p. 242
Marvelous Shells 'n' Cheese *(Runner-Up)*....p. 242
Potluck Ham and Pasta *(Runner-Up)*....p. 249
Turkey Cabbage Bake *(Runner-Up)*....p. 247
Sneaky Lasagna *(Runner-Up)*....p. 246
Dijon Scalloped Potatoes *(Runner-Up)*....p. 134

She Used Refrigerated Dough to Delight Judges

GREAT TASTE, ease and handy ingredients are the top priorities when Jaime Keeling is planning meals for husband Ryan and herself. "Our lives are busy, so I often tweak recipes to make them fit our time frame," she says from Keizer, Oregon.

Her scrumptious recipe for Pull-Apart Caramel Coffee Cake is a classic example—it requires just four everyday ingredients and 10 minutes of prep time. Our panel of judges gave it top honors in the "It's All About the Dough" recipe contest.

It's All About the Dough Contest Winners

Pull-Apart Caramel Coffee Cake *(Grand Prize)*....p. 152
Ham and Cheese Loaf *(2nd Place)*....p. 185
Tomato Cheese Pizza *(3rd Place)*....p. 201
Surprise Monkey Bread *(4th Place)*....p. 148
Beef-Stuffed Crescents *(Runner-Up)*....p. 283
Breakfast Pizza *(Runner-Up)*....p. 172
Crescent Apple Dessert *(Runner-Up)*....p. 222
Garlic-Cheese Crescent Rolls *(Runner-Up)*....p. 151
Mini Toffee Rolls *(Runner-Up)*....p. 149
Pizza Loaf *(Runner-Up)*....p. 275
Spicy Chicken Bundles *(Runner-Up)*....p. 183
Stromboli Slices *(Runner-Up)*....p. 276

Her Grilled Entree Had a Special Spark

FOR CREATIVE COOKS like Shawn Solley of Morgantown, West Virginia, one good recipe often leads to another. That's exactly what happened with her Grilled Asian Flank Steak—the first-place entry in our "All Fired Up" contest.

"The flank steak my mom and aunt served up for years was a longtime family favorite," Shawn writes. "I decided to try combining it with my own marinade for venison tenderloin...and was thrilled with the results!"

All Fired Up Contest Winners

Grilled Asian Flank Steak *(Grand Prize)*....................p. 235
Chipotle Chicken Fajitas *(2nd Place)*........................p. 304
Best Barbecue Wings *(3rd Place)*..............................p. 280
Barbecued Pork Chops *(4th Place)*............................p. 194
Chipotle Pork Tenderloins *(Runner-Up)*....................p. 306
Feta Salmon Salad *(Runner-Up)*................................p. 139
Flank Steak Sandwiches *(Runner-Up)*........................p. 189
Greek Lemon Chicken *(Runner-Up)*...........................p. 97
Grilled Sweet Onions *(Runner-Up)*............................p. 132
Mayonnaise Lovers' Chicken *(Runner-Up)*..................p. 307
Pineapple Beef Kabobs *(Runner-Up)*..........................p. 305
Tomato-Basil Shrimp Skewers *(Runner-Up)*................p. 304

Frosty Pie Takes the Heat Off of Busy Cook

MARRIED for more than 60 years, Velma Jo Brown still fixes three sit-down meals a day for husband Robert and herself on their Turner Station, Kentucky farm. "And I'll host our daughters and their families on special occasions," she notes.

After so many years, you might say Velma has cooking for a family "down cold." Her irresistible Coffee Ice Cream Pie is just one example...and ended up receiving the Grand Prize in our "Easy Freezer Desserts" contest.

Easy Freezer Desserts Contest Winners

Coffee Ice Cream Pie *(Grand Prize)*..........................p. 220
Frozen Raspberry Cheesecake *(2nd Place)*..................p. 210
Frosty Mallow Fruit Dessert *(3rd Place)*....................p. 221
Nutty Cookies & Cream Dessert *(4th Place)*..............p. 215
Swirled Sherbet Dessert *(Runner-Up)*.........................p. 217
Frozen Banana Split Pie *(Runner-Up)*.........................p. 227
Maple Mocha Pops *(Runner-Up)*..................................p. 75
Bing Cherry Sherbet *(Runner-Up)*...............................p. 86
Rainbow Sherbet Dessert *(Runner-Up)*........................p. 213
Mint Sundae Brownie Squares *(Runner-Up)*................p. 213
Fruit Juice Pops *(Runner-Up)*......................................p. 79
Watermelon Bombe *(Runner-Up)*..................................p. 212

Her Frightful Appetizer Scares Up Halloween Fun

"MY HUSBAND and I have two young children, and it can be a challenge to find wholesome foods they'll eat," says Heather Snow of Salt Lake City, Utah.

This stay-at-home mom has her own bag of tricks when it comes to making meals special. Our judges took notice and awarded her Yummy Mummy with Veggie Dip top honors in the "Halloween Spooktacular" contest.

"I created this appetizer for our annual Halloween get-together," Heather writes, "and it was a big hit."

Halloween Spooktacular Contest Winners

Yummy Mummy with Veggie Dip *(Grand Prize)*........p. 31
Squirmy Wormy Sandwiches *(2nd Place)*...................p. 30
Ogre Eyes Hot Cocoa *(3rd Place)*..............................p. 30
Black Cat Brownie *(4th Place)*...................................p. 32
Bat Cupcakes *(Runner-Up)*...p. 32
Bloodshot Eyeballs *(Runner-Up)*...............................p. 33
Chili-Filled Coffin *(Runner-Up)*.................................p. 35
Crunchy Monster Claws *(Runner-Up)*.........................p. 35
Ghostly Graveyard *(Runner-Up)*..................................p. 34
Ghoul Punch *(Runner-Up)*...p. 33
Gruesome Green Toes *(Runner-Up)*.............................p. 31
Jack-o'-Lantern Sloppy Joe Pie *(Runner-Up)*...............p. 34

She Wrapped Up Contest with a Tasteful Gift

ON MOST NIGHTS, Diane Willey doesn't know what she'll make for dinner until an hour or so before mealtime. "But I always manage to come up with something," she laughs.

The same casual approach extends to this Bozman, Maryland cook's baking—and gives rise to treats such as Pecan Toffee Fudge, the Grand Prize winner in the "Greatest Gift Recipe" contest.

"I make this fudge at least once every 3 weeks, and I always give a portion of it away," Diane relates.

Greatest Gift Recipe Contest Winners

Pecan Toffee Fudge *(Grand Prize)*...............................p. 217
Apricot Bars *(2nd Place)*..p. 215
Peanut Butter Clusters *(3rd Place)*..............................p. 79
Peppermint Meltaways *(4th Place)*..............................p. 301
Chili Seasoning Mix *(Runner-Up)*................................p. 38
Pecan Shortbread Diamonds *(Runner-Up)*..................p. 225
Christmas Mice Cookies *(Runner-Up)*.........................p. 38
Cranberry Banana Bread *(Runner-Up)*.........................p. 152
Hawaiian Turtle Cups *(Runner-Up)*.............................p. 91
Oatmeal Cranberry Cookie Mix *(Runner-Up)*..............p. 39
Pretzel Cereal Crunch *(Runner-Up)*.............................p. 39
Strawberry Sundae Sauce *(Runner-Up)*.......................p. 223

Chapter 1

Readers' Favorite Fast Meals

WHETHER your personal recipe collection contains a few dozen recipes or a few thousand, you likely have a small number of favorites that you turn to and rely on time and again.

These can't-do-without dishes have home-style taste but don't require lots of fuss in the kitchen. And when dinnertime is near and your family's hungry, that's important!

In this chapter, six on-the-go cooks just like you share their favorite tried-and-true menus. Each meal can be prepared in just 30 minutes...or less.

From entrees such as Monterey Barbecued Chicken and Family-Pleasing Pizza to Dream Clouds and other desserts, these recipes are sure to become regulars in your household.

MAINSTAY MENU. Sweet 'n' Sour Coleslaw, Garlic New Potatoes and Mustard Fried Catfish (all recipes on p. 14).

Chicken Dinner Is Special and Satisfying

FOR self-proclaimed "foodie" Jennifer Shaw, cooking is more than putting dinner on the table. "It's my primary hobby," she writes from her home in Dorchester, Massachusetts.

She loves just "puttering around" in the kitchen, coming up with new recipes. But occasionally, the hustle and bustle of working in nearby Boston can take its toll.

"Sometimes, I just want to get in and out of the kitchen in order to maximize the time spent eating lazily in front of the TV," she says.

For this single workingwoman, cooking came naturally but with lots of inspiration from her grandmother. Now, she cooks mostly for herself—but often ends up with leftovers. "I find that I cook enough to feed about four people," she admits. "I have trouble showing restraint in the kitchen!"

The meal she shares here serves four and holds nothing back when it comes to flavor and ease. Her menu begins with Zippy Paprika Chicken. "It has a unique flavor and hint of classic Hungarian paprika chicken, but with a modern twist," she relates.

Serve the chicken with her Smashed Potatoes and Roasted Asparagus for a hearty dinner. "I wouldn't dream of making this chicken without the potatoes to soak up the sauce," Jennifer notes. "And asparagus is always a great choice as a quick side dish."

Zippy Paprika Chicken

Prep/Total Time: 30 min.

2 tablespoons paprika
1 to 2 tablespoons Southwest marinade mix
1/8 teaspoon salt
1/8 teaspoon pepper
4 boneless skinless chicken breast halves (4 ounces *each*)
2 tablespoons olive oil
1/4 cup water
2 tablespoons soy sauce
5 teaspoons lemon juice
1/2 cup sour cream

In a large resealable plastic bag, combine the paprika, marinade mix, salt and pepper; add chicken. Seal bag; shake to coat. Refrigerate for 10 minutes.

In a large skillet, cook chicken in oil over medium heat for 5-6 minutes on each side or until juices run clear. Remove and keep warm.

Add water, soy sauce and lemon juice to the skillet; cook for 1-2 minutes, stirring to loosen browned bits. Remove from the heat; stir in the sour cream until blended. Serve with chicken. **Yield:** 4 servings.

Editor's Note: This recipe was tested with McCormick Grill Mates Southwest Marinade seasoning packet.

Smashed Potatoes

Prep/Total Time: 25 min.

7 to 8 medium red potatoes (about 2 pounds), quartered
1/4 cup sour cream
1/4 cup milk
2 tablespoons butter
1/4 teaspoon salt
1/4 teaspoon pepper
Pinch ground nutmeg

Place potatoes in a large saucepan; cover with water. Bring to a boil. Reduce heat; cover and cook for 10-15 minutes or until tender. Drain. In a large mixing bowl, mash potatoes with the sour cream, milk, butter, salt, pepper and nutmeg. **Yield:** 4 servings.

Roasted Asparagus

Prep/Total Time: 15 min.

✓ This recipe includes Nutrition Facts and Diabetic Exchanges.

1 pound fresh asparagus, trimmed
1 tablespoon olive oil
1/4 teaspoon salt
1/8 teaspoon pepper

Place the asparagus on an ungreased baking sheet. Drizzle with the oil. Sprinkle with salt and pepper; turn to coat. Bake at 425° for 10-15 minutes or until tender. **Yield:** 4 servings.

Nutrition Facts: 1 serving equals 43 calories, 4 g fat (trace saturated fat), 0 cholesterol, 154 mg sodium, 2 g carbohydrate, 1 g fiber, 1 g protein. **Diabetic Exchanges:** 1 vegetable, 1/2 fat.

About Asparagus

WHEN buying asparagus, look for spears that are firm, straight and of uniform size. The tips should be closed with crisp stalks.

It's best to use asparagus within a few days of purchase. For a little longer storage, place bundled stalks upright in a bowl filled with 1 inch of water and refrigerate. Or wrap the cut ends in moist paper towels. Cover the towel with plastic wrap and refrigerate.

To clean asparagus, soak it in cold water. Cut or snap off the tough white portion.

Supper Goes From Ordinary To Amazing

TO BUSY COOK Tabitha Freeman, no two meals are the same. But they always have one thing in common—they have to be fast!

"For the past 10 years, I've either worked two jobs or been going to school while working, so I know all about having no kitchen time to spare," she says. "Usually, I'm racing the clock when I get home. I typically spend just 15-20 minutes making dinner." But what she whips up in that time is amazing!

Take, for example, the delicious supper the Meriden, Connecticut cook shares here. "I can't remember exactly how I put it together," she relates. "But I remember it comes together quick!"

It all starts with a sandwich—no ordinary sandwich, mind you. Her Portobello Roast Beef Hoagies feature mushrooms, roast beef and provolone cheese. "It doesn't get much easier than this," she notes.

For a side dish, Tabitha fixes Pepperoncini Arugula Salad. "I'm trying to cut processed foods out of my life. I'm not obsessive about it, but fresh food, close to its original source, is where it's at for me," she says. "This refreshing salad is a great choice."

To round out the menu, serve elegant Chocolate Cake with Coconut Sauce. "It's guaranteed to make your sweet tooth happy," Tabitha assures.

Portobello Roast Beef Hoagies

Prep/Total Time: 15 min.

4 whole wheat hoagie buns, split
4 tablespoons butter, softened, *divided*
1 teaspoon Italian seasoning
1/4 teaspoon garlic salt
3/4 pound sliced deli roast beef, julienned
1/2 pound sliced baby portobello mushrooms
1 teaspoon dried rosemary, crushed
1/4 teaspoon pepper
1/2 pound sliced provolone cheese
1/2 cup sour cream
1 tablespoon prepared horseradish

Spread cut sides of buns with 2 tablespoons butter; sprinkle with Italian seasoning and garlic salt. Set aside.

In a large skillet, saute the beef, mushrooms, rosemary and pepper in remaining butter until the mushrooms are tender. Spoon onto buns; top with cheese.

Place on a baking sheet. Broil 2-3 in. from the heat for 2-4 minutes or until cheese is melted. In a small bowl, combine sour cream and horseradish; serve with sandwiches. **Yield:** 4 servings.

Pepperoncini Arugula Salad

Prep/Total Time: 5 min.

✓ This recipe includes Nutrition Facts and Diabetic Exchanges.

2 cups fresh arugula *or* baby spinach
2 cups torn romaine
1/4 cup chopped red onion
2 pepperoncinis, sliced
1 medium tomato, sliced
1/4 cup balsamic vinaigrette

In a large salad bowl, combine the arugula, romaine, onion, pepperoncinis and tomato. Drizzle with vinaigrette; gently toss to coat. **Yield:** 4 servings.

Editor's Note: Look for pepperoncinis (pickled peppers) in the pickle and olive section of your grocery store.

Nutrition Facts: 1-1/4 cups equals 50 calories, 3 g fat (trace saturated fat), 0 cholesterol, 197 mg sodium, 6 g carbohydrate, 1 g fiber, 1 g protein. **Diabetic Exchanges:** 1 vegetable, 1/2 fat.

Chocolate Cake With Coconut Sauce

Prep/Total Time: 30 min.

1 package (19.6 ounces) frozen chocolate fudge layer cake
1/2 cup flaked coconut
1/2 cup sweetened condensed milk
1/2 teaspoon vanilla extract
1/4 cup red raspberry preserves
4 scoops vanilla ice cream

Cut cake in half. Return half to the freezer. Let remaining cake stand at room temperature to thaw.

Meanwhile, in a small saucepan, combine the coconut, milk and vanilla. Cook and stir over medium heat for 2-3 minutes or until heated through.

Cut cake into four slices; place on dessert plates. Spread with preserves. Top with coconut mixture and ice cream. **Yield:** 4 servings.

Editor's Note: This recipe was tested with Pepperidge Farm frozen three-layer cake.

Wrapping Up Salad

FOR A CASUAL TWIST, Tabitha likes to make fun and tasty lettuce wraps from her Pepperoncini Arugula Salad ingredients (recipe above). She layers one romaine leaf and two arugula leaves, then the other ingredients. To finish, she simply folds the lettuce leaves over and dips the wrap into balsamic vinaigrette.

She Barbecues Indoors...In Mere Minutes

A QUICK, well-rounded meal is important to Linda Coleman of Cedar Rapids, Iowa. "When you have three young, extremely active children who need to be in three different places at once, there's no time for elaborate meals," she writes.

Although Linda doesn't have time for fussy dinners, she makes an effort to provide her family with quality meals. "I don't want to compromise on giving my family a wholesome supper," she relates. "So I have several mealtime strategies.

"For one thing, I like to have all of the recipe ingredients and kitchen tools I need to prepare a meal sitting out before I begin cooking. Then I don't have to waste valuable time searching for things.

"But most importantly, I have a range of dishes that I can prepare and cook in 30 minutes or less." Linda shares a few of her favorites recipes here.

She turns regular chicken into a savory dish with barbecue sauce, crisp bacon and melty cheese. Her Monterey Barbecued Chicken gets even better with a sprinkling of fresh tomato and green onions.

That barbecue flavor keeps going with Linda's In-a-Flash Beans. No one will guess this recipe begins with a can. Chopped onion and green pepper lend a little crunch and lots of home-cooked flavor.

Strawberry Pound Cake Dessert adds a pretty and refreshing finish to Linda's meal. This simple, classic dessert comes together in moments and adds a pop of color. You can use fresh strawberries if you have the time to slice 3 cups of them—just add 2 to 3 tablespoons of sugar and let the berries sit for 15 minutes to juice up.

"I like to prepare this menu even if I'm not hurrying to take the kids somewhere," Linda notes. "That way, I can fix it and rush out to do one of my own passions—habitat gardening."

Monterey Barbecued Chicken

Prep/Total Time: 25 min.

4 bacon strips
4 boneless skinless chicken breast halves (4 ounces *each*)
1 tablespoon butter
1/2 cup barbecue sauce
3 green onions, chopped
1 medium tomato, chopped
1 cup (4 ounces) shredded cheddar cheese

Cut the bacon strips in half widthwise. In a large skillet, cook the bacon over medium heat until cooked but not crisp. Remove the bacon to paper towels to drain; keep warm.

Drain the bacon drippings from the skillet; cook the chicken in butter over medium heat for 5-6 minutes on each side or until the chicken juices run clear.

Top each chicken breast half with barbecue sauce, green onions, tomato and two reserved bacon pieces; sprinkle with the cheddar cheese. Cover and cook for 5 minutes or until cheese is melted. **Yield:** 4 servings.

In-a-Flash Beans

Prep/Total Time: 15 min.

1 can (15-3/4 ounces) pork and beans
1/2 cup barbecue sauce
1/2 cup chopped onion
1/4 cup chopped green pepper, optional

In a large saucepan, combine the beans, barbecue sauce, onion and green pepper if desired. Cook and stir bean mixture over medium heat until heated through. **Yield:** 4 servings.

Strawberry Pound Cake Dessert

Prep/Total Time: 10 min.

1 loaf (10-3/4 ounces) frozen pound cake, thawed
2 containers (16 ounces *each*) frozen sweetened sliced strawberries, thawed and drained
1-1/2 cups whipped topping

Slice the pound cake loaf into eight pieces. Place one cake slice on each of four dessert plates. Top each cake slice with 1/2 cup strawberries, 3 tablespoons whipped topping and another cake slice. Serve the desserts with the remaining strawberries and whipped topping. **Yield:** 4 servings.

Step-by-Step Strategy

BREAKING down meal preparation into steps can make the process more efficient—and therefore even faster! To make preparing the delicious meal here as fast and fuss-free as can be, follow these steps:

1. Cut and cook the bacon strips for the Monterey Barbecued Chicken.

2. While the bacon is cooking, chop the green and onions and tomato.

3. Drain the bacon drippings and cook the chicken breast halves.

4. As the chicken cooks, assemble and cook In-a-Flash Beans.

5. Prepare Strawberry Pound Cake Dessert and finish making the main course.

Her Home-Style Fish Fry Is A Great Catch

WHILE many people enjoy curling up with a good novel, Barbara Keith of Faucett, Missouri chooses different reading material—a good cookbook. "I love spending time in the kitchen and have been collecting cookbooks for years," she says.

Her husband, Keith, four kids, 10 grandchildren and seven great-grandchildren couldn't be happier about Barbara's passion for cooking. And they're not the only ones! "When I'm not cooking meals for my family, I like to prepare dishes for neighbors and relatives who are sick or recovering from surgery," Barbara relates.

Cooking for others seems to be second nature for Barbara, whose parents owned a small cafe. "I did a lot of cooking there as a teenager when my mom was working her other job," she says. "I would make pies, fried chicken and big pots of chili and soup."

It's no wonder Barbara and her husband also welcomed friends and family over for "whole-hog" barbecues and large fish fries when they had the time. "I was often asked for recipes at these gatherings, so I began taping copies to the bottom of each dish I prepared and kept extras in the house," she says.

Here, Barbara shares some of her favorite recipes, including her popular fried fish. "I make this meal on a monthly basis," she writes of her Mustard Fried Catfish. "The fish is so delicious and flaky, and it's easy to prepare, too." If you can't find catfish, try orange roughy or cod instead.

Tender fried fish just wouldn't be the same without a side of cool, creamy coleslaw. Barbara's Sweet 'n' Sour Coleslaw comes together in just 5 minutes and brings bright flavor and crunch to the menu. "This was my mother's recipe, and I'm always asked to share it," she explains.

To round out the menu, Barbara turns to buttery Garlic New Potatoes. "I have yet to meet a person who doesn't enjoy this simple but tasty dish," she says. "The potatoes complement just about any entree and are quick to prepare."

Mustard Fried Catfish

Prep/Total Time: 20 min.

2/3 cup yellow cornmeal
1/3 cup all-purpose flour
1/2 teaspoon salt
1/4 teaspoon paprika
1/4 teaspoon pepper
1/8 teaspoon cayenne pepper
1/2 cup prepared mustard
4 catfish fillets (6 ounces *each*)
Oil for frying

In a shallow bowl, combine the first six ingredients. Spread mustard over both sides of fillets; coat with cornmeal mixture.

In an electric skillet or deep-fat fryer, heat oil to 375°. Fry fillets, a few at a time, for 2-3 minutes on each side or until fish flakes easily with a fork. Drain on paper towels. **Yield:** 4 servings.

Sweet 'n' Sour Coleslaw

Prep/Total Time: 5 min.

5-1/2 cups coleslaw mix
1/2 cup heavy whipping cream
1/3 cup sugar
3 tablespoons white vinegar
1/2 teaspoon salt

Place coleslaw mix in a serving bowl. In a jar with a tight-fitting lid, combine the remaining ingredients; shake well. Pour over coleslaw mix and toss to coat. Chill until serving. **Yield:** 4 servings.

Garlic New Potatoes

Prep/Total Time: 25 min.

16 small red potatoes
3 tablespoons butter, melted
1-1/2 teaspoons minced garlic
1-1/2 teaspoons dried parsley flakes
Salt and pepper to taste

Place the potatoes in a steamer basket; place in a large saucepan over 1 in. of water. Bring to a boil; cover and steam for 15-20 minutes or until tender. Transfer to a serving bowl.

Combine the butter, garlic, dried parsley flakes, salt and pepper; pour over the potatoes and toss to coat. **Yield:** 4 servings.

Meal Planning Pointers

HERE ARE some handy tips to keep in mind when preparing this scrumptious meal from Barbara:

- The recipe for Mustard Fried Catfish calls for frying the fillets in an electric skillet or deep-fat fryer. If baking is a more convenient choice, feel free to put the fillets in the oven instead. Make sure to grease the bottom of the baking dish.
- To speed up the preparation of Garlic New Potatoes, use bottled minced garlic from the supermarket instead of mincing fresh garlic yourself.

Pizza Menu Is Better Than Delivery

AS A VOLUNTEER for the American Heart Association, Judy Sellgren of Wyoming, Michigan always seems to put others first. In fact, those who know her best would probably tell you that for Judy, cooking is as much an act of looking after friends and family as it is of feeding them.

"I typically make dinner for my husband, John, and myself, but we really enjoy having our kids and two grandchildren over, too," she says. "I also help out with preparing dinners at church and for funerals."

No matter how many people she's serving, Judy tries to tailor her menu to suit their tastes. A number of her family's favorite recipes came from friends.

"I truly can't remember who gave me the recipe for Family-Pleasing Pizza," Judy says. "But I've used it for unexpected company or as a busy weekend meal for years. Add whatever fresh veggies you have on hand."

Bacon and chow mein noodles bring lively crunch to Tangy Spinach Salad, which goes super-fast when you use store-bought hard-cooked eggs. "I made this for two of my best girlfriends, and they loved it. One still fixes it regularly for her husband!"

Top off the meal with sweet and creamy Cake with Pineapple Pudding, a five-ingredient delight. "This recipe was given to me by a dear friend," Judy says. "It's wonderfully light and refreshing."

Family-Pleasing Pizza

Prep/Total Time: 30 min.

1/2 pound bulk pork sausage
1 tube (13.8 ounces) refrigerated pizza crust
2 teaspoons butter, melted
2 tablespoons grated Parmesan cheese
1 teaspoon garlic powder
2 cups (8 ounces) shredded part-skim mozzarella cheese
2 medium Roma tomatoes, thinly sliced
2 teaspoons Italian seasoning

In a large skillet, cook sausage over medium heat until no longer pink. Drain and set aside.

Meanwhile, press pizza dough into a greased 13-in. x 9-in. x 2-in. baking dish. Brush with butter; sprinkle with Parmesan cheese and garlic powder. Layer with 1 cup mozzarella, sausage and tomatoes. Sprinkle with remaining mozzarella and Italian seasoning.

Bake at 400° for 20-25 minutes or until crust is golden brown and cheese is melted. **Yield:** 6 servings.

Tangy Spinach Salad

Prep/Total Time: 10 min.

3 tablespoons sugar
3 tablespoons cider vinegar
3 tablespoons vegetable oil
3 tablespoons ketchup
1-1/2 teaspoons Worcestershire sauce
1 teaspoon dried minced onion
1 package (6 ounces) fresh baby spinach
3 hard-cooked eggs, chopped
1/3 cup chow mein noodles
1/3 cup real bacon bits

In a jar with a tight-fitting lid, combine the first six ingredients; shake well. In a large bowl, combine spinach, eggs, chow mein noodles and bacon. Drizzle with dressing. Refrigerate leftovers. **Yield:** 6 servings.

Cake with Pineapple Pudding

Prep/Total Time: 10 min.

✓ This recipe includes Nutrition Facts.

2 cups milk
1 package (3.4 ounces) instant French vanilla pudding mix
1 can (8 ounces) unsweetened crushed pineapple, drained
1 cup whipped topping
6 slices angel food cake

In a large bowl, whisk milk and pudding mix for 2 minutes. Let stand for 2 minutes or until soft-set. Fold in pineapple and whipped topping. Chill until serving. Serve with cake. **Yield:** 6 servings.

Nutrition Facts: 1 slice with 2/3 cup pudding equals 236 calories, 5 g fat (4 g saturated fat), 8 mg cholesterol, 470 mg sodium, 43 g carbohydrate, 1 g fiber, 4 g protein.

Asian-Inspired Dinner Has Restaurant Flair

BUSY COOKS know it's a challenge to prepare a nice meal during a hectic week. Just ask Tonya Michelle Burkhard of Englewood, Florida. "I'm a wife and a mom to two children, and I have a full-time job. I need fast meals, but I want my kids to know there are other foods besides burgers and French fries."

Instead of turning to a drive through, Tonya relies on no-fuss recipes. "I make meals that can be done simply, yet offer maximum taste," she explains, and that certainly shows in the menu she's sharing.

Although elegant enough to be from a restaurant, Tonya's Sweet-and-Sour Scallops are filled with homemade flavor. They put a delicious twist on a classic.

"This meal will change your traditional way of serving sweet and sour," she writes. "The scallops are so tender, they practically melt in your mouth."

A side of fragrant Almond Rice is perfect with the scallops and lets you enjoy every drop of the sweet-tangy sauce. "The rice absorbs all the great flavors," Tonya says. "When I serve this, I sprinkle the edges of a large serving platter with fresh parsley, add the Almond Rice and top it with the scallops."

Cap off the meal with a dessert that's just as lovely. With their refreshing orange flavor, Dream Clouds complement this menu's Asian-inspired recipes and are sure to satisfy anyone's sweet tooth.

Sweet-and-Sour Scallops

Prep/Total Time: 20 min.

2 cans (8 ounces *each*) pineapple chunks
1 pound sea scallops (about 16)
1 tablespoon vegetable oil
1/3 cup chopped onion
1/3 cup julienned green pepper
1/4 cup butter, cubed
1/4 cup sugar
2 tablespoons cornstarch
1/2 teaspoon ground mustard
1/4 teaspoon salt
1/2 cup white vinegar
2 tablespoons soy sauce
2/3 cup cherry tomatoes, halved

Drain the pineapple chunks, reserving the juice; set the pineapple and juice aside. In a large skillet, saute the scallops in oil until firm and opaque; drain. Remove scallops from pan and keep warm. In the same pan, saute the onion and green pepper in butter for 3-4 minutes or until crisp-tender.

Meanwhile, in a small bowl, combine the sugar, cornstarch, ground mustard and salt. Whisk in the vinegar, soy sauce and reserved pineapple juice until smooth. Gradually stir into the pan. Bring to a boil; cook and stir for 2 minutes or until thickened. Stir in the cherry tomatoes, scallops and reserved pineapple chunks; heat through. **Yield:** 4 servings.

Almond Rice

Prep/Total Time: 10 min.

1-1/2 cups water
1-1/2 cups uncooked instant rice
1 tablespoon butter
1/2 cup slivered almonds, toasted
1/4 teaspoon salt
1/4 teaspoon pepper
1 tablespoon minced fresh parsley

In a large saucepan, bring the water, rice and butter to a boil. Remove from heat. Cover and let stand for 5 minutes or until water is absorbed.

Stir in the slivered almonds, salt and pepper. Sprinkle with fresh parsley. **Yield:** 4 servings.

Dream Clouds

Prep/Total Time: 10 min.

1 pint vanilla ice cream, softened
1 pint orange sherbet, softened
2 cups whipped topping
1 can (11 ounces) mandarin oranges, drained

Place the ice cream and sherbet in a large bowl. Using a knife, swirl sherbet into ice cream.

Spoon 1/2 cup whipped topping into each of four individual serving dishes. Top the whipped topping with the ice cream-sherbet mixture and mandarin oranges. **Yield:** 4 servings.

Chapter 2

Holiday and Seasonal Pleasers

FROM CHRISTMAS and Easter to summer picnics and Halloween parties, holidays and other special occasions give creative cooks the chance to add to the celebration—by preparing foods with festive flair.

You'll have fun all year long thanks to the themed recipes in this timely chapter. Delight family and friends with a Valentine's Day dinner...a star-filled spread for July Fourth...Christmas cookies you can whip up in advance...and much more.

Think these dressed-up treats will require hours and hours in the kitchen? Not so! Each one was created with convenience in mind, so it's easy to fit them into hectic schedules.

A LITTLE SPARKLE. Star Pastry Snacks and Strawberry Salsa (both recipes on p. 29).

Tempting Treats for Sweethearts

ON VALENTINE'S DAY or any time you want to show someone special how much they're loved, try these delectable dishes. They'll send the message in an unforgettable, taste-tempting way.

Whether you're cooking for two, doubling a recipe for guests or preparing a bounty of desserts, the occasion will be as simple as it is memorable. All that's left to do is decide whether to serve an entree, a side dish or a dessert—or all three!

Vanilla Chip Dessert

(Pictured below)

Prep: 30 min. + chilling

With vanilla flavor and a creamy filling, this dessert is so luscious. Sometimes I garnish it with shaved chocolate.
—Melanie Budd, Anaconda, Montana

3 cups vanilla wafer crumbs (about 60 wafers)
1/2 cup butter, melted
3 tablespoons brown sugar
1 package (10 to 12 ounces) vanilla *or* white chips
2 packages (8 ounces *each*) cream cheese, softened
2 cups (16 ounces) sour cream
1 carton (8 ounces) frozen whipped topping, thawed
Chocolate ice cream topping, optional

In a small bowl, combine the wafer crumbs, butter and brown sugar. Press onto the bottom of a greased 13-in. x 9-in. x 2-in. baking dish. Bake at 350° for 5-8 minutes or until lightly browned. Cool.

In a microwave-safe bowl, melt vanilla chips; stir until smooth. Cool. In a large mixing bowl, beat cream cheese and sour cream until smooth. Add melted chips; beat well. Fold in whipped topping.

Pour over crust. Cover and refrigerate for 2 hours or until set. Drizzle with chocolate topping if desired. **Yield:** 15 servings.

Vanilla Chip Dessert

Strawberry Valentine Cookies

Strawberry Valentine Cookies

(Pictured above)

Prep: 50 min. **Bake:** 10 min./batch + cooling

Start a new Valentine's Day tradition with these pretty, heart-shaped cookies. I think the strawberry flavor is the perfect complement to the rich chocolate glaze.
—Marna Heitz, Farley, Iowa

2/3 cup butter, softened
2/3 cup sugar
1 egg
1 tablespoon lemon juice
2 cups all-purpose flour
1/3 cup strawberry drink mix
2 teaspoons baking powder
1/2 teaspoon salt
GLAZE:
1 cup (6 ounces) semisweet chocolate chips
1 teaspoon shortening
FROSTING:
1/3 cup butter, softened
2 tablespoons strawberry drink mix
1/8 teaspoon salt
3 cups confectioners' sugar
3 to 5 tablespoons milk

In a small mixing bowl, cream butter and sugar. Beat in egg and lemon juice. Combine the flour, drink mix, baking powder and salt; gradually add to creamed mixture and mix well.

On a lightly floured surface, roll out dough to 1/4-in. thickness. Cut with a floured 2-1/2- to 3-in. heart-shaped cookie cutter. Place 2 in. apart on ungreased baking sheets. Bake at 350° for 8-10 minutes or until set and edges begin to brown. Cool for 2 minutes before removing to wire racks to cool completely.

In a small microwave-safe bowl, melt chocolate chips and shortening; stir until smooth. Spread over cookies; let stand until set.

In a small mixing bowl, cream the butter, drink mix and salt. Gradually beat in confectioners' sugar. Add enough milk to achieve desired consistency. Decorate cookies. **Yield:** about 2 dozen.

Seafood Alfredo Baskets

(Pictured at right)

Prep: 10 min. **Bake:** 25 min.

Your dinner companion will think you slaved over this sophisticated main dish for two, featuring seafood on flaky puff pastry shells. But with just a few convenient ingredients, the little baskets go together in a "heartbeat!"
—Diana Smarrit, Blackwood, New Jersey

- **4 frozen puff pastry shells**
- **6 cups water**
- **1/2 pound bay scallops**
- **1/4 pound uncooked medium shrimp, peeled and deveined**
- **1 cup Alfredo sauce, warmed**
- **1/2 to 1 teaspoon garlic powder**

Bake shells according to package directions. Meanwhile, in a large saucepan, bring water to a boil. Add scallops and shrimp. Cook for 2-5 minutes or until scallops are firm and opaque and shrimp turn pink; drain.

Combine Alfredo sauce and garlic powder; drizzle over shells. Top with seafood. **Yield:** 2 servings.

Seafood Alfredo Baskets
Lemon-Pepper Green Beans

Lemon-Pepper Green Beans

(Pictured at right)

Prep/Total Time: 20 min.

Created in the Simple & Delicious Test Kitchen, these delicious beans bring refreshing flavor and a dash of color to the table. They're just the right partner for a rich entree.

✓ This recipe includes Nutrition Facts and Diabetic Exchanges.

- **1/2 pound fresh green beans, trimmed**
- **1 tablespoon olive oil**
- **1-1/2 teaspoons cider vinegar**
- **1/4 to 1/2 teaspoon Italian seasoning**
- **1/4 teaspoon onion salt**
- **1/8 teaspoon lemon-pepper seasoning**

Place the beans in a steamer basket; place in a large saucepan over 1 in. of water. Bring to a boil; cover and steam for 8-10 minutes or until crisp-tender.

Meanwhile, in a small bowl, combine the oil, vinegar and seasonings until blended. Transfer beans to a serving bowl; drizzle with seasoning mixture and toss to coat. **Yield:** 2 servings.

Nutrition Facts: 3/4 cup equals 92 calories, 7 g fat (1 g saturated fat), 0 cholesterol, 261 mg sodium, 8 g carbohydrate, 3 g fiber, 2 g protein. **Diabetic Exchanges:** 1-1/2 fat, 1 vegetable.

Easter Dinner with Ease

FEWER INGREDIENTS add up to less preparation fuss—which is especially nice on busy holidays. So you'll love every delicious recipe here. Each dish in this delightful Easter spread takes no more than a handful of ingredients and a few moments of time.

Fluffy Chocolate Pie

(Pictured below)

Prep: 15 min. + chilling

Kids and adults alike love this pie. Because it's so easy to make, you can even let children help with the preparation.
—Wanda Lois Lewis, Springfield, Kentucky

2-1/2 cups miniature milk chocolate kisses
1 carton (12 ounces) frozen whipped topping, thawed, *divided*
1 graham cracker crust (9 inches)
20 miniature peanut butter cups, chopped

In a large microwave-safe bowl, melt chocolate kisses; stir until smooth. Cool slightly. Fold in 3-1/2 cups whipped topping until blended.

Spread half of the chocolate mixture into crust; sprinkle with peanut butter cups. Top with remaining chocolate mixture. Chill for at least 30 minutes. Top with remaining whipped topping. **Yield:** 8 servings.

Fluffy Chocolate Pie

Polka-Dot Macaroons

Polka-Dot Macaroons

(Pictured above)

Prep: 15 min. **Bake:** 10 min./batch

These chewy cookies mix up fast and go over big with folks of all ages. I've been baking for 35 years, and believe me, these never last long! The baking bits make them festive for special occasions. *—Janice Lass, Dorr, Michigan*

✓ This recipe includes Nutrition Facts and Diabetic Exchanges.

5 cups flaked coconut
1 can (14 ounces) sweetened condensed milk
1/2 cup all-purpose flour
1-1/2 cups M&M's miniature baking bits

In a large bowl, combine the coconut, milk and flour. Stir in baking bits.

Drop by rounded tablespoonfuls 2 in. apart onto baking sheets coated with cooking spray. Bake at 350° for 8-10 minutes or until edges are lightly browned. Remove to wire racks. **Yield:** about 4-1/2 dozen.

Nutrition Facts: 1 cookie equals 99 calories, 5 g fat (4 g saturated fat), 3 mg cholesterol, 31 mg sodium, 13 g carbohydrate, 1 g fiber, 1 g protein. **Diabetic Exchanges:** 1 starch, 1 fat.

Brie Mashed Potatoes
Beer-Glazed Ham

Beer-Glazed Ham

(Pictured above)

Prep: 5 min. **Bake:** 1 hour 40 min.

My motto is, "Anything that has brown sugar in it has to be good." And this main course really is! With only five ingredients, it features a fuss-free way to "fancy up" your Easter ham that everyone at the table will enjoy.
—Kim Ryon, Factoryville, Pennsylvania

1 boneless fully cooked ham (3 pounds)
1 can (12 ounces) beer *or* nonalcoholic beer
1 cup packed brown sugar
2 tablespoons balsamic vinegar
2 teaspoons ground mustard

Place the ham on a rack in a shallow roasting pan. Score the surface of the ham, making diamond shapes 1/2 in. deep. Set aside 2 tablespoons beer. Pour the remaining beer over the ham. Bake, uncovered, at 350° for 1 hour.

In a small bowl, combine the brown sugar, vinegar, mustard and reserved beer; spread over the ham. Bake 40-45 minutes longer or until a meat thermometer reads 140°, basting occasionally. **Yield:** 8 servings.

Brie Mashed Potatoes

(Pictured above)

Prep/Total Time: 30 min.

These rich, buttery whipped potatoes are delicately flavored with Brie and fresh thyme...and are so tasty, they're likely to become a tradition for your special occasions.
—Yvonne Starlin, Portland, Tennessee

4 pounds potatoes (about 12 medium), peeled and cubed
1 cup milk
1 round (8 ounces) Brie cheese, rind removed and cubed
2 tablespoons butter
2 teaspoons minced fresh thyme
1 teaspoon salt
1/2 teaspoon pepper

Place potatoes in a Dutch oven and cover with water. Bring to a boil. Reduce heat; cover and simmer for 10-15 minutes or until tender; drain.

In a large mixing bowl, mash the potatoes with the milk, Brie cheese, butter, thyme, salt and pepper. **Yield:** 8-10 servings.

Creations from the Campfire

WHETHER you prefer an RV, a tent or just sleeping under the stars, your next camping trip is about to get better! The low-maintenance dishes featured here are so delicious, you'd think they came from a gourmet kitchen instead of the campfire.

Summer Sausage Hobo Packets

(Pictured below)

Prep: 25 min. **Grill:** 20 min.

This family favorite really satisfies after a day of outdoor activities. Plus, the foil packet makes cleanup a breeze.
—Tonia Anne Carrier, Elizabethton, Tennessee

- **1 pound summer sausage, cut into 1-inch pieces**
- **4 medium potatoes, peeled and cut into 1/2-inch cubes**
- **3 cups shredded cabbage**
- **1 large sweet onion, halved and sliced**
- **1 medium green pepper, cut into strips**
- **1 medium sweet red pepper, cut into strips**
- **1 small zucchini, sliced**
- **1 small yellow summer squash, sliced**
- **1 pound chicken tenderloins, cut into 1-inch pieces**
- **2 medium tomatoes, cut into wedges**
- **1/2 cup butter, cut into eight cubes**
- **1/4 cup prepared Italian salad dressing**

Summer Sausage Hobo Packets

Peanut Butter S'Mores

In a large bowl, combine the first eight ingredients. Gently stir in the chicken and tomatoes. Divide mixture among eight double thicknesses of heavy-duty foil (about 12 in. square). Top each with a butter cube.

Fold foil around mixture and seal tightly. Grill, covered, over medium heat for 20-25 minutes or until chicken juices run clear and vegetables are tender. Carefully open foil to allow steam to escape; drizzle with dressing. **Yield:** 8 servings.

Peanut Butter S'Mores

(Pictured above)

Prep/Total Time: 10 min.

I always depend on these four-ingredient goodies when dessert is a last-minute thought. On cold or rainy days when I'm not using the grill, I simply microwave these for a few seconds until the marshmallows are soft.
—Lillian Julow, Gainesville, Florida

- **8 large chocolate chip cookies**
- **4 teaspoons hot fudge ice cream topping**
- **4 large marshmallows**
- **4 peanut butter cups**

Spread the bottoms of four chocolate chip cookies with the fudge topping.

Using a long-handled fork, grill marshmallows 6 in. from medium-hot heat until golden brown, turning occasionally. Carefully place a marshmallow and peanut butter cup on each fudge-topped cookie; top with remaining cookies. Serve immediately. **Yield:** 4 servings.

Breakfast Eggs in Foil Bowls

Grilled Caesar Salad

Prep/Total Time: 20 min.

My aunt shared this recipe, which is great when it's too hot to cook inside and you want something more than a typical salad. I can toss this together in just 20 minutes.
—Debbie Clark, Northglenn, Colorado

3 tablespoons butter, melted
1/2 teaspoon minced garlic
2 bunches romaine hearts, halved lengthwise
1 cup Caesar salad dressing, *divided*
3/4 cup salad croutons
1/4 cup shredded Parmesan cheese

Prepare grill for indirect medium heat. In a small bowl, combine butter and garlic; let stand for 5 minutes. Brush over the cut side of each romaine half; lightly brush with 2-3 tablespoons salad dressing.

Grill, covered, for 3-4 minutes or until outer leaves begin to wilt and romaine is heated through, turning once. Coarsely chop romaine, discarding cores.

Transfer to a salad bowl. Sprinkle with croutons and Parmesan cheese. Serve with remaining salad dressing. **Yield:** 6 servings.

Breakfast Eggs in Foil Bowls

(Pictured above)

Prep/Total Time: 30 min.

Breakfast around the campfire couldn't be easier thanks to these clever egg bowls. They'll give you a terrific start to the day. *—Jennifer Meadows, Mattoon, Illinois*

6 eggs
1/3 cup milk
1/8 teaspoon salt
1/8 teaspoon garlic powder
1/8 teaspoon pepper
1/2 cup shredded cheddar cheese
1/4 cup chopped green pepper
4 brown-and-serve sausage links, chopped
4 bacon strips, cooked and crumbled
2 green onions, chopped

Prepare the grill for indirect medium heat. In a small bowl, whisk the first five ingredients. Pour into three 4-1/2-in. disposable foil tart pans coated with cooking spray. Sprinkle with cheese, green pepper, sausage, bacon and onions.

Cover each foil tart pan with foil. Grill, covered, for 20-22 minutes or until eggs are completely set. **Yield:** 3 servings.

Bowled Over

CAN'T FIND the foil tart pans for the eggs (pictured above)? Make your own with heavy-duty aluminum foil. Simply invert a 10-ounce custard cup onto a work surface and place three 9-in.-square pieces of foil over the cup, forming a bowl shape. Remove the foil bowl and repeat as needed.

Star-Spangled Picnic Spread

LOOKING for a sparkling menu for the Fourth of July, Labor Day or another summer gathering with family and friends? Try this fresh and fast selection of reader favorites, from a sensational sandwich to fun star-shaped treats. They're sure to add a little patriotic pizzazz to your picnic table.

Italian Muffuletta

(Pictured below)

Prep/Total Time: 25 min.

I first fixed this hearty sandwich for friends and family when they were helping my husband and me build our deck. The muffuletta was a hit, and I've served it several times since. It also makes an impressive party entree.
—Dana Schmitt, Ames, Iowa

2/3 cup pimiento-stuffed olives, chopped
1 can (4-1/4 ounces) chopped ripe olives
6 tablespoons shredded Parmesan cheese
1/4 cup Italian salad dressing
2 teaspoons minced garlic
1 round loaf (22 ounces) unsliced Italian bread
1/2 pound sliced deli turkey
1/4 pound sliced Swiss cheese
1/4 pound thinly sliced hard salami
1/4 pound sliced provolone cheese
1/4 pound thinly sliced bologna

In a small bowl, combine the first five ingredients; set aside. Cut bread in half horizontally; carefully hollow out top and bottom, leaving a 1-in. shell (discard removed bread or save for another use).

Spoon half of olive mixture over bottom half of bread. Layer with turkey, Swiss cheese, salami, provolone cheese, bologna and remaining olive mixture. Replace bread top. Cut into six wedges. **Yield:** 6 servings.

Italian Muffuletta

Mushroom Spinach Salad

Prep/Total Time: 25 min.

I'm a fan of salads, especially recipes that have fresh flavor. This simple medley really fills the bill and is also very adaptable. *—Michelle Bagwell, Alamosa, Colorado*

3 cups torn iceberg lettuce
3 cups fresh baby spinach
1/4 pound sliced fresh mushrooms
1 cup (4 ounces) shredded part-skim mozzarella cheese
2 tablespoons chopped red onion
1 tablespoon real bacon bits

DRESSING:

6 tablespoons vegetable oil
3 tablespoons sugar
3 tablespoons cider vinegar
1/4 to 1/2 teaspoon poppy seeds
1/8 teaspoon prepared mustard

In a large bowl, combine the first six ingredients; set aside. In a jar with a tight-fitting lid, combine the dressing ingredients; shake well. Drizzle over salad; toss to coat. Serve immediately. Refrigerate any leftover dressing. **Yield:** 8 servings.

Speedier Salad

IN A HURRY to pull together your picnic menu? Instead of creating the homemade dressing for your Mushroom Spinach Salad (recipe above), simply purchase your favorite bottled variety of dressing and drizzle the salad with that instead.

Star Pastry Snacks
Strawberry Salsa

Strawberry Salsa

(Pictured above)

Prep: 20 min. + chilling

This refreshing salsa is strawberry-sweet with just a hint of bite. It'll add a tongue-tingling twist to fish, chicken or tortilla chips. —Nancy Whitford, Edwards, New York

✓ This recipe includes Nutrition Facts and Diabetic Exchanges.

1-1/2 cups sliced fresh strawberries
1-1/2 cups chopped sweet red pepper
1 cup chopped green pepper
1 cup seeded chopped tomato
1/4 cup chopped Anaheim pepper
2 tablespoons minced fresh cilantro
1/2 teaspoon salt
1/2 teaspoon crushed red pepper flakes
1/4 teaspoon pepper
2 tablespoons plus 2 teaspoons honey
2 tablespoons lemon juice

In a large bowl, combine the first nine ingredients. In a small bowl, combine honey and lemon juice; gently stir into strawberry mixture. Cover and refrigerate for at least 4 hours. Stir just before serving. Serve with a slotted spoon. **Yield:** 4 cups.

Editor's Note: When cutting hot peppers, disposable gloves are recommended. Avoid touching your face.

Nutrition Facts: 1/4 cup salsa equals 25 calories, trace fat (trace saturated fat), 0 cholesterol, 76 mg sodium, 6 g carbohydrate, 1 g fiber, 1 g protein. **Diabetic Exchange:** 1/2 starch.

Star Pastry Snacks

(Pictured above)

Prep: 15 min. **Bake:** 10 min./batch

I made up this recipe and was really happy with the results. It's so simple, any young "chef" in your house could help create the star-shaped snacks. You could also use cookie cutters of different shapes for other occasions.
—Kathleen Tribble, Buellton, California

✓ This recipe includes Nutrition Facts and Diabetic Exchanges.

1 package (15 ounces) refrigerated pie pastry
2 tablespoons butter, melted
2 tablespoons plus 2-1/2 teaspoons sugar
1/2 teaspoon ground cinnamon
1/3 cup miniature chocolate chips

Unfold the pie pastry onto a lightly floured surface. Cut the pastry with a 2-1/2-in. star-shaped cookie cutter. Remove the excess dough and reroll the scraps for more cutouts if desired.

Place 1 in. apart on baking sheets coated with cooking spray; brush with butter. In a small bowl, combine sugar and cinnamon; sprinkle over stars. Sprinkle with chocolate chips.

Bake at 400° for 6-8 minutes or until the edges of the stars are golden brown. Remove the stars to wire racks. **Yield:** 4 dozen.

Nutrition Facts: 1 star equals 52 calories, 3 g fat (1 g saturated fat), 3 mg cholesterol, 36 mg sodium, 6 g carbohydrate, trace fiber, trace protein. **Diabetic Exchanges:** 1/2 starch, 1/2 fat.

Halloween Hocus-Pocus

TO CONJURE UP fun for October 31, we collected a bewitching buffet of munchies, beverages, desserts and more that you can fix in a flash. Just cast your eyes on these creepy recipes and choose your favorites. Whether for kids or adults, your Halloween bash will be a spellbinding good time!

Ogre Eyes Hot Cocoa

(Pictured below)

Prep/Total Time: 25 min.

Here's looking at you! Halloween guests of all ages will get a kick out of these eerie "ogre eyes" staring out from a mug of hot cocoa...and they couldn't be simpler to create.
—Jeannie Klugh, Lancaster, Pennsylvania

- **8 cups milk, *divided***
- **1 cup mint chocolate chips**
- **1 cup instant hot cocoa mix**
- **16 large marshmallows**
- **16 Crows candies**
- **16 lollipop sticks**

Ogre Eyes Hot Cocoa

Squirmy Wormy Sandwiches

In a large saucepan, combine 1 cup milk, chocolate chips and cocoa mix. Cook and stir over low heat until chips are melted. Stir in remaining milk; heat through.

Meanwhile, cut a slit in top of each marshmallow; insert a candy. Carefully insert a lollipop stick through the bottom of each marshmallow and into each candy.

Pour hot cocoa into mugs or cups; place two prepared marshmallows in each cup. Serve immediately. **Yield:** 8 servings.

Squirmy Wormy Sandwiches

(Pictured above)

Prep/Total Time: 20 min.

My sister and I invented these sandwiches while trying to come up with ghoulish foods for a Halloween party menu. You could also serve the hot dog "worms" as an appetizer with party picks and barbecue sauce for dipping.
—Diane Eaton, Campbell, California

- **1 package (16 ounces) hot dogs**
- **1 tablespoon vegetable oil**
- **1/2 cup ketchup**
- **1 tablespoon brown sugar**
- **2 teaspoons Worcestershire sauce**
- **1/2 teaspoon spicy brown mustard**
- **Dash Liquid Smoke, optional**
- **6 hamburger buns, split**

Cut each hot dog into eight strips. In a large skillet, saute hot dogs in oil until golden brown.

Stir in the ketchup, brown sugar, Worcestershire sauce, mustard and Liquid Smoke if desired; heat through. Serve on buns. **Yield:** 6 servings.

Gruesome Green Toes

(Pictured below)

Prep: 25 min. + standing

With only four ingredients and no baking, these treats will have you out of the kitchen in no time so you can mingle with your guests. The recipe is also a great one to make with children—even the youngest kids can press on the candy "nails." —*Jamey Jackson, Gile, Wisconsin*

12 ounces white candy coating, coarsely chopped
Green paste food coloring
22 peanut butter cream-filled sandwich cookies
11 Crows candies, halved lengthwise

In a microwave-safe bowl, melt candy coating; stir until smooth. Tint green.

Dip one sandwich cookie into the tinted candy coating. Let the excess drip off and place on waxed paper. Immediately place a candy half, cut side down, on the cookie for toenail. Repeat. Let stand for 15 minutes or until set. **Yield:** 22 cookies.

Editor's Note: This recipe was tested in a 1,100-watt microwave.

Yummy Mummy with Veggie Dip

(Pictured at right)

Prep: 25 min. **Bake:** 20 min. + cooling

I came up with this idea for dressing a veggie tray for our annual Halloween party, and everyone got really "wrapped up" in it. Frozen bread dough and dip mix make this an easy appetizer that's as fun to display as it is to eat.
—*Heather Snow, Salt Lake City, Utah*

Gruesome Green Toes

Yummy Mummy with Veggie Dip

1 loaf (1 pound) frozen bread dough, thawed
3 pieces string cheese
2 cups (16 ounces) sour cream
1 envelope fiesta ranch dip mix
1 pitted ripe olive
Assorted crackers and fresh vegetables

Let dough rise according to package directions. Place dough on a greased baking sheet. For mummy, roll out dough into a 12-in. oval that is narrower at the bottom. For the head, make an indentation about 1 in. from the top. Let rise in a warm place for 20 minutes.

Bake at 350° for 20-25 minutes or until golden brown. Arrange strips of string cheese over bread; bake 1-2 minutes longer or until cheese is melted. Remove from pan to a wire rack to cool.

Meanwhile, in a small bowl, combine sour cream and dip mix. Chill until serving.

Cut mummy in half horizontally. Hollow out bottom half, leaving a 3/4-in. shell. Cut removed bread into cubes; set aside. Place bread bottom on a serving plate. Spoon dip into shell. Replace top. For eyes, cut olive and position on head. Serve with crackers, vegetables and reserved bread. **Yield:** 16 servings (2 cups dip).

Black Cat Brownie

Black Cat Brownie

(Pictured above)

Prep: 25 min. **Bake:** 20 min. + cooling

My mom baked this frosted, cat-shaped brownie for my brother and me every Halloween when we were growing up. Now, my own daughter enjoys this treat each year. It's a yummy October tradition to pass on.
—Janice Korsmeyer, Highland, Illinois

1 package fudge brownie mix (13-inch x 9-inch pan size)
1 can (16 ounces) chocolate frosting
2 large yellow gumdrops
1 large green gumdrop
1 large black gumdrop
2 pieces black shoestring licorice
6 candy corns

Line two 9-in. round baking pans with parchment paper; coat with cooking spray and set aside.

Prepare brownie mix batter according to package directions. Pour into prepared pans. Bake at 350° for 20-25 minutes or until a toothpick comes out clean. Cool for 10 minutes before removing from pans to wire racks to cool completely; remove parchment paper.

For cat's body, place one brownie circle on a covered board. From one side of the remaining brownie, cut a 1-in.-wide crescent-shaped slice; position tail on board. From the center of the opposite side, measure 2-3/4 in. toward the center. Make a vertical cut, forming a small half circle; cut in half and trim if desired, forming two ears. For the head, position the remaining brownie with the flat side against the cat's body; add the ears.

Spread with frosting. Flatten yellow gumdrops. Cut two thin rounds from green gumdrop; position yellow and green gumdrops for eyes. Press black gumdrop into frosting for nose. Cut licorice into desired lengths for whiskers and a mouth; press lightly into frosting. Arrange candy corns at base for toes. **Yield:** 20 servings.

Bat Cupcakes

(Pictured below)

Prep: 25 min. **Bake:** 20 min. + cooling

Even my adult children love these creepy cupcakes! We always have them at our annual pumpkin-carving party. If you like, you could assemble some of the bats with the fudge stripes on their wings facing up for variety.
—Joyce Moynihan, Lakeville, Minnesota

1 package (18-1/4 ounces) chocolate cake mix
1 can (16 ounces) chocolate frosting
24 fudge-striped cookies, halved
24 milk chocolate kisses
Red decorating icing

Prepare and bake cake batter according to package directions for cupcakes; cool completely.

Set aside 2 tablespoons chocolate frosting. Frost cupcakes with remaining frosting. For wings, cut cookies in half and add scalloped edges if desired. Insert two cookie halves into each cupcake. Gently press chocolate kisses into frosting for heads. Pipe ears with reserved frosting; add eyes with decorating icing. **Yield:** 2 dozen.

Bat Cupcakes

Bloodshot Eyeballs

Bloodshot Eyeballs

(Pictured above)

Prep: 40 min. + standing

Keep your eyes peeled for Halloween fun by making these gruesome-looking but delicious deviled eggs. Serve them within 2 hours for the best "bloodshot" effect.
—Bernice Janowski, Stevens Point, Wisconsin

6 eggs
3 cups hot water
2 tablespoons red food coloring
1 tablespoon white vinegar
1/3 cup mayonnaise
1/4 cup chopped green onions
2 tablespoons minced fresh cilantro
2 teaspoons Dijon mustard
12 sliced ripe olives
1 teaspoon ketchup

Place eggs in a single layer in a large saucepan; add enough cold water to cover by 1 in. Cover and bring to a boil over high heat. Remove from the heat; cover and let stand for 15 minutes. Place in ice water until completely cooled. Gently crack eggs (do not peel).

In a large bowl, combine 3 cups hot water, food coloring and vinegar. Add eggs. (If eggs are not completely covered by colored water, add more hot water.) Let stand for 30 minutes. Remove eggs with a slotted spoon; peel.

Cut eggs in half widthwise. Place yolks in a small bowl; set whites aside. Mash yolks with a fork; stir in the mayonnaise, onions, cilantro and mustard.

To level egg white halves, cut a small slice from the bottom of each; place on a platter. Pipe or stuff yolk mixture into center of whites. Place an olive slice on each; fill olives with ketchup. Refrigerate until serving. Recipe is best eaten the day it is prepared. **Yield:** 1 dozen.

Ghoul Punch

(Pictured below)

Prep: 10 min. + freezing

Because my son's birthday is so close to Halloween, I stir up this ghoulish beverage for his party every year. The punch is a sure hit with kids—they get a kick out of the ice "hand" and "spider" ice cubes floating in the bowl.
—Katheryn Sipos, Canon City, Colorado

12 gummy spiders
1 vinyl glove
1 gallon green fruit punch, chilled
2 liters lemon-lime soda, chilled
1 quart raspberry sherbet

Pour water into an ice cube tray; add a gummy spider to each of 12 compartments. Freeze for at least 4 hours. Fill the vinyl glove with water; tie or seal and freeze for at least 4 hours.

In a 7-qt. punch bowl, combine the green fruit punch and lemon-lime soda. Add the raspberry sherbet and gummy-spider ice cubes. Remove the vinyl glove from the hand-shaped ice; add to punch. Serve immediately. **Yield:** 32 servings (6 quarts).

Ghoul Punch

Jack-o'-Lantern Sloppy Joe Pie

(Pictured below)

Prep/Total Time: 30 min.

This meat pie is so much fun to assemble—and because kids love it, you'll never have to worry about leftovers! It even goes over well with adults...but you may want to increase the heat level with a hotter salsa or seasonings.

—Bonnie Hawkins, Elkhorn, Wisconsin

1-1/2 pounds lean ground beef
1/2 cup chopped onion
2 teaspoons all-purpose flour
1 cup salsa
1/2 cup chili sauce
1 cup frozen corn
1 can (4 ounces) chopped green chilies
2 tablespoons brown sugar
1 sheet refrigerated pie pastry
1 egg
Orange paste food coloring

In a large skillet, cook beef and onion over medium heat until meat is no longer pink; drain. In a small bowl, combine the flour, salsa and chili sauce until blended; stir into skillet. Add the corn, chilies and brown sugar.

Transfer to a deep-dish 9-in. pie plate. Unroll pastry; place over filling. With a sharp knife, cut out a face to resemble a jack-o'-lantern; flute edges. Beat egg and food coloring; brush over pastry.

Bake at 450° for 9-11 minutes or until crust is golden brown and filling is bubbly. **Yield:** 6 servings.

Jack-o'-Lantern Sloppy Joe Pie

Ghostly Graveyard

Ghostly Graveyard

(Pictured above)

Prep: 30 min. **Cook:** 10 min.

I created these dressed-up cereal squares for my youngest daughter's October birthday. Then my son requested them for a school treat. But I knew for certain they were a hit when my oldest daughter took them to a class Halloween party, and even her teacher asked for the recipe!

—Angie Dierikx, Taylor Ridge, Illinois

4 cups miniature marshmallows
1/4 cup butter, cubed
6 cups crisp rice cereal
12 oval cream-filled chocolate sandwich cookies
1 tube white decorating gel
1 can (16 ounces) chocolate frosting
Halloween sprinkles

In a large saucepan, combine marshmallows and butter. Cook and stir over medium-low heat until melted and blended. Remove from the heat; stir in cereal. Press into a greased 13-in. x 9-in. x 2-in. dish; cool. Cut into 12 squares and set aside.

Cut a 1/2-in. piece from the bottom of each sandwich cookie. Crush removed cookie pieces; set aside. Write "RIP" on each cookie, using white decorating gel.

Position cereal squares on a large serving tray. With 2 tablespoons frosting, form a circle on each cereal square; top each with a decorated cookie. Sprinkle reserved crumbs around tombstones; add Halloween sprinkles. **Yield:** 12 servings.

Crunchy Monster Claws

(Pictured below)

Prep/Total Time: 30 min.

This recipe makes a creepy appetizer to serve at an October 31st gathering. The claws will really "grab" guests' attention! Plus, Cajun seasoning adds great flavor, and a crunchy coating helps keep the chicken nice and moist.
—Mary Ann Dell, Phoenixville, Pennsylvania

1 small sweet yellow pepper
2 tablespoons all-purpose flour
2 teaspoons plus 1 tablespoon Cajun seasoning, *divided*
3 eggs, lightly beaten
1-1/2 cups cornflake crumbs
2 tablespoons chopped green onion
1 pound boneless skinless chicken breasts, cut lengthwise into 3/4-inch strips
Barbecue sauce

Cut the yellow pepper into 15 triangles; set aside. In a large resealable plastic bag, combine flour and 2 teaspoons Cajun seasoning. Place eggs in a shallow bowl. In another shallow bowl, combine the cornflake crumbs, green onion and remaining Cajun seasoning.

Place a few pieces of chicken in bag; seal and shake to coat. Dip in eggs, then in crumb mixture. Place on a greased baking sheet. Repeat. Bake at 350° for 15-20 minutes or until juices run clear.

Cut a small slit into one end of each chicken strip; insert a pepper triangle into each. Serve with barbecue sauce. **Yield:** 15 appetizers.

Crunchy Monster Claws

Chili-Filled Coffin

Chili-Filled Coffin

(Pictured above)

Prep: 45 min. + cooling **Cook:** 10 min.

Here's a fuss-free main dish that's festive enough to double as a centerpiece on a party table. The hearty, meatless chili is spiced up with colorful peppers and onions.
—Agnes Ward, Stratford, Ontario

2 packages (8-1/2 ounces *each*) corn bread/muffin mix
2/3 cup milk
2 eggs
1/4 teaspoon black paste food coloring
1 medium sweet red pepper, sliced
1 serrano pepper, seeded and finely chopped
1/3 cup chopped onion
1 tablespoon vegetable oil
2 cans (15 ounces *each*) fat-free vegetarian chili
1 tablespoon process cheese sauce
1 tablespoon ketchup

In a large bowl, combine corn bread mix, milk, eggs and food coloring until moistened. Pour into a greased 9-in. x 5-in. x 3-in. loaf pan. Bake at 400° for 30-35 minutes until a toothpick inserted near the center comes out clean. Cool for 10 minutes; remove from pan to a wire rack to cool completely.

Cut top fourth off loaf of bread; carefully hollow out bottom, leaving a 1-in. shell (discard removed bread or save for another use).

In a large skillet, saute peppers and onion in oil until tender. Set aside 1/4 cup pepper mixture. Stir chili into remaining pepper mixture; heat through. Spoon 2-1/2 to 3 cups chili mixture into bread coffin; arrange reserved pepper mixture over chili. Replace bread top. Transfer remaining chili to a serving bowl.

Place cheese sauce in a heavy-duty resealable plastic bag; cut a small hole in a corner of bag. Write "RIP" with cheese sauce, then repeat with ketchup. Serve immediately. **Yield:** 6 servings.

Editor's Note: When cutting hot peppers, disposable gloves are recommended. Avoid touching your face.

Thanksgiving Extras They'll Crave

WHEN TURKEY DAY is over and there are lots of holiday leftovers in the fridge, what's a cook to do? You don't want perfectly good food to go to waste...but at the same time, you don't want to keep feeding your family the same thing for a week!

For the solution to that dilemma, just look here. These creative recipes make deliciously different use of cooked turkey, as well as extra cans of cranberry sauce you may have stocked in the cupboard.

Club-Style Turkey Enchiladas

(Pictured below)

Prep: 25 min. **Bake:** 30 min.

Bacon, shredded turkey and Swiss cheese are the basis of these unusual but delightful enchiladas. You'll need approximately 1-3/4 cups of leftover turkey for this recipe.
—Anna Ginsberg, Austin, Texas

8 bacon strips, chopped
1/2 cup chopped sweet red pepper
1/3 cup chopped onion
10 ounces thinly sliced cooked turkey, shredded
1-1/2 cups (6 ounces) shredded Swiss cheese, *divided*
1/4 teaspoon salt
1/4 teaspoon pepper
8 yellow corn tortillas (6 inches), warmed
1 carton (10 ounces) refrigerated Alfredo sauce
1/4 cup milk

Club-Style Turkey Enchiladas

Crescent Turkey Casserole

2 cups shredded lettuce
1 can (14-1/2 ounces) diced tomatoes, well drained

In a large skillet, saute the bacon, red pepper and onion until bacon is crisp and vegetables are tender; drain. Cool slightly.

In a large bowl, combine the turkey, bacon mixture, 1 cup cheese, salt and pepper. Place 1/2 cup turkey mixture down the center of each tortilla. Roll up and place seam side down in a greased 13-in. x 9-in. x 2-in. baking dish. In a small bowl, combine Alfredo sauce and milk; pour over top.

Cover and bake at 350° for 25 minutes. Uncover; sprinkle with remaining cheese. Bake 5-10 minutes longer or until cheese is melted. Garnish with lettuce and tomatoes. **Yield:** 4 servings.

Crescent Turkey Casserole

(Pictured above)

Prep/Total Time: 30 min.

This comforting bake features the creamy filling and golden crust of a potpie. Plus, the casserole is ready in just 30 minutes.
—Daniela Essman, Perham, Minnesota

1/2 cup mayonnaise
2 tablespoons all-purpose flour
1 teaspoon chicken bouillon granules
1/8 teaspoon pepper
3/4 cup milk
1-1/2 cups cubed cooked turkey breast
1 package (10 ounces) frozen mixed vegetables, thawed
1 tube (4 ounces) refrigerated crescent rolls

In a large saucepan, combine the mayonnaise, flour, bouillon and pepper. Gradually add milk; stir until smooth. Bring to a boil over medium heat; cook and stir for 2 minutes or until thickened. Add turkey and vegetables; cook 3-4 minutes longer, stirring occasionally. Spoon into a greased 8-in. square baking dish.

Unroll crescent dough and separate into two rectangles. Seal seams and perforations. Place over turkey mixture. Bake at 375° for 15-20 minutes or until golden brown. **Yield:** 4 servings.

Cranberry Chili Meatballs

(Pictured below)

Prep/Total Time: 30 min.

Using packaged meatballs for this recipe helps me save time in the kitchen. My friends look forward to these at holiday gatherings—and there are never leftovers!
—Amy Scamerhorn, Indianapolis, Indiana

✓ This recipe includes Nutrition Facts and Diabetic Exchanges.

1 can (16 ounces) jellied cranberry sauce
1 bottle (12 ounces) chili sauce
3/4 cup packed brown sugar
1/2 teaspoon chili powder
1/2 teaspoon ground cumin
1/4 teaspoon cayenne pepper
1 package (38 ounces) frozen fully cooked home-style meatballs, thawed

In a large saucepan over medium heat, combine the first six ingredients; stir until sugar is dissolved. Add meatballs; cook for 20-25 minutes or until hot, stirring occasionally. **Yield:** about 6 dozen.

Nutrition Facts: 1 meatball equals 51 calories, 2 g fat (1 g saturated fat), 12 mg cholesterol, 80 mg sodium, 6 g carbohydrate, trace fiber, 2 g protein. **Diabetic Exchanges:** 1/2 starch, 1/2 lean meat.

Cranberry Chili Meatballs

Cranberry Pork Chops with RIce

Cranberry Pork Chops with Rice

(Pictured above)

Prep/Total Time: 30 min.

This is a satisfying, wholesome and delicious meal-in-one for your family. Best of all, it goes together in just half an hour and looks special enough to serve guests.
—Mary Bilyeu, Ann Arbor, Michigan

1/3 cup all-purpose flour
1/2 teaspoon salt
1/2 teaspoon seasoned salt
1/4 teaspoon pepper
4 boneless pork loin chops (1/2 inch thick and 4 ounces *each*)
2 tablespoons olive oil
1 can (16 ounces) whole-berry cranberry sauce
1 tablespoon balsamic vinegar

CRANBERRY RICE:

1-3/4 cups chicken broth
2 cups instant brown rice
1/2 cup dried cranberries

In a large resealable plastic bag, combine the flour, salt, seasoned salt and pepper. Add pork chops, one at a time, and shake to coat. In a large skillet, cook pork in oil over medium-high heat for 4-5 minutes on each side or until juices run clear.

In a small bowl, combine cranberry sauce and vinegar; pour over chops. Bring to a boil. Reduce heat; cover and simmer for 10 minutes.

Meanwhile, in a large saucepan, bring chicken broth to a boil. Add rice and cranberries. Return to a boil. Reduce heat; cover and simmer for 5 minutes. Remove from the heat. Let stand for 5 minutes or until the broth is absorbed. Serve pork chops with sauce and rice. **Yield:** 4 servings.

Merry Gifts from the Kitchen

SEEMS like everyone is looking for ways to cut down on Christmastime expenses...and the hustle and bustle of gift shopping at the mall. Here, busy cooks share their secrets for cooking and baking up easy seasonal gifts guaranteed to please.

From a flavor-packed seasoning mix that'll kick-start a chili dinner to yummy Yuletide mice cookies for sweet tooths, these goodies go together fast—and are likely to disappear just as quickly as soon as your family and friends receive them!

Chili Seasoning Mix

(Pictured below)

Prep/Total Time: 10 min.

I created this recipe as a Christmas present, packaged in fun cups from garage sales and wrapped in bright cellophane bags with an easy chili recipe. Now, I'm filling requests all year! —Caroline Munoz, Austin, Minnesota

1/2 cup dried parsley flakes
1/2 cup chili powder
1/4 cup dried minced onion
2 tablespoons salt
2 tablespoons cornstarch
2 tablespoons dried minced garlic
2 tablespoons ground cumin
1 tablespoon ground coriander
1 tablespoon *each* dried cilantro flakes, basil and oregano

Chili Seasoning Mix

Christmas Mice Cookies

1 tablespoon crushed red pepper flakes
1-1/2 teaspoons pepper

In a small bowl, combine all ingredients. Store in an airtight container for up to 6 months. Use as a rub for pork or sprinkle on fish or as a seasoning for chili. **Yield:** 1-3/4 cups.

Christmas Mice Cookies

(Pictured above)

Prep: 30 min. + chilling

These whimsical little mice taste like truffles and have been a family favorite for 15 years. We really enjoy the smiles and laughs they get. At holiday time, we make sure to have enough for friends, neighbors and parties.
—Deborah Zabor, Fort Erie, Ontario

✓ This recipe includes Nutrition Facts and Diabetic Exchanges.

2/3 cup semisweet chocolate chips
2 cups chocolate wafer crumbs (about 40 wafers), *divided*
1/3 cup sour cream
36 red nonpareils
1/4 cup sliced almonds
18 pieces black shoestring licorice (2 inches *each*)

In a microwave-safe bowl, melt chocolate chips; stir until smooth. Stir in 1 cup crumbs and sour cream. Cover and refrigerate for 1 hour or until easy to handle.

For each mouse, roll about 1 tablespoon chocolate mixture into a ball, tapering one end to resemble a mouse. Roll in remaining chocolate crumbs to coat. Position nonpareils for eyes, almond slices for ears and licorice pieces for tails. **Yield:** 1-1/2 dozen.

Nutrition Facts: 1 cookie equals 135 calories, 5 g fat (2 g saturated fat), 3 mg cholesterol, 89 mg sodium, 22 g carbohydrate, 1 g fiber, 2 g protein. **Diabetic Exchanges:** 1-1/2 starch, 1/2 fat.

Pretzel Cereal Crunch

(Pictured below)

Prep: 20 min. + cooling

A festive container of this salty-sweet snack was left in my mailbox several Christmases ago—and was gone in no time! My neighbor shared the quick and easy recipe. I've since added peanut butter because I love that flavor.
—Cindy Lund, Walley Center, California

1-1/4 cups Golden Grahams
1-1/4 cups Apple Cinnamon Cheerios
1-1/4 cups miniature pretzels
1 cup chopped pecans, toasted
1 package (10 to 12 ounces) vanilla *or* white chips
2 tablespoons creamy peanut butter

In a large bowl, combine the cereals, pretzels and pecans. In a microwave-safe bowl, melt chips; stir until smooth. Stir in peanut butter. Drizzle over cereal mixture; toss to coat. Spread evenly on a waxed paper-lined baking sheet. Cool completely; break into pieces. Store in an airtight container. **Yield:** about 9 cups.

Editor's Note: This recipe was tested in a 1,100-watt microwave.

Pretzel Cereal Crunch

Oatmeal Cranberry Cookie Mix

Oatmeal Cranberry Cookie Mix

(Pictured above)

Prep: 15 min. **Bake:** 10 min./batch

Who wouldn't like to find a jar of this scrumptious cookie mix under the tree? Be sure to include the list of added ingredients and instructions for baking. Yum!
—Sarah Wilson, Republic, Washington

✓ This recipe includes Nutrition Facts and Diabetic Exchanges.

1/2 cup all-purpose flour
1/4 teaspoon baking soda
1/4 teaspoon salt
1/4 cup sugar
1/4 cup packed brown sugar
1 cup old-fashioned oats
1 cup chopped walnuts
1/2 cup Shredded Wheat, crushed
1/2 cup dried cranberries
ADDITIONAL INGREDIENTS:
1/2 cup butter, softened
1 egg
2 tablespoons water
1/2 teaspoon vanilla extract

In a small bowl, combine the flour, baking soda and salt. In a 1-qt. glass container, layer the flour mixture, sugar, brown sugar, oats, walnuts, cereal and cranberries. Cover and store in a cool dry place for up to 6 months. **Yield:** 1 batch (about 4 cups total).

To prepare cookies: In a large bowl, beat butter, egg, water and vanilla until blended. Add cookie mix and mix well. Drop by rounded tablespoonfuls 2 in. apart onto ungreased baking sheets. Bake at 350° for 10-12 minutes or until golden brown. Cool for 1 minute before removing to wire racks to cool completely. Store in an airtight container. **Yield:** about 2-1/2 dozen.

Nutrition Facts: 1 cookie equals 89 calories, 5 g fat (2 g saturated fat), 14 mg cholesterol, 51 mg sodium, 9 g carbohydrate, 1 g fiber, 2 g protein. **Diabetic Exchanges:** 1 fat, 1/2 starch.

Make-Ahead Christmas Cookies

WHETHER you're a novice baker or a pro, it's easy to fill your holiday tray with these festive treats. You can even whip them up in advance and freeze them. Just pick your favorites, and have a merry time!

Chocolate Reindeer Cookies

(Pictured at right)

Prep: 55 min. **Bake:** 15 min./batch

These Rudolph treats from our Test Kitchen home economists add a touch of whimsy to Christmas cookie trays.

1-1/2 cups packed brown sugar
3/4 cup butter, cubed
2 tablespoons water
2 cups (12 ounces) semisweet chocolate chips
2 eggs
1/2 teaspoon almond extract
2-3/4 cups all-purpose flour
1-1/4 teaspoons baking soda
1/2 teaspoon salt
Miniature pretzels
Red shoestring licorice, cut into 1-inch pieces
1 can (16 ounces) chocolate frosting
M&M's miniature baking bits, cherry sour balls and nonpareil-coated chocolate candies

In a large saucepan over low heat, cook the brown sugar, butter and water until butter is melted. Remove from the heat; stir in chocolate chips until smooth. Cool for 5 minutes. Stir in eggs and extract. Combine the flour, baking soda and salt; fold into chocolate mixture.

Drop dough by rounded teaspoonfuls onto baking sheets; cover and freeze until firm. Transfer frozen dough to a resealable plastic freezer bag. May be frozen up to 3 months.

To use frozen dough: Place 2 in. apart on greased baking sheets. Bake at 350° for 13-15 minutes or until surface cracks. Cool on wire racks.

Meanwhile, cut two rounded sides from each pretzel. Make a 3/4-in. cut in each licorice piece. For each cookie, frost and position pretzels for antlers, M&M's for eyes and sour ball for nose. Shape licorice for mouth. Add nonpareil candies for collar. **Yield:** about 5 dozen.

Chocolate Reindeer Cookies

Chocolate-Dipped Cranberry Cookies

Prep: 25 min. **Bake:** 15 min. + cooling

Your family and friends will love the combination of rich chocolate and tangy cranberries in this special cookie.
—Barbara Nowakowski, North Tonawanda, New York

✓ This recipe includes Nutrition Facts and Diabetic Exchanges.

1 cup shortening
1 cup sugar
1 egg
1 teaspoon vanilla extract
2 cups all-purpose flour
1 teaspoon baking powder
1/2 teaspoon salt
2 cups coarsely chopped fresh *or* frozen cranberries
2 cups (12 ounces) semisweet chocolate chips
2 tablespoons shortening
1-1/4 cups chopped walnuts, optional

In a large bowl, cream shortening and sugar until fluffy. Beat in egg and vanilla. Combine flour, baking powder and salt; gradually add to creamed mixture. Using paper towels, pat cranberries dry; stir into dough. Drop by rounded teaspoonfuls onto baking sheets; cover and freeze until firm. Transfer dough to a resealable plastic freezer bag. May be frozen up to 3 months.

To use frozen dough: Place 2 in. apart on baking sheets coated with cooking spray. Bake at 350° for 15-17 minutes or until lightly browned. Cool on wire racks.

In a microwave, melt chocolate chips and shortening; stir until smooth. Dip cookies halfway into chocolate mixture; sprinkle chocolate with walnuts if desired. Place on waxed paper until set. **Yield:** 3-1/2 dozen.

Editor's Note: To prepare the cookies without freezing, drop the dough by rounded teaspoonfuls 2 in. apart on baking sheets coated with cooking spray. Bake at 350° for 11-13 minutes or until lightly browned. Cool on wire racks.

Nutrition Facts: 1 cookie (calculated without nuts) equals 130 calories, 8 g fat (3 g saturated fat), 5 mg cholesterol, 40 mg sodium, 15 g carbohydrate, 1 g fiber, 1 g protein. **Diabetic Exchanges:** 1-1/2 fat, 1 starch.

Thumbprint Cookies

(Pictured below)

Prep: 20 min. **Bake:** 20 min./batch + cooling

These nutty treats are so pretty with the preserves in the center. —Georgia MacDonald, Dover, New Hampshire

✓ This recipe includes Nutrition Facts and Diabetic Exchanges.

1/2 cup butter, softened
1/4 cup packed brown sugar
1 egg yolk
1/2 teaspoon vanilla extract
1 cup all-purpose flour
1/4 teaspoon salt
1 egg white, lightly beaten
3/4 cup finely chopped pecans *or* walnuts
1/2 cup preserves *or* jelly of your choice

In a large bowl, cream butter and brown sugar until fluffy. Beat in egg yolk and vanilla. Combine flour and salt; gradually add to creamed mixture.

Shape dough into 1-in. balls; roll in egg white, then in pecans. Using the end of a wooden spoon handle, make an indentation in the center of each ball. Cover and freeze until firm. Transfer dough to a resealable plastic freezer bag. May be frozen up to 3 months.

To use frozen dough: Place 2 in. apart on baking sheets coated with cooking spray. Bake at 350° for 17-20 minutes or until set. Remove to wire racks. While warm, fill each with a teaspoonful of preserves. Cool completely. **Yield:** about 1-1/2 dozen.

Editor's Note: To prepare cookies without freezing, shape dough into 1-in. balls; roll in egg white, then in nuts. Place 2 in. apart on baking sheets coated with cooking spray. Using the end of a wooden spoon handle, make an indentation in the center of each ball. Bake at 350° for 12-14 minutes or until lightly browned. Remove to wire racks. While warm, fill each with a teaspoonful of preserves. Cool completely.

Nutrition Facts: 1 cookie equals 142 calories, 9 g fat (4 g saturated fat), 25 mg cholesterol, 73 mg sodium, 15 g carbohydrate, 1 g fiber, 2 g protein. **Diabetic Exchanges:** 2 fat, 1 starch.

Thumbprint Cookies

Crisp Lemon Tea Cookies

Crisp Lemon Tea Cookies

(Pictured above)

Prep: 40 min. + chilling **Bake:** 10 min. + cooling

Our Test Kitchen staff had fun "sprucing up" these frosted goodies using colorful chocolate baking bits.

✓ This recipe includes Nutrition Facts and Diabetic Exchanges.

1/2 cup butter, softened
1/2 cup sugar
1 tablespoon milk
1/2 teaspoon vanilla extract
1-1/4 cups all-purpose flour
1/2 teaspoon ground cinnamon

FROSTING:

2 tablespoons plus 1 teaspoon butter
1-1/2 cups confectioners' sugar
2 tablespoons lemon juice
Assorted M&M's miniature baking bits

In a small bowl, cream butter and sugar until fluffy. Beat in milk and vanilla. Gradually add flour and cinnamon to creamed mixture. Shape dough into an 8-in. x 2-in. roll; wrap in plastic wrap and freeze.

To use frozen dough: Unwrap and let stand at room temperature for 10 minutes. Cut into 1/4-in. slices. Place 2 in. apart on ungreased baking sheets. Bake at 375° for 8-10 minutes or until lightly browned. Cool on wire racks.

For frosting, in a small bowl, cream butter and confectioners' sugar. Gradually beat in lemon juice. Frost cookies. Decorate with baking bits. **Yield:** 2 dozen.

Editor's Note: This recipe does not use eggs.

Nutrition Facts: 1 frosted cookie (calculated without baking bits) equals 113 calories, 5 g fat (3 g saturated fat), 13 mg cholesterol, 35 mg sodium, 17 g carbohydrate, trace fiber, 1 g protein. **Diabetic Exchanges:** 1 starch, 1 fat.

Chapter 3

30 Minutes to Mealtime

IS GETTING dinner on the table for your family one of the most challenging parts of your day? Thanks to this extra-big chapter, it might now become the *easiest* part!

Just page through to find 26 plate-filling meals you'll be able to serve your family in a flash. Each sure-to-please recipe can be prepared from start to finish in only 30 minutes—or less.

Fast food from a restaurant simply can't compare to wholesome home cooking such as Kielbasa Bow Tie Skillet, Colorful Chicken Pizza, Three-Cheese Garlic Bread and Raisin Sauce for Pound Cake.

So choose any of these fast but flavorful dinners you like—and enjoy it tonight!

SUPPER IN A SNAP. Lemon Rice and Pork Chops with Onion Gravy (both recipes on p. 49).

Quick-Fix Greek Supper

WHEN YOUR FAMILY is craving a cozy dinner, this menu will hit the spot. Hearty Greek-Style Supper from Alice Bower of Roanoke, Illinois is a meal-in-one dish that's sure to be a favorite. Better still, there's minimal prep work and cleanup!

Add a little crunch to the menu with Garlic-Sesame Pita Chips—all you need is 15 minutes and a few basic ingredients. With their crisp texture, these nibbles from Helen Forsythe of Puyallup, Washington are a wonderful addition to any meal. Enjoy!

Greek-Style Supper

Prep/Total Time: 30 min.

✓ This recipe includes Nutrition Facts and Diabetic Exchanges.

1/2 pound ground beef
1/2 cup chopped onion
1 can (14-1/2 ounces) beef broth
1 can (14-1/2 ounces) diced tomatoes, undrained
1-1/2 cups uncooked penne pasta
1-1/2 cups frozen cut green beans, thawed
2 tablespoons tomato paste
2 teaspoons dried oregano
1/2 teaspoon garlic powder
1/4 teaspoon ground cinnamon
3/4 cup crumbled feta cheese

In a large skillet, cook beef and onion over medium heat until meat is no longer pink. Meanwhile, in a large saucepan, bring broth and tomatoes to a boil; add pasta. Reduce heat; simmer, uncovered, for 15-20 minutes or until pasta is tender, stirring occasionally.

Drain beef mixture; add to pasta. Stir in beans, tomato paste, oregano, garlic powder and cinnamon; heat through. Sprinkle with feta cheese. **Yield:** 4 servings.

Nutrition Facts: 1-1/2 cups equals 300 calories, 10 g fat (5 g saturated fat), 39 mg cholesterol, 792 mg sodium, 33 g carbohydrate, 6 g fiber, 20 g protein. **Diabetic Exchanges:** 2 lean meat, 2 vegetable, 1-1/2 starch, 1/2 fat.

Garlic-Sesame Pita Chips

Prep/Total Time: 15 min.

2 whole wheat pita breads (6 inches)
3 tablespoons olive oil
1 teaspoon sesame oil
1 tablespoon sesame seeds
1/2 teaspoon garlic salt

Cut pita breads in half. Split each half in two; cut into strips. Place on ungreased baking sheets. In a small bowl, combine the oils; brush over strips. Sprinkle with sesame seeds and garlic salt.

Bake at 400° for 3-5 minutes or until golden brown. Remove to wire racks. **Yield:** about 4 dozen.

Greek-Style Supper
Garlic-Sesame Pita Chips

Sensational Skillet Dinner

THIS SPECIAL MENU couldn't make dinnertime simpler! Not only is Kielbasa Bow Tie Skillet a real crowd-pleaser, it comes together in just one pan. Plus, it freezes and reheats beautifully, so you'll want to fix extras for a fast entree later.

"My daughters are picky eaters," says Lori Daniels of Beverly, West Virginia, "but this reminds them of macaroni and cheese, and they gobble it up!"

When plates are scraped clean, it's time for Raisin Sauce for Pound Cake, a homey dessert that takes moments to prepare. "I often substitute white cupcakes for the pound cake," says Charlene Turnbull, Wainwright, Alberta. "It's one of our favorite desserts."

Kielbasa Bow Tie Skillet

Prep/Total Time: 25 min.

8 ounces uncooked bow tie pasta
1 pound fully cooked kielbasa *or* smoked Polish sausage, cut into 1/4-inch slices
1 jar (4-1/2 ounces) sliced mushrooms, drained
2 teaspoons minced garlic
2 tablespoons butter
1 tablespoon cornstarch
1-1/2 cups milk
1-1/2 cups fresh *or* frozen snow peas
1 cup (4 ounces) shredded cheddar cheese

Cook pasta according to package directions. Meanwhile, in a large skillet, saute the sausage, mushrooms and garlic in butter.

Combine cornstarch and milk until smooth; gradually add to the skillet. Bring to a boil; cook and stir for 2 minutes or until thickened. Drain pasta; add to sausage mixture. Stir in the peas and cheese; cook until cheese is melted. **Yield:** 4 servings.

Raisin Sauce for Pound Cake

Prep/Total Time: 15 min.

1 loaf (10-3/4 ounces) frozen pound cake
1/2 cup packed brown sugar
2 tablespoons all-purpose flour
1/4 teaspoon salt
Dash ground cinnamon and nutmeg
1 cup water
2 tablespoons raisins
1/2 teaspoon vanilla extract
1/8 teaspoon maple flavoring
Vanilla ice cream

Raisin Sauce for Pound Cake
Kielbasa Bow Tie Skillet

With a serrated knife, cut pound cake in half widthwise; cut one half into four slices and set aside to thaw. Freeze remaining cake for another use.

In a small saucepan, combine the brown sugar, flour, salt, cinnamon and nutmeg; stir in water until smooth. Add raisins. Bring to a boil over medium heat; cook and stir for 1-2 minutes or until thickened.

Remove from the heat; stir in vanilla and maple flavoring. Top each slice of cake with a scoop of ice cream; drizzle with raisin sauce. **Yield:** 4 servings.

Second-Day Sauce

IF YOU HAVE leftover sauce from Raisin Sauce for Pound Cake (recipe at left), just store it in the refrigerator. The next morning, simply warm the sauce, and you'll have a delicious topping to put over pancakes, waffles or French toast for breakfast.

Restaurant Taste at Home

Three-Cheese Garlic Bread
Broccoli with Smoked Almonds
Lemon Teriyaki Chicken

TOO HUNGRY to spend a long time cooking? You don't have to stop for takeout. With this restaurant-quality menu, you'll be able to cook fast and eat well.

The main star is Lemon Teriyaki Chicken, sauteed on the stovetop. The moist chicken dish has mild, family-pleasing flavor. "I like to serve it over rice," says Clara Coulston, Washington Court House, Ohio.

Colorful, attractive Broccoli with Smoked Almonds will complement the chicken nicely. "The recipe came from my mom," says Gertrudis Miller, Evansville, Indiana. "I consider it her best skillet side dish."

Let Three-Cheese Garlic Bread from Judy Schut of Grand Rapids, Michigan tie your dinner together. The warm, gooey bread is bound to be a hit!

Lemon Teriyaki Chicken

Prep/Total Time: 25 min.

☑ This recipe includes Nutrition Facts and Diabetic Exchanges.

4 boneless skinless chicken breast halves (4 ounces *each*)
2 tablespoons all-purpose flour
3 tablespoons butter
1/4 cup teriyaki sauce
2 tablespoons lemon juice
3/4 teaspoon minced garlic
1/2 teaspoon sugar

Flatten chicken to 1/2-in. thickness; coat with flour. In a large skillet, cook chicken in butter over medium heat for 4-5 minutes on each side or until juices run clear. Remove and keep warm.

Add the teriyaki sauce, lemon juice, garlic and sugar to the skillet; stir to loosen browned bits. Return the chicken to the pan. Bring to a boil. Reduce heat; simmer, uncovered, for 2-3 minutes or until heated through. **Yield:** 4 servings.

Nutrition Facts: 1 chicken breast half equals 231 calories, 11 g fat (6 g saturated fat), 86 mg cholesterol, 752 mg sodium, 6 g carbohydrate, trace fiber, 24 g protein. **Diabetic Exchanges:** 3 very lean meat, 2 fat, 1/2 starch.

Broccoli with Smoked Almonds

Prep/Total Time: 15 min.

1 package (14 ounces) frozen broccoli florets, thawed
1/2 teaspoon minced garlic
1 tablespoon olive oil
1/2 cup water
1/4 teaspoon salt
1/3 cup smoked *or* roasted salted almonds, coarsely chopped
1 jar (2 ounces) sliced pimientos, drained

In a large skillet, saute broccoli and garlic in oil for 2 minutes or until garlic is golden brown. Add water and salt; bring to a boil. Reduce heat; cover and cook for 2-3 minutes or until broccoli is tender.

Add almonds and pimientos. Cook, uncovered, for 1 minute or until water is evaporated. **Yield:** 4 servings.

Three-Cheese Garlic Bread

Prep/Total Time: 15 min.

1 loaf (1 pound) unsliced Italian bread
1/4 cup butter, softened
1/2 cup shredded part-skim mozzarella cheese
1/2 cup shredded cheddar cheese
1 tablespoon grated Parmesan cheese
1/4 teaspoon garlic powder
1/8 teaspoon Worcestershire sauce
Dash paprika and pepper

Cut bread in half widthwise; cut one portion in half lengthwise. Save remaining bread for another use. In a small mixing bowl, combine the remaining ingredients. Spread evenly over cut sides of bread.

Place on a baking sheet. Bake at 400° for 10-12 minutes or until cheese is melted. Slice and serve warm. **Yield:** 4 servings.

Easy Breakfast Foods Anytime

SAY GOODBYE to the winter doldrums! When it's cold outside, you can create a little sunshine by serving this bright breakfast.

Apple Spice Waffles are cozy and comforting anytime, morning or evening. "The recipe comes from a recipe booklet I made for my daughter one Christmas," writes Jane Sims of De Leon, Texas.

Try savory Pork Sausage Patties on the side. "My sons grew up enjoying them and still love them today," says Carole Thomson, Komarno, Manitoba.

Add a little fruit or glasses of juice, and you've got a pretty, perfect breakfast...or dinner. You choose!

Apple Spice Waffles

Prep/Total Time: 30 min.

2 cups biscuit/baking mix
2 teaspoons ground cinnamon
1 teaspoon ground nutmeg
2 eggs
1-1/2 cups milk
6 tablespoons butter, melted
1 cup chopped peeled apple

In a large bowl, combine the biscuit/baking mix, cinnamon and nutmeg. Combine the eggs and milk; stir into the dry ingredients until smooth. Stir in the melted butter and apple.

Bake waffle batter in a preheated waffle iron according to the manufacturer's directions until golden brown. **Yield:** 12 waffles.

Pork Sausage Patties

Prep/Total Time: 15 min.

1 egg, beaten
1/3 cup milk
1/2 cup chopped onion
2 tablespoons all-purpose flour
1/8 teaspoon salt
Dash pepper
1 pound sage bulk pork sausage

In a large bowl, combine the first six ingredients. Crumble the sausage over the mixture and mix well. Shape into six patties.

In a large skillet, cook the patties over medium heat for 6 minutes on each side or until the meat is no longer pink, turning occasionally. **Yield:** 6 servings.

Pork Sausage Patties
Apple Spice Waffles

Confetti Corn
Salmon with Curry Chutney Sauce

Seafood with a Taste of Spring

WHEN SPRINGTIME is in the air, your family's appetite for heavy food may just go the way of melting snow! They might begin to crave lighter menus... such as the scrumptious seafood dinner featured here. And the entire meal can be on your table in less than 30 minutes.

Tropical-flavored Salmon with Curry Chutney Sauce starts off this special spread that whispers of warmer weather. Carla Newman whips up the main dish in her Mequon, Wisconsin kitchen.

Looking for a fresh and colorful new way to fix corn for her kids, Glenda Watts of Charleston, Illinois stirred in water chestnuts, red pepper and chopped carrot—adding extra nutrition at the same time! Her easy Confetti Corn will dress up almost any entree.

Salmon with Curry Chutney Sauce

Prep/Total Time: 20 min.

2 tablespoons all-purpose flour
2 teaspoons curry powder
1/4 teaspoon salt
4 salmon fillets (6 ounces *each*)
2 tablespoons butter
3/4 cup chicken broth
1/3 cup mango chutney
1/4 teaspoon hot pepper sauce

In a large resealable plastic bag, combine the flour, curry and salt. Add salmon; seal bag and shake to coat. In a large skillet, cook salmon in butter for 5-6 minutes on each side or until fish flakes easily with a fork.

Meanwhile, in a small saucepan, combine the chicken broth, mango chutney and hot pepper sauce. Bring to a boil. Reduce heat; simmer, uncovered, for 3-5 minutes or until heated through. Serve over salmon. **Yield:** 4 servings.

Confetti Corn

Prep/Total Time: 15 min.

✓ This recipe includes Nutrition Facts and Diabetic Exchanges.

1/4 cup chopped carrot
1 tablespoon olive oil
2-3/4 cups fresh *or* frozen corn, thawed
1/4 cup chopped water chestnuts
1/4 cup chopped sweet red pepper
1 teaspoon dried parsley flakes

In a large skillet, saute carrot in oil until crisp-tender. Stir in the corn, water chestnuts, red pepper and parsley; heat through. **Yield:** 4 servings.

Nutrition Facts: 3/4 cup equals 140 calories, 4 g fat (1 g saturated fat), 0 cholesterol, 7 mg sodium, 26 g carbohydrate, 3 g fiber, 4 g protein. **Diabetic Exchanges:** 1-1/2 starch, 1/2 fat.

Cold-Weather Comfort Food

WARM UP chilly days with a super-fast, savory meal that will please everyone—including the cook! Just ask Amy Radyshewsky of Great Falls, Montana. "I created my Pork Chops with Onion Gravy as a quick dinner for my finicky husband," she says. "He always gives these tender chops a thumbs-up."

Table-ready in just 15 minutes, colorful Lemon Rice delivers a refreshing splash of citrus flavor. It's a favorite from Pat Stevens, Granbury, Texas.

Pork Chops with Onion Gravy

Prep/Total Time: 30 min.

✓ This recipe includes Nutrition Facts and Diabetic Exchanges.

4 boneless pork loin chops (1/2 inch thick and 4 ounces *each*)
1/4 teaspoon pepper
1/8 teaspoon salt
1 small onion, sliced and separated into rings
1 tablespoon canola oil
1/4 cup reduced-sodium chicken broth
1 envelope pork gravy mix
1/8 teaspoon garlic powder
3/4 cup water

Sprinkle pork chops with pepper and salt. In a large skillet, cook the chops and onion in oil over medium heat for 2-3 minutes on each side or until the chops are lightly browned; drain.

Add broth. Bring to a boil. Reduce heat; cover and simmer for 14-16 minutes or until meat is no longer pink, turning once.

In a small bowl, whisk gravy mix, garlic powder and water. Pour over the pork chops. Bring to a boil. Reduce heat; simmer, uncovered, for 3-4 minutes or until thickened, stirring occasionally. **Yield:** 4 servings.

Nutrition Facts: 1 pork chop with 3 tablespoons gravy equals 210 calories, 10 g fat (3 g saturated fat), 55 mg cholesterol, 528 mg sodium, 6 g carbohydrate, trace fiber, 22 g protein. **Diabetic Exchanges:** 3 lean meat, 1/2 starch, 1/2 fat.

Lemon Rice

Prep/Total Time: 15 min.

✓ This recipe includes Nutrition Facts and Diabetic Exchanges.

1-1/2 cups chicken broth
1-1/2 cups uncooked instant rice
1 tablespoon butter
1 to 1-1/2 teaspoons grated lemon peel
1/2 teaspoon minced garlic
Dash salt
2 tablespoons minced fresh parsley
2 tablespoons diced pimientos
1/8 teaspoon pepper

In a small saucepan, bring broth to a boil. Stir in the rice, butter, lemon peel, garlic and salt; cover and remove from the heat. Let stand for 5 minutes. Stir in the parsley, pimientos and pepper. **Yield:** 4 servings.

Nutrition Facts: 3/4 cup equals 169 calories, 3 g fat (2 g saturated fat), 8 mg cholesterol, 418 mg sodium, 31 g carbohydrate, 1 g fiber, 4 g protein. **Diabetic Exchanges:** 2 starch, 1/2 fat.

Lemon Rice
Pork Chops with Onion Gravy

Meal with Malt Shop Appeal

YOU'LL SATISFY the whole family when you serve the diner-inspired meal here. Juicy Change-of-Pace Burgers from Nita Smith, Bellefonte, Pennsylvania feature veggies and chili sauce. The menu gets even better with Loaded Waffle Fries from Jeffrey Viccone of Decatur, Illinois, plus Chocolate Banana Smoothies from Renee Zimmer, Tacoma, Washington.

Change-of-Pace Burgers

Prep/Total Time: 20 min.

1/4 cup finely chopped onion
1/4 cup finely chopped green pepper
3 tablespoons chopped fresh mushrooms
3 tablespoons chili sauce
1 pound ground beef
4 hamburger buns, split
Ketchup and mustard, optional

In a large bowl, combine the onion, green pepper, mushrooms and chili sauce. Crumble beef over mixture and mix well. Shape into four patties.

In a large skillet, cook the patties over medium heat for 5-6 minutes on each side or until the meat is no longer pink. Serve patties on buns with ketchup and mustard, if desired. **Yield:** 4 servings.

Loaded Waffle Fries

Prep/Total Time: 30 min.

4 cups frozen waffle-cut fries
1/2 to 1-1/2 teaspoons steak seasoning
1 cup (4 ounces) shredded cheddar cheese
2 tablespoons chopped green onions
2 tablespoons real bacon bits

Arrange waffle fries in a greased 15-in. x 10-in. x 1-in. baking pan. Bake at 450° for 20-25 minutes or until lightly browned.

Sprinkle with steak seasoning; toss to coat. Top with cheese, onions and bacon. Bake 2-3 minutes longer or until cheese is melted. **Yield:** 4 servings.

Editor's Note: This recipe was tested with McCormick's Montreal Steak Seasoning. Look for it in the spice aisle of your grocery store.

Chocolate Banana Smoothies

Prep/Total Time: 10 min.

1 cup milk
1 cup vanilla yogurt
1/2 cup chocolate syrup
2 medium bananas, halved
8 ice cubes

In a blender, combine all ingredients; cover and process until smooth. Pour into chilled glasses; serve immediately. **Yield:** 4 servings.

Chocolate Banana Smoothies
Change-of-Pace Burgers
Loaded Waffle Fries

Chicken Pasta Toss
Carrot Coins with Thyme

Winning Chicken Dinner

SOME NIGHTS call for a straightforward meal that delivers on flavor...and that's just what you'll find in this simple but tasty menu.

Jazzed up with herbs and seasonings, Chicken Pasta Toss will appeal to any family member's taste buds. The rich and creamy sauce takes minimal effort, notes Margaret Penaflor of Thornton, Colorado.

Brighten everyone's dinner plate with colorful Carrot Coins with Thyme from Edna Hoffman, Hebron, Indiana. Her convenient side dish requires only 15 minutes from start to finish, and its mild flavors will complement just about any main course.

Chicken Pasta Toss

Prep/Total Time: 25 min.

10 ounces uncooked spaghetti
1 teaspoon minced garlic
2 tablespoons butter
3/4 pound boneless skinless chicken breasts, cubed
1/3 cup chopped green onions
1 teaspoon salt
1/2 teaspoon dried thyme
1/4 teaspoon *each* onion powder, rubbed sage, white pepper and black pepper
Dash cayenne pepper
1 cup heavy whipping cream
1/2 cup shredded Parmesan cheese
2 tablespoons minced fresh parsley

Cook the spaghetti according to package directions. Meanwhile, in a large skillet, saute garlic in butter. Add chicken, onions and seasonings; cook, uncovered, for 3-5 minutes or until juices run clear.

Stir in cream. Bring to a boil. Reduce heat; simmer, uncovered, for 4-5 minutes or until slightly thickened.

Drain spaghetti; toss with chicken mixture. Sprinkle with Parmesan cheese and parsley. **Yield:** 4 servings.

Carrot Coins with Thyme

Prep/Total Time: 15 min.

4 cups frozen sliced carrots, thawed
1 cup sliced celery
1/2 cup chopped onion
1/4 cup butter, cubed
2 teaspoons lemon juice
1/2 teaspoon salt
1/4 teaspoon dried thyme
1/4 teaspoon pepper

In a large skillet, saute the carrots, celery and onion in butter until tender. Stir in the lemon juice, salt, thyme and pepper; heat through. **Yield:** 4 servings.

Maple-Glazed Chicken
Stir-Fried Asparagus

Simply Elegant Meal Anytime

NEED A MEAL that's both pretty and easy? You found it! Maple-Glazed Chicken from Taryn Kuebelbeck of Plymouth, Minnesota offers sweet and savory flavors thanks to a pleasant maple sauce. Tender and loaded with appeal, this entree is sure to please.

Add a burst of color to your menu with a green vegetable. "Asparagus is one of my favorites," says Carolyn Sutter of Orangevale, California.

"I grew up in Stockton, California, where there's an annual festival to celebrate that vegetable," she relates. "I like it best stir-fried." One bite of her Stir-Fried Asparagus recipe, and you'll see why!

Maple-Glazed Chicken

Prep/Total Time: 20 min.

✓ This recipe includes Nutrition Facts and Diabetic Exchanges.

4 boneless skinless chicken breast halves (5 ounces *each*)
1/4 teaspoon salt
1/8 teaspoon pepper
1 tablespoon canola oil
1/2 teaspoon cornstarch
1/2 cup apple cider *or* unsweetened apple juice
2 tablespoons maple syrup
1/2 teaspoon onion powder

Flatten chicken to 1/2-in. thickness. Sprinkle with salt and pepper. In a large skillet, cook chicken in oil for 5-6 minutes on each side or until juices run clear. Remove and keep warm.

Meanwhile, in a small bowl, combine cornstarch and cider until smooth. Stir in syrup and onion powder; add to skillet. Bring to a boil; cook and stir for 2 minutes or until thickened. Add chicken and turn to coat. **Yield:** 4 servings.

Nutrition Facts: 1 chicken breast half with 2 tablespoons glaze equals 226 calories, 7 g fat (1 g saturated fat), 78 mg cholesterol, 220 mg sodium, 11 g carbohydrate, trace fiber, 29 g protein. **Diabetic Exchanges:** 4 very lean meat, 1 starch, 1/2 fat.

Stir-Fried Asparagus

Prep/Total Time: 20 min.

1-1/2 pounds fresh asparagus, trimmed and cut into 2-inch pieces (about 4 cups)
2 tablespoons butter
1 tablespoon vegetable oil
3 tablespoons chicken broth
1 teaspoon lemon juice
1 teaspoon soy sauce
1/4 teaspoon pepper
2 tablespoons slivered almonds, toasted

In a large skillet or wok, stir-fry asparagus in butter and oil for 2 minutes. Stir in broth, juice, soy sauce and pepper. Cover; cook for 2-3 minutes or until asparagus is tender. Sprinkle with almonds. **Yield:** 4 servings.

Pizza Parlor At Home

PUT DOWN the phone—there's no need to call for delivery tonight! With these recipes, you'll have a mouth-watering homemade pizza pie in no time, as well as a rich dressing for your favorite salad greens.

"I threw together Colorful Chicken Pizza on a hot summer night when I needed something quick to satisfy my fiance and me," writes Kelli Stone of Boise, Idaho. "It was an experiment with ingredients I had in the kitchen." Without a doubt, her fast, first attempt was a smashing success.

A side salad tossed with Mom's Blue Cheese Dressing is an ideal partner for the pizza. "My mom made this creamy dressing for years," says Donna Schulken, Santa Nella, California.

"It stores well in the refrigerator and is delicious over all types of greens. We love it for everything from weeknight family meals to dinner parties."

Colorful Chicken Pizza

Prep/Total Time: 25 min.

1 prebaked Italian bread shell crust (14 ounces)
2 tablespoons olive oil
1 package (6 ounces) ready-to-serve grilled chicken breast strips
1/2 cup barbecue sauce
1/3 cup chopped onion
1-1/2 teaspoons minced garlic
1-1/2 cups (6 ounces) shredded pizza cheese blend
1/4 cup chopped sweet red pepper
1/4 cup chopped green pepper
2 ounces smoked Gouda cheese, shredded
2 tablespoons minced fresh basil

Place the crust on an ungreased 12-in. pizza pan. Brush with oil. Combine the chicken, barbecue sauce, onion and garlic; spoon half over crust.

Sprinkle with pizza cheese. Top with remaining chicken mixture. Sprinkle with peppers, Gouda cheese and basil. Bake at 450° for 10-12 minutes or until cheese is melted. **Yield:** 6 slices.

Dessert in a Dash

WANT to round out this dinner with a dessert that's effortless? Serve up scoops of your family's favorite ice cream, frozen yogurt or sherbet. Provide bowls of yummy toppings for each family member to choose from, and you're sure to have smiles all around.

Mom's Blue Cheese Dressing

Prep/Total Time: 5 min.

1/2 cup mayonnaise
1/4 cup buttermilk
2 tablespoons crumbled blue cheese
1/4 teaspoon minced garlic
1 to 2 drops hot pepper sauce

In a small bowl, combine all ingredients until blended. Cover and refrigerate the salad dressing until serving. **Yield:** 3/4 cup.

Mom's Blue Cheese Dressing
Colorful Chicken Pizza

Elegant Broccoli
Parmesan Pork Chops

Pork Chop Perfection

LOOKING for the perfect menu you can assemble on the spot for your family or guests? Moist, golden-crusted Parmesan Pork Chops from Terri McKitrick of Delafield, Wisconsin are a great choice as the main course. Flavored with fresh rosemary and Parmesan cheese, they're ready in no time.

A citrusy splash of lemon brightens Sarah Smith's Elegant Broccoli, a mouth-watering side dish. "It's easy to throw together in a few minutes, and that's especially helpful when the entree is more elaborate," she says from Edgewood, Kentucky.

"Plus, everyone likes it—even people who say they usually don't care for broccoli."

For a no-fuss dessert, layer frozen yogurt and fresh blueberries in parfait glasses...and dinner's done!

Parmesan Pork Chops

Prep/Total Time: 30 min.

1/4 cup biscuit/baking mix
1 egg, beaten
1 cup shredded Parmesan cheese
1/4 cup dry bread crumbs
2 teaspoons minced fresh rosemary
4 boneless pork loin chops (1/2 inch thick and 6 ounces *each*)
2 tablespoons vegetable oil

Place biscuit mix and egg in separate shallow bowls. In another shallow bowl, combine the Parmesan cheese, bread crumbs and rosemary. Coat pork chops with biscuit mix, dip in egg, then coat with Parmesan mixture.

In a large skillet, brown chops on both sides in oil. Cook, uncovered, over medium heat for 10-15 minutes or until juices run clear, turning once. **Yield:** 4 servings.

Elegant Broccoli

Prep/Total Time: 15 min.

1-1/2 pounds fresh broccoli, cut into florets
1/4 cup water
1/3 cup mayonnaise
1/4 cup shredded cheddar cheese
1 tablespoon lemon juice
1 tablespoon Dijon mustard
Dash cayenne pepper

Place broccoli and water in a large microwave-safe bowl. Cover and microwave on high for 3-4 minutes or until tender; drain and keep warm.

For sauce, in a small microwave-safe bowl, combine the remaining ingredients. Cover and microwave on high for 1-2 minutes or until warmed, stirring once. Serve over broccoli. **Yield:** 4 servings.

Editor's Note: Reduced-fat or fat-free mayonnaise is not recommended for this recipe. This recipe was tested in a 1,100-watt microwave.

Seafood Fit For Summer

WHEN SUMMER WEATHER beckons you outdoors, who wants to fuss with complicated dinners? This casual meal will have you out of the kitchen in a flash.

Start with lip-smacking Lemon Butter Salmon from Karla Seville of Waynesboro, Pennsylvania. The simple but flavorful main course is jazzed up with just a few everyday ingredients.

From Deerfield, Wisconsin, Jessica Grettie shares her fluffy, fruit-filled Curried Apricot Couscous side dish. "It tastes a lot like one I tried in Israel," she notes. "It's so quick, colorful and easy, too."

Lemon Butter Salmon

Prep/Total Time: 20 min.

2 teaspoons minced garlic
1/2 cup butter, cubed
6 tablespoons lemon juice
2 teaspoons salt
1/2 teaspoon pepper
1/2 teaspoon hot pepper sauce
5 salmon fillets *or* steaks (6 ounces *each*)

In a small skillet, saute garlic in butter; whisk in lemon juice, salt, pepper and pepper sauce. Transfer 2/3 cup to a serving bowl; set aside.

Place salmon in a greased 15-in. x 10-in. x 1-in. baking pan. Drizzle with remaining lemon butter. Broil 4-6 in. from the heat for 10-15 minutes or until fish flakes easily with a fork. Serve with reserved lemon butter. **Yield:** 5 servings.

Curried Apricot Couscous

Prep/Total Time: 20 min.

1/3 cup chopped onion
3 tablespoons butter
1-1/2 cups chicken broth
1 cup chopped dried apricots
1/4 teaspoon curry powder
1 cup uncooked couscous

In a small saucepan, saute onion in butter. Stir in broth, apricots and curry. Bring to a boil. Stir in couscous.

Cover and remove from the heat; let stand for 5-10 minutes or until liquid is absorbed. Fluff with a fork. **Yield:** 5 servings.

Lemon Butter Salmon
Curried Apricot Couscous

Easy, Everyday Italian Food

COME HOME from a busy day of work or errands to a two-skillet, Italian-style menu. You'll be enjoying a hot, satisfying meal in no time flat!

In one skillet, pepperoni and mozzarella cheese punch up Pizza Pork Chops with a taste both kids and adults are bound to love. From Vance Werner, Jr. of Franklin, Wisconsin, this entree goes together in minutes using prepared sauce.

In the other skillet, dried basil adds its rich herb flavor to creamy Orzo with Parmesan & Basil. It's a favorite from Anna Chaney, Antigo, Wisconsin.

To round out your dinner, serve these dishes with fresh broccoli or green beans on the side...and finish with scoops of lemon sherbet or sorbet.

Expecting company? This memorable dinner is easy to double for guests. Enjoy!

Pizza Pork Chops

Prep/Total Time: 30 min.

2 cups sliced fresh mushrooms
2 tablespoons butter
4 boneless pork loin chops (1/2 inch thick and 4 ounces *each*)
1/4 teaspoon salt
1/4 teaspoon pepper
2 tablespoons olive oil
2 cups marinara *or* spaghetti sauce
16 slices pepperoni
1 cup (4 ounces) shredded part-skim mozzarella cheese

In a large skillet, saute mushrooms in butter until tender. Remove and keep warm. Sprinkle pork chops with salt and pepper. In the same skillet, brown chops in oil on both sides; drain.

Add marinara sauce; bring to a boil. Reduce heat; simmer, uncovered, for 8-10 minutes until a meat thermometer reaches 160°, turning once. Layer pork with pepperoni, mushrooms and cheese. Remove from the heat. Cover and let stand for 2-3 minutes or until cheese is melted. **Yield:** 4 servings.

Orzo with Parmesan & Basil

Prep/Total Time: 20 min.

1 cup uncooked orzo pasta
2 tablespoons butter
1 can (14-1/2 ounces) chicken broth
1/2 cup grated Parmesan cheese
2 teaspoons dried basil
1/8 teaspoon pepper

In a large skillet, saute orzo in butter for 3-5 minutes or until lightly browned.

Stir in broth. Bring to a boil. Reduce heat; cover and simmer for 10-15 minutes or until liquid is absorbed and orzo is tender. Stir in the Parmesan cheese, basil and pepper. **Yield:** 4 servings.

Pizza Pork Chops
Orzo with Parmesan & Basil

Avocado Tomato Salad
Spicy Bronzed Chicken

Super-Fast Supper Combo

IT'S A SNAP to pack a nutritious sit-down meal into busy weeknights. Just consider Spicy Bronzed Chicken—it's ready in only 20 minutes!

"My husband and I really like this chicken, which tastes great cold, too," writes Kathy Rajkovich from St. Petersburg, Russia. "The spicy seasoning blend also makes a good coating for pork and fish."

Pair that entree with Dawn McKnight's Avocado Tomato Salad. "We have a monthly pitch-in lunch at work, and this popular dish has made several appearances," she relates from Zionsville, Indiana.

Avocado Ease

TO PREPARE the avocado for the salad recipe (at right), wash the avocado and cut it in half lengthwise, cutting around the seed. Twist the halves in opposite directions to separate them, then slip a tablespoon under the seed to loosen it from the fruit.

To remove the flesh from the skin, loosen it from the skin with a large spoon and scoop the flesh out. Then slice the peeled avocado as desired.

Spicy Bronzed Chicken

Prep/Total Time: 20 min.

- **4 boneless skinless chicken breasts (5 ounces *each*)**
- **1 teaspoon *each* garlic powder, salt and paprika**
- **1/2 teaspoon *each* onion powder, ground cumin, chili powder and pepper**
- **1/4 teaspoon cayenne pepper**
- **1/4 cup butter, melted**

Flatten chicken to 1/2-in. thickness. In a small bowl, combine seasonings. Dip the chicken in butter; sprinkle with the seasonings.

In a large skillet, cook chicken over medium heat for 4-5 minutes on each side or until chicken juices run clear. **Yield:** 4 servings.

Avocado Tomato Salad

Prep/Total Time: 10 min.

- **2-1/2 cups torn mixed salad greens**
- **1 cup cherry tomatoes**
- **1 medium ripe avocado, peeled and sliced**
- **1/4 cup real bacon bits**
- **2 tablespoons vegetable oil**
- **1 tablespoon cider vinegar**
- **1/2 teaspoon salt**

Divide the salad greens, tomatoes and avocado among four salad plates; sprinkle with bacon. In a jar with a tight-fitting lid, combine the remaining ingredients; shake well. Drizzle over salads; serve immediately. **Yield:** 4 servings.

Marinated Beef Tenderloins
Anytime Cucumber Salad

Marinated In Minutes

GRILLING is a great way to enjoy the outdoors. But who's got the time? You do! This dinner gets your grill going and food on the table without a fuss.

To begin preparing melt-in-your-mouth Marinated Beef Tenderloins, you simply marinate the steaks for 15 minutes. "It really couldn't be much easier," notes Karen Haskell of Tempe, Arizona.

In the meantime, you can quickly put together a refreshing complement—Anytime Cucumber Salad from Barbara Moravek of Jay, Florida.

"In 10 minutes, you have a terrific salad," Barbara says. "And you only need five ingredients!"

Marinated Beef Tenderloins

Prep/Total Time: 30 min.

1 can (12 ounces) beer *or* nonalcoholic beer
1/2 cup chopped green onions
1/2 cup teriyaki sauce
2 tablespoons soy sauce
1 tablespoon Worcestershire sauce
2 teaspoons minced garlic
4 beef tenderloin steaks (8 ounces *each*)

In a small bowl, combine the first six ingredients. Set aside 3/4 cup for basting. Pour remaining marinade into a large resealable plastic bag; add the steaks. Seal bag and turn to coat; refrigerate for at least 15 minutes.

Drain and discard marinade. Grill steaks, covered, over medium heat for 4-6 minutes on each side or until meat reaches desired doneness (for medium-rare, a meat thermometer should read 145°; medium, 160°; well-done, 170°), basting with reserved marinade. **Yield:** 4 servings.

Anytime Cucumber Salad

Prep/Total Time: 10 min.

1-1/2 cups chopped peeled cucumbers
1 cup seedless red grapes
1 can (8 ounces) pineapple chunks, drained
1/3 cup chopped pecans, toasted
1/2 cup bacon ranch salad dressing

In a large bowl, combine the cucumbers, red grapes, pineapple and pecans. Pour dressing over salad; toss to coat. **Yield:** 4 servings.

Catch of The Kitchen

WHEN SEAFOOD is the order of the day, look no further than this memorable menu. It stars Lemon Parsley Swordfish, always a top dinnertime choice for Nathan Leopold of Mechanicsburg, Pennsylvania.

Pair it with Erika Maxwell's superb Mushroom Feta Pasta, and you've got a menu combination that's hard to beat. "This side dish is great 'company's coming' food, too," Erika says from Monroe, Michigan.

Lemon Parsley Swordfish

Prep/Total Time: 25 min.

4 swordfish steaks (7 ounces *each*)
1/2 teaspoon salt
1/2 cup minced fresh parsley, *divided*
1/3 cup olive oil
1 tablespoon lemon juice
2 teaspoons minced garlic
1/4 teaspoon crushed red pepper flakes

Place swordfish steaks in a greased 13-in. x 9-in. x 2-in. baking dish; sprinkle with salt. Combine 1/4 cup parsley, oil, lemon juice, garlic and red pepper flakes; spoon over the fish.

Bake, uncovered, at 425° for 15-20 minutes or until fish flakes easily with a fork, basting occasionally. Sprinkle with remaining parsley. **Yield:** 4 servings.

Mushroom Feta Pasta

Prep/Total Time: 20 min.

4 ounces uncooked angel hair pasta
1/2 pound sliced fresh mushrooms
1/2 cup chopped onion
1-1/2 teaspoons minced garlic
2 tablespoons butter
1/4 cup white wine *or* chicken broth
1/4 teaspoon salt
1/8 teaspoon pepper
1 package (4 ounces) crumbled tomato and basil feta cheese

Cook the angel hair pasta according to the package directions. Meanwhile, in a large skillet, saute the mushrooms, onion and garlic in butter until tender. Add the wine or broth, salt and pepper. Bring to a boil; cook, uncovered, over medium heat for 5-7 minutes or until liquid is evaporated.

Drain pasta. Stir into the mushroom mixture; sprinkle with feta. Toss to coat. **Yield:** 4 servings.

Lemon Parsley Swordfish
Mushroom Feta Pasta

Classics from The Southwest

SAY "ADIOS" to boring dinners and "Olé!" to these creamy Cheese and Chicken Enchiladas from Christine Taylor. In Greenfield, Wisconsin, she uses the microwave to fix this mild, family-pleasing entree.

Complete the menu with fresh-tasting Confetti Corn Salad from Tonia Mahnke of Sun Prairie, Wisconsin. You'll be surprised at just how quickly it comes together...and how deliciously different it is!

Cheese and Chicken Enchiladas

Prep/Total Time: 20 min.

1/2 cup chopped onion
1/2 teaspoon minced garlic
1 package (9 ounces) frozen diced cooked chicken breast, thawed and chopped
4 ounces cream cheese, cubed
1 can (4 ounces) chopped green chilies
1/4 cup chicken broth
2 teaspoons chili powder
1/2 teaspoon ground cumin
6 flour tortillas (8 inches), warmed
4 ounces process cheese (Velveeta), cubed
1/2 cup diced fresh tomato, *divided*
2 tablespoons milk

In a large microwave-safe bowl, combine onion and garlic. Cover and microwave on high for 30-60 seconds or until onion is tender, stirring twice. Stir in the chicken, cream cheese, green chilies, broth, chili powder and cumin. Cover and microwave on high for 45-90 seconds or until cream cheese is melted, stirring twice.

Spoon about 1/3 cup down the center of each tortilla. Roll up and place seam side down in an ungreased microwave-safe 8-in. square dish.

In a microwave-safe bowl, combine the process cheese, 1/4 cup tomato and milk. Microwave, uncovered, on high for 30-60 seconds or until cheese is melted, stirring twice; drizzle over enchiladas. Top with remaining tomato. Microwave enchiladas, uncovered, on high for 45-90 seconds or until heated through. **Yield:** 3 servings.

Editor's Note: This recipe was tested in a 1,100-watt microwave.

Confetti Corn Salad

Prep/Total Time: 10 min.

1 can (7 ounces) whole kernel corn, drained
1 can (2-1/4 ounces) sliced ripe olives, drained
1/2 cup chopped green pepper
1/2 cup chopped sweet red pepper
2 radishes, sliced
1/4 cup prepared Italian salad dressing

In a small bowl, combine the corn, olives, peppers and radishes. Add salad dressing; toss to coat. Refrigerate until serving. **Yield:** 3 servings.

Cheese and Chicken Enchiladas
Confetti Corn Salad

Cranberry-Pineapple Pork Chops
Walnut Rice

Elegant and Effortless Menu

WHY NOT ADD a touch of class to your weekdays? It's a breeze with this colorful, special menu!

For the main course, enjoy Cranberry-Pineapple Pork Chops from Priscilla Gilbert of Indian Harbour Beach, Florida. The dressed-up chops feature a tangy sauce Priscilla also serves with her Christmas ham.

Accent that entree with Vera Whisner's Walnut Rice. "I always get compliments when I make it, and there are never any leftovers," she writes from Elkton, Maryland. "The short preparation and cooking times are a definite bonus as well!"

Cranberry-Pineapple Pork Chops

Prep/Total Time: 25 min.

4 boneless pork loin chops (1 inch thick and 6 ounces *each*)
1 tablespoon vegetable oil
1 can (20 ounces) unsweetened pineapple tidbits
1/2 cup sugar
4 teaspoons cornstarch
1 can (6 ounces) unsweetened pineapple juice
2 tablespoons butter
1/3 cup dried cranberries

In a large skillet, cook pork in oil for 8-10 minutes on each side or until a meat thermometer reaches 160°.

Meanwhile, drain pineapple, reserving the juice and 3/4 cup pineapple (save remaining pineapple for another use). In a small saucepan, combine sugar and cornstarch. Gradually stir in pineapple juice and reserved juice. Bring to a boil; cook and stir for 2 minutes or until thickened.

Stir in the butter, cranberries and reserved pineapple. Serve with pork. **Yield:** 4 servings.

Walnut Rice

Prep/Total Time: 20 min.

2/3 cup chopped walnuts
1/3 cup chopped onion
1 tablespoon sesame seeds
1/4 teaspoon salt
1/4 teaspoon garlic powder
3 tablespoons butter
1-1/2 cups hot water
2 tablespoons soy sauce
1-1/2 cups frozen broccoli florets
1 cup uncooked instant rice

In a large skillet, saute the walnuts, onion, sesame seeds, salt and garlic powder in butter until onion is tender and sesame seeds are golden brown. Add water and soy sauce; bring to a boil. Stir in broccoli and rice. Cover and remove from the heat. Let stand for 5 minutes or until rice is tender. **Yield:** 4 servings.

Fresh Broccoli Salad
Texas Toast Steak Sandwiches

Standout Salad And Sandwich

GETTING a delicious, wholesome meal on the table can be a challenge during hectic weekdays. This casual dinner goes together in minutes...and goes beyond the ordinary sandwich-and-salad combo!

Enjoy Taryn Kuebelbeck's zippy, open-faced Texas Toast Steak Sandwiches. The Plymouth, Minnesota cook layers them with spinach, cheese and tomato.

They go perfectly with Fresh Broccoli Salad from Sherry Thompson of Seneca, South Carolina. Her creamy medley is jazzed up with apple and bacon.

Texas Toast Steak Sandwiches

Prep/Total Time: 30 min.

- **1/3 cup mayonnaise**
- **2 teaspoons minced chipotle pepper in adobo sauce**
- **6 slices Texas toast**
- **6 beef cube steaks (1-1/2 pounds)**
- **2 cups fresh baby spinach**
- **6 Muenster cheese slices (1/2 ounce *each*)**
- **6 tomato slices**

In a small bowl, combine mayonnaise and chipotle pepper. Heat Texas toast on a foil-lined baking sheet according to package directions.

Meanwhile, in a large skillet coated with cooking spray, cook beef in batches over medium heat until no longer pink.

Layer warmed Texas toast with spinach, steaks, mayonnaise mixture, cheese and tomato. Broil 3-4 in. from the heat for 1-2 minutes or until cheese is melted. **Yield:** 6 servings.

Fresh Broccoli Salad

Prep/Total Time: 15 min.

- **3/4 pound chopped fresh broccoli**
- **1 small green apple, chopped**
- **1/2 cup chopped red onion**
- **3 tablespoons real bacon bits**
- **1/2 cup ranch salad dressing**
- **4-1/2 teaspoons sugar**

In a large bowl, combine broccoli, apple, onion and bacon. In a small bowl, combine dressing and sugar. Pour over salad; toss to coat. **Yield:** 6 servings.

Hooked on Flavorful Fish

FEEL LIKE a fish dinner—but need it *fast*? Try Baked Parmesan Roughy from Patti Bailey of Chanute, Kansas and add Potatoes, Peas & Pearl Onions from Priscilla Gilbert, Indian Harbour Beach, Florida.

Table-ready in less than 30 minutes, this fuss-free supper leaves you plenty of time to unwind after a busy day...and to reel in the rave reviews!

Baked Parmesan Roughy

Prep/Total Time: 25 min.

3/4 cup crushed cornflakes
1/2 cup grated Parmesan cheese
1/2 teaspoon salt
2 eggs, lightly beaten
2 tablespoons milk
2 pounds orange roughy fillets

In a large resealable plastic bag, combine cornflakes, Parmesan cheese and salt. In a shallow bowl, combine eggs and milk. Dip fish in egg mixture, then shake in cornflake mixture. Transfer to a greased 15-in. x 10-in. x 1-in. baking pan. Bake at 450° for 15-20 minutes or until fish flakes easily with a fork. **Yield:** 6 servings.

Potatoes, Peas & Pearl Onions

Prep/Total Time: 20 min.

1 package (20 ounces) refrigerated red potato wedges
1/3 cup water
1-1/3 cups frozen pearl onions, thawed
3 tablespoons butter
2/3 cup heavy whipping cream
1/3 cup chicken broth
1/4 teaspoon salt
1/4 teaspoon ground nutmeg
1/4 teaspoon pepper
2/3 cup frozen peas, thawed
3 tablespoons chopped green onions

Place potatoes and water in a 2-qt. microwave-safe bowl. Cover and microwave on high for 8-10 minutes or until potatoes are tender; drain and set aside.

Meanwhile, in a large skillet, saute pearl onions in butter for 2 minutes. Add the cream, broth, salt, nutmeg and pepper. Bring to a boil. Reduce heat; simmer, uncovered, for 5-7 minutes or until onions are tender. Stir in the peas, green onions and reserved potatoes; heat through. **Yield:** 6 servings.

Editor's Note: This recipe was tested in a 1,100-watt microwave.

Potatoes, Peas & Pearl Onions
Baked Parmesan Roughy

Traditional Turkey Taste

WHEN AUTUMN arrives, savor the flavors of the season with this meal from Margaret Wilson of Hemet, California. Her elegant Turkey Sweet Potato Supper is a streamlined version of a classic turkey dinner.

Even kids are likely to go for microwave-quick, cheesy Crumb-Topped Brussels Sprouts—the perfect complement to Margaret's main course.

Turkey Sweet Potato Supper

Prep/Total Time: 30 min.

- **2 turkey breast tenderloins (8 ounces *each*)**
- **1 tablespoon butter**
- **1 can (2 pounds, 8 ounces) sweet potatoes, drained**
- **1/3 cup dried cranberries**
- **1/3 cup maple syrup**
- **1/4 cup orange juice**
- **1/4 teaspoon ground cinnamon**
- **1/2 teaspoon cornstarch**
- **1 tablespoon cold water**

In a large skillet, brown turkey in butter on each side. Arrange sweet potatoes around turkey. Combine the cranberries, maple syrup, orange juice and cinnamon; pour over top. Bring to a boil. Reduce heat; cover and simmer for 15-20 minutes or until turkey juices run clear.

Remove turkey and potatoes to a platter. Combine cornstarch and cold water until smooth; add to skillet. Bring to a boil. Cook and stir for 1 minute or until thickened. Serve with turkey and potatoes. **Yield:** 4 servings.

Crumb-Topped Brussels Sprouts

Prep/Total Time: 15 min.

- **1 package (16 ounces) frozen brussels sprouts**
- **2 tablespoons water**
- **2/3 cup condensed cheddar cheese soup, undiluted**
- **1 tablespoon milk**
- **1/4 cup dry bread crumbs**
- **3 tablespoons chopped walnuts**
- **2 tablespoons butter, melted**
- **Dash of pepper**

In a microwave-safe bowl, combine brussels sprouts and water. Cover and microwave on high for 5-7 minutes or until crisp-tender, stirring once. Drain.

Stir in soup and milk. In a small bowl, combine the bread crumbs, walnuts, butter and pepper; sprinkle over brussels sprouts. Microwave, uncovered, on high for 2-3 minutes or until heated through. **Yield:** 4 servings.

Editor's Note: This recipe was tested in a 1,100-watt microwave.

Turkey Sweet Potato Supper
Crumb-Topped Brussels Sprouts

Basil-Garlic Cheese Bread
Two-Meat Spaghetti Sauce

Popular Pasta In a Snap

AT HECTIC TIMES of the year, savvy cooks look for convenient meals that cut out the fuss. From Shirley Klinner of Medford, Wisconsin, Two-Meat Spaghetti Sauce gets you well on your way toward an Italian feast. Then just add scrumptious Basil-Garlic Cheese Bread from Deni Adkins, Scottsboro, Alabama.

Two-Meat Spaghetti Sauce

Prep/Total Time: 30 min.

✓ This recipe includes Nutrition Facts.

- **10 ounces uncooked spaghetti**
- **1/2 pound ground beef**
- **2 packages (3 ounces *each*) sliced pepperoni**
- **1 cup water**
- **1 can (8 ounces) tomato sauce**
- **1 can (6 ounces) tomato paste**
- **1 can (4 ounces) mushroom stems and pieces, drained**
- **2 tablespoons dried minced onion**
- **2 tablespoons dried parsley flakes**
- **1 teaspoon dried oregano**
- **1 teaspoon chili powder**
- **3/4 to 1 teaspoon sugar**
- **1/2 teaspoon garlic powder**

Cook spaghetti according to package directions; drain. Meanwhile, in a large skillet, cook beef and pepperoni over medium heat until beef is no longer pink; drain. Stir in water, tomato sauce and paste, mushrooms, onion, parsley, oregano, chili powder, sugar and garlic powder.

Bring to a boil. Reduce heat; simmer, uncovered, for 15-20 minutes or until heated through. Serve with spaghetti. **Yield:** 5 servings.

Nutrition Facts: 1 cup spaghetti with 3/4 cup sauce equals 358 calories, 5 g fat (2 g saturated fat), 22 mg cholesterol, 358 mg sodium, 59 g carbohydrate, 5 g fiber, 18 g protein.

Basil-Garlic Cheese Bread

Prep/Total Time: 10 min.

- **1/2 cup butter, softened**
- **2 tablespoons grated Parmesan cheese**
- **2 tablespoons olive oil**
- **1 tablespoon lemon juice**
- **2 teaspoons minced garlic**
- **1 to 2 teaspoons dried basil**
- **1 loaf (1 pound) unsliced French bread, halved lengthwise**

In a small bowl, combine the first six ingredients; spread over cut sides of bread. Place on an ungreased baking sheet. Broil 4-6 in. from heat for 2-3 minutes or until lightly browned. Cut into 2-in. slices. **Yield:** 10 servings.

Mango-Chutney Baby Carrots
Dijon Crumb Chicken

Irresistible Family Dinner

ON RUSHED EVENINGS, draw your family to the table with a delicious dinner that begins with Dijon Crumb Chicken. Shared by Ann Wilson of Holland, Michigan, it's delightfully crunchy...and goes wonderfully with Mango-Chutney Baby Carrots. Writes Patricia Nieh in Portola Valley, California, "We pull baby carrots from our garden for this side dish recipe, which is one of our favorites."

Dijon Crumb Chicken

Prep/Total Time: 25 min.

2 eggs
2 tablespoons Dijon mustard
1 cup seasoned bread crumbs
1/2 cup grated Parmesan cheese
1-1/2 teaspoons onion powder
1-1/2 teaspoons garlic powder
4 boneless skinless chicken breast halves (4 ounces *each*)
3 tablespoons vegetable oil

In a shallow bowl, beat eggs and mustard. In another shallow bowl, combine the bread crumbs, Parmesan cheese, onion powder and garlic powder. Flatten chicken to 1/4-in. thickness. Dip the chicken in egg mixture, then coat with crumb mixture.

In a large skillet, cook chicken in oil over medium heat for 15-20 minutes or until juices run clear and chicken is golden brown, turning once. **Yield:** 4 servings.

Mango-Chutney Baby Carrots

Prep/Total Time: 15 min.

✓ This recipe includes Nutrition Facts and Diabetic Exchanges.

1 package (16 ounces) fresh baby carrots
2 tablespoons water
1/4 cup orange juice
2 tablespoons mango chutney
2 tablespoons butter
1-1/2 teaspoons minced fresh gingerroot
1/2 teaspoon minced garlic
1 teaspoon curry powder
3 tablespoons minced fresh parsley

Place carrots and water in a microwave-safe bowl. Cover; microwave on high for 4-6 minutes or until tender.

Meanwhile, in a large bowl, combine the orange juice, chutney, butter, ginger, garlic and curry. Cover and microwave on high for 45 seconds or until butter is melted. Drain carrots; add to orange juice mixture and toss to coat. Garnish with parsley. **Yield:** 4 servings.

Editor's Note: This recipe was tested in a 1,100-watt microwave.

Nutrition Facts: 3/4 cup equals 131 calories, 6 g fat (4 g saturated fat), 15 mg cholesterol, 216 mg sodium, 19 g carbohydrate, 2 g fiber, 1 g protein. **Diabetic Exchanges:** 2 vegetable, 1 fat, 1/2 starch.

Quick Calzones Tonight!

THE END OF THE WEEK means the beginning of the weekend. What better way to celebrate than with a fun meal? If you like pizza, you'll love Zippy Calzones from Mary Addy of West Point, Nebraska.

Pair them with Herbed Green Beans—easy to fix while the calzones bake. Says Nanci Keatley of Salem, Oregon, "They're wonderful warm or chilled...and even as a centerpiece on an antipasto tray."

Zippy Calzones

Prep/Total Time: 30 min.

1 tube (13.8 ounces) refrigerated pizza crust
1 cup (4 ounces) shredded part-skim mozzarella cheese
32 slices pepperoni
3/4 cup 1% cottage cheese
3/4 cup julienned green, sweet red *and/or* yellow pepper
1/4 cup finely chopped onion

Unroll pizza crust; roll into a 12-in. square. Cut into four 6-in. squares. Sprinkle 2 tablespoons mozzarella cheese over half of each square to within 1/2 in. of edges. Top with eight slices pepperoni and 3 tablespoons cottage cheese. Combine pepper and onion; place 1/4 cup mixture on each square; top with 2 tablespoons cottage cheese. Fold dough over filling; press edges with a fork to seal.

Transfer calzones to a lightly greased baking sheet. Bake at 400° for 13-18 minutes or until golden brown. **Yield:** 4 servings.

Herbed Green Beans

Prep/Total Time: 15 min.

1/2 cup white wine vinegar
1/4 cup olive oil
1/2 to 3/4 teaspoon dried basil
1/2 teaspoon dried oregano
1/2 teaspoon garlic salt
1 package (16 ounces) frozen cut green beans, thawed
2 tablespoons water
1/3 cup sliced almonds, toasted
1/4 cup grated Parmesan cheese

In a small saucepan, bring vinegar, oil, basil, oregano and garlic salt to a boil. Reduce heat; simmer, uncovered, for 5 minutes. Meanwhile, place beans and water in a 1-qt. microwave-safe dish. Cover and microwave on high for 4-5 minutes or until crisp-tender; drain.

Pour vinegar mixture over beans; sprinkle with almonds and cheese. Toss to coat. **Yield:** 4 servings.

Editor's Note: This recipe was tested in a 1,100-watt microwave.

Herbed Green Beans
Zippy Calzones

Special Pesto Entree, Presto!

YOUR GUESTS will feel like they're in a fancy restaurant when you serve this mouth-watering meal. It's a bounty of veggies, chicken and pasta tossed with tongue-tingling pesto. No one will believe you prepared it in less than 30 minutes!

"Chicken Pesto Pasta is a terrific recipe because it's easy, yet looks and tastes like I spent all day making it," says Barbara Christensen of Arvada, Colorado. "Plus, it includes my favorite ingredients."

In West Lakeland, Minnesota, Viki Ailport appreciates the simplicity of Savory Parmesan Sticks. "Their aroma during baking really whets your appetite, and they look so pretty on the table, too," she says.

Chicken Pesto Pasta

Prep/Total Time: 25 min.

1 package (16 ounces) bow tie pasta
1 cup cut fresh asparagus (1-inch pieces)
1-1/4 cups sliced fresh mushrooms
1 medium sweet red pepper, sliced
1-1/2 teaspoons minced garlic
2 tablespoons olive oil
2 cups cubed cooked chicken
1 can (14 ounces) water-packed artichoke hearts, rinsed and drained
2 jars (3-1/2 ounces *each*) prepared pesto
1 jar (7 ounces) oil-packed sun-dried tomatoes, drained and chopped
1 teaspoon salt
1/8 teaspoon crushed red pepper flakes
1 cup (4 ounces) shredded Parmesan cheese
2/3 cup pine nuts, toasted

Cook pasta according to package directions, adding asparagus during the last 3 minutes of cooking.

Meanwhile, in a large skillet, saute the mushrooms, red pepper and garlic in oil until tender. Reduce the heat; stir in the chicken, artichokes, pesto, tomatoes, salt and pepper flakes. Cook 2-3 minutes longer or until heated through.

Drain pasta; toss with chicken mixture. Sprinkle with cheese and pine nuts. **Yield:** 8 servings.

Savory Parmesan Sticks

Prep/Total Time: 20 min.

1 package (17.3 ounces) frozen puff pastry, thawed
1 egg, beaten
1-1/2 cups grated Parmesan cheese
1 tablespoon dried rosemary, crushed

Brush one side of each puff pastry sheet with egg; sprinkle with Parmesan cheese and rosemary. Cut each sheet into ten 1-in. strips. Place 1 in. apart on greased baking sheets.

Bake at 400° for 10-13 minutes or until golden brown. **Yield:** 20 breadsticks.

Savory Parmesan Sticks
Chicken Pesto Pasta

Fresh Fare From the Grill

A JUICY BURGER from the grill and a creamy pasta salad capture the essence of summer as few other foods can. Treat your friends and family to the best with the delectable, all-American spread here.

To shake up your usual burger routine, try Guacamole Burgers from Patricia Collins of Imbler, Oregon. She takes classic bacon cheeseburgers to a whole new level with a dollop of guacamole, zippy green chilies and melted Monterey Jack.

Scoop up a big spoonful of Vegetable Macaroni Salad to go with each sandwich. "This salad is so easy and versatile," notes Mary Kay Dillingham of Overland Park, Kansas. "And the bonus is that any leftovers taste great the next day."

Each recipe requires just 30 minutes or less to pull together, proving that a great meal doesn't have to take a great deal of time and effort. So pour some ice-cold lemonade, fire up that grill and relax!

Guacamole Burgers
Vegetable Macaroni Salad

Guacamole Burgers

Prep/Total Time: 30 min.

8 bacon strips
1/2 cup chopped onion
1 can (4 ounces) chopped green chilies
1 pound ground beef
4 slices Monterey Jack cheese
4 sandwich buns, split and toasted
1/4 cup guacamole

In a large skillet, cook bacon over medium heat until crisp. Remove to paper towels to drain. Meanwhile, in a small bowl, combine onion and green chilies; set aside. Shape beef into eight patties. Top half of patties with onion mixture. Cover with remaining patties and firmly press edges to seal.

Grill, covered, over medium heat for 5-7 minutes on each side or until no longer pink. Top each with bacon and cheese. Grill 1 minute longer or until cheese is melted. Serve on buns with guacamole. **Yield:** 4 servings.

Vegetable Macaroni Salad

Prep/Total Time: 20 min.

1 cup uncooked elbow macaroni
1/2 cup mayonnaise
1/4 cup sliced celery
1/4 cup chopped pitted green olives
1/4 cup sliced green onions
1/4 cup shredded cheddar cheese
2 tablespoons sliced radishes
1 tablespoon minced fresh parsley
1 tablespoon white vinegar
1 teaspoon prepared mustard
1/4 to 1/2 teaspoon salt
1/4 teaspoon celery seed
Dash pepper

Cook macaroni according to package directions. Meanwhile, in a large bowl, combine the remaining ingredients. Drain macaroni and rinse in cold water. Add macaroni to mayonnaise mixture; toss to coat. Chill until serving. **Yield:** 4 servings.

Big on Burgers

FOR THE BEST burgers every time, keep these tips from our Test Kitchen experts in mind:

- Try not to flatten the burgers with a spatula when grilling them. It presses out the flavorful juices that keep the meat moist.
- Cook burgers to 160°. Check their temperature with a meat thermometer inserted horizontally from the side into the center of the meat.

Chapter 4

Fun Foods For Kids

IT'S CHILD'S PLAY to create the kid-friendly foods in this chapter. Each recipe is not only fast to fix, but it's also sure to put a smile on children's faces.

Whether you're searching for main dishes, sides, snacks, desserts or school treats, you'll find lots of child-pleasing choices. For example, Taco Macaroni and Pizza Noodle Bake are terrific ways to get youngsters to eat a wholesome supper.

Round out the meal with Potato Wedges and Peanut Butter Jumbos. Then keep Berry Yogurt Cups in mind for breakfast... and send kids off to class with a batch of Cookie Pops for fellow students and teachers.

No matter what kind of tot-inspired delight you need, look here for the youthful solution!

PLAYFUL FARE. Caramel Cashew Chewies (p. 74).

Scooter Snacks

(Pictured above)

Prep/Total Time: 30 min.

Feel like building a little fun into those after-school routines...or rainy weekend afternoons? Let the kids help you construct these nutritious, fast snacks to rev things up!
—Didi Desjardins, Dartmouth, Massachusetts

8 slices zucchini (1/4 inch thick)
6 pretzel sticks, *divided*
2 pieces string cheese (1 ounce *each*)
2 pretzel rods, cut into 3-inch pieces
2 tablespoons spreadable garden vegetable cream cheese
4 cherry tomatoes, halved
2 pimiento-stuffed olives, halved

For each of the four axles, thread two zucchini slices through a pretzel stick, leaving a 1-in. space in the center. For each scooter, position a piece of string cheese between the two axles.

Attach a pretzel rod with cream cheese to each scooter; top each with a pretzel stick for handlebars. Add tomato hubcaps and olive headlights and taillights with cream cheese. **Yield:** 2 scooters.

Child's Play

YOU CAN BUILD on the idea for Scooter Snacks (recipe above) to form all sorts of fun food creations. For example, skip the string cheese and handlebars—replace them with an oval cheese slice and place it on top of the wheels for a skateboard.

Upside-Down Pizza Bake

(Pictured below)

Prep: 20 min. **Bake:** 25 min.

This super-easy but delicious recipe is one I've been serving to my children, and now my grandchildren, for over 30 years! Adults like it just as much as kids do.
—Sandy Bastian, Tinley Park, Illinois

1/2 pound Italian sausage links, cut into 1/4-inch slices
1 cup spaghetti sauce
1/2 cup sliced fresh mushrooms
1/2 cup julienned green pepper
1 cup (4 ounces) shredded part-skim mozzarella cheese, *divided*
1 cup biscuit/baking mix
1 egg
1/2 cup milk

In a large skillet, cook the sausage over medium heat until meat is no longer pink; drain.

Pour the spaghetti sauce into a greased 8-in. square baking dish. Top with the mushrooms, green pepper, sausage and 1/2 cup mozzarella cheese.

In a small bowl, combine the biscuit/baking mix, egg and milk until blended. Pour over the top of casserole. Sprinkle with the remaining mozzarella cheese. Bake, uncovered, at 400° for 25-30 minutes or until golden brown. **Yield:** 4 servings.

Homemade Fudge Pops

Prep: 30 min. + freezing

On hot summer afternoons, these are my children's favorite frozen treats. To avoid the messy hands that can result when eating popsicles, try this idea—slide a paper coffee filter onto the stick so your hand is covered.
—*Lyssa Prasek, Vita, Manitoba*

☑ This recipe includes Nutrition Facts and Diabetic Exchanges.

- **1/4 cup butter, cubed**
- **1/2 cup all-purpose flour**
- **4 cups milk**
- **1-1/3 cups packed brown sugar**
- **1/3 cup baking cocoa**
- **1 teaspoon salt**
- **2 teaspoons vanilla extract**
- **20 Popsicle molds *or* disposable plastic cups (3 ounces *each*) and Popsicle sticks**

In a large saucepan, melt butter over medium heat. Stir in flour until smooth; gradually add milk. Stir in brown sugar, cocoa and salt. Bring to a boil; cook and stir for 2 minutes or until thickened.

Remove from the heat; stir in vanilla. Cool for 20 minutes, stirring several times.

Pour 1/4 cupfuls of mixture into the Popsicle molds or disposable plastic cups; top the molds with holders or insert Popsicle sticks into cups. Freeze until firm. **Yield:** 20 servings.

Nutrition Facts: 1 fudge pop equals 121 calories, 4 g fat (2 g saturated fat), 11 mg cholesterol, 159 mg sodium, 20 g carbohydrate, trace fiber, 2 g protein. **Diabetic Exchanges:** 1 starch, 1 fat.

Potato Wedges

(Pictured above right)

Prep/Total Time: 30 min.

Youngsters will love the Parmesan flavor and cornflake crunch in these better-than-frozen fries. Let your little helpers sprinkle the cornflake mixture on each wedge.
—*Melissa Tatum, Greensboro, North Carolina*

- **4 medium baking potatoes**
- **1/3 cup finely crushed cornflakes**
- **1/3 cup grated Parmesan cheese**
- **2 teaspoons paprika**
- **1/2 teaspoon salt**
- **1/4 cup ranch salad dressing**
- **Additional ranch salad dressing, optional**

Scrub and pierce potatoes; place on a microwave-safe plate. Microwave, uncovered, on high for 18-20 minutes or until tender, turning once. Cool slightly.

Meanwhile, in a small bowl, combine the cornflake crumbs, Parmesan cheese, paprika and salt. Cut each potato lengthwise into quarters; brush with salad dressing and sprinkle with cornflake mixture.

Place the potato wedges on a broiler pan. Broil 4 in. from the heat for 2-3 minutes or until lightly browned. Serve the wedges with additional salad dressing if desired. **Yield:** 4 servings.

Editor's Note: This recipe was tested in a 1,100-watt microwave.

Mini Subs
Potato Wedges

Mini Subs

(Pictured above)

Prep/Total Time: 10 min.

I created these for my daughter, Ashelen, when we ran out of bread one day. Now, she prefers to have the hot dog buns. They make the perfect kid-size submarine sandwich—and best of all, there's no crust! I like to serve the mini subs with my Potato Wedges (recipe at left).
—*Melissa Tatum, Greensboro, North Carolina*

- **3 tablespoons mayonnaise**
- **4 hot dog buns, split**
- **4 slices process American cheese**
- **1/4 pound sliced deli ham**
- **1/4 pound sliced deli turkey**
- **4 slices tomato, halved**
- **1 cup shredded lettuce**

Spread the mayonnaise over the cut side of the hot dog bun bottoms. Layer with the cheese, deli ham, deli turkey, tomato and lettuce; replace the tops of buns. **Yield:** 4 servings.

Caramel Cashew Chewies

Caramel Cashew Chewies

(Pictured above and on page 70)

Prep: 30 min. **Bake:** 10 min. + cooling

These chocolaty treats can turn ordinary days into something special! Let the kids unwrap the caramels, counting as they go, to see who unwraps the most.
—Amber Kieffer, Aurora, Colorado

☑ This recipe includes Nutrition Facts and Diabetic Exchanges.

3/4 cup butter, softened
3/4 cup packed brown sugar
1 egg
1-1/2 cups all-purpose flour
1 cup old-fashioned oats
1 package (14 ounces) caramels
1/3 cup half-and-half cream
1 cup semisweet chocolate chunks
1 cup salted cashew halves, chopped

In a large mixing bowl, cream butter and brown sugar. Beat in egg. Stir in flour and oats. Press into a 13-in. x 9-in. x 2-in. baking pan coated with cooking spray. Bake at 350° for 15-18 minutes or until golden brown.

Meanwhile, in a small saucepan, combine caramels and cream. Cook over low heat for 4-5 minutes or until caramels are melted, stirring occasionally. Pour over crust. Sprinkle with chocolate chunks and cashews.

Bake for 8-10 minutes or until chocolate is melted. Cool on a wire rack before cutting. **Yield:** about 3 dozen.

Nutrition Facts: 1 bar equals 158 calories, 8 g fat (4 g saturated fat), 16 mg cholesterol, 89 mg sodium, 20 g carbohydrate, 1 g fiber, 2 g protein. **Diabetic Exchanges:** 1-1/2 starch, 1 fat.

Pizza Noodle Bake

Prep: 25 min. **Bake:** 15 min.

It's a snap to assemble this family-pleasing casserole for a quick weeknight meal. Plus, the recipe can easily be doubled and frozen for another busy-day dinner.
—Bernice Knutson, Soldier, Iowa

10 ounces uncooked egg noodles
1-1/2 pounds ground beef
1/2 cup finely chopped onion
1/4 cup chopped green pepper
1 jar (14 ounces) pizza sauce
1 can (4 ounces) mushroom stems and pieces, drained
1 cup (4 ounces) shredded cheddar cheese
1 cup (4 ounces) shredded part-skim mozzarella cheese
1 package (3-1/2 ounces) sliced pepperoni

Cook the egg noodles according to the package directions. Meanwhile, in a large skillet, cook the ground beef, onion and green pepper over medium heat until meat is no longer pink; drain.

Add pizza sauce and mushrooms. Bring to a boil. Reduce heat; simmer, uncovered, for 2-3 minutes or until heated through. Drain noodles.

In a greased 13-in. x 9-in. x 2-in. baking dish, layer half of the noodles, beef mixture, cheeses and pepperoni. Repeat layers. Cover and bake at 350° for 15-20 minutes or until heated through. **Yield:** 6 servings.

Orange Ice Cream Pops

Prep: 10 min. + freezing

Orange juice and vanilla ice cream are great together in these pops. And you'll need only two other ingredients!
—Antoinette Ronzio, North Providence, Rhode Island

☑ This recipe includes Nutrition Facts and Diabetic Exchanges.

1 cup cold milk
2 cups vanilla ice cream
1 can (6 ounces) frozen orange juice concentrate, partially thawed
12 Popsicle molds *or* disposable plastic cups (3 ounces *each*) and Popsicle sticks

In a blender, combine the milk, ice cream and orange juice concentrate; cover and process until smooth.

Pour 1/4 cupfuls into Popsicle molds or plastic cups; top molds with holders or insert Popsicle sticks into cups. Freeze until firm. **Yield:** 1 dozen.

Nutrition Facts: 1 ice cream pop equals 79 calories, 3 g fat (2 g saturated fat), 12 mg cholesterol, 26 mg sodium, 12 g carbohydrate, trace fiber, 2 g protein. **Diabetic Exchanges:** 1 starch, 1/2 fat.

Fluffy Apple Dip

Prep/Total Time: 10 min.

This is an annual family favorite, beginning with the apple harvest in autumn and extending right on through New Year's. Plus, our friends like this fast dip just as much as we do! To add extra color to my serving tray, I cut apple wedges from red, green and yellow varieties.
—Sharon Parks, Adair, Illinois

1 package (8 ounces) cream cheese, softened
1 tablespoon peanut butter
1/2 teaspoon pumpkin pie spice
1 jar (7 ounces) marshmallow creme
Assorted apple wedges

In a small mixing bowl, beat the cream cheese, peanut butter and pumpkin pie spice until blended; fold in the marshmallow creme. Serve the dip with apple wedges. **Yield:** 2 cups.

Taco Macaroni

Prep/Total Time: 30 min.

With plenty of noodles, ground beef, cheddar cheese and taco flavor, this stovetop meal-in-one is always popular with families. It's a terrific way to fill everyone up after an activity-packed day at school and work.
—Marissa Undercofler, Howard, Pennsylvania

1 package (16 ounces) elbow macaroni
1 pound ground beef
3/4 cup chopped onion
1 can (14-1/2 ounces) diced tomatoes, undrained
1 can (10-3/4 ounces) condensed tomato soup, undiluted
1 can (8 ounces) tomato sauce
1 envelope taco seasoning
Shredded cheddar cheese

Cook the macaroni according to the package directions. Meanwhile, in a Dutch oven, cook the ground beef and onion over medium heat until the meat is no longer pink; drain.

Stir in the tomatoes, soup, tomato sauce and taco seasoning. Bring to a boil. Reduce heat; simmer, uncovered, for 8-10 minutes or until thickened.

Drain macaroni; stir into meat mixture and heat through. Sprinkle with cheese. **Yield:** 6 servings.

From Pops to Cups

Want a wonderful, hot-weather treat for your adult guests? Turn the Maple Mocha Pops recipe (above right) into a frozen coffee drink for grown-ups. Simply freeze the mixture in serving cups and top each one with a dollop of whipped cream. Yum!
—Caroline Sperry, Shelby Township, Michigan

Maple Mocha Pops

(Pictured below)

Prep: 15 min. + freezing

"One just isn't enough," my husband says whenever I surprise him with these creamy pops. They're a breeze to make on the spur of the moment...and both kids and adults like the maple-mocha taste combination.
—Caroline Sperry, Shelby Township, Michigan

2 cups heavy whipping cream
1/2 cup half-and-half cream
1/4 cup maple syrup
1/4 cup chocolate syrup
1 tablespoon instant coffee granules
12 Popsicle molds *or* paper cups (3 ounces *each*) and Popsicle sticks

In a small bowl, whisk the heavy whipping cream, half-and-half cream, maple syrup, chocolate syrup and coffee granules until the coffee is dissolved. Fill each Popsicle mold or paper cup with 1/4 cup cream mixture; top with the holders or insert Popsicle sticks into cups. Freeze. **Yield:** 1 dozen.

Maple Mocha Pops

Taco Salad Waffles

(Pictured below)

Prep/Total Time: 25 min.

Here's a fast and easy twist on the usual Mexican fare. Taco salad and waffles may sound like a strange combination, but you'll be surprised at how tasty it is. This recipe is perfect for a build-your-own party for teenagers, and I've even served it at brunch with rave reviews.
—Trisha Kruse, Eagle, Idaho

1 pound ground beef
1 cup salsa
1 can (4 ounces) chopped green chilies
1 envelope taco seasoning
8 frozen waffles
Shredded cheddar cheese, shredded lettuce, chopped tomatoes, cubed avocado, salsa and sour cream, optional

In a large skillet, cook ground beef over medium heat until no longer pink; drain. Stir in the salsa, chilies and taco seasoning. Bring to a boil. Reduce heat; simmer for 5 minutes.

Meanwhile, toast the waffles according to the package directions. Spoon about 1/4 cup ground beef mixture onto each waffle. If desired, top with cheddar cheese, lettuce, tomatoes, avocado, salsa and sour cream. **Yield:** 4 servings.

Taco Salad Waffles

Silver Dollar Oat Pancakes

Silver Dollar Oat Pancakes

(Pictured above)

Prep/Total Time: 25 min.

I combined two of my grandson Joshua's favorite foods—applesauce and oatmeal—to create these wholesome little pancakes. *—Margaret Wilson, Hemet, California*

✓ This recipe includes Nutrition Facts and Diabetic Exchanges.

1/2 cup all-purpose flour
1/2 cup quick-cooking oats
1-1/2 teaspoons sugar
1 teaspoon baking powder
1/2 teaspoon baking soda
1/2 teaspoon salt
1 egg
3/4 cup buttermilk
1/2 cup cinnamon applesauce
2 tablespoons butter, melted
Maple syrup *or* topping of your choice

In a large bowl, combine the dry ingredients. In a small bowl, beat the egg, buttermilk, applesauce and butter; stir into the dry ingredients just until moistened.

Pour batter by 2 tablespoonfuls onto a lightly greased hot griddle; turn when bubbles form on top. Cook until the second side is golden brown. Serve with maple syrup. **Yield:** 4 servings.

Nutrition Facts: 5 pancakes (calculated without syrup) equals 211 calories, 8 g fat (4 g saturated fat), 70 mg cholesterol, 660 mg sodium, 29 g carbohydrate, 2 g fiber, 6 g protein. **Diabetic Exchanges:** 2 starch, 1-1/2 fat.

Peanut Butter Jumbos

(Pictured below)

Prep: 15 min. **Bake:** 15 min./batch

Eyes always light up when I present a plate of these big cookies fresh from the oven. They look fun and festive dotted with the miniature baking bits. Whip up a batch for a school event or your next bake sale at church.
—Deborah Huffer, Staunton, Virginia

☑ This recipe includes Nutrition Facts and Diabetic Exchanges.

1-1/2 cups peanut butter
1/2 cup butter, softened
1 cup sugar
1 cup packed brown sugar
3 eggs
1 teaspoon vanilla extract
4-1/2 cups quick-cooking oats
2 teaspoons baking soda
1 cup miniature semisweet chocolate chips
1 cup M&M's miniature baking bits

In a large mixing bowl, cream peanut butter, butter and sugars. Add eggs, one at a time, beating well after each addition. Beat in vanilla. Combine oats and baking soda; gradually add to creamed mixture. Stir in chocolate chips and baking bits.

Drop by heaping tablespoonfuls 2 in. apart onto ungreased baking sheets. Bake at 350° for 12-14 minutes or until edges are browned. Remove cookies to wire racks. **Yield:** 9 dozen.

Editor's Note: Reduced-fat or generic brands of peanut butter are not recommended for this recipe.

Nutrition Facts: 1 cookie equals 76 calories, 4 g fat (2 g saturated fat), 9 mg cholesterol, 53 mg sodium, 9 g carbohydrate, 1 g fiber, 2 g protein. **Diabetic Exchanges:** 1 fat, 1/2 starch.

Peanut Butter Jumbos

Golden Chicken Nuggets

Golden Chicken Nuggets

(Pictured above)

Prep: 30 min. **Bake:** 15 min.

My grandchildren all love chicken nuggets, and they think these homemade bites are better than those from fast-food restaurants. Add a simple green salad to round out the menu, and you have a complete, kid-pleasing meal.
—Donna Louderback, Arkansas City, Kansas

1/2 cup mayonnaise
3 tablespoons milk
1/2 teaspoon ground cumin
1/4 teaspoon onion powder
1/4 teaspoon garlic powder
1/4 teaspoon cayenne pepper
1-1/4 cups crushed sesame snack crackers (about 38 crackers)
1-1/4 pounds boneless skinless chicken breasts, cut into 1-inch pieces

In a shallow bowl, combine the first six ingredients. Place crackers in another shallow bowl. Dip chicken in mayonnaise mixture, then coat with cracker crumbs.

Place on a foil-lined baking sheet. Bake at 400° for 8-10 minutes on each side or until chicken is no longer pink. **Yield:** 5 servings.

Dipping Delight

Dipping sauce makes any food more fun for kids. Let children help you mix 1/2 cup of mayonnaise with 1/2 cup of salsa for their nuggets. You could even spoon some sauce over mixed greens for a side salad.
—Donna Louderback, Arkansas City, Kansas

Cookie Pops

Cookie Pops

(Pictured above)

Prep/Total Time: 30 min.

Children will have a blast helping to assemble these fun chocolate-covered treats. Decorate them to make flower shapes, smiley faces, rainbows...whatever you like!
—Maria Regakis, Somerville, Massachusetts

✓ This recipe includes Nutrition Facts and Diabetic Exchanges.

1/4 cup creamy peanut butter
20 vanilla wafers
10 Popsicle sticks
4 ounces milk chocolate candy coating, chopped
1 teaspoon shortening
M&M's miniature baking bits, optional

Spread peanut butter over the flat side of 10 vanilla wafers, about 1 tsp. on each. Top each with a Popsicle stick and another wafer. Place on a waxed paper-lined baking sheet; freeze for 7 minutes.

In a small microwave-safe bowl, melt candy coating and shortening; stir until smooth. Dip pops into chocolate, allowing excess to drip off. Return to baking sheet. Decorate with baking bits if desired. Freeze for 5-6 minutes or until chocolate is set. Store in an airtight container at room temperature. **Yield:** 10 servings.

Nutrition Facts: 1 cookie pop (calculated without baking bits) equals 133 calories, 8 g fat (4 g saturated fat), 1 mg cholesterol, 53 mg sodium, 15 g carbohydrate, 1 g fiber, 2 g protein. **Diabetic Exchanges:** 1-1/2 fat, 1 starch.

Breaded Chicken Tenders With Noodles

Prep/Total Time: 25 min.

My daughter, Chelsea, and her friend Becca created this dish for my husband and me. It was an impressive surprise and a real treat. *—Jodi Harre, Nashville, Illinois*

5 cups uncooked egg noodles
1 tablespoon lemon juice
1 tablespoon lime juice
1/2 cup seasoned bread crumbs
8 chicken tenderloins
1 teaspoon minced garlic
6 tablespoons butter, *divided*
1/8 teaspoon garlic salt
1/8 teaspoon garlic powder

Cook noodles according to package directions. Meanwhile, combine the lemon and lime juices in a small bowl; set aside.

Place the bread crumbs in a large resealable plastic bag; add chicken, one piece at a time, and shake to coat. In a large skillet, cook chicken and garlic in 2 tablespoons butter over medium heat for 3 minutes on each side or until chicken juices run clear, basting occasionally with citrus juice mixture.

Melt remaining butter. Drain noodles; toss with garlic salt, garlic powder and melted butter. Serve with chicken tenders. **Yield:** 4 servings.

Berry Yogurt Cups

Prep/Total Time: 10 min.

Blueberries and strawberries jazz up vanilla yogurt in this summery dessert. Feel free to use any fruits your children may like. *—Shannon Mink, Columbus, Ohio*

✓ This recipe includes Nutrition Facts and Diabetic Exchanges.

1-1/2 cups sliced fresh strawberries
1-1/2 cups fresh blueberries
1 carton (6 ounces) vanilla yogurt
1 teaspoon sugar
1/8 to 1/4 teaspoon ground cinnamon

Divide the strawberries and blueberries among four individual serving dishes. In a small bowl, combine the vanilla yogurt, sugar and cinnamon; spoon over fruit. **Yield:** 4 servings.

Nutrition Facts: 3/4 cup fruit with 3 tablespoons yogurt equals 98 calories, 2 g fat (1 g saturated fat), 4 mg cholesterol, 29 mg sodium, 20 g carbohydrate, 3 g fiber, 3 g protein. **Diabetic Exchanges:** 1 fruit, 1/2 milk.

Peanut Butter Clusters

Prep: 20 min. + chilling

This yummy, chocolate-coated crunch is great to keep on hand for drop-in guests. I make a batch at Christmastime and frequently during the rest of the year, too.
—Pat Maxwell, Taft, California

✓ This recipe includes Nutrition Facts and Diabetic Exchanges.

2 cups peanut butter chips
1 cup milk chocolate chips
1-1/2 cups dry roasted peanuts
1 cup crushed ridged potato chips

In a microwave-safe bowl, melt peanut butter chips and chocolate chips; stir until smooth. Stir in peanuts and potato chips. Drop by level tablespoonfuls onto waxed paper-lined baking sheets. Refrigerate until firm. Store in an airtight container. **Yield:** about 3-1/2 dozen.

Editor's Note: This recipe was tested in a 1,100-watt microwave.

Nutrition Facts: 1 piece equals 96 calories, 6 g fat (2 g saturated fat), 1 mg cholesterol, 70 mg sodium, 8 g carbohydrate, 1 g fiber, 3 g protein. **Diabetic Exchanges:** 1 fat, 1/2 starch.

Fruit Juice Pops

Prep: 25 min. + freezing

My kids always enjoyed these more than any other pops. Try them with either pineapple or orange juice. You could also freeze and serve them in cups made from hollowed-out oranges.
—Barbara Stewart, Garland, Texas

✓ This recipe includes Nutrition Facts.

2 cups water
1-1/2 cups sugar
4 cups unsweetened apple juice
1 cup unsweetened pineapple *or* orange juice
1/2 cup lemon juice
12 Popsicle molds *or* paper cups (3 ounces *each*) and Popsicle sticks

In a large saucepan, combine water and sugar; bring to a boil. Reduce heat; simmer, uncovered, for 3-4 minutes or until sugar is dissolved, stirring occasionally. Remove from the heat; stir in juices.

Fill molds or cups with 1/4 cup juice mixture; top with holders or insert sticks into cups. Freeze. **Yield:** 1 dozen.

Nutrition Facts: 1 juice pop equals 149 calories, trace fat (trace saturated fat), 0 cholesterol, 3 mg sodium, 38 g carbohydrate, trace fiber, trace protein.

Animal Ideas

THE FACES of the Mice Cupcakes (recipe above right) could easily be altered to resemble other critters. For example, try creating teddy bears, puppies, kittens or monkeys using different varieties of candies, frosting and cookies as the decorations.

Mice Cupcakes

(Pictured below)

Prep: 45 min. **Bake:** 20 min. + cooling

During a visit several years ago, we let our 3-year-old grandson, Robert, help decorate the Mice Cupcakes I was making for a party. It was quite a project...and so fun!
—Beverly Arnold, Green Valley, Arizona

1 package (18-1/4 ounces) chocolate cake mix
2 cans (16 ounces *each*) vanilla frosting
48 vanilla wafers
Red-hot candies, red gumdrops and red shoestring licorice

Prepare cake batter and bake according to package directions for cupcakes, using foil- or paper-lined muffin tins. Remove from pans to wire racks to cool completely.

Frost cupcakes generously with vanilla frosting. For ears, position two vanilla wafers on each cupcake.

Add red-hots for eyes and gumdrops for noses. Insert short pieces of licorice for whiskers and longer pieces for tails. **Yield:** 2 dozen.

Mice Cupcakes

Chapter 5

Give Me 5 or Fewer

CAN DISHES as great-tasting and special-looking as Crumb-Coated Ranch Chicken, Pesto Tortellini Salad and Coconut Brownies really come together with only a handful of ingredients? It may seem impossible, but it's true!

Those specialties are just a sampling of the short-but-sweet recipes here. Each one calls for only five ingredients or less (not including the basics of water, salt and pepper)...so you won't need a grocery bag full of items in order to get cooking.

And there's an added bonus: You'll save time not just in the kitchen, but also in the supermarket thanks to a short shopping list. Simply turn to this chapter—and fix it with five!

TAKE FIVE FOR FLAVOR. Bacon-Wrapped Appetizers (p. 97).

Surprise Spice Cake

(Pictured below)

Prep: 15 min. **Bake:** 30 min. + cooling

An unusual ingredient—canned tomato soup—is the secret in this yummy spice cake. That "surprise" adds nutrition and color...but no one ever detects it! Topped with cream cheese frosting, a big piece of this dessert makes a wonderful treat for your family or guests anytime.
—Hannah Thompson, Scotts Valley, California

1 package (18-1/4 ounces) spice cake mix
1 can (10-3/4 ounces) condensed tomato soup, undiluted
3 eggs
1/2 cup water
1 can (16 ounces) cream cheese frosting

In a large mixing bowl, combine the spice cake mix, tomato soup, eggs and water; beat on low speed for 30 seconds. Beat on medium for 2 minutes. Pour into a greased 13-in. x 9-in. x 2-in. baking dish.

Bake at 350° for 30-33 minutes or until a toothpick inserted near the center of cake comes out clean. Cool on a wire rack. Frost with cream cheese frosting. **Yield:** 12 servings.

Surprise Spice Cake

Fettuccine with Sausage and Leeks

Prep/Total Time: 20 min.

This 20-minute dinner has been a lifesaver in our household for more than 25 years. It gets raves from all of my friends. —Mary Jane McConahay, Indianapolis, Indiana

8 ounces uncooked fettuccine
1 pound bulk Italian sausage
2 medium leeks (white portion only), sliced
1/2 pound sliced fresh mushrooms
3/4 cup heavy whipping cream

Cook fettuccine according to package directions. Meanwhile, in a large skillet, cook sausage and leeks over medium heat until meat is no longer pink and leeks are tender; drain. Add mushrooms; cook for 3-4 minutes or until tender.

Stir in whipping cream. Reduce heat; cook and stir for 2-3 minutes or until heated through (do not boil).

Drain the fettuccine; serve with the sausage mixture. **Yield:** 4 servings.

Apple Cherry Salad

Prep: 20 min. + chilling

The popularity of this salad comes from its crunch and blend of different textures. It's my mother's recipe.
—Karen Harrington, Le Mars, Iowa

✓ This recipe includes Nutrition Facts and Diabetic Exchanges.

1 package (3 ounces) cherry gelatin
1 cup boiling water
1 can (21 ounces) cherry pie filling
4 medium apples, chopped
1 cup chopped celery

In a large bowl, dissolve gelatin in boiling water. Stir in the pie filling, apples and celery. Refrigerate for 30 minutes or until chilled. **Yield:** 8-10 servings.

Nutrition Facts: 3/4 cup equals 134 calories, trace fat (trace saturated fat), 0 cholesterol, 40 mg sodium, 33 g carbohydrate, 2 g fiber, 1 g protein. **Diabetic Exchange:** 2 fruit.

Learning About Leeks

A MEMBER of the onion family, leeks have a very subtle flavor. Buy leeks with crisp, brightly colored leaves and an unblemished white stalk. Leeks that are larger than 1-1/2 inches in diameter will be less tender.

Refrigerate leeks in a plastic bag for up to 5 days. Before using them, cut off the roots and trim the tough leaf ends. Slit the leek from end to end and wash it thoroughly under cold water to remove dirt trapped between the leaf layers. Chop or slice the white portion to use in a variety of dishes, such as Fettuccine with Sausage and Leeks (recipe at top).

Roasted Potatoes and Peppers
Crumb-Coated Ranch Chicken

Roasted Potatoes and Peppers

(Pictured above)

Prep: 10 min. **Bake:** 40 min.

This colorful side dish has such a delicious, tangy taste. I've also had success using the fat-free variety of salad dressing. —Joan Hallford, North Richland Hills, Texas

✓ This recipe includes Nutrition Facts and Diabetic Exchanges.

2 pounds small red potatoes, quartered
1 medium green pepper, coarsely chopped
1 medium sweet red pepper, coarsely chopped
1 medium red onion, coarsely chopped
1/2 cup creamy garlic salad dressing

In a 15-in. x 10-in. x 1-in. baking pan coated with cooking spray, combine potatoes, peppers and onion. Drizzle with dressing and toss to coat.

Bake at 400° for 40-45 minutes or until potatoes are tender, stirring occasionally. **Yield:** 8 servings.

Nutrition Facts: 3/4 cup equals 149 calories, 6 g fat (1 g saturated fat), 0 cholesterol, 188 mg sodium, 22 g carbohydrate, 3 g fiber, 3 g protein. **Diabetic Exchanges:** 1-1/2 starch, 1 fat.

Crumb-Coated Ranch Chicken

(Pictured above)

Prep: 10 min. **Bake:** 30 min.

How do you get lots of flavor from only five ingredients? In this recipe, the key is the ranch salad dressing! Along with Italian seasoning and garlic powder, it makes chicken a treat. Enjoy this simple entree on busy weeknights or even with company for special occasions. —LaDonna Reed, Ponca City, Oklahoma

2/3 cup ranch salad dressing
2 cups coarsely crushed cornflakes
1 tablespoon Italian seasoning
1 teaspoon garlic powder
4 boneless skinless chicken breast halves (8 ounces *each*)

Pour the ranch salad dressing into a shallow bowl. In another shallow bowl, combine the cornflake crumbs, Italian seasoning and garlic powder. Dip the chicken breast halves in the salad dressing, then coat with the crumb mixture.

Place coated chicken in a greased shallow baking pan. Bake at 400° for 30-35 minutes or until the juices run clear. **Yield:** 4 servings.

Asparagus Ham Roll-Ups

Asparagus Ham Roll-Ups

(Pictured above)

Prep/Total Time: 25 min.

Asparagus and red pepper make these tasty roll-ups ideal for a celebration. They have a fussed-over look but are a cinch to make. —Rhonda Struthers, Ottawa, Ontario

✓ This recipe includes Nutrition Facts and Diabetic Exchanges.

16 fresh asparagus spears, trimmed
1 medium sweet red pepper, cut into 16 strips
8 ounces Havarti cheese, cut into 16 strips
8 thin slices deli ham *or* prosciutto, cut in half lengthwise
16 whole chives

In a large skillet, bring 1 in. of water to a boil. Add asparagus; cover and cook for 3 minutes. Drain and immediately place the asparagus in ice water. Drain and pat dry.

Place an asparagus spear, a red pepper strip and a cheese strip on each slice of ham. Roll up tightly; tie with a chive. Refrigerate until serving. **Yield:** 16 servings.

Nutrition Facts: 1 roll-up equals 69 calories, 5 g fat (3 g saturated fat), 18 mg cholesterol, 180 mg sodium, 2 g carbohydrate, trace fiber, 6 g protein. **Diabetic Exchanges:** 1 fat, 1/2 vegetable.

Snipped in a Snap

SNIPPING herbs, such as the fresh dill for Dilled Mashed Potatoes (recipe above right), means to cut the herbs into small pieces using a kitchen shears. Simply hold the dill or other herbs over a small bowl and make 1/8-inch to 1/4-inch cuts.

Dilled Mashed Potatoes

(Pictured below)

Prep/Total Time: 30 min.

Round out any holiday meal or Sunday dinner with these delightful mashed potatoes. The dill flavor is guaranteed to please your family and guests. I also add a bit of cottage cheese to give the potatoes a pleasantly creamy texture. —Sandi Guettler, Bay City, Michigan

✓ This recipe includes Nutrition Facts and Diabetic Exchanges.

2 pounds Yukon Gold potatoes, peeled and cubed
2/3 cup 4% cottage cheese
1/3 cup shredded cheddar cheese
2 teaspoons butter
2 teaspoons snipped fresh dill *or* 1/2 teaspoon dill weed
1/2 teaspoon salt

Place potatoes in a large saucepan and cover with water; cover and bring to a boil over medium-high heat. Cook for 15-20 minutes or until tender; drain.

Transfer to a large mixing bowl. Add the cottage cheese, cheddar cheese, butter, dill and salt; beat until smooth and fluffy. **Yield:** 6 servings.

Nutrition Facts: 2/3 cup equals 185 calories, 4 g fat (3 g saturated fat), 16 mg cholesterol, 350 mg sodium, 28 g carbohydrate, 2 g fiber, 8 g protein. **Diabetic Exchanges:** 2 starch, 1 fat.

Dilled Mashed Potatoes

Microwave Acorn Squash

Chocolate-Peanut Butter Cookies

(Pictured below)

Prep: 15 min. **Bake:** 10 min./batch

Children will love baking a batch of these fuss-free goodies with Mom, Dad or the grandparents. The nutty frosted cookies are dense and rich...and absolutely perfect for dunking. Be sure to have big glasses of cold milk ready to go!
—Elaine Stephens, Carmel, Indiana

✓ This recipe includes Nutrition Facts and Diabetic Exchanges.

2 cans (16 ounces *each*) chocolate fudge frosting
1 egg
1 cup chunky peanut butter
1-1/2 cups all-purpose flour
Granulated sugar

Set aside 1 can plus 1/3 cup frosting. In a large bowl, combine egg, peanut butter and remaining frosting. Stir in flour until moist.

Drop by rounded tablespoons 2 in. apart on greased baking sheets. Flatten cookies with a fork dipped in sugar. Bake at 375° for 8-11 minutes or until set. Remove to wire racks. Cool completely; spread with frosting. **Yield:** 3-1/2 dozen.

Nutrition Facts: 1 cookie equals 143 calories, 7 g fat (1 g saturated fat), 5 mg cholesterol, 79 mg sodium, 18 g carbohydrate, 1 g fiber, 2 g protein. **Diabetic Exchanges:** 1 starch, 1 fat.

Chocolate Peanut-Butter Cookies

Microwave Acorn Squash

(Pictured above)

Prep/Total Time: 20 min.

When it comes to acorn squash, it's hard to beat this recipe combining brown sugar, butter and honey. Yum!
—Kara de la Vega, Santa Rosa, California

✓ This recipe includes Nutrition Facts.

2 medium acorn squash
1/4 cup packed brown sugar
2 tablespoons butter
4 teaspoons honey
1/4 teaspoon salt
1/4 teaspoon pepper

Cut squash in half; discard seeds. Place squash cut side down in a microwave-safe dish. Cover and microwave on high for 10-12 minutes or until tender.

Turn squash cut side up. Fill centers of squash with brown sugar, butter and honey; sprinkle with salt and pepper. Cover and microwave on high for 2-3 minutes or until heated through. **Yield:** 4 servings.

Editor's Note: This recipe was tested in a 1,100-watt microwave.

Nutrition Facts: 1 squash half equals 216 calories, 6 g fat (4 g saturated fat), 15 mg cholesterol, 200 mg sodium, 43 g carbohydrate, 3 g fiber, 2 g protein.

Bing Cherry Sherbet

Bing Cherry Sherbet

(Pictured above)

Prep: 30 min. + freezing

To whip up this pretty pink sherbet studded with dark, sweet cherries, you'll need an ice cream maker—and a total of just four ingredients. For a change of flavor, try this recipe with sliced peaches and peach soda.
—Helen Humble, Longview, Texas

✓ This recipe includes Nutrition Facts.

4 cups fresh *or* frozen pitted dark sweet cherries, quartered
1 cup sugar
2 liters black cherry soda, chilled
1 can (14 ounces) sweetened condensed milk

In a large saucepan, bring cherries and sugar to a boil over medium heat, stirring constantly. Reduce heat; cover and simmer for 10 minutes, stirring occasionally. Cool slightly. Transfer to a large bowl; cover and refrigerate until chilled.

Stir in soda and milk. Fill ice cream freezer cylinder two-thirds full; freeze according to manufacturer's directions. Refrigerate remaining mixture until ready to freeze. Transfer to a freezer container; freeze for 2-4 hours or until firm. Remove from the freezer 10 minutes before serving. **Yield:** about 3 quarts.

Nutrition Facts: 3/4 cup equals 201 calories, 2 g fat (1 g saturated fat), 8 mg cholesterol, 45 mg sodium, 44 g carbohydrate, 1 g fiber, 2 g protein.

Sausage-Stuffed Mushrooms

(Pictured below)

Prep: 20 min. **Bake:** 20 min.

My family snatches up these warm snacks just as fast as I can make them, so I'm glad they're a cinch to prepare! The little oven-baked mushroom caps are irresistible with their simple stuffing of sausage, mozzarella cheese, chopped mushrooms and seasoned bread crumbs.
—Kathryn Schumacker, Batesville, Indiana

30 to 35 large fresh mushrooms
1/2 pound bulk pork sausage
1/2 cup shredded part-skim mozzarella cheese
1/4 cup seasoned bread crumbs

Remove the stems from the mushrooms and finely chop; set the caps aside. In a large skillet, cook the sausage and mushrooms over medium heat until meat is no longer pink; drain.

Remove from the heat. Stir in the cheese and bread crumbs. Fill each mushroom cap with about 1 tablespoon of filling.

Place on foil-lined baking sheets. Bake at 400° for 16-20 minutes or until the mushrooms are tender. **Yield:** 30-35 appetizers.

Sausage-Stuffed Mushrooms

Salami Roll-Ups
Mexican Salsa Pizza

Mexican Salsa Pizza

(Pictured above)

Prep/Total Time: 25 min.

My guests have a hard time believing that such a terrific-tasting appetizer can be so simple. Like things spicier? Kick up the heat a bit with a hot salsa and pepper Jack cheese. —*Carla McMahon, Hermiston, Oregon*

✓ This recipe includes Nutrition Facts and Diabetic Exchanges.

- **1 prebaked Italian bread shell crust (14 ounces)**
- **1 cup (4 ounces) shredded Monterey Jack cheese, *divided***
- **3/4 cup salsa**
- **2 tablespoons minced fresh cilantro**

Place crust on an ungreased baking sheet or pizza pan. In a small bowl, combine 1/2 cup cheese, salsa and cilantro. Spread over crust to within 1/2 in. of edges. Sprinkle with remaining cheese. Bake at 350° for 20-25 minutes or until cheese is melted. Cut into wedges. **Yield:** 2 dozen.

Nutrition Facts: 1 wedge equals 64 calories, 2 g fat (1 g saturated fat), 4 mg cholesterol, 143 mg sodium, 8 g carbohydrate, trace fiber, 3 g protein. **Diabetic Exchanges:** 1/2 starch, 1/2 fat.

Salami Roll-Ups

(Pictured above)

Prep/Total Time: 25 min.

These bite-size snacks are great for tiding your family over until dinnertime. And the roll-ups are so easy to make, kids can help. —*Jean Baffuto, Apache Junction, Arizona*

✓ This recipe includes Nutrition Facts.

- **1 carton (8 ounces) whipped cream cheese**
- **1/4 pound hard salami, finely chopped**
- **2 tablespoons dill pickle relish**
- **4 flour tortillas (10 inches), room temperature**

In a small bowl, combine the cream cheese, salami and pickle relish. Spread over tortillas. Roll up tightly; wrap in plastic wrap. Refrigerate for 15 minutes. Unwrap and cut each tortilla into 1-in. slices. **Yield:** 3-1/2 dozen.

Nutrition Facts: 1 roll-up equals 49 calories, 3 g fat (2 g saturated fat), 9 mg cholesterol, 120 mg sodium, 4 g carbohydrate, 1 g fiber, 2 g protein.

Bacon Chicken Roll-Ups

(Pictured below)

Prep: 20 min. **Bake:** 35 min.

I get many requests for these bacon-wrapped chicken rolls. And to me, nothing's better than a dish that impresses everyone but is actually simple to prepare! The chicken cooks a little longer than weeknight recipes, but it'll leave you hands-free time to spend with your guests.
—Sandi Guettler, Bay City, Michigan

12 bacon strips
6 boneless skinless chicken breast halves (4 ounces *each*)
1 package (8 ounces) cream cheese, softened
1 medium sweet onion, halved and cut into slices
Dash salt and pepper

In a large skillet, cook bacon over medium heat until cooked but not crisp. Remove to paper towels to drain.

Meanwhile, flatten the chicken breast halves to 1/8-in. thickness. Spread the cream cheese down the center of each chicken breast; top with onion. Roll up from a long side; tuck the ends in. Sprinkle with salt and pepper. Wrap two bacon strips around each piece of chicken; secure with toothpicks.

Place the wrapped chicken rolls in a greased 13-in. x 9-in. x 2-in. baking dish. Bake at 350° for 35-40 minutes or until chicken juices run clear. Discard the toothpicks before serving. **Yield:** 6 servings.

Spinach Pizza

Bacon Chicken Roll-Ups

Spinach Pizza

(Pictured above)

Prep/Total Time: 25 min.

This tasty meatless pie goes together quickly with purchased Alfredo sauce, spinach, tomatoes and shredded cheese over an easy crust from a mix. It's an unusual taste twist on pizza, but everyone in my family—including my young daughter—loves this veggie-filled meal.
—Dawn Bartholomew, Raleigh, North Carolina

1 package (6-1/2 ounces) pizza crust mix
1/2 cup Alfredo sauce
4 cups chopped fresh spinach
2 medium tomatoes, chopped
2 cups (8 ounces) shredded Italian cheese blend

Prepare pizza dough according to package directions. With floured hands, press dough onto a greased 12-in. pizza pan.

Spread the Alfredo sauce over the pizza dough to within 1 in. of the edges. Top with the spinach, tomatoes and cheese. Bake at 450° for 10-15 minutes or until the cheese is melted and the crust is golden brown. **Yield:** 4-6 servings.

Skillet Mac & Cheese

Prep/Total Time: 25 min.

What could be better than the ultimate comfort food—homemade macaroni and cheese—made super-simple? This skillet version is sure to please. You could use salt and pepper to taste, but we don't feel it's necessary.
—Ann Bowers, Rockport, Texas

- **2 cups uncooked elbow macaroni**
- **2 tablespoons butter**
- **2 tablespoons all-purpose flour**
- **1-1/2 cups half-and-half cream**
- **3/4 pound process cheese (Velveeta), cubed**

Cook macaroni according to the package directions. Meanwhile, in a large nonstick skillet, melt butter over medium heat. Stir in flour until smooth. Gradually add cream; bring to a boil. Cook and stir for 2 minutes or until thickened. Reduce heat. Stir in cheese until melted.

Drain the macaroni; add to the cheese mixture. Cook and stir for 3-4 minutes or until heated through. **Yield:** 4 servings.

Slow-Cooked Ribs

Prep: 15 min. **Cook:** 6 hours

A few convenience items produce the sweet and tangy flavor of these saucy ribs...and my slow cooker makes them fuss-free. *—Sharon Crider, St. Robert, Missouri*

- **4 pounds boneless country-style pork ribs**
- **1 cup barbecue sauce**
- **1 cup Catalina salad dressing**
- **1/2 teaspoon minced garlic**
- **2 tablespoons all-purpose flour**
- **1/4 cup cold water**

Cut ribs into serving-size pieces. Place in a 5-qt. slow cooker. Combine barbecue sauce and salad dressing; pour over ribs. Sprinkle with garlic. Cover and cook on low for 6-7 hours or until meat is tender.

Remove ribs and keep warm. Strain cooking liquid into a small saucepan; skim fat. Combine flour and water until smooth; stir into cooking liquid. Bring to a boil; cook and stir for 2 minutes or until thickened. Spoon sauce over the ribs. **Yield:** 8 servings.

Golden Chicken with Rice

Prep: 10 min. **Bake:** 2 hours

The combo of chicken and rice has never been so easy—or so delicious! These tender chicken legs are served over creamy wild rice for a wonderful, home-style main dish.
—Sharon Juart, Rochester Mills, Pennsylvania

- **1 package (6 ounces) long grain and wild rice mix**
- **1 can (10-3/4 ounces) condensed cream of mushroom soup, undiluted**
- **1 can (10-3/4 ounces) condensed cream of celery soup, undiluted**
- **1-1/2 cups water**
- **4 chicken leg quarters**
- **1 envelope onion soup mix**

In a large bowl, combine the rice, contents of seasoning packet, cream soups and water. Spread into a greased 13-in. x 9-in. x 2-in. baking dish. Top with chicken; sprinkle with onion soup mix.

Cover and bake at 350° for 2 hours or until a meat thermometer reads 180° and the rice is tender. **Yield:** 4 servings.

Buttery-Onion Corn on the Cob

(Pictured below)

Prep/Total Time: 20 min.

My mother has been making this oven recipe for years. No one can believe that the scrumptious cobs of corn require only butter and an envelope of onion soup mix.
—Lisa Denson, Decatur, Alabama

- **1/2 cup butter, melted**
- **1 envelope onion soup mix**
- **4 medium ears sweet corn, husks removed**

In a small bowl, combine the butter and onion soup mix; rub over the corn. Place each ear of corn on a 12-in. x 10-in. piece of heavy-duty foil. Fold foil over corn and seal tightly.

Bake at 450° for 15-20 minutes or until corn is tender, turning once. **Yield:** 4 servings.

Buttery-Onion Corn on the Cob

Peppermint Stick Sauce

Peppermint Stick Sauce

(Pictured above)

Prep/Total Time: 25 min.

Turn ice cream into an extra-special treat with this yummy sauce. People of all ages love its cool, sweet flavor.
—Kelly Ann Gray, Beaufort, South Carolina

1-1/2 cups crushed peppermint candies
1 cup heavy whipping cream
1 jar (7 ounces) marshmallow creme

In a heavy saucepan, combine the crushed peppermint candies, heavy whipping cream and marshmallow creme. Cook and stir over low heat until the peppermint candy is completely melted and the mixture is smooth. Remove from the heat. Store sauce in the refrigerator. **Yield:** 2-1/4 cups.

Creamy Potato Soup

Prep/Total Time: 25 min.

A friend brought me this soup when I was sick. It tastes like it simmered for hours, but basic ingredients make it a snap to prepare. A big bowlful is guaranteed to chase away the chills! *—Pat Maruca, Philippi, West Virginia*

1 package (30 ounces) frozen shredded hash brown potatoes
6 cups water
1/3 cup chopped onion
2 cans (10-3/4 ounces *each*) condensed cream of celery soup, undiluted
4 ounces process cheese (Velveeta), cubed
1 cup (8 ounces) sour cream
1/2 teaspoon salt
1/4 teaspoon pepper

In a large saucepan, combine the hash brown potatoes, water and onion. Bring to a boil. Reduce the heat; stir in the soup and cheese. Cook and stir until cheese is melted.

Stir in the sour cream, salt and pepper. Cook and stir until heated through (do not boil). **Yield:** 13 servings (about 3 quarts).

Hot Dog Spaghetti Rings

Prep/Total Time: 25 min.

I used to make this dinner when I was a teenager. It's so easy—you just cook the pasta, then stir all of the ingredients together and heat the mixture in the microwave. Add a tossed green salad for a complete meal.
—Jared Graetz, Andover, Minnesota

1 package (7 ounces) ring macaroni
1 can (10-3/4 ounces) condensed cheddar cheese soup, undiluted
1 can (10-3/4 ounces) condensed tomato soup, undiluted
5 hot dogs, halved lengthwise and thinly sliced

Cook the macaroni according to the package directions; drain. Place in a 2-qt. microwave-safe dish; stir in the cheese soup, tomato soup and hot dogs. Cover and microwave on high for 3-4 minutes or until heated through. **Yield:** 6 servings.

Editor's Note: This recipe was tested in a 1,100-watt microwave.

Chocolate Wafer Ice Cream

Prep: 5 min. + freezing

Orange and chocolate make a mouth-watering combination in this effortless dessert. It dresses up ordinary vanilla ice cream with crushed chocolate wafers and orange marmalade. Whole wafers make a fun garnish.
—Lillian Julow, Gainesville, Florida

8 chocolate wafers, *divided*
1-1/2 cups vanilla ice cream, softened
2 tablespoons orange marmalade

Crush two chocolate wafers. In a small mixing bowl, beat the vanilla ice cream and orange marmalade until blended. Fold in the crushed chocolate wafers. Freeze until firm.

Divide the ice cream between two parfait glasses. Serve ice cream with the remaining chocolate wafers. **Yield:** 2 servings.

Crab Crescents

(Pictured below)

Prep/Total Time: 25 min.

When your guests start snatching from a platter of these warm little bites, no one will guess how quickly you were able to put them together. The simple appetizers combine prepared pesto and crab inside store-bought crescent roll dough. They're delicious...and decadent, too!
—Stephanie Howard, Oakland, California

☑ This recipe includes Nutrition Facts and Diabetic Exchanges.

1 tube (8 ounces) refrigerated crescent rolls
3 tablespoons prepared pesto
1/2 cup fresh crabmeat

Unroll the crescent roll dough; separate into eight triangles. Cut each triangle in half lengthwise, forming two triangles. Spread 1/2 teaspoon pesto over each triangle; place 1 rounded teaspoonful of crab along the wide end of each triangle.

Roll up the triangles from the wide ends and place with the point side down 1 in. apart on an ungreased baking sheet. Bake at 375° for 10-12 minutes or until golden brown. Serve warm. **Yield:** 16 appetizers.

Nutrition Facts: 1 appetizer equals 74 calories, 4 g fat (1 g saturated fat), 5 mg cholesterol, 144 mg sodium, 6 g carbohydrate, trace fiber, 2 g protein. **Diabetic Exchanges:** 1 fat, 1/2 starch.

Crab Crescents

Hawaiian Turtle Cups

Hawaiian Turtle Cups

(Pictured above)

Prep: 20 min. + chilling

My mother-in-law loves macadamia nuts, and my daughter prefers white chocolate to milk chocolate. To please both of them, I came up with this fun twist on classic turtle candy. *—Larisa Sarver, LaSalle, Illinois*

1-1/2 cups vanilla *or* white chips
1/2 cup macadamia nuts, chopped
18 caramels
2 teaspoons heavy whipping cream
12 dried pineapple pieces, chopped

In a microwave-safe bowl, melt vanilla chips; stir until smooth. Pour by teaspoonfuls into greased miniature muffin cups; set aside the remaining melted chips. Sprinkle the center of each muffin cup with nuts.

In a microwave-safe bowl, melt caramels and cream; stir until smooth. Pour over nuts. Reheat reserved chips if necessary; pour over caramel mixture. Top each with pineapple. Chill for 30 minutes or until set. Carefully run a knife around the edge of each muffin cup to loosen candy. **Yield:** 1 dozen.

Crescent Creations

THE RECIPE for Crab Crescents (above left) is wonderfully versatile. For example, if you don't have prepared pesto on hand or just want a different flavor, try replacing the pesto with purchased Alfredo sauce. You could also use canned crabmeat instead of fresh.

Spinach Pasta Salad

Spinach Pasta Salad

(Pictured above)

Prep/Total Time: 20 min.

This colorful pasta salad from our Test Kitchen boasts a crisp blend of fruit-and-veggie flavors. It's a lovely choice for a light dinner or luncheon.

✓ This recipe includes Nutrition Facts and Diabetic Exchanges.

1 cup uncooked bow tie pasta
1 package (10 ounces) fresh baby spinach
1 medium sweet yellow pepper, diced
1/2 cup chopped dried apricots
1/2 cup balsamic vinaigrette

Cook pasta according to package directions. Meanwhile, in a large serving bowl, combine the spinach, yellow pepper and apricots.

Drain pasta and rinse in cold water; add to spinach mixture. Drizzle with vinaigrette and toss to coat. **Yield:** 8-10 servings.

Nutrition Facts: 3/4 cup equals 63 calories, 2 g fat (trace saturated fat), 0 cholesterol, 127 mg sodium, 10 g carbohydrate, 1 g fiber, 2 g protein. **Diabetic Exchange:** 1 starch.

Berry Rhubarb Fool

Prep: 30 min. + chilling

"Fool" is a classic British dessert that's usually made with whipped cream and cooked fruit. Try my quicker version that features tangy rhubarb and strawberries.
—Cheryl Miller, Fort Collins, Colorado

3 cups sliced fresh *or* frozen rhubarb (1-inch pieces)
1/3 cup sugar
1/4 cup orange juice
Dash salt
1 cup heavy whipping cream
1 pint fresh strawberries, halved

In a large saucepan, combine the rhubarb, sugar, orange juice and salt. Bring to a boil. Reduce heat; cover and simmer for 6-8 minutes or until the rhubarb is tender. Cool slightly.

In a blender, process the rhubarb mixture until smooth. Transfer to a large bowl. Cover and refrigerate until chilled.

Just before serving, whip cream until soft peaks form. Fold into the rhubarb mixture. In parfait glasses, alternately layer cream mixture and strawberries. **Yield:** 6 servings.

Lemon Fudge

(Pictured below)

Prep: 20 min. + chilling

It's amazing that something this smooth and luscious can be made with so few ingredients—and in such little time! The pastel-yellow fudge is a pretty treat for Easter celebrations, as well as bridal and baby showers.
—Rozanne Born, Zumbrota, Minnesota

✓ This recipe includes Nutrition Facts and Diabetic Exchanges.

1-1/2 teaspoons plus 6 tablespoons butter, *divided*
2 packages (10 to 12 ounces *each*) vanilla *or* white chips
2/3 cup sweetened condensed milk
2/3 cup marshmallow creme
1-1/2 teaspoons lemon extract

Line a 9-in. square pan with foil. Grease foil with 1-1/2 teaspoons butter; set aside. In a large saucepan, melt remaining butter over low heat. Add the vanilla chips and milk; cook and stir for 10-12 minutes or until the chips are melted.

Stir in marshmallow creme and extract; cook and stir 3-4 minutes longer or until smooth. Pour into prepared pan. Chill until set.

Using the foil, lift the fudge out of pan. Discard foil; cut fudge into squares. Store in the refrigerator. **Yield:** about 2 pounds.

Nutrition Facts: 1 piece equals 72 calories, 4 g fat (3 g saturated fat), 6 mg cholesterol, 25 mg sodium, 8 g carbohydrate, 0 fiber, 1 g protein. **Diabetic Exchanges:** 1 fat, 1/2 starch.

Lemon Fudge

Shrimp Canapes

Shrimp Canapes

(Pictured above)

Prep/Total Time: 30 min.

Here's a cool, elegant way to kick-start your party. With shrimp, flavored cream cheese and cocktail sauce on bread triangles, this simple but oh-so-special appetizer is a festive finger food that will disappear in a flash.
—Sarah Vasques, Milford, New Hampshire

✓ This recipe includes Nutrition Facts and Diabetic Exchanges.

2/3 cup spreadable chive and onion cream cheese
8 slices pumpernickel bread, crusts removed
32 cooked large shrimp, peeled and deveined
1/2 cup seafood cocktail sauce
1 medium lemon, cut into wedges and halved

Spread the cream cheese on one side of each slice of bread. Cut each slice into four triangles. Top with the shrimp and seafood sauce. Garnish with lemon. **Yield:** 32 servings.

Nutrition Facts: 1 canape equals 43 calories, 2 g fat (1 g saturated fat), 16 mg cholesterol, 104 mg sodium, 4 g carbohydrate, 1 g fiber, 2 g protein. **Diabetic Exchanges:** 1/2 starch, 1/2 fat.

Marshmallow Method

To easily remove marshmallow creme from a jar, try this technique: Place the jar in a pan of very hot water. Repeat this once or twice, then simply spoon out the marshmallow creme with a wooden spoon.
—Mary French, Port Orange, Florida

Pesto Bruschetta

Pesto Bruschetta

(Pictured above)

Prep/Total Time: 20 min.

My daughter came up with this scrumptious recipe. If you like, switch up the flavor a bit using different types of pesto. —Shirley Dickstein, Parma, Idaho

✓ This recipe includes Nutrition Facts and Diabetic Exchanges.

1 loaf (1 pound) French bread, cut into slices
1 jar (7 ounces) prepared pesto
2 medium tomatoes, seeded and finely chopped
1 package (4 ounces) crumbled feta cheese

Arrange bread slices on an ungreased baking sheet. Spread with pesto; top with tomatoes and cheese. Broil 4 in. from the heat for 3-5 minutes or until edges are lightly browned. **Yield:** 29 appetizers.

Nutrition Facts: 1 appetizer equals 93 calories, 4 g fat (1 g saturated fat), 4 mg cholesterol, 196 mg sodium, 10 g carbohydrate, 1 g fiber, 4 g protein. **Diabetic Exchanges:** 1 fat, 1/2 starch.

Corn Clue

Try this technique for buttering corn on the cob—swipe a tablespoon or two of seasoned butter down the center of a slice of bread. Then roll an ear of hot corn on the bread while holding it in the palm of your hand. You'll want to eat the bread, too—it tastes like buttery sweet corn! *—Diana Fill, Mantua, Ohio*

Corn on the Cob with Lemon-Pepper Butter

Prep: 10 min. + soaking **Grill:** 25 min.

This method of preparing corn on the cob is as old as the Ozark hills in which I was raised. You'll want to roast plenty—the buttery, seasoned corn is a favorite! —Allene Bary-Cooper, Ramona, Oklahoma

8 medium ears sweet corn
1 cup butter, softened
2 tablespoons lemon-pepper seasoning

Carefully peel back corn husks to within 1 in. of bottoms; remove silk. Rewrap corn in husks and secure with kitchen string. Place in a large kettle; cover with cold water. Soak for 20 minutes; drain.

Meanwhile, in a small bowl, combine butter and lemon-pepper; set aside. Grill corn, covered, over medium heat for 25-30 minutes or until tender, turning often. Serve with butter mixture. **Yield:** 8 servings.

Pesto Tortellini Salad

(Pictured below)

Prep/Total Time: 20 min.

I tried re-creating a pasta salad I had at a wedding rehearsal, and this recipe was the delicious result. Now it's requested whenever I'm invited to a potluck or party. Everyone enjoys the cheese tortellini, Parmesan and bacon. —Danielle Weets Grandview, Washington

1 package (19 ounces) frozen cheese tortellini
3/4 cup shredded Parmesan cheese
1 can (2-1/4 ounces) sliced ripe olives, drained
5 bacon strips, cooked and crumbled
1/4 cup prepared pesto

Cook tortellini according to package directions; drain and rinse in cold water. Place in a small bowl. Add remaining ingredients; toss to coat. Serve immediately. **Yield:** 5 servings.

Pesto Tortellini Salad

Tomato Cucumber Salad
Grilled Pork Tenderloin

Grilled Pork Tenderloin

(Pictured above)

Prep: 10 min. + marinating **Grill:** 25 min.

We've been serving this grilled entree for years, and guests who sample the tender, marinated tenderloin always want the recipe. We often double it so we're sure to have leftovers...and then we enjoy them the next day on a green salad.
—Debbie Wigle, Williamson, New York

✓ This recipe includes Nutrition Facts and Diabetic Exchanges.

1/2 cup Italian salad dressing
1/4 cup reduced-sodium soy sauce
1 pork tenderloin (1 pound)
1/2 teaspoon steak seasoning

In a large resealable plastic bag, combine salad dressing and soy sauce; add the pork. Seal bag and turn to coat; refrigerate for up to 4 hours.

Coat grill rack with cooking spray before starting the grill. Prepare grill for indirect heat. Drain and discard marinade. Rub pork with steak seasoning.

Grill pork, covered, over indirect medium-hot heat for 25-40 minutes or until a meat thermometer reads 160°. Let stand for 5 minutes before slicing. **Yield:** 4 servings.

Editor's Note: This recipe was tested with McCormick's Montreal Steak Seasoning. Look for it in the spice aisle.

Nutrition Facts: 3 ounces cooked pork equals 171 calories, 8 g fat (2 g saturated fat), 63 mg cholesterol, 500 mg sodium, 1 g carbohydrate, trace fiber, 23 g protein. **Diabetic Exchanges:** 3 lean meat, 1/2 fat.

Tomato Cucumber Salad

(Pictured above)

Prep/Total Time: 25 min.

Red wine vinaigrette perks up this medley of crisp cucumber, bright red tomatoes and cubed mozzarella cheese. The refreshing salad looks just as good as it tastes!
—Renae Boothroyd, Raeford, North Carolina

5 plum tomatoes, chopped
1 medium cucumber, coarsely chopped
8 ounces cubed part-skim mozzarella cheese
1 cup red *or* white wine vinaigrette

In a large resealable plastic bag, combine the tomatoes, cucumber and cheese. Add dressing; seal bag and turn to coat. Refrigerate for at least 15 minutes. Serve with a slotted spoon. **Yield:** 8 servings.

Mozzarella Rye Snacks

Mozzarella Rye Snacks

(Pictured above)

Prep/Total Time: 20 min.

This finger food is a staple at our summer deck parties and is also ideal for unexpected guests or as a fast snack. The creamy topping pairs perfectly with crisp rye bread.
—Missie Klei, Cincinnati, Ohio

- **1 cup (4 ounces) shredded part-skim mozzarella cheese**
- **1/2 cup mayonnaise**
- **1/2 cup sour cream**
- **1 tablespoon Italian salad dressing mix**
- **1 loaf (16 ounces) snack rye bread**

In a small bowl, combine the mozzarella, mayonnaise, sour cream and salad dressing mix until blended. Spread 1 tablespoonful over each slice of bread.

Place on greased baking sheets. Bake at 350° for 5-7 minutes or until cheese is melted and bubbly. Serve immediately. **Yield:** 2 dozen.

Buckeye Bars

Prep/Total Time: 30 min.

I often use my mom's recipe for yummy chocolate bars. When you want to satisfy a sweet tooth, these definitely fill the bill! *—Rachel Dillon, Flemington, New Jersey*

✓ This recipe includes Nutrition Facts and Diabetic Exchanges.

- **1 cup butter, cubed**
- **1-1/2 cups creamy peanut butter, *divided***
- **3-3/4 cups confectioners' sugar**
- **5 Nestlé Crunch candy bars (1.55 ounces *each*), chopped**

In a large microwave-safe mixing bowl, combine butter and 1 cup peanut butter. Microwave, uncovered, on high for 1 minute or until butter is melted, stirring once. Beat in the confectioners' sugar. Spread into a greased 13-in. x 9-in. x 2-in. pan.

In a microwave-safe bowl, melt candy bars and remaining peanut butter; stir until blended. Spread over peanut butter layer. Refrigerate until cool.

Cut into 1-1/2-in. x 1-in. bars. Store in an airtight container in the refrigerator. **Yield:** 6-1/2 dozen.

Nutrition Facts: 1 bar equals 87 calories, 6 g fat (2 g saturated fat), 7 mg cholesterol, 43 mg sodium, 9 g carbohydrate, trace fiber, 1 g protein. **Diabetic Exchanges:** 1 fat, 1/2 starch.

Coconut Brownies

(Pictured below)

Prep: 10 min. **Bake:** 30 min. + cooling

These lickety-split brownies are in the pan and ready for the oven in just 10 minutes. Best of all, they've proven to be a can't-miss treat—no one seems to tire of them! For an extra-special dessert, put the warm brownies in bowls and top them with a big scoop of vanilla ice cream.
—Barbara Carlucci, Orange Park, Florida

✓ This recipe includes Nutrition Facts and Diabetic Exchanges.

- **1 package fudge brownie mix (13-inch x 9-inch pan size)**
- **1 cup (8 ounces) sour cream**
- **1 cup coconut-pecan frosting**
- **2 eggs**
- **1/4 cup water**
- **1 cup (6 ounces) semisweet chocolate chips**

Coconut Brownies

In a large bowl, combine the brownie mix, sour cream, frosting, eggs and water just until moistened.

Pour into a 13-in. x 9-in. x 2-in. baking dish coated with cooking spray. Bake at 350° for 30-35 minutes or until center is set (do not overbake). Sprinkle with chocolate chips; let stand for 5 minutes. Spread chips over brownies to frost. **Yield:** 2 dozen.

Nutrition Facts: 1 brownie equals 203 calories, 9 g fat (4 g saturated fat), 25 mg cholesterol, 117 mg sodium, 29 g carbohydrate, 1 g fiber, 3 g protein. **Diabetic Exchanges:** 2 starch, 2 fat.

Greek Lemon Chicken

Prep: 10 min. + marinating **Grill:** 10 min.

This refreshing main dish is a favorite of my family and friends, especially in summertime. The recipe's five simple ingredients add up to fantastic Mediterranean flavor.
—Dawn Ellen, Bishopville, South Carolina

- **1-1/4 cups Greek vinaigrette, *divided***
- **4 boneless skinless chicken breast halves (5 ounces *each*)**
- **1 medium lemon, quartered**
- **3 tablespoons sliced oil-packed sun-dried tomatoes**
- **1/4 cup crumbled feta cheese**

Pour 3/4 cup vinaigrette into a large resealable plastic bag; add chicken. Seal bag and turn to coat; refrigerate for up to 4 hours. Cover and refrigerate remaining vinaigrette for basting.

Drain and discard the marinade. Grill the chicken, covered, over medium heat for 4 minutes. Turn and baste with some of the reserved vinaigrette. Grill 4-5 minutes longer or until chicken juices run clear, basting occasionally.

Squeeze lemon wedges over chicken. Sprinkle with tomatoes and cheese. **Yield:** 4 servings.

Orange Salmon with Rice

Prep/Total Time: 20 min.

Want an elegant meal that looks as good as it tastes... and is on the table in just 20 minutes? Here it is! The tender salmon fillets take on Asian flavors thanks to a tongue-tingling sauce and a side of fluffy rice.
—Jolanthe Erb, Harrisonburg, Virginia

- **2 cups uncooked instant rice**
- **4 salmon fillets (5 ounces *each*)**
- **1/4 teaspoon salt**
- **1/4 teaspoon pepper**
- **6 tablespoons orange juice**
- **6 tablespoons soy sauce**
- **1 teaspoon sesame oil**

Cook rice according to package directions. Meanwhile, sprinkle salmon with salt and pepper. In a large skillet coated with cooking spray, cook salmon over medium-high heat for 3 minutes on each side. Cover and cook 2-3 minutes longer or until fish flakes easily with a fork.

Bacon-Wrapped Appetizers

Remove salmon and keep warm. Add orange juice and soy sauce to the skillet; cook over high heat for 1-2 minutes. Stir in sesame oil. Spoon over salmon; serve with rice. **Yield:** 4 servings.

Bacon-Wrapped Appetizers

(Pictured above and on page 80)

Prep: 25 min. **Bake:** 25 min.

These are always a hit at our family birthdays and Christmas parties. Crunchy water chestnuts and sweet pineapple are perfect with the sweet-and-sour sauce.
—Nancy Harrold, Broken Bow, Nebraska

✓ This recipe includes Nutrition Facts and Diabetic Exchanges.

- **1 pound sliced bacon**
- **1 can (8 ounces) whole water chestnuts, drained**
- **1 can (8 ounces) unsweetened pineapple chunks, drained**
- **1 jar (10 ounces) sweet-and-sour sauce**

Cut each bacon strip in half widthwise. Wrap a strip around each chestnut or pineapple chunk; secure with toothpicks. Place in an ungreased 15-in. x 10-in. x 1-in. baking pan. Bake at 400° for 25-35 minutes or until bacon is crisp.

Pour sweet-and-sour sauce into a microwave-safe bowl. Cover and microwave on high for 1-2 minutes or until heated through. Serve with appetizers. **Yield:** about 2-1/2 dozen.

Nutrition Facts: 1 appetizer equals 45 calories, 2 g fat (1 g saturated fat), 4 mg cholesterol, 133 mg sodium, 4 g carbohydrate, trace fiber, 2 g protein. **Diabetic Exchange:** 1/2 fat.

Chapter 6

10 Minutes to the Table

WHAT daily tasks can you complete from start to finish in a mere 10 minutes? Chances are, there aren't many. But now you can add cooking to that done-in-a-dash list—thanks to this amazing chapter!

You won't believe your eyes when you see all of the incredible recipes that come together in just 10 minutes. From White Chili to Parmesan-Coated Brie and Smooth Chocolate Fondue, each fast favorite is ready to serve in a snap.

And the quick cooking time will be your little secret. That's because your family will be so impressed, they'll never guess how speedy and fuss-free these delicious dishes actually are!

QUICK AS CAN BE. Cajun Shrimp and Rice (p. 105).

Maple Salad Dressing

(Pictured above)

Prep/Total Time: 10 min.

I tell people, "I know you'll love this recipe." And they always do! Sweet and tangy like French dressing, it gives greens great taste. —Janet Lawton, St. Albans, Vermont

✓ This recipe includes Nutrition Facts and Diabetic Exchanges.

7 tablespoons maple syrup
1/4 cup cider vinegar
1/4 cup ketchup
3 tablespoons plus 1 teaspoon canola oil
2 tablespoons water
1/2 teaspoon prepared horseradish
1/4 teaspoon salt
1/8 teaspoon celery salt

In a jar with a tight-fitting lid, combine all ingredients; shake well. Cover and refrigerate until serving. **Yield:** 1-1/4 cups.

Nutrition Facts: 2 tablespoons equals 85 calories, 5 g fat (trace saturated fat), 0 cholesterol, 156 mg sodium, 11 g carbohydrate, trace fiber, trace protein. **Diabetic Exchanges:** 1 starch, 1 fat.

Pudding Preference

FEEL FREE to replace the lemon pudding in Lemon Fruit Dip (recipe above right) with any pudding flavor you prefer. For example, substitute chocolate, vanilla or coconut. Try fresh fruits such as strawberries, blackberries, apples and pineapple for dipping.

Lemon Fruit Dip

(Pictured below)

Prep/Total Time: 5 min.

My husband's a construction worker, and this fruit dip is a yummy treat to put in his lunch with whatever fresh fruit he wants. It keeps well in the fridge all week. —Megan Wilkinson, Morgan, Utah

✓ This recipe includes Nutrition Facts and Diabetic Exchanges.

1 cup cold milk
1 package (3.4 ounces) instant lemon pudding mix
1 cup (8 ounces) sour cream
Assorted fresh fruit

In a small bowl, whisk milk and pudding mix for 2 minutes. Let stand for 2 minutes or until soft-set. Whisk in sour cream. Chill until serving. Serve with fruit. **Yield:** 1-2/3 cups.

Nutrition Facts: 2 tablespoons (calculated without fruit) equals 75 calories, 4 g fat (3 g saturated fat), 14 mg cholesterol, 106 mg sodium, 9 g carbohydrate, 0 fiber, 1 g protein. **Diabetic Exchanges:** 1/2 starch, 1/2 fat.

Hot Dog Bean Soup

Hot Dog Bean Soup

(Pictured above)

Prep/Total Time: 10 min.

Our three children liked this soup when they were growing up, and now they prepare it for their own families. It's a real favorite on camping trips or any time at all.
—Mary Ann Kime, Sturgis, Michigan

3 hot dogs, halved lengthwise and cut into 1/4-inch pieces
1 teaspoon vegetable oil
1 can (16 ounces) kidney beans, rinsed and drained
1 can (11-1/2 ounces) condensed bean and bacon soup, undiluted
1-1/4 cups water
1 teaspoon dried minced onion
1/4 teaspoon pepper

In a large skillet, cook the hot dogs in oil over medium heat for 3-4 minutes or until browned. Meanwhile, in a 2-qt. microwave-safe bowl, combine the remaining ingredients. Cover and microwave on high for 2-3 minutes or until heated through, stirring once. Stir in hot dogs. **Yield:** 4 servings.

Editor's Note: This recipe was tested in a 1,100-watt microwave.

Apple Salad

Prep/Total Time: 10 min.

I turn to this delicious recipe on long days when I come home tired and ready to relax. The colorful salad tastes fantastic, has a wonderful crunch and is nutritious, too.
—Kathy Everette, Menlo, Georgia

✓ This recipe includes Nutrition Facts and Diabetic Exchanges.

3 medium red apples, diced
1/2 cup chopped celery
1/4 cup chopped pecans
1/4 cup dried cranberries
1/4 cup miniature marshmallows
2 tablespoons raisins
3/4 cup whipped topping
1/4 cup sour cream

In a large bowl, combine the apples, celery, pecans, dried cranberries, marshmallows and raisins. Combine the whipped topping and sour cream; spoon over the apple mixture and toss to coat. Serve immediately. **Yield:** 6 servings.

Nutrition Facts: 3/4 cup equals 152 calories, 7 g fat (3 g saturated fat), 7 mg cholesterol, 15 mg sodium, 22 g carbohydrate, 3 g fiber, 1 g protein. **Diabetic Exchanges:** 1-1/2 fat, 1 fruit, 1/2 starch.

Pine Nut Salad Dressing

Prep/Total Time: 10 min.

This low-calorie dressing tastes great. I think the flavors blend especially well in basic salads with feta cheese sprinkled on top. —Renee Dwyer, Kenosha, Wisconsin

✓ This recipe includes Nutrition Facts and Diabetic Exchanges.

6 tablespoons cranberry juice
1 tablespoon pine nuts, toasted
1 tablespoon olive oil
1 tablespoon balsamic vinegar
1/4 teaspoon pepper
1/8 teaspoon salt

In a jar with a tight-fitting lid, combine all ingredients; shake well. Cover and refrigerate dressing until serving. **Yield:** 1/2 cup.

Nutrition Facts: 2 tablespoons equals 56 calories, 4 g fat (1 g saturated fat), 0 cholesterol, 75 mg sodium, 4 g carbohydrate, trace fiber, 1 g protein. **Diabetic Exchange:** 1 fat.

Simple Shrimp Scampi

(Pictured below)

Prep/Total Time: 10 min.

Here's a no-fuss recipe designed to impress your guests. Serve it for your next dinner party, and just wait for the rave reviews! —Lisa Boehm, Deepwater, Missouri

Simple Shrimp Scampi

Pineapple Shakes

3/4 cup butter, cubed
2 pounds uncooked medium shrimp, peeled and deveined
5 teaspoons lemon-pepper seasoning
2 teaspoons garlic powder
8 lemon wedges, optional

In a large skillet over medium heat, melt butter. Add the shrimp, lemon-pepper and garlic powder; cook for 5-8 minutes or until shrimp turn pink. Transfer to individual serving dishes. Serve with lemon wedges if desired. **Yield:** 8 servings.

Pineapple Shakes

(Pictured above)

Prep/Total Time: 5 min.

Your family will love this yummy, citrusy new take on milkshakes. With refreshing pineapple and a dash of cinnamon, the frosty beverages make you want to sip every last drop. —Fran Scott, Birmingham, Michigan

1/4 cup cold milk
2 cups vanilla ice cream
1 can (5-1/2 ounces) unsweetened pineapple chunks, undrained
1/4 teaspoon ground cinnamon

In a blender, combine all ingredients; cover and process until smooth. Pour into chilled glasses; serve immediately. **Yield:** 3 servings.

Smooth Chocolate Fondue

Prep/Total Time: 10 min.

This tempting treat is fun to dip into and makes the perfect ending to a special meal. As the chocolate cools, it just gets better! —Kim Terhune, Mountain Lakes, New Jersey

1 can (14 ounces) sweetened condensed milk
2 cups (12 ounces) semisweet chocolate chips
1 cup heavy whipping cream
1-1/4 teaspoons vanilla extract
Assorted fresh fruit *or* cubed pound cake

In a microwave-safe bowl or heavy saucepan, combine milk, chocolate chips, cream and vanilla. Heat just until chips are melted, stirring occasionally. Transfer to a fondue pot and keep warm. Serve with fruit or cake. **Yield:** 3-1/2 cups.

Meat 'n' Veggie Pockets

(Pictured below)

Prep/Total Time: 10 min.

When you want something that'll please everyone, try these versatile pockets. You can replace any of the ingredients you like. —Danielle Binkley, Huber Heights, Ohio

1 small cucumber, chopped
1/2 cup chopped onion
1 can (2-1/4 ounces) sliced ripe olives, drained
1/2 cup Italian salad dressing
4 pita breads (6 inches), halved
1/2 pound thinly sliced deli ham
1/2 pound thinly sliced deli turkey
4 slices process American cheese

In a small bowl, combine cucumber, onion, olives and salad dressing. Fill pita halves with ham, turkey and cheese; top with cucumber mixture. **Yield:** 4 servings.

Black Bean Pineapple Salad

Prep/Total Time: 10 min.

I created this medley when I had very little in the fridge and needed something fast. The beans and pineapple go really well together. —Julie Muccillo, Chicago, Illinois

✓ This recipe includes Nutrition Facts and Diabetic Exchanges.

6 cups fresh baby spinach
1 can (15-1/2 ounces) unsweetened pineapple chunks, drained
1 can (15 ounces) black beans, rinsed and drained
1/2 cup *each* chopped sweet red and orange peppers
1/2 cup crumbled feta cheese
1/4 cup prepared balsamic vinaigrette

In a large bowl, combine the spinach, pineapple, beans, peppers and cheese. Drizzle with vinaigrette; toss to coat. Serve with a slotted spoon. **Yield:** 6 servings.

Nutrition Facts: 2/3 cup equals 149 calories, 3 g fat (1 g saturated fat), 5 mg cholesterol, 338 mg sodium, 23 g carbohydrate, 5 g fiber, 6 g protein. **Diabetic Exchanges:** 1 lean meat, 1 vegetable, 1/2 starch, 1/2 fruit.

Meat 'n' Veggie Pockets

Tropical Fruit Smoothies

(Pictured below)

Prep/Total Time: 10 min.

Need a fast thirst-quencher? Try these smoothies featuring four kinds of fruit. Sweetened with honey, they'll cool you off in a hurry. —*Susan Voigt, Plymouth, Minnesota*

☑ This recipe includes Nutrition Facts and Diabetic Exchanges.

1-1/2 cups orange juice
1 can (8 ounces) crushed pineapple, undrained
1 medium mango, peeled and cut into chunks
1 cup halved fresh strawberries
2 medium kiwifruit, peeled and quartered
1 tablespoon honey
14 ice cubes
1/2 cup club soda, chilled

Place half of the orange juice, pineapple, mango, strawberries, kiwi, honey and ice cubes in a blender; cover and process until blended. Stir in 1/4 cup soda. Pour into chilled glasses; serve immediately. Repeat with remaining ingredients. **Yield:** 7 servings.

Nutrition Facts: 1 cup equals 97 calories, trace fat (trace saturated fat), 0 cholesterol, 6 mg sodium, 25 g carbohydrate, 2 g fiber, 1 g protein. **Diabetic Exchanges:** 1 fruit, 1/2 starch.

Tropical Fruit Smoothies

Calypso Coleslaw

Prep/Total Time: 10 min.

My family just loves this coleslaw variation. Its refreshing flavor and speedy preparation make it ideal for backyard barbecues. —*Cathy Heacox, Sikeston, Missouri*

4 cups shredded cabbage
1 can (11 ounces) Mexicorn, drained
1/2 cup finely chopped onion
1/4 cup shredded cheddar cheese
2 tablespoons sliced ripe olives
1 cup mayonnaise
2 tablespoons sugar
2 tablespoons cider vinegar
4 teaspoons prepared mustard
1/2 teaspoon celery seed

In a large bowl, combine cabbage, corn, onion, cheese and olives. In a jar with a tight-fitting lid, combine the remaining ingredients; shake well. Pour over salad and toss to coat. Chill until serving. **Yield:** 6 servings.

White Chili

Prep/Total Time: 10 min.

This chicken chili recipe started as a mistake but became a success. I created it by accident...and the final results got raves. —*Cynthia Lynn Bloemker, Effingham, Illinois*

☑ This recipe includes Nutrition Facts and Diabetic Exchanges.

1 jar (48 ounces) great northern beans, rinsed and drained
2 cans (one 10 ounces, one 5 ounces) chunk white chicken, drained
1-1/4 cups milk
1 cup (8 ounces) sour cream
1 can (4 ounces) chopped green chilies
1 teaspoon salt-free seasoning blend
1 cup (4 ounces) shredded Italian cheese blend
2 tablespoons minced fresh cilantro
Additional sour cream, optional

In a large saucepan, combine the first six ingredients. Bring to a boil over medium-high heat; remove from the heat. Add cheese and cilantro; stir until cheese is melted. Garnish with additional sour cream if desired. **Yield:** 8 servings (2 quarts).

Nutrition Facts: 1 cup (calculated without additional sour cream) equals 310 calories, 11 g fat (7 g saturated fat), 60 mg cholesterol, 788 mg sodium, 29 g carbohydrate, 9 g fiber, 23 g protein. **Diabetic Exchanges:** 3 lean meat, 2 starch.

Cajun Shrimp and Rice

Cajun Shrimp and Rice

(Pictured above and on page 98)

Prep/Total Time: 10 min.

I have a friend who has celiac disease, so she has specific dietary restrictions. This delicious meal-in-one fits her diet, and I serve it often when she visits. It's also popular with people who don't have to watch what they eat.
—Ruth Miller, Boyertown, Pennsylvania

✓ This recipe includes Nutrition Facts and Diabetic Exchanges.

1 package (8.8 ounces) ready-to-serve long grain rice
1 pound uncooked medium shrimp, peeled and deveined
1-1/2 teaspoons minced garlic
2 teaspoons Cajun seasoning
1 tablespoon olive oil
1 tablespoon butter
1 package (6 ounces) frozen snow peas, thawed

Cook rice according to package directions. Meanwhile, in a large skillet, saute the shrimp, garlic and Cajun seasoning in oil and butter until shrimp turn pink. Add the peas and rice. Cook 2-3 minutes longer or until heated through. **Yield:** 4 servings.

Nutrition Facts: 1 cup equals 269 calories, 8 g fat (3 g saturated fat), 176 mg cholesterol, 550 mg sodium, 23 g carbohydrate, 1 g fiber, 21 g protein. **Diabetic Exchanges:** 3 lean meat, 1-1/2 starch, 1/2 fat.

Surefire Shrimp Technique

THE RECIPE for Cajun Shrimp and Rice (at left) calls for uncooked shrimp that are peeled and deveined. To peel and devein, just follow these simple steps:

1. Start on the underside of the shrimp by the head area to remove the shell from the shrimp. Pull the legs and the first section of the shell to one side. Continue pulling the shell up around the top and to the other side. Pull off the shell by the tail if desired.

2. Remove the black vein running down the back of the shrimp by making a shallow slit with a paring knife along the back from the head area to the tail. After cutting the slit, rinse the shrimp under cold water to remove the vein.

Parmesan-Coated Brie

Parmesan-Coated Brie

(Pictured above)

Prep/Total Time: 10 min.

When you serve this wonderful appetizer, your guests are sure to be impressed...and no one will have a clue that it took a mere 10 minutes to create. The golden exterior gives way to warm cheese, perfect for crackers or sliced French bread. Add some fresh fruit such as apple slices or grapes.
—Karen Grant, Tulare, California

1 egg
1 tablespoon water
1/2 cup seasoned bread crumbs
1/4 cup grated Parmesan cheese
1 round (8 ounces) Brie cheese *or* Brie cheese with herbs
1/4 cup vegetable oil
Assorted crackers *and/or* fresh fruit

In a shallow bowl, combine the egg and water. In another bowl, combine the seasoned bread crumbs and Parmesan cheese. Dip the Brie cheese in the egg mixture, turning to coat all sides; coat with the bread crumb mixture. Repeat.

In a small skillet, cook the Brie cheese in oil over medium heat for 2 minutes on each side or until golden brown. Serve with assorted crackers and/or fresh fruit. **Yield:** 8 servings.

Baked Beans with Ham

Prep/Total Time: 10 min.

My husband and I enjoy ham and beans, and this combination is so good. Plus, it couldn't be easier to prepare. You just combine the ingredients, then microwave.
—Gloria Warczak, Cedarburg, Wisconsin

1 can (28 ounces) baked beans
2 cups cubed fully cooked ham
1/4 cup tomato paste
2 tablespoons molasses
1 tablespoon brown sugar
1 tablespoon Worcestershire sauce
1 teaspoon dried minced onion
1 teaspoon taco seasoning
1 teaspoon minced fresh cilantro

In a 1-1/2-qt. microwave-safe bowl, combine all ingredients. Cover and microwave on high for 3-5 minutes or until heated through, stirring once. **Yield:** 5 servings.

Editor's Note: This recipe was tested in a 1,100-watt microwave.

Minty Sugar Snap Peas

Prep/Total Time: 10 min.

I think mint is one of the most distinctive herbs. Use it to flavor salads, tea and chocolate desserts—as well as these yummy peas! —*Alice Kaldahl, Ray, North Dakota*

☑ This recipe includes Nutrition Facts and Diabetic Exchanges.

3 cups fresh sugar snap peas, trimmed
1/4 teaspoon sugar
2 to 3 tablespoons minced fresh mint
2 tablespoons butter

In a large skillet, bring 1 in. of water, peas and sugar to a boil. Reduce heat; cover and simmer for 4-5 minutes or until crisp-tender; drain. Stir in mint and butter. **Yield:** 4 servings.

Nutrition Facts: 3/4 cup equals 102 calories, 6 g fat (4 g saturated fat), 15 mg cholesterol, 45 mg sodium, 9 g carbohydrate, 3 g fiber, 4 g protein. **Diabetic Exchanges:** 2 vegetable, 1 fat.

Blue Cheese Pear Salad

(Pictured below)

Prep/Total Time: 10 min.

With just five ingredients, this elegant salad is a cinch to put together. Chopped pear balances the rich blue cheese, while almonds lend crunch and extra sweetness.
—*Ginger Smiser, Blanco, Texas*

3 cups hearts of romaine salad mix
1 large pear, chopped
1/3 cup slivered almonds
1/2 cup crumbled blue cheese
1/3 cup Italian salad dressing

Blue Cheese Pear Salad

Crouton-Topped Broccoli

In a large bowl, combine the salad mix, pear, almonds and blue cheese. Drizzle with dressing and toss to coat. Serve immediately. **Yield:** 4 servings.

Crouton-Topped Broccoli

(Pictured above)

Prep/Total Time: 10 min.

We love this super-fast side dish—even my children are crazy for it! It goes well with any meat and can easily be doubled for holidays. —*Kathy Fry, Brockville, Ontario*

1 package (16 ounces) frozen chopped broccoli
2 tablespoons water
1 can (10-3/4 ounces) condensed cream of mushroom soup, undiluted
1/2 cup shredded Swiss cheese
1/2 cup shredded cheddar cheese
1/4 cup milk
1-1/2 cups cheese-and-garlic croutons

Place broccoli and water in a microwave-safe 2-qt. dish. Cover and microwave on high for 6-8 minutes or until tender; drain.

Stir in the soup, cheeses and milk. Cover and microwave for 2 minutes or until cheeses are melted. Sprinkle with croutons. **Yield:** 5 servings.

Editor's Note: This recipe was tested in a 1,100-watt microwave.

Chapter 7

Shop Once...Eat All Week

WITH everything else that's on your daily to-do list, wouldn't it be great to limit your grocery shopping to just one day per week...and end up with five weeknights of dinners?

The home economists in our Test Kitchen have made it possible with this handy chapter. They've created dinner recipes and put them into a six-week planner, complete with a grocery list for each week.

Use a list, and you can shop just once to get everything you need for an entire workweek's worth of dinners. There's no guesswork, no fuss and no planning on your part...just 30 days of terrific meals such as Ravioli Skillet, Beef Fried Rice and Garlic Ranch Chicken. Enjoy!

IT'S A PLAN. Chicken over Curly Noodles and Broccoli Side Dish (both recipes on p. 114).

Week 1

Shopping List

Check for these staples:

- all-purpose flour
- butter
- chicken bouillon granules
- chicken broth
- dried parsley flakes
- dried tarragon
- eggs
- grated Parmesan cheese
- Italian seasoning
- milk
- minced garlic
- onions
- pepper
- quick-cooking tapioca
- salad dressing of your choice
- salt
- walnuts

Shop for these items:

5 medium green peppers
4 medium carrots
1 medium celery rib
1 package (5 ounces) spring mix salad greens
1 loaf (1 pound) Italian bread
2 jars (26 ounces *each*) spaghetti sauce
1 jar (7 ounces) roasted sweet red peppers
1 can (2.25 ounces) sliced ripe olives
1 package (16 ounces) orzo pasta
1 package (8.8 ounces) ready-to-serve long grain and wild rice
1 package (40 ounces) biscuit/baking mix
1 package (8 ounces) shredded part-skim mozzarella cheese
1 carton (1 pint) half-and-half cream
1 package (16 ounces) frozen broccoli-cauliflower blend
7 boneless skinless chicken breast halves (6 ounces *each*)
2 pounds ground beef
3 ounces prosciutto
1 package (25 ounces) frozen ravioli
2 packages (7.6 ounces *each*) frozen Cajun blackened grilled fish fillets

Time-Saving Tips

- Three of the cooked chicken breasts from Monday's main dish will be saved for Wednesday's Chicken Wild Rice Chowder. The extra chicken could also make a great base for chicken salad.
- On Wednesday, when you're chopping 1/2 cup onion, consider chopping an extra 1/2 cup and storing it in the refrigerator. You'll save time on Thursday when preparing Stuffed Peppers for Four.

Creamy Tarragon Chicken

Monday

Creamy Tarragon Chicken

(Pictured above)

Prep: 10 min. **Cook:** 6-1/4 hours

Start the week on an easy note with this all-in-one recipe. A cup of prepared chicken broth may be substituted for the water and chicken bouillon granules listed.

7 boneless skinless chicken breast halves (6 ounces *each*)
1 cup chopped onion
1 cup water
2 ounces prosciutto *or* deli ham, chopped
3 tablespoons quick-cooking tapioca
2 teaspoons chicken bouillon granules
2 teaspoons dried tarragon
1 teaspoon minced garlic
1/4 teaspoon salt
1/4 teaspoon pepper
3 cups frozen broccoli-cauliflower blend, thawed
1/2 cup half-and-half cream
1-1/2 cups uncooked orzo pasta

In a 5-qt. slow cooker, combine the first 10 ingredients. Cover and cook on low for 6-7 hours or until chicken juices run clear.

Remove three chicken breast halves; cool. Cover and refrigerate for Chicken Wild Rice Chowder (recipe on page 111) or save for another use.

Stir vegetables and cream into the slow cooker. Cover and cook 15 minutes longer or until vegetables are heated through. Meanwhile, cook orzo according to package directions. Serve with chicken and vegetables. **Yield:** 4 servings.

Tuesday

Ravioli Skillet

(Pictured below)

Prep/Total Time: 30 min.

Store-bought cheese ravioli gets a mouth-watering makeover with ground beef, prosciutto and mozzarella in this memorable weekday dinner.

1 pound ground beef
3/4 cup chopped green pepper
1 ounce prosciutto *or* deli ham, chopped
3 cups spaghetti sauce
3/4 cup water
1 package (25 ounces) frozen cheese ravioli
1 cup (4 ounces) shredded part-skim mozzarella cheese

In a large skillet, cook beef, green pepper and prosciutto over medium heat until meat is no longer pink; drain.

Stir in spaghetti sauce and water; bring to a boil. Add ravioli. Reduce heat; cover and simmer for 7-9 minutes or until ravioli is tender, stirring once. Sprinkle with cheese. Simmer, uncovered, 1-2 minutes longer or until cheese is melted. **Yield:** 4 servings.

Ravioli Skillet

Wednesday

Chicken Wild Rice Chowder

(Pictured above right)

Prep/Total Time: 25 min.

This soothing chicken soup is comfort food at its finest—perfect to help get you through "hump day" Wednesday and ready for the rest of the week.

2 cups sliced fresh carrots
1/2 cup chopped onion

Chicken Wild Rice Chowder
Parmesan Walnut Muffins

1/2 cup chopped celery
2 tablespoons butter
3 tablespoons all-purpose flour
2 cans (14-1/2 ounces *each*) chicken broth
2-2/3 cups cubed cooked chicken breast
1 package (8.8 ounces) ready-to-serve long grain and wild rice
1/4 cup half-and-half cream
1/8 teaspoon pepper

In a large saucepan, saute the carrots, onion and celery in butter until tender. Stir in flour until blended; gradually add broth. Bring to a boil; cook and stir for 2 minutes or until thickened. Stir in the chicken, rice, cream and pepper; heat through. **Yield:** 4 servings.

Parmesan Walnut Muffins

(Pictured above)

Prep/Total Time: 30 min.

These golden-brown muffins go wonderfully with Chicken Wild Rice Chowder (recipe below left), but they'd also be welcome alongside many other main dishes.

3 cups biscuit/baking mix
1/4 cup plus 1 tablespoon grated Parmesan cheese, *divided*
3/4 teaspoon dried parsley flakes
1/2 teaspoon Italian seasoning
2 eggs
1 cup milk
2 tablespoons butter, melted, *divided*
2 tablespoons chopped walnuts

In a large bowl, combine the biscuit mix, 1/4 cup Parmesan cheese, parsley and Italian seasoning. In a small bowl, whisk the eggs, milk and 1 tablespoon butter; stir into dry ingredients just until moistened.

Fill greased or paper-lined muffin cups three-fourths full. Pour remaining butter over tops; sprinkle with walnuts and remaining Parmesan cheese.

Bake at 400° for 15-17 minutes or until a toothpick comes out clean. Cool for 5 minutes before removing from pan to a wire rack. Serve warm. **Yield:** 1 dozen.

Thursday

Stuffed Peppers for Four

(Pictured above)

Prep/Total Time: 30 min.

Truly a meal-in-one, this satisfying entree has everything: vegetables, meat, pasta and sauce, all packed into tender green peppers and cooked to perfection.

4 medium green peppers
1/4 cup water
1/2 cup uncooked orzo pasta
1 pound ground beef
1/2 cup chopped onion
2 cups spaghetti sauce
1 cup frozen broccoli-cauliflower blend, thawed and chopped
1/2 cup grated Parmesan cheese, *divided*

Cut tops off peppers and remove seeds; replace tops. Place in an ungreased shallow round 3-qt. microwave-safe dish; add the water. Cover and microwave on high for 8-10 minutes or until crisp-tender.

Meanwhile, cook orzo according to package directions. In a large skillet, cook beef and onion over medium heat until meat is no longer pink; drain. Drain orzo; stir into meat mixture. Add the spaghetti sauce, vegetables and 1/4 cup Parmesan cheese.

Spoon into peppers. Sprinkle with remaining Parmesan cheese. Microwave, uncovered, on high for 1-2 minutes or until heated through. **Yield:** 4 servings.

Editor's Note: This recipe was tested in a 1,100-watt microwave.

Friday

Fish Sandwich Loaf

(Pictured at right)

Prep/Total Time: 30 min.

Roasted red peppers give this beautiful sandwich fantastic flavor. The Cajun fillets are surprisingly mild, so kids will enjoy the spices as much as adults.

1 loaf (1 pound) Italian bread
2 packages (7.6 ounces *each*) frozen Cajun blackened grilled fish fillets
3 tablespoons butter, melted
1 teaspoon minced garlic
1/2 cup roasted sweet red peppers, patted dry
1 cup (4 ounces) shredded part-skim mozzarella cheese

Cut the top half off the loaf of bread; carefully hollow out top and bottom, leaving a 1/2-in. shell (save removed bread for another use).

Microwave fish fillets according to package directions. Meanwhile, combine butter and garlic; spread over cut sides of bread. In bread bottom, layer fish, red peppers and cheese. Replace bread top. Wrap loaf in foil. Bake at 350° for 15-20 minutes or until cheese is melted. Slice and serve immediately. **Yield:** 6 servings.

Italian Side Salad

(Pictured below)

Prep/Total Time: 5 min.

Round out your end-of-the-week dinner with an effortless four-ingredient side salad. Feel free to vary the dressing or toppings to suit your family's tastes.

1 package (5 ounces) spring mix salad greens
2 tablespoons sliced ripe olives, drained
1/4 cup Italian salad dressing *or* salad dressing of your choice
1/4 cup chopped walnuts

In a large salad bowl, combine the greens and olives. Drizzle with dressing; toss to coat. Sprinkle with walnuts. Serve immediately. **Yield:** 6 servings.

Week 2

Shopping List

Check for these staples:

- salt
- pepper
- dill weed
- cumin
- onion salt
- paprika
- crushed red pepper flakes
- dried rosemary
- dried thyme
- dried basil
- Italian seasoning
- dried bread crumbs
- brown sugar
- sugar
- onion
- butter
- cider vinegar
- peanut butter
- milk
- soy sauce
- minced garlic
- olive oil

Shop for these items:

1 pound sliced fresh mushrooms
2 large sweet red peppers
2 medium bunches broccoli
1 package (6 ounces) fresh baby spinach
1 package (5.7 ounces) instant creamy chicken-flavored rice and sauce mix
1 package (16 ounces) linguine
3 packages (3 ounces *each*) chicken ramen noodles
1 can (16 ounces) refried beans
1 can (14-1/2 ounces) diced tomatoes with mild green chilies
1 can (14 ounces) bean sprouts
1 can (11 ounces) Mexicorn
12 flour tortillas (8 inches)
1 package (8 ounces) shredded cheddar cheese
1 container (8 ounces) spreadable chive and onion cream cheese
1 container (8 ounces) sour cream
1 pound boneless skinless chicken breasts
4 boneless skinless chicken breasts (5 ounces *each*)
4 fresh *or* frozen orange roughy fillets (6 ounces *each*)
1-3/4 pounds boneless beef top round steak

Time-Saving Tip

Don't have a panini maker or indoor grill for making Friday's Grilled Beef Fajitas? No problem! Put the fajitas in a skillet and top them with aluminum foil and a heavy skillet. Then just flip the fajitas when browned and repeat on the other side.

Orange Roughy with Rice

Monday

Orange Roughy with Rice

(Pictured above)

Prep/Total Time: 25 min.

Orange roughy fillets pair with a creamy, chicken-flavored rice mix for this terrific meal. You could also prepare the recipe using flounder, sole or red snapper.

✓ This recipe includes Nutrition Facts and Diabetic Exchanges.

1 package (5.7 ounces) instant creamy chicken-flavored rice and sauce mix
2 cups water
1 tablespoon butter, optional
1 cup fresh broccoli florets
1/4 teaspoon onion salt
1/4 teaspoon pepper
1/8 teaspoon dill weed
1/8 teaspoon paprika
4 fresh *or* frozen orange roughy fillets (6 ounces *each*)
1 tablespoon olive oil

In a large saucepan, combine the rice mix, water and butter if desired. Bring to a boil; stir in the broccoli. Reduce the heat; cover and simmer for 7 minutes or until the rice is tender.

Meanwhile, combine the onion salt, pepper, dill and paprika; sprinkle over fillets. In a large skillet, cook fillets in oil over medium heat for 4-6 minutes on each side or until fish flakes easily with a fork.

Remove rice from the heat; let stand for 2 minutes. Serve with fish. **Yield:** 4 servings.

Nutrition Facts: 1 fillet with 3/4 cup rice (calculated without butter) equals 320 calories, 8 g fat (1 g saturated fat), 34 mg cholesterol, 719 mg sodium, 31 g carbohydrate, 2 g fiber, 30 g protein. **Diabetic Exchanges:** 4 very lean meat, 2 starch, 1/2 fat.

Tuesday

Mushroom Steak 'n' Linguine

Prep/Total Time: 30 min.

Mushrooms and rosemary make this pasta entree special enough for guests. It's sure to be a family favorite!

8 ounces uncooked linguine
1 pound boneless beef top round steak, cut into thin strips
1/4 teaspoon salt
1/4 teaspoon pepper
3 teaspoons olive oil, *divided*
1 cup chopped sweet red pepper
1/2 cup chopped onion
1/2 pound sliced fresh mushrooms
1 cup coarsely chopped fresh spinach
1/2 teaspoon dried rosemary, crushed
3/4 cup spreadable chive and onion cream cheese
1/2 cup sour cream
1 tablespoon milk

Cook linguine according to package directions. Meanwhile, sprinkle beef with salt and pepper. In a large skillet, saute beef in 2 teaspoons oil until juices run clear. Remove and keep warm.

In the same pan, saute red pepper and onion in remaining oil until tender. Add mushrooms; saute 1-2 minutes longer or until tender. Add spinach and rosemary; cook and stir just until spinach is wilted. Stir in the cream cheese, sour cream and milk; heat through (do not boil). Drain linguine; top with mushroom mixture and beef. **Yield:** 4 servings.

Wednesday

Chicken over Curly Noodles

(Pictured at right and on page 108)

Prep/Total Time: 30 min.

In this dish, ramen noodles get a big pick-me-up thanks to a simple Asian-style sauce and tender chicken.

1/4 cup packed brown sugar
1/4 cup creamy peanut butter
1/4 cup soy sauce
1 teaspoon minced garlic
1/2 cup dry bread crumbs
3 packages (3 ounces *each*) chicken ramen noodles
4 boneless skinless chicken breast halves (5 ounces *each*)
1 tablespoon olive oil
1 can (14 ounces) bean sprouts, drained

In a small bowl, combine brown sugar, peanut butter, soy sauce and garlic; set aside. In a large resealable plastic bag, combine bread crumbs and contents of two noodle seasoning packets (discard remaining packet or save for another use). Add chicken, one piece at a time, and shake to coat.

In a large skillet, cook the chicken in oil over medium heat for 5-6 minutes on each side or until the juices run clear. Meanwhile, cook the noodles according to the package directions.

Remove chicken and keep warm. Add peanut butter mixture to skillet; cook and stir until heated through. Drain noodles. Add noodles and bean sprouts to skillet; toss to coat. Serve with chicken. **Yield:** 4 servings.

Broccoli Side Dish

(Pictured below and on page 108)

Prep/Total Time: 10 min.

Requiring just a handful of everyday ingredients, this microwave broccoli makes a great plate-filler for dinner.

✓ This recipe includes Nutrition Facts and Diabetic Exchanges.

5 cups fresh broccoli florets
2 tablespoons butter, melted
4 teaspoons soy sauce
2 teaspoons brown sugar
1/2 teaspoon minced garlic

Place broccoli in a large microwave-safe bowl. Combine the remaining ingredients; pour over broccoli. Cover and microwave on high for 3-4 minutes or until tender. Serve with a slotted spoon. **Yield:** 4 servings.

Editor's Note: This recipe was tested in a 1,100-watt microwave.

Nutrition Facts: 3/4 cup equals 88 calories, 6 g fat (4 g saturated fat), 15 mg cholesterol, 389 mg sodium, 7 g carbohydrate, 3 g fiber, 3 g protein. **Diabetic Exchanges:** 1 vegetable, 1 fat.

Chicken over Curly Noodles
Broccoli Side Dish

Thursday

Chicken Tortilla Bake

Prep: 25 min. **Bake:** 25 min.

Pop this casserole in the oven, then enjoy some hands-free time while it's baking. Your family will be thrilled with dinner's south-of-the-border flavor.

- **1 pound boneless skinless chicken breasts, cut into 1-inch cubes**
- **1/2 teaspoon ground cumin**
- **1/4 teaspoon salt**
- **1 tablespoon plus 1 teaspoon olive oil, *divided***
- **1 can (16 ounces) refried beans**
- **1 can (14-1/2 ounces) diced tomatoes with mild green chilies, drained**
- **8 flour tortillas (8 inches), cut into 1-inch strips**
- **1 can (11 ounces) Mexicorn, drained**
- **2 cups (8 ounces) shredded cheddar cheese**

In a large skillet, saute the chicken, cumin and salt in 1 tablespoon oil until chicken is no longer pink.

Combine the refried beans and tomatoes; spread 1 cup into a greased 11-in. x 7-in. x 2-in. baking dish. Top with 24 tortilla strips; layer with half of the corn, bean mixture, chicken and cheese. Repeat layers.

Using remaining tortilla strips, make a lattice crust over filling; brush with remaining oil. Bake, uncovered, at 350° for 25-30 minutes or until heated through and cheese is melted. **Yield:** 6 servings.

Friday

Zesty Spinach Salad

(Pictured above right)

Prep/Total Time: 10 min.

This 10-minute recipe's homemade dressing, featuring garlic and basil, makes the salad especially tasty.

This recipe includes Nutrition Facts and Diabetic Exchanges.

- **4 cups fresh baby spinach**
- **1 cup sliced fresh mushrooms**
- **3 tablespoons olive oil**
- **1 tablespoon cider vinegar**
- **1/2 teaspoon dried basil**
- **1/2 teaspoon minced garlic**
- **1/4 teaspoon sugar**
- **1/8 teaspoon salt**
- **1/8 teaspoon dried thyme**
- **1/8 teaspoon pepper**
- **Dash crushed red pepper flakes**

In a salad bowl, combine spinach and mushrooms. In a jar with a tight-fitting lid, combine the remaining ingredients; shake well. Pour over salad and toss to coat.

Zesty Spinach Salad
Grilled Beef Fajitas

Serve immediately. **Yield:** 4 servings.

Nutrition Facts: 1 cup equals 71 calories, 7 g fat (1 g saturated fat), 0 cholesterol, 72 mg sodium, 2 g carbohydrate, 1 g fiber, 1 g protein. **Diabetic Exchanges:** 1 vegetable, 1 fat.

Grilled Beef Fajitas

(Pictured above)

Prep/Total Time: 25 min.

With their cream cheese filling and crispy shells, these fajitas will end the week with a mouth-watering sizzle!

- **1 cup julienned sweet red pepper**
- **1/2 cup sliced onion**
- **2 tablespoons olive oil, *divided***
- **3/4 pound boneless beef top round steak, cut into thin strips**
- **1 teaspoon Italian seasoning**
- **1/4 teaspoon salt**
- **1/4 teaspoon pepper**
- **1/4 cup spreadable chive and onion cream cheese**
- **4 flour tortillas (8 inches), warmed**

In a large skillet, saute red pepper and onion in 1 tablespoon oil until crisp-tender; remove and set aside.

In the same skillet, saute the steak, Italian seasoning, salt and pepper in remaining oil for 2-4 minutes or until meat reaches desired doneness. Return vegetables to the pan; heat through.

Spread 1 tablespoon of cream cheese off-center on each tortilla; top with beef mixture. Fold in sides and roll up. Cook on a panini maker or indoor grill for 3-4 minutes or until tortilla is browned. **Yield:** 4 servings.

Week 3

Shopping List

Check for these staples:

- biscuit/baking mix
- olive oil
- butter
- onion powder
- celery salt
- pepper
- chicken bouillon granules
- prepared horseradish
- cider vinegar
- prepared mustard
- dried basil
- salt
- dried thyme
- seasoned salt
- eggs
- soy sauce
- all-purpose flour
- grated Parmesan
- ground cumin
- instant rice
- mayonnaise
- milk
- minced garlic

Shop for these items:

1 small onion
4 croissants
1 package (16 ounces) bow tie pasta
1 can (15-3/4 ounces) lemon pie filling
1 head lettuce
1 package (16 ounces) coleslaw mix
1-1/4 pounds fresh asparagus
1 bunch seedless red grapes
1 small apple
1 bunch fresh parsley
2 medium tomatoes
1 pint fresh raspberries
1 package (8 ounces) shredded cheddar cheese
1 carton (6 ounces) raspberry yogurt
7 boneless beef petite sirloin steaks (5 ounces *each*)
4 bone-in chicken breast halves (12 ounces *each*)
3/4 pound sliced deli ham
1 package (8 ounces) bacon
1 package (19.6 ounces) frozen vanilla layer cake

Time-Saving Tips

- While Monday's chicken bakes, cook 2 cups of rice according to the package directions and refrigerate it for Friday's meal. Also, reserve 1/3 cup of lemon pie filling for Wednesday's coleslaw.
- On Tuesday, save 1/2 pound of uncut asparagus for Beef Fried Rice on Friday and keep four ham slices for Cobb Salad Sandwiches on Thursday.
- Beef Fried Rice will also use 2-1/2 cups of coleslaw mix left over from Wednesday's Fruity Coleslaw.

Lemon Chicken with Rice

Monday

Lemon Chicken with Rice

(Pictured above)

Prep: 25 min. **Bake:** 40 min.

Start the week off right with this delightful entree. Lemon pie filling is the "secret" ingredient in the flavorful sauce.

1/3 cup biscuit/baking mix
1 teaspoon seasoned salt
1/2 teaspoon pepper
4 bone-in chicken breast halves (12 ounces *each*), skin removed
1/4 cup olive oil
1-1/3 cups lemon pie filling
1/2 cup water
1/3 cup cider vinegar
1/4 cup soy sauce

TOMATO PARSLEY RICE:

2 cups water
1 teaspoon chicken bouillon granules
1/8 teaspoon pepper
2 cups uncooked instant rice
1 medium tomato, seeded and chopped
3 tablespoons minced fresh parsley

In a large resealable plastic bag, combine the biscuit mix, seasoned salt and pepper. Add chicken, one piece at a time, and shake to coat.

In a large skillet, brown chicken in oil on both sides; drain. Transfer to a 13-in. x 9-in. x 2-in. baking dish. In a small bowl, combine the pie filling, water, vinegar and soy sauce; pour over chicken. Bake, uncovered, at 375° for 40-45 minutes or until chicken juices run clear.

In a large saucepan, bring water, bouillon and pepper to a boil. Stir in the rice, tomato and parsley. Cover and remove from the heat; let stand for 5 minutes. Fluff with a fork. Serve with chicken. **Yield:** 4 servings.

Tuesday

Ham 'n' Cheese Pasta

(Pictured below)

Prep/Total Time: 30 min.

Both kids and adults are guaranteed to like this dressed-up version of creamy macaroni and cheese.

3 cups uncooked bow tie pasta
3/4 pound fresh asparagus, trimmed and cut into 1-inch pieces
2 tablespoons butter
1 teaspoon minced garlic
2 tablespoons all-purpose flour
1/4 teaspoon onion powder
1/4 teaspoon pepper
1/8 to 1/4 teaspoon dried thyme
2 cups milk
2 cups (8 ounces) shredded cheddar cheese
1/2 cup grated Parmesan cheese
1/2 pound sliced deli ham, chopped

Cook pasta according to package directions, adding asparagus during the last 3 minutes.

Meanwhile, in a large saucepan, melt butter; add garlic. Stir in the flour, onion powder, pepper and thyme until blended; gradually add milk. Bring to a boil; cook and stir for 2 minutes or until thickened.

Reduce heat. Add cheeses; stir until melted. Stir in ham; heat through. Drain pasta and asparagus; toss with cheese mixture. **Yield:** 4 servings.

Ham 'n' Cheese Pasta

Wednesday

Grilled Sirloin Steaks

(Pictured above right)

Prep/Total Time: 25 min.

Here, tender steaks are treated to a buttery topping that's mixed with garlic, parsley and cumin. Delicious!

Grilled Sirloin Steaks
Fruity Coleslaw

2 tablespoons prepared mustard
1/4 teaspoon pepper
4 boneless beef petite sirloin steaks (5 ounces *each*)
1/4 cup butter, softened
3 tablespoons minced fresh parsley
1 teaspoon minced garlic
1/2 teaspoon ground cumin

Combine the mustard and pepper; rub over both sides of the steaks. Grill, covered, over medium heat or broil 4 in. from the heat for 4-5 minutes on each side or until meat reaches desired doneness (for medium-rare, a meat thermometer should read 145°; medium, 160°; well-done, 170°).

In a small bowl, combine the butter, parsley, garlic and cumin. Serve with steaks. **Yield:** 4 servings.

Fruity Coleslaw

(Pictured above)

Prep/Total Time: 15 min.

You'll love the fresh tang of lemon in this crunchy slaw. It nicely accents Grilled Sirloin Steaks (recipe below left).

4 cups coleslaw mix
1 cup seedless red grapes, halved
1 small apple, chopped
3/4 cup mayonnaise
1/3 cup lemon pie filling
1 teaspoon cider vinegar
1/4 teaspoon celery salt
1/8 teaspoon salt
1/8 teaspoon pepper

In a large serving bowl, combine the coleslaw, grapes and apple. In a small bowl, combine the remaining ingredients; pour over coleslaw and toss to coat. Chill until serving. **Yield:** 6 servings.

Vanilla Cake with Raspberries
Cobb Salad Sandwiches

Thursday

Cobb Salad Sandwiches

(Pictured above)

Prep/Total Time: 20 min.

Satisfy everyone with these fun, hearty sandwiches. It's easy to customize them to suit each person's tastes.

1/4 cup mayonnaise
1/2 teaspoon prepared horseradish
1/4 teaspoon dried basil
4 croissants, split
4 lettuce leaves
1 medium tomato, sliced
4 cooked bacon strips, halved
4 slices deli ham
3 hard-cooked eggs, sliced

In a small bowl, combine the mayonnaise, horseradish and basil; spread over cut side of croissant bottoms. Layer with lettuce, tomato, bacon, ham and eggs; replace tops. **Yield:** 4 servings.

Vanilla Cake with Raspberries

(Pictured above)

Prep: 5 min. + standing

This simple-to-fix, pretty and refreshing dessert will make your Thursday night feel extra special.

1 package (19.6 ounces) frozen vanilla layer cake
3/4 cup fresh raspberries
1 carton (6 ounces) raspberry yogurt

Cut cake in half. Return half to the freezer. Let remaining cake stand at room temperature to thaw.

Cut cake into eight slices. Place four slices on dessert plates; sprinkle with raspberries. Top with remaining cake slices; dollop with yogurt. **Yield:** 4 servings.

Editor's Note: This recipe was tested with Pepperidge Farm frozen three-layer cake.

Friday

Beef Fried Rice

(Pictured below)

Prep/Total Time: 30 min.

End the week with a touch of the Orient. Moist beef strips, crisp asparagus and coleslaw create a standout dish.

1 tablespoon plus 1 teaspoon olive oil, *divided*
3 eggs, lightly beaten
3 boneless beef petite sirloin steaks (5 ounces *each*), cut into thin strips
2-1/2 cups coleslaw mix
1/2 pound fresh asparagus, trimmed and cut into 1-1/2-inch pieces
1/2 cup chopped onion
4 cups cold cooked instant rice
3 tablespoons butter, cubed
3 tablespoons soy sauce
1/8 teaspoon pepper

In a large skillet or wok, heat 1 tablespoon oil until hot. Add eggs; cook and stir over medium heat until completely set. Remove and keep warm.

In the same pan, stir-fry the beef, coleslaw, asparagus and onion in remaining oil for 4-6 minutes or until vegetables are crisp-tender.

Add rice and butter; cook and stir over medium heat for 1-2 minutes or until heated through. Add eggs; stir in soy sauce and pepper. **Yield:** 6 servings.

Beef Fried Rice

Week 4

Shopping List

Check for these staples:

- all-purpose flour
- brown sugar
- butter
- chicken bouillon granules
- eggs
- garlic salt
- Louisiana-style hot sauce
- minced garlic
- olive oil
- onion powder
- onions
- pepper
- salad dressing
- salt
- seasoned bread crumbs

Shop for these items:

1 can (8 ounces) sliced pineapple
1 can (14-1/2 ounces) diced tomatoes
1 jar (24 ounces) marinara *or* spaghetti sauce
1 envelope fajita seasoning mix
1 package (8 ounces) red beans and rice mix
1 package flour tortillas (8 inches)
1 package (5 ounces) spring mix salad greens
4 medium zucchini
3/4 pound fresh green beans
1 medium sweet red pepper
2 medium ripe avocados
1 package (16 ounces) fresh strawberries
1 large navel orange
1 tube (11-1/2 ounces) refrigerated corn bread twists
1 package (8 ounces) shredded Monterey Jack cheese
2 pork tenderloins (1 pound *each*)
1/2 pound smoked sausage
1 pound ground beef
1-1/2 pounds cooked medium shrimp, peeled and deveined

Time-Saving Tips

- For Refreshing Shrimp Salad on Monday, keep in mind that strawberries say fresher if stored unwashed with the stems on. Also, remember to save the orange peel for Wednesday's beans.
- Bring some helping hands into the kitchen and spend a little quality time with the kids, too. Let them scoop out the zucchini to make the "boats" for Beef-Stuffed Zucchini on Tuesday.
- Feel like having guests over for dinner midweek? Feel free! The main course on Wednesday—Pork Medallions with Garlic-Strawberry Sauce—is simple to double and comes together quickly.

Sweet & Savory Breadsticks
Refreshing Shrimp Salad

Monday

Refreshing Shrimp Salad

(Pictured above)

Prep/Total Time: 15 min.

Balsamic and raspberry vinaigrette dressings are great finishing touches for this fresh-tasting, light entree salad.

✓ This recipe includes Nutrition Facts and Diabetic Exchanges.

1 package (5 ounces) spring mix salad greens
1 pound cooked medium shrimp, peeled and deveined
1 large navel orange, peeled and sectioned
1 medium ripe avocado, peeled and sliced
1 cup sliced fresh strawberries
1/2 cup thinly sliced onions
Salad dressing of your choice

On each of four serving plates, arrange salad greens, shrimp, orange, avocado, strawberries and onions. Drizzle with dressing. **Yield:** 4 servings.

Nutrition Facts: 3 cups (calculated without salad dressing) equals 239 calories, 9 g fat (1 g saturated fat), 172 mg cholesterol, 181 mg sodium, 16 g carbohydrate, 6 g fiber, 25 g protein. **Diabetic Exchanges:** 3 very lean meat, 1-1/2 fat, 1 vegetable, 1/2 fruit.

Peeling Pointer

With avocados, I've found that using a grapefruit knife works wonders. Just slide the knife around the inside of the skin after slicing the avocado in half, and you can lift the entire half out or cut it according to your needs. *—Karlene Lantz, Felton, California*

Sweet & Savory Breadsticks

(Pictured on page 119)

Prep/Total Time: 25 min.

Give these a try tonight...they're so good, you may want to pair them with Thursday's jambalaya, too!

1 tube (11-1/2 ounces) refrigerated corn bread twists
1/4 cup butter, melted
1/3 cup packed brown sugar
1/2 teaspoon garlic salt
1/4 teaspoon onion powder

Unroll and separate bread twists into 16 pieces. Place butter in a shallow bowl. Combine the brown sugar, garlic salt and onion powder in another shallow bowl. Roll bread pieces in butter, then in brown sugar mixture.

Twist two pieces together. Pinch ends to seal. Place on an ungreased baking sheet. Repeat. Bake at 375° for 12-14 minutes or until golden brown. Serve warm. **Yield:** 4 servings.

Tuesday

Beef-Stuffed Zucchini

Prep/Total Time: 25 min.

You'll add a dash of fun to Tuesday with these "boats." For variety, substitute barbecue sauce for the marinara.

4 medium zucchini
1 pound ground beef
1/2 cup chopped onion
1 egg
3/4 cup marinara *or* spaghetti sauce
1/4 cup seasoned bread crumbs
1/4 teaspoon salt
1/4 teaspoon pepper
1 cup (4 ounces) shredded Monterey Jack cheese, *divided*
Additional marinara *or* spaghetti sauce

Cut zucchini in half lengthwise; cut a thin slice from the bottom of each with a sharp knife to allow zucchini to sit flat. Scoop out pulp, leaving 1/4-in. shells.

Place shells in an ungreased 13-in. x 9-in. x 2-in. microwave-safe dish. Turn off microwave turntable setting. Cover and microwave on high for 3 minutes or until crisp-tender; drain and set aside.

Meanwhile, in a large skillet, cook beef and onion over medium heat until meat is no longer pink; drain. Remove from the heat; stir in the egg, marinara sauce, bread crumbs, salt, pepper and 1/2 cup cheese.

Spoon about 1/4 cup into each shell. Microwave, uncovered, on high for 4 minutes. Sprinkle with remaining cheese. Microwave 3-4 minutes longer or until a thermometer inserted into filling reads 160° and zucchini are tender. Serve with additional sauce. **Yield:** 4 servings.

Editor's Note: If your microwave does not have a turntable setting, microwave zucchini in two batches, using an 11-in. x 7-in. x 2-in. microwave-safe dish. This recipe was tested in a 1,100-watt microwave.

Wednesday

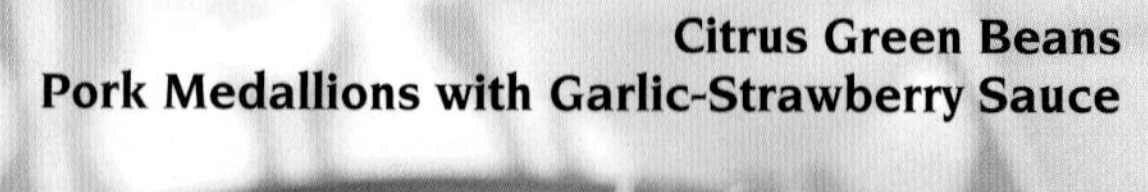

Pork Medallions with Garlic-Strawberry Sauce

(Pictured above)

Prep: 15 min. **Cook:** 20 min.

These crispy pork medallions are treated to a refreshing berry sauce. They'll make your weeknight feel special.

1 pork tenderloin (1 pound), cut into 1/2-inch slices
1/4 teaspoon salt
1/4 teaspoon pepper
1/2 cup all-purpose flour
2 eggs, beaten
2/3 cup seasoned bread crumbs
1/2 cup butter, *divided*
2 cups fresh strawberries
1 teaspoon minced garlic
1/4 cup hot water
1 teaspoon chicken bouillon granules
Sliced fresh strawberries, optional

Flatten pork to 1/4-inch thickness; sprinkle with salt and pepper. Place flour, eggs and crumbs in separate shallow bowls. Dip pork in flour, eggs, then crumbs.

In a large skillet over medium heat, cook pork in 1/4 cup butter until juices run clear; remove and keep warm.

Meanwhile, place strawberries in a food processor. Cover and process until blended; set aside.

In the same skillet, saute garlic in remaining butter. Add the pureed strawberries, water and bouillon; heat through. Serve pork with sauce. Garnish with sliced strawberries if desired. **Yield:** 4 servings.

Citrus Green Beans

(Pictured below left)

Prep/Total Time: 20 min.

Orange flavor really perks up these beans. You could also try using lemon peel...or a blend of orange and lemon.

☑ This recipe includes Nutrition Facts and Diabetic Exchanges.

3/4 pound fresh green beans, trimmed
2 teaspoons olive oil
1 to 2 teaspoons grated orange peel
Dash salt and pepper

Place green beans in a steamer basket; place in a large saucepan over 1 in. of water. Bring to a boil; cover and steam for 8-10 minutes or until crisp-tender.

Transfer beans to a small bowl. Add the oil, peel, salt and pepper; toss to coat. **Yield:** 4 servings.

Nutrition Facts: 3/4 cup equals 44 calories, 2 g fat (trace saturated fat), 0 cholesterol, 41 mg sodium, 5 g carbohydrate, 3 g fiber, 1 g protein. **Diabetic Exchanges:** 1 vegetable, 1/2 fat.

Thursday

Jiffy Jambalaya

(Pictured below)

Prep/Total Time: 30 min.

Your family will love this hearty, smoky dish. The bean-and-rice mix gets a quick makeover for a delicious meal.

1 package (8 ounces) red beans and rice mix
1/2 pound smoked sausage, sliced
1/2 cup chopped onion
1 tablespoon olive oil
1/2 pound cooked medium shrimp, peeled and deveined
1 can (14-1/2 ounces) diced tomatoes, drained
1 teaspoon brown sugar
1/4 teaspoon Louisiana-style hot sauce, optional

Cook bean and rice mix according to package directions. Meanwhile, in a large skillet, saute sausage and onion in oil until onion is tender. Add shrimp, tomatoes, sugar and sauce if desired. Cook for 3-4 minutes or until heated through. Stir in rice mixture. **Yield:** 4 servings.

Jiffy Jambalaya

Friday

Pork Tenderloin Fajitas

Pork Tenderloin Fajitas

(Pictured above)

Prep: 15 min. + marinating **Grill:** 20 min.

Grilled pineapple gives these fajitas a tangy twist. If you have time, let the pork marinate for up to an hour.

1 can (8 ounces) sliced pineapple
1 envelope fajita seasoning mix
1 pork tenderloin (1 pound)
1 medium sweet red pepper, sliced
1 medium onion, sliced
4 flour tortillas (8 inches), warmed
1 cup (4 ounces) shredded Monterey Jack cheese
1 medium ripe avocado, peeled and sliced

Drain pineapple, reserving juice; set pineapple aside. In a large resealable plastic bag, combine seasoning mix and reserved juice; add pork. Seal bag and turn to coat; refrigerate for 15 minutes.

Meanwhile, place the red pepper, onion and pineapple on a double thickness of heavy-duty foil (about 12 in. square). Fold foil around mixture and seal tightly.

Prepare grill for indirect heat. Drain and discard marinade from pork. Grill pork and foil packet, covered, over indirect medium heat for 25-40 minutes or until a meat thermometer inserted in the pork reads 160° and vegetables are tender. Remove from the grill. Cover pork and let stand for 5 minutes. Cut pork into strips; place on tortillas. Top with vegetable mixture, cheese and avocado; fold in sides. **Yield:** 4 servings.

Week 5

Shopping List

Check for these staples:

- butter
- dill pickle slices
- flour
- garlic salt
- Italian seasoning
- ketchup
- mayonnaise
- milk
- minced garlic
- olive oil
- onions
- pepper
- prepared mustard
- salt
- Worcestershire sauce

Shop for these items:

1 package (8 count) hamburger buns
1 package (16 ounces) penne pasta
1 envelope ranch salad dressing mix
1 can (15 ounces) tomato puree
1 can (14-1/2 ounces) beef broth
1 can (10-3/4 ounces) condensed cream of mushroom soup
2 cans (6 ounces *each*) tuna
2 packages (10 ounces *each*) shredded lettuce
3 packages (9 ounces *each*) fresh spinach
4 medium tomatoes
1/2 pint heavy whipping cream
1 package (8 ounces) sliced process American cheese
2 packages (8 ounces *each*) shredded part-skim mozzarella cheese
1 package (16 ounces) frozen mixed vegetables
2 pounds ground beef
1 package (16 ounces) bacon
4 boneless skinless chicken breast halves (5 ounces *each*)
1 pound boneless skinless chicken breasts

Time-Saving Tips

- Have leftover cooked bacon from Monday's Bacon Cheeseburger Salad? Make good use of it by sprinkling it on a salad to go along with Garlic Ranch Chicken on Thursday.
- Save the excess mixed vegetables from Wednesday's sandwiches for Friday. The veggies can make a side dish to complement your Hearty Penne Beef.
- Remember to keep the extra ranch salad dressing mix from Wednesday. You'll use it to flavor Thursday's chicken breasts.
- On Friday, you should still have some leftover spinach. Chop it to use in Hearty Penne Beef.

Bacon Cheeseburger Salad

Monday

Bacon Cheeseburger Salad

(Pictured above)

Prep/Total Time: 30 min.

Think children won't eat salad? Try this one, and you'll change your mind! It features lettuce topped with ground beef and other popular burger ingredients.

2 hamburger buns, cut into 1-inch cubes
2 teaspoons olive oil
1/8 teaspoon garlic salt
1 pound ground beef
3/4 cup chopped onion
3/4 cup ketchup
1 tablespoon prepared mustard
1/8 teaspoon pepper
8 cups shredded lettuce
2 cups chopped tomatoes
4 slices process American cheese, cut into strips
1/2 cup crumbled cooked bacon
8 dill pickle slices

For croutons, place bun cubes on a baking sheet. Drizzle with oil and sprinkle with garlic salt; toss to coat. Broil 4 in. from the heat for 4-6 minutes or until golden brown, turning once.

In a large skillet, cook beef and onion over medium heat until meat is no longer pink; drain. Add the ketchup, mustard and pepper; heat through.

Divide lettuce among four dinner plates; top each with tomatoes, meat mixture, cheese and bacon. Garnish with croutons and pickles. **Yield:** 4 servings.

Tuesday

Creamy Spinach Chicken Dinner

(Pictured below)

Prep/Total Time: 30 min.

This all-in-one pasta supper is a breeze to fix. To make things even easier, don't bother chopping the spinach—just tear it with your hands.

1-1/2 cups uncooked penne pasta
1 pound boneless skinless chicken breasts, cut into 1-inch cubes
1/2 cup chopped onion
2 teaspoons olive oil
1 can (10-3/4 ounces) condensed cream of mushroom soup, undiluted
1 cup heavy whipping cream
10 cups coarsely chopped fresh spinach
2 cups (8 ounces) shredded part-skim mozzarella cheese
1/8 teaspoon pepper

Cook the pasta according to package directions. Meanwhile, in a Dutch oven over medium heat, cook and stir the chicken and onion in oil for 5 minutes or until chicken juices run clear.

Stir in soup and cream. Bring to a boil over medium heat. Reduce heat; simmer, uncovered, for 2 minutes. Stir in the spinach, cheese and pepper; cook for 1-2 minutes or until spinach is wilted and cheese is melted.

Drain pasta; add to chicken mixture and toss to coat. **Yield:** 4 servings.

Creamy Spinach Chicken Dinner

Hot Tuna Sandwiches

Wednesday

Hot Tuna Sandwiches

(Pictured above)

Prep/Total Time: 25 min.

Mixed veggies really perk up this oven-baked sandwich. Serve it with fruit cups and your favorite chips.

2 cans (6 ounces *each*) tuna, drained
1/2 cup frozen mixed vegetables, thawed and chopped
1/3 cup mayonnaise
2 tablespoons finely chopped onion
1 tablespoon ranch salad dressing mix
4 hamburger buns, split

In a large bowl, combine the first five ingredients. Spoon tuna mixture onto bun bottoms; replace tops.

Place each sandwich on a piece of heavy-duty foil (about 12 in. square). Fold foil around each sandwich and seal tightly; place packets on a baking sheet. Bake at 400° for 10-15 minutes or until heated through. **Yield:** 4 servings.

Pasta Pointers

- To cook pasta more evenly, prevent it from sticking together and avoid boil-overs, cook pasta in a large kettle or Dutch oven.
- To test for doneness, use a fork to remove a piece of pasta from the boiling water. Rinse it in cold water and taste it. Pasta should be cooked until "al dente," or firm yet tender. Test often to avoid overcooking, which can result in a soft or mushy texture.
- As soon as the pasta tests done, pour it into a large colander to drain, being careful of the steam.

Garlic Ranch Chicken

Thursday

Garlic Ranch Chicken

(Pictured above)

Prep/Total Time: 30 min.

Simple ingredients are all you'll need to give this entree family-pleasing flavor. Whip up a no-nonsense side salad to round out the meal.

✓ This recipe includes Nutrition Facts and Diabetic Exchanges.

4 boneless skinless chicken breast halves (5 ounces *each*)
1/4 cup milk
1/2 teaspoon minced garlic
1/4 cup all-purpose flour
1 tablespoon ranch salad dressing mix
1/8 teaspoon pepper
1 tablespoon olive oil
1 tablespoon butter

Flatten chicken slightly; set aside. In a shallow bowl, combine milk and garlic. In another shallow bowl, combine the flour, salad dressing mix and pepper. Dip chicken in milk mixture, then coat with flour mixture.

In a large skillet, cook chicken in oil and butter over medium heat for 6-8 minutes on each side or until juices run clear. **Yield:** 4 servings.

Nutrition Facts: 1 chicken breast half equals 264 calories, 12 g fat (4 g saturated fat), 88 mg cholesterol, 125 mg sodium, 7 g carbohydrate, trace fiber, 30 g protein. **Diabetic Exchanges:** 4 very lean meat, 1-1/2 fat, 1/2 starch.

Friday

Hearty Penne Beef

(Pictured below)

Prep/Total Time: 30 min.

What a great way to end the week—with a comforting casserole sure to please everyone at the table. This main dish is delicious, easy and a smart way to sneak some spinach into dinner for extra nutrition.

1-3/4 cups uncooked penne pasta
1 pound ground beef
1 teaspoon minced garlic
1 can (15 ounces) tomato puree
1 can (14-1/2 ounces) beef broth
1-1/2 teaspoons Italian seasoning
1 teaspoon Worcestershire sauce
1/4 teaspoon salt
1/4 teaspoon pepper
2 cups chopped fresh spinach
2 cups (8 ounces) shredded part-skim mozzarella cheese

Cook the pasta according to package directions. Meanwhile, in a Dutch oven, cook the beef and garlic over medium heat until meat is no longer pink; drain. Stir in the tomato puree, broth, Italian seasoning, Worcestershire sauce, salt and pepper.

Bring to a boil. Reduce heat; simmer, uncovered, for 10-15 minutes or until slightly thickened. Add spinach; cook for 1-2 minutes or until spinach is wilted.

Drain pasta; stir into beef mixture. Sprinkle with cheese; cover and cook for 3-4 minutes or until cheese is melted. **Yield:** 4 servings.

Hearty Penne Beef

Week 6

Shopping List

Check for these staples:

- all-purpose flour
- brown sugar
- butter
- chili sauce
- cider vinegar
- curry powder
- Dijon mustard
- dried basil
- dried parsley
- dried thyme
- egg
- garlic powder
- ground cumin
- instant rice
- Italian seasoning
- minced garlic
- olive oil
- onions
- pepper
- salt
- seasoned bread crumbs

Shop for these items:

1 loaf (1 pound) Italian bread
1 can (14 ounces) coconut milk
2 cans (14-1/2 ounces *each*) vegetable broth
1 can (10-3/4 ounces) condensed cream of celery soup
1 can (4 ounces) chopped green chilies
2 cans (15-1/2 ounces *each*) great northern beans
1 can (15-1/2 ounces) sloppy joe sauce
1 jar (26 ounces) spaghetti sauce
1 package (8 ounces) shredded part-skim mozzarella cheese
1 package (10 ounces) shredded lettuce
1 pound red potatoes
1 package (6 ounces) baby spinach
2 medium tomatoes
2 pounds ground beef
1-1/2 pounds boneless skinless chicken breasts
1 package (8 ounces) bacon strips
1 pound smoked kielbasa
1 package (16 ounces) frozen chopped broccoli
1 package (16 ounces) frozen mixed vegetables
1 package (27 ounces) frozen hash brown patties

Time-Saving Tips

- On Monday, cut all of the chicken and chop the onion for both Monday's and Wednesday's meals.
- Do you use the microwave to cook bacon? When making Thursday's Potato Kielbasa Skillet, wait until the potatoes are done, then cook your bacon while everything else is on the stovetop.

Chicken & Kielbasa with Curried Rice

Monday

Chicken & Kielbasa With Curried Rice

(Pictured above)

Prep: 25 min. **Cook:** 15 min.

Chunks of chicken and sausage slices form a hearty base for this fast-to-fix entree, which has everything you need for dinner. Curry powder carries the flavor, while the coconut milk is on the mild side.

3/4 pound boneless skinless chicken breasts, cut into 1/2-inch cubes
1/4 pound smoked kielbasa *or* Polish sausage, cut into 1/4-inch slices
1/2 cup chopped onion
1 tablespoon olive oil
3 cups frozen chopped broccoli, thawed
1 can (14 ounces) coconut milk
1 can (10-3/4 ounces) condensed cream of celery soup, undiluted
1 cup uncooked instant rice
1/3 cup water
1 tablespoon curry powder
1/4 teaspoon salt
1 medium tomato, chopped

In a large skillet, saute the chicken, kielbasa and onion in oil until the chicken juices run clear. Add the broccoli, coconut milk, cream of celery soup, rice, water, curry powder and salt.

Bring to a boil. Reduce the heat; cover and simmer for 10-15 minutes or until rice is tender. Garnish with tomato. **Yield:** 4 servings.

Tuesday

Sloppy Joe Hash Browns

(Pictured above)

Prep: 10 min. **Cook:** 25 min.

These golden brown patties are topped off with sloppy-joe beef and other tasty ingredients. You could use cheddar, Monterey Jack or American cheese instead of mozzarella.

- **8 frozen hash brown patties**
- **1 pound ground beef**
- **1/4 cup chopped onion**
- **1 can (15-1/2 ounces) sloppy joe sauce**
- **1 tablespoon chili sauce**
- **1/4 teaspoon pepper**
- **1 cup (4 ounces) shredded part-skim mozzarella cheese**
- **2 cups shredded lettuce**
- **1 medium tomato, chopped**

Cook hash browns in batches according to package directions. Meanwhile, in a large skillet, cook beef and onion over medium heat until meat is no longer pink; drain. Add the sloppy joe sauce, chili sauce and pepper; bring to a boil. Reduce heat; simmer, uncovered, for 3-5 minutes or until heated through.

Place two hash brown patties on each plate; top with the meat sauce, mozzarella cheese, lettuce and tomato. **Yield:** 4 servings.

Kids in the Kitchen

TUESDAY'S SUPPER of Sloppy Joe Hash Browns (recipe above) gives you an opportunity to bring children in on the action. This simple main dish is easy enough for the kids to help with—by adding their own toppings to the hash brown patties.

Wednesday

Chunky Chicken Soup

(Pictured below)

Prep: 20 min. **Cook:** 20 min.

With lots of beans, chicken and vegetables, this quick soup is guaranteed to fill up your hungry family.

- **3/4 pound boneless skinless chicken breasts, cut into 1/2-inch cubes**
- **1/2 cup chopped onion**
- **1-1/2 teaspoons minced garlic**
- **2 teaspoons olive oil**
- **2 tablespoons all-purpose flour**
- **2 cans (14-1/2 ounces *each*) vegetable broth**
- **2 cans (15-1/2 ounces *each*) great northern beans, rinsed and drained**
- **1-1/2 cups frozen mixed vegetables, thawed**
- **1 cup frozen chopped broccoli, thawed**
- **1 can (4 ounces) chopped green chilies**
- **3/4 teaspoon Italian seasoning**
- **1/2 teaspoon ground cumin**
- **1/4 teaspoon pepper**
- **1/2 cup shredded part-skim mozzarella cheese**

In a Dutch oven, saute the chicken, onion and garlic in oil until chicken juices run clear. Stir in flour until blended; gradually add broth. Bring to a boil; cook and stir for 2 minutes.

Reduce heat; stir in the beans, vegetables and seasonings. Cook, stirring occasionally, for 8-10 minutes or until the vegetables are tender. Garnish with mozzarella cheese. **Yield:** 7 cups.

Potato Kielbasa Skillet

Thursday

Potato Kielbasa Skillet

(Pictured above)

Prep/Total Time: 30 min.

Slices of smoky kielbasa steal the show in this home-style, hearty supper. On those chilly late-fall and early-winter nights, you'll hear raves when you serve up big helpings of piping-hot sausage and potatoes.

1 pound red potatoes, cubed
3 tablespoons water
3/4 pound smoked kielbasa *or* Polish sausage, cut into 1/4-inch slices
1/2 cup chopped onion
1 tablespoon olive oil
2 tablespoons brown sugar
2 tablespoons cider vinegar
1 tablespoon Dijon mustard
1/2 teaspoon dried thyme
1/4 teaspoon pepper
4 cups fresh baby spinach
5 bacon strips, cooked and crumbled

Place the potatoes and water in a microwave-safe dish. Cover and microwave on high for 4 minutes or until tender; drain.

In a large skillet, saute kielbasa and onion in oil until onion is tender. Add potatoes; saute 3-5 minutes longer or until kielbasa and potatoes are lightly browned.

Combine the brown sugar, cider vinegar, Dijon mustard, thyme and pepper; stir into the skillet. Bring to a boil. Reduce the heat; simmer, uncovered, for 2-3 minutes or until heated through.

Add the spinach and bacon; cook and stir until the spinach is wilted. **Yield:** 4 servings.

Friday

Italian Patty Melts

(Pictured below)

Prep/Total Time: 30 min.

This casual main course will usher in your weekend on a fun note. Prepare the Italian-style beef burgers as traditional sandwiches...or serve them as open-faced sandwiches alongside a bowl of extra sauce.

1 egg
1/2 cup spaghetti sauce, *divided*
3 tablespoons seasoned bread crumbs
1/4 teaspoon pepper
1 pound ground beef
2 tablespoons butter, melted
1/4 teaspoon dried basil
1/4 teaspoon dried parsley flakes
1/8 teaspoon garlic powder
8 slices Italian bread
1/2 cup shredded part-skim mozzarella cheese

In a large bowl, combine the egg, 1/4 cup spaghetti sauce, bread crumbs and pepper. Crumble the ground beef over the mixture and mix well. Shape into four oval patties; set aside.

Combine butter and seasonings; brush over both sides of the bread. In a large skillet, toast bread until lightly browned; set aside.

In the same skillet, cook the beef patties over medium heat for 4-6 minutes on each side or until no longer pink. Spoon the remaining spaghetti sauce over the patties; sprinkle with mozzarella cheese. Cover and cook for 1 minute or until the cheese is melted. Place the burgers on four slices of toast; top with the remaining toast. **Yield:** 4 servings.

Italian Patty Melts

Chapter 8

Speedy Sides and Salads

YOU'VE CHOSEN the perfect main course—now you need just the right dish on the side. It not only has to complement your entree, but it also needs to get on the table in a flash.

What to do? The solution is easy! Just look to the exceptional recipes in this chapter. From tossed greens and pasta to vegetables and rice, these special accompaniments make standout additions to menus.

Choose from favorites such as Mashed Potatoes Supreme, Apple Stuffing and Seafood Pasta Salad. You even get Layered Italian Chicken Salad, Garden Primavera Fettuccine and other hearty selections that can make a meal all by themselves!

TOSS IT IN. Spicy Teriyaki Beef Salad (p. 131).

Green Beans in Beer Sauce

Green Beans in Beer Sauce

(Pictured above)

Prep/Total Time: 25 min.

Think green beans as a side dish are boring? Jazz them up with some diced bacon and a tangy-sweet sauce. Don't be surprised if your guests ask for seconds!
—Lynn Thomas, London, Ontario

1/3 pound sliced bacon, diced
1 package (16 ounces) frozen cut green beans, thawed
1/3 cup beer *or* nonalcoholic beer
1/3 cup butter, cubed
3 tablespoons brown sugar
3 tablespoons white vinegar
4 teaspoons cornstarch
2 teaspoons grated onion

In a large skillet, cook the bacon over medium heat until crisp. Meanwhile, in a large saucepan, bring the beans, beer and butter to a boil. Reduce the heat; cover and simmer for 8-10 minutes or until the beans are crisp-tender. Using a slotted spoon, remove bacon to paper towels to drain. Remove beans with a slotted spoon and keep warm.

In a small bowl, combine the brown sugar, vinegar, cornstarch and onion until blended. Stir into the saucepan. Bring to a boil; cook and stir for 1-2 minutes or until thickened. Add beans; heat through. Sprinkle with bacon. **Yield:** 4 servings.

Pimiento Brussels Sprouts

(Pictured below)

Prep/Total Time: 15 min.

This is very pretty any time you want a special side dish, but it's especially nice on a Christmas dinner table. Tarragon and vinegar flavor the packaged brussels sprouts, and pimientos add the perfect splash of festive red color.
—Carolyn Hayes, Johnston City, Illinois

✓ This recipe includes Nutrition Facts and Diabetic Exchanges.

1 package (16 ounces) frozen brussels sprouts
4-1/2 teaspoons butter
4-1/2 teaspoons white vinegar
3/4 teaspoon dried tarragon
1/4 teaspoon salt
1 jar (2 ounces) diced pimientos, drained

Cook the brussels sprouts according to the package directions. Drain, reserving 1 tablespoon liquid; keep brussels sprouts warm.

In a small saucepan, melt the butter; stir in the vinegar, tarragon, salt and reserved cooking liquid. Pour over sprouts and toss to coat. Sprinkle with pimientos. **Yield:** 4 servings.

Nutrition Facts: 3/4 cup equals 88 calories, 5 g fat (3 g saturated fat), 11 mg cholesterol, 191 mg sodium, 10 g carbohydrate, 5 g fiber, 5 g protein. **Diabetic Exchanges:** 2 vegetable, 1 fat.

Pimiento Brussels Sprouts

Spicy Teriyaki Beef Salad

Spicy Teriyaki Beef Salad

(Pictured above and on page 128)

Prep/Total Time: 30 min.

Cool cucumber and avocado combine with spiced-up steak for this tongue-tingling main course. If the spice is a bit too much for your taste, simply skip the cayenne pepper and red pepper flakes in the avocado mixture.
—Ning Watson, San Diego, California

1 cup teriyaki sauce
2 tablespoons minced garlic
4-1/2 teaspoons sesame oil
1 teaspoon crushed red pepper flakes, *divided*
1 teaspoon cayenne pepper, *divided*
1 pound boneless beef sirloin steak, cut into thin strips
1 medium ripe avocado, peeled and chopped
1 cup chopped cucumber
1 cup soy sauce
1/2 cup red wine vinegar
1 tablespoon sugar
1 large portobello mushroom, sliced
2 cups hearts of romaine salad mix

In a large resealable plastic bag, combine the teriyaki sauce, garlic, sesame oil, 1/2 teaspoon pepper flakes and 1/2 teaspoon cayenne; add the steak. Seal bag and turn to coat; refrigerate for 10 minutes.

Meanwhile, in a large bowl, combine the avocado, cucumber, soy sauce, vinegar, sugar, and remaining pepper flakes and cayenne; set aside.

Drain and discard marinade. In a large nonstick skillet, saute steak and mushroom until meat reaches desired doneness and mushroom is tender. Divide salad mix among four plates; top with avocado mixture and meat mixture. **Yield:** 4 servings.

Italian Spinach Salad

(Pictured below)

Prep/Total Time: 25 min.

Here's a quick, colorful veggie medley that's as refreshing as springtime itself. It's also an attractive salad choice for special occasions. Keep it in mind for Easter, when you need to use up all of those extra hard-cooked eggs!
—Gloria Warczak, Cedarburg, Wisconsin

4 cups fresh baby spinach
2 medium tomatoes, quartered
8 large fresh mushrooms, sliced
2 hard-cooked eggs, quartered
1/2 cup real bacon bits
1 small red onion, sliced and separated into rings
3 tablespoons snipped fresh dill
1-1/2 cups Italian salad dressing
1 teaspoon sugar
1/3 cup seasoned croutons

On eight salad plates, arrange the spinach, tomatoes, mushrooms, hard-cooked eggs, bacon, red onion and dill if desired.

In a small saucepan, cook the salad dressing and sugar over low heat until sugar is dissolved. Drizzle over the salads; sprinkle with the croutons. Serve immediately. **Yield:** 8 servings.

Italian Spinach Salad

Mashed Potatoes Supreme

(Pictured below)

Prep: 40 min. **Bake:** 20 min.

I received this recipe from my sister some 60 years ago, and countless people have requested it since then. With three kinds of cheese, green pepper and onions, the rich and creamy potatoes taste like the twice-baked variety.
—Julia Daubresse, Sun City Center, Florida

3 pounds medium red potatoes, quartered
2 packages (3 ounces *each*) cream cheese, cubed
1/2 cup butter, cubed
1/2 cup half-and-half cream *or* milk
1 medium green pepper, chopped
4 green onions, thinly sliced
1 jar (2 ounces) sliced pimientos, drained
1/2 teaspoon salt
1/4 teaspoon pepper
1/2 cup shredded cheddar cheese, *divided*
1/2 cup grated Parmesan cheese, *divided*

Place potatoes in a large saucepan; cover with water. Bring to a boil. Reduce heat; cover and cook for 15-20 minutes or until tender. Drain.

In a large mixing bowl, mash the potatoes. Add the cream cheese, butter and cream; beat until blended.

Stir in the green pepper, onions, pimientos, salt and pepper. Stir in 1/3 cup cheddar cheese and 1/3 cup Parmesan cheese.

Transfer to a greased 11-in. x 7-in. x 2-in. baking dish. Sprinkle with remaining cheeses. Bake, uncovered, at 350° for 20-25 minutes or until heated through. **Yield:** 8 servings.

Mashed Potatoes Supreme

Grilled Sweet Onions

Grilled Sweet Onions

(Pictured above)

Prep: 15 min. **Grill:** 35 min.

These are so good, we prepare them all year long—on the grill in summer and in an oven preheated to 350° for the same amount of time in winter. Add a small green salad and some bread, and you can even have a light meal.
—Mary Bilke, Eagle River, Wisconsin

4 large sweet onions
4 teaspoons beef bouillon granules
4 tablespoons butter
1/2 teaspoon dried thyme
1/4 teaspoon salt
1/4 teaspoon pepper
4 teaspoons white wine *or* beef broth, optional

With a sharp knife, carefully remove a 1-in. core from the center of each onion. Cut each onion into four wedges to within 1/2 in. of root end.

Place each onion on a double thickness of heavy-duty foil (about 12 in. square). Place bouillon in the centers of onions; top with butter, thyme, salt and pepper. Drizzle with wine or broth if desired. Fold foil around onions and seal tightly.

Prepare grill for indirect heat. Grill onions, covered, over indirect medium heat for 35-40 minutes or until tender. Open foil carefully to allow steam to escape. **Yield:** 4 servings.

Angel Hair with Walnuts

Prep/Total Time: 20 min.

I worked in an Italian restaurant that served pasta with olive oil, garlic and a sprinkling of walnuts. I enjoyed that combination so much, I tried to duplicate it with this recipe for an important dinner. The result was a hit!
—Nancy Beckman, Helena, Montana

8 ounces uncooked angel hair pasta
1-1/2 to 2 teaspoons minced garlic
1/4 cup olive oil
1/2 cup chopped walnuts
1/8 to 1/4 teaspoon crushed red pepper flakes
1/8 teaspoon salt
2 tablespoons minced fresh parsley
1/2 cup shredded Romano cheese

Cook pasta according to package directions. Meanwhile, in a large skillet, saute garlic in oil until tender. Stir in the walnuts, pepper flakes and salt. Cook for 2-3 minutes or until walnuts are toasted.

Remove from the heat; stir in parsley. Drain the pasta; add to the skillet. Add Romano cheese; toss to coat. **Yield:** 4 servings.

Mixed Herb Rice

Prep/Total Time: 20 min.

Marjoram offers a mild, slightly sweet flavor that makes it ideal for meats, veggies and this delicious rice medley. Oregano can be substituted for the marjoram, but use less than the recipe calls for because oregano is stronger.
—Randeen Rumps, Garden City, Michigan

1 cup chopped onion
3 tablespoons butter, cubed
1-1/2 cups hot water
2-1/4 teaspoons chicken bouillon granules
1-1/2 cups uncooked instant rice
1 tablespoon minced fresh savory *or* 1 teaspoon dried savory
1-1/2 teaspoons minced fresh marjoram *or* 1/2 teaspoon dried marjoram
1-1/2 teaspoons minced fresh rosemary *or* 1/2 teaspoon dried rosemary, crushed
1/2 teaspoon salt

In a small saucepan, saute onion in butter until tender. Add water and bouillon. Bring to a boil. Stir in the remaining ingredients. Remove from the heat. Cover and let stand for 5 minutes. **Yield:** 4 servings.

Antipasto Salad with Basil Dressing

(Pictured at right)

Prep/Total Time: 30 min.

With salami, feta cheese, croutons and more, this Italian-style salad has fantastic taste and looks great in a glass bowl. You won't want to skip the homemade dressing!
—Hunter Marlo, Blacksburg, Virginia

1 package (6 ounces) torn mixed salad greens
6 thin slices hard salami, quartered
1 jar (7-1/2 ounces) marinated quartered artichoke hearts, drained
1 large sweet red pepper, sliced
1/2 cup pitted Greek olives
1 small red onion, thinly sliced
1-1/2 cups (6 ounces) crumbled feta cheese
15 cherry tomatoes, halved
1/2 cup chopped walnuts
1 cup salad croutons

BASIL SALAD DRESSING:

1/2 cup olive oil
1/4 cup balsamic vinegar
5 fresh basil leaves, thinly sliced
1/2 teaspoon sugar
1/2 teaspoon garlic powder
1/4 teaspoon salt
1/4 teaspoon pepper

In a 3-1/2-qt. glass bowl, layer the first 10 ingredients in order listed. Cover and chill until serving.

In a jar with a tight-fitting lid, combine the salad dressing ingredients; shake well. Just before serving, drizzle the salad dressing over the salad; toss to coat. **Yield:** 8 servings.

Antipasto Salad with Basil Dressing

Dijon Scalloped Potatoes

Dijon Scalloped Potatoes

(Pictured above)

Prep: 25 min. **Bake:** 50 min. + standing

My family loves this creamy and colorful recipe for cheesy potatoes. And what's not to love? It has both sweet and white potatoes, lots of rich, buttery flavor and a golden crumb topping. —*Carolyn Putnam, Norwalk, Ohio*

2/3 cup chopped onion
2 teaspoons vegetable oil
1 can (14-1/2 ounces) chicken broth
2 packages (3 ounces *each*) cream cheese, cubed
1 tablespoon Dijon mustard
3 medium russet potatoes, peeled and thinly sliced
2 medium sweet potatoes, peeled and thinly sliced
1-1/2 to 2 cups crushed butter-flavored crackers
3 tablespoons grated Parmesan cheese
2 tablespoons butter, melted
2 teaspoons minced fresh parsley

In a Dutch oven, saute onion in oil until tender. Reduce heat to medium; stir in the chicken broth, cream cheese and mustard until blended. Remove from the heat. Stir in the potatoes.

Transfer to a greased 13-in. x 9-in. x 2-in. baking dish. Combine the crushed crackers, Parmesan cheese and butter; sprinkle over the top.

Bake, uncovered, at 350° for 50-60 minutes or until potatoes are tender. Sprinkle with parsley. Let stand for 10 minutes before serving. **Yield:** 8 servings.

Taco Salad

Prep/Total Time: 30 min.

This Southwestern main-dish salad takes just 30 minutes to fix. It'll give your family a satisfying dinner and leave you time to relax. —*Marie Noguerole, Portland, Oregon*

1-1/2 pounds ground beef
1/2 cup chopped onion
2 cans (15 ounces *each*) pinto beans, rinsed and drained
1 can (16 ounces) kidney beans, rinsed and drained
1 can (14-1/2 ounces) stewed tomatoes, undrained
1 can (4 ounces) chopped green chilies
2 teaspoons hot pepper sauce
1/2 teaspoon salt
8 cups corn chips
2 cups shredded lettuce
1 cup (4 ounces) shredded Mexican cheese blend
1/2 cup sour cream
1/4 cup sliced ripe olives

In a large skillet, cook beef and onion over medium heat until meat is no longer pink; drain. Add the beans, tomatoes, chilies, hot pepper sauce and salt. Bring to a boil. Reduce heat; simmer, uncovered, for 5 minutes.

Serve over corn chips. Top with lettuce, cheese, sour cream and olives. **Yield:** 8 servings.

Tangy Pasta 'n' Peas

Prep/Total Time: 25 min.

Fresh-picked peas are wonderful in this change-of-pace dish, but frozen ones are just fine when the garden is covered with snow! —*Janice Mitchell, Aurora, Colorado*

✓ This recipe includes Nutrition Facts and Diabetic Exchanges.

4 ounces uncooked angel hair pasta
2 cups fresh *or* frozen snow peas
1/2 cup chopped red onion
2 teaspoons butter
6 tablespoons sour cream
3 tablespoons white wine *or* chicken broth
1 jar (2 ounces) sliced pimientos, drained
1 tablespoon Dijon mustard

Cook pasta according to package directions, adding peas during the last 2-3 minutes. Meanwhile, in a large skillet, saute onion in butter until tender. Reduce the heat. Stir in the sour cream, wine or broth, pimientos and mustard; heat through.

Drain pasta and peas; add to sauce and toss to coat. **Yield:** 5 servings.

Nutrition Facts: 3/4 cup equals 179 calories, 5 g fat (3 g saturated fat), 16 mg cholesterol, 107 mg sodium, 24 g carbohydrate, 3 g fiber, 6 g protein. **Diabetic Exchanges:** 1-1/2 starch, 1 fat.

Calico Corn Cakes

(Pictured below)

Prep/Total Time: 25 min.

These colorful corn cakes from our Test Kitchen are great with south-of-the-border entrees. Just add a bowl of your favorite salsa or dollops of sour cream.

1/4 cup chopped onion
1/4 cup chopped green pepper
1 teaspoon canola oil
1/4 cup all-purpose flour
2 tablespoons yellow cornmeal
1/2 teaspoon sugar
1/4 teaspoon salt
1/4 teaspoon dried oregano
1/8 teaspoon baking powder
1/8 teaspoon ground cumin
1 egg, beaten
1/4 cup milk
1 cup frozen corn, thawed
1 tablespoon diced pimientos
1/2 cup salsa

In a small skillet, saute onion and green pepper in oil until tender; set aside. In a large bowl, whisk the flour, cornmeal, sugar, salt, oregano, baking powder, cumin, egg and milk just until combined. Fold in the corn, pimientos and onion mixture.

Heat a large skillet coated with cooking spray; drop batter by 1/4 cupfuls into skillet. Cook cakes for 3 minutes on each side or until golden brown. Serve with salsa. **Yield:** 3 servings.

Calico Corn Cakes

Grilled Steak Tossed Salad

Grilled Steak Tossed Salad

(Pictured above)

Prep/Total Time: 20 min.

My grandmother gave me this recipe—it's the perfect solution when you have leftover grilled steak from the night before. On hot summer days or evenings, you'll have a delicious lunch or dinner without heating up the kitchen.
—Warren Paulson, Mesa, Arizona

4 cups Italian-blend salad greens
1/2 pound cooked boneless beef sirloin steak, thinly sliced
4 tomato wedges
1/2 cup fresh whole kernel corn
1/3 cup prepared balsamic vinaigrette
1/4 cup shredded Romano cheese

In a large bowl, combine the salad greens, steak, tomato wedges and corn. Drizzle with the balsamic vinaigrette and toss to coat; sprinkle with Romano cheese. **Yield:** 2 servings.

Cut to the Quick

Here's my speedy technique for taking corn off the cob. First, I carefully put the cob on an ice pick. Then I use an electric knife to cut the corn off. It only takes a few seconds, and you have fresh corn to use in salads, side dishes and other recipes.
—Faye Howery, Max Meadows, Virginia

Turkey Salad with Blueberry Vinaigrette

(Pictured below)

Prep/Total Time: 20 min.

This deliciously different salad has become a favorite. For a special touch, I serve it with French bread slices cut into stars, sprinkled with ground ginger and then broiled.
—Josephine Piro, Easton, Pennsylvania

- **1/2 small cantaloupe, seeded and peeled**
- **2 packages (5 ounces *each*) spring mix salad greens**
- **2 cups cubed deli smoked turkey**
- **1 cup fresh blueberries**
- **1/2 cup pine nuts, toasted**
- **1/2 cup crumbled blue cheese**

VINAIGRETTE:

- **1/3 cup raspberry vinegar**
- **1/3 cup vegetable oil**
- **1 cup fresh blueberries**
- **1 shallot, chopped**
- **1 tablespoon sugar**
- **1 tablespoon minced fresh gingerroot**
- **1/8 teaspoon salt**

Cut melon half into 16 wedges. On eight salad plates, arrange the greens, turkey, melon, blueberries, pine nuts and blue cheese.

In a blender, combine the vinaigrette ingredients; cover and process for 2-3 minutes or until blended. Drizzle over the salads. Serve immediately. **Yield:** 8 servings (1-1/3 cups vinaigrette).

Turkey Salad with Blueberry Vinaigrette

Confetti Mashed Potatoes

Confetti Mashed Potatoes

(Pictured above)

Prep/Total Time: 25 min.

When ordinary mashed potatoes just won't do, try this tasty twist that features Mexican-style cheese, onion and bright peppers. It gives you all the homey comfort of the traditional dish but adds flavor and color.
—LaDonna Reed, Ponca City, Oklahoma

- **6 medium red potatoes, cubed**
- **3 tablespoons chopped sweet red pepper**
- **3 tablespoons chopped green pepper**
- **3 tablespoons finely chopped onion**
- **3/4 cup shredded Mexican cheese blend**
- **3 tablespoons butter, softened**
- **1/8 to 1/4 teaspoon salt**
- **1/8 to 1/4 teaspoon pepper**

Place the potatoes in a large saucepan and cover with water. Bring to a boil. Reduce heat; cover and cook for 5 minutes.

Add peppers and onion; cook 5 minutes longer or until potatoes and vegetables are tender. Drain; mash the potato mixture with cheese, butter, salt and pepper. **Yield:** 4 servings.

Seafood Pasta Salad

Prep/Total Time: 25 min.

This salad's sweet dressing has a bit of kick that blends perfectly with the pasta, seafood and veggies. It's a great dish when you need something for a get-together.
—Elizabeth Halfman, Davenport, Iowa

8 ounces uncooked spiral pasta
1/2 cup mayonnaise
1/2 cup Thousand Island salad dressing
3 to 4 drops hot pepper sauce
1 package (8 ounces) imitation crabmeat, chopped
1 package (5 ounces) frozen cooked salad shrimp, thawed
1 cup fresh broccoli florets
1 cup fresh caulifloweretts
1/2 cup diced celery

Cook pasta according to package directions. Meanwhile, in a large bowl, combine the mayonnaise, salad dressing and hot pepper sauce. Stir in the crab, shrimp, broccoli, cauliflower and celery.

Drain pasta and rinse in cold water. Gently stir into shrimp mixture. Cover and refrigerate until serving. **Yield:** 10 servings.

Salami Asparagus Salad

Prep: 20 min. + chilling

Everyone oohs and aahs when I take this fresh asparagus medley to potlucks. At home, we often have it with sliced French bread and Brie cheese for a light supper.
—Patricia Smith, Golden, Colorado

1 pound fresh asparagus, trimmed
1/2 medium sweet red pepper, cut into 2-inch strips
1 small onion, thinly sliced and separated into rings
1/4 pound hard salami, cut into strips
1/2 cup crumbled feta cheese
1/3 cup olive oil
1/4 cup sugar
1/4 cup white vinegar
1/4 cup rice wine vinegar
1-1/2 teaspoons minced garlic
1/2 teaspoon salt
1/2 teaspoon dried basil

In a large skillet, bring 1 in. of water to a boil. Add asparagus; cover and cook for 3 minutes or until tender. Drain and immediately place in ice water. Drain and pat dry.

In a large bowl, combine the asparagus, red pepper, onion, salami and feta cheese. In a small bowl, whisk the remaining ingredients. Pour over the vegetable mixture and toss to coat.

Cover and refrigerate for at least 20 minutes, stirring occasionally. Serve the salad with a slotted spoon. **Yield:** 4 servings.

Garden Primavera Fettuccine

(Pictured below)

Prep/Total Time: 30 min.

I created this side dish while I was trying to make broccoli Alfredo. I just kept adding fresh veggies—and loved the result! *—Tammy Perrault, Lancaster, Ohio*

✓ This recipe includes Nutrition Facts and Diabetic Exchanges.

1 package (12 ounces) fettuccine
1 cup fresh caulifloweretts
1 cup fresh broccoli florets
1/2 cup julienned carrot
1 small sweet red pepper, julienned
1/2 small yellow summer squash, sliced
1/2 small zucchini, sliced
1 cup Alfredo sauce
1 teaspoon dried basil
Shredded Parmesan cheese, optional

In a large saucepan, cook the fettuccine according to the package directions, adding the vegetables during the last 4 minutes. Drain and return to the pan.

Add Alfredo sauce and basil; toss to coat. Cook over low heat for 1-2 minutes or until heated through. Sprinkle with the cheese if desired. **Yield:** 10 servings.

Nutrition Facts: 3/4 cup (calculated without cheese) equals 165 calories, 3 g fat (2 g saturated fat), 7 mg cholesterol, 121 mg sodium, 28 g carbohydrate, 3 g fiber, 7 g protein. **Diabetic Exchanges:** 2 starch, 1/2 fat.

Garden Primavera Fettuccine

Carrot Tortellini Salad

Bacon-Almond Green Beans

Prep/Total Time: 30 min.

I adapted this recipe from one in a magazine. The new version is much quicker to prepare than the original but still tastes great. —Jackie Matthews, Yucca Valley, California

1-1/2 pounds fresh green beans, trimmed and cut into 1-1/2-inch pieces
3 tablespoons butter
3 tablespoons brown sugar
2-1/4 teaspoons soy sauce
2-1/4 teaspoons Worcestershire sauce
4 to 5 tablespoons real bacon bits
4 to 5 tablespoons sliced almonds, toasted

Place beans in a large saucepan and cover with water. Bring to a boil; cook, uncovered, for 8-10 minutes or until crisp-tender.

Meanwhile, melt the butter in a large skillet over medium heat. Stir in the brown sugar, soy sauce and Worcestershire sauce. Cook for 1 minute or until the sugar is dissolved.

Drain the beans; add to the skillet. Cook and stir for 2 minutes or until heated through. Sprinkle with bacon and almonds; toss to coat. Serve with a slotted spoon. **Yield:** 6 servings.

Greek Tossed Salad

Prep/Total Time: 15 min.

When I brought this to a work luncheon, everyone raved about it. Using convenience items makes it a time-saver, too. —Susan Harman, Pacifica, California

4 cups spring mix salad greens
1 cup sliced fresh mushrooms
1 cup cherry tomatoes
1 cup pitted ripe olives, drained
1 cup (4 ounces) crumbled feta cheese
1/4 cup sliced pepperoncinis
2/3 cup creamy Parmesan Romano salad dressing

In a large salad bowl, combine the first six ingredients. Drizzle with dressing and toss to coat. Serve immediately. **Yield:** 5 servings.

Editor's Note: Look for pepperoncinis (pickled peppers) in the pickle/olive section of your grocery store.

Carrot Tortellini Salad

(Pictured above)

Prep: 20 min. + chilling

Two kinds of tortellini, crunchy carrots and fresh basil star in this pasta salad. When you're craving something different, try this! —Hasel King, Nacogdoches, Texas

1 package (10 ounces) refrigerated cheese-filled spinach tortellini
1 package (9 ounces) refrigerated cheese-filled tortellini
2 medium carrots, thinly sliced
2/3 cup Italian salad dressing
2 green onions, sliced
8 to 12 small fresh basil leaves
1 tablespoon grated Parmesan cheese
1/4 teaspoon pepper

Cook both types of tortellini according to package directions. Drain and rinse in cold water.

In a large bowl, combine tortellini and remaining ingredients. Cover and refrigerate for 2 hours before serving, stirring occasionally. **Yield:** 7 servings.

Best Bean Dish

PLAN TO MAKE Bacon-Almond Green Beans (recipe at top)? Keep in mind that 1-1/2 pounds of fresh green beans equals about 6 cups cut up.

To trim fresh green beans quickly, simply place the beans on your cutting board and line up the ends. Then use a chef's knife to slice several at a time.

Want to give your bean dish added crispness? Try tossing in some sliced water chestnuts.

Feta Salmon Salad

(Pictured below)

Prep/Total Time: 25 min.

My son, David, always ordered the salmon sandwich at a local pub. Trying to duplicate that favorite at home, he came up with this salad instead. It's the only recipe he's ever created—and our whole family thinks it's terrific!
—Susan Griffiths, Mt. Pleasant, South Carolina

1/4 teaspoon salt
1/4 teaspoon garlic powder
1/4 teaspoon ground ginger
1/4 teaspoon dried parsley flakes
1/4 teaspoon pepper
4 salmon fillets (6 ounces *each*)
1 package (5 ounces) spring mix salad greens
1 large cucumber, chopped
1 large tomato, chopped
1/2 cup crumbled feta cheese
1/4 cup red wine vinaigrette

Coat the grill rack with cooking spray before starting the grill. Combine the seasonings; sprinkle over the salmon fillets. Grill, covered, over medium heat or broil 4 in. from the heat for 8-12 minutes or until the fish flakes easily with a fork.

In a large bowl, combine the salad greens, cucumber, tomato and feta cheese; divide among four plates. Top with salmon; drizzle with vinaigrette. **Yield:** 4 servings.

Feta Salmon Salad

Berry Gelatin Mold

Berry Gelatin Mold

(Pictured above)

Prep: 15 min. + chilling

This refreshing gelatin is always a hit. Sometimes I add a scoop of whipped topping for festive, red-white-and-blue color. *—Anne Marie Papineau, Hanover, Connecticut*

✓ This recipe includes Nutrition Facts and Diabetic Exchanges.

2 packages (3 ounces *each*) strawberry gelatin
2 cups boiling cranberry juice
1-1/2 cups club soda, chilled
1 teaspoon lemon juice
1 cup *each* fresh blueberries, raspberries and sliced strawberries
Lettuce leaves
Additional mixed fresh berries, optional

In a large bowl, dissolve the gelatin in boiling cranberry juice. Let stand for 10 minutes. Stir in the club soda and lemon juice; refrigerate for 45 minutes or until partially set.

Fold in the berries. Pour into a 6-cup ring mold coated with cooking spray. Refrigerate for 4 hours or until set. Unmold onto a lettuce-lined platter; fill center with additional berries if desired. **Yield:** 8 servings.

Nutrition Facts: 1 slice (calculated without additional mixed berries) equals 131 calories, trace fat (trace saturated fat), 0 cholesterol, 59 mg sodium, 32 g carbohydrate, 2 g fiber, 3 g protein. **Diabetic Exchanges:** 1 starch, 1 fruit.

Dilly Grilled Veggies

(Pictured below)

Prep/Total Time: 30 min.

A wonderfully delicate herb, dill works in a wide variety of recipes. I think it really enhances the grilled zucchini, mushrooms, broccoli and red pepper in this side dish. Give it a try in potato salad, white sauces and eggs, too.
—Fran Scott, Birmingham, Michigan

✓ This recipe includes Nutrition Facts and Diabetic Exchanges.

2 cups sliced fresh mushrooms
2 cups sliced fresh zucchini
2 cups fresh broccoli florets
1/2 medium sweet red pepper, cut into strips
2 tablespoons olive oil
2 tablespoons minced fresh dill *or* 2 teaspoons dill weed
1/8 teaspoon garlic salt
1/8 teaspoon pepper

Place vegetables on a double thickness of heavy-duty foil (about 18 in. square). Drizzle with oil; sprinkle with dill, garlic salt and pepper. Fold foil around vegetables and seal tightly.

Grill, covered, over medium heat for 15 minutes or until vegetables are tender. **Yield:** 6 servings.

Nutrition Facts: 3/4 cup equals 61 calories, 5 g fat (1 g saturated fat), 0 cholesterol, 49 mg sodium, 4 g carbohydrate, 2 g fiber, 2 g protein. **Diabetic Exchanges:** 1 vegetable, 1 fat.

Dilly Grilled Veggies

Savory Bean & Tomato Salad

Savory Bean & Tomato Salad

(Pictured above)

Prep/Total Time: 25 min.

I like using savory to spruce up everything from beans and fresh vegetables to rich cuts of meat. The homemade dressing for this side salad also boasts blue cheese, lime juice, minced garlic and pine nuts for crunch. Delicious!
—Carol Gano, Ballwin, Missouri

✓ This recipe includes Nutrition Facts and Diabetic Exchanges.

1 pound fresh green beans, trimmed
6 medium tomatoes (about 2 pounds), sliced
3 green onions, coarsely chopped

DRESSING:

1/4 cup lime juice
2 ounces crumbled blue cheese
5 teaspoons olive oil
1/2 teaspoon minced garlic
1/8 teaspoon salt
1/8 teaspoon pepper
1 tablespoon pine nuts
2 tablespoons fresh savory leaves

Place beans in a large saucepan and cover with water. Bring to a boil. Cook, uncovered, for 8-10 minutes or until crisp-tender.

Drain and immediately place the beans in ice water. Drain and pat dry. Cut into 2-in. pieces. Divide the tomatoes, green onions and cut green beans among six salad plates.

For dressing, in a blender, combine the lime juice, blue cheese, oil, garlic, salt and pepper until blended.

Drizzle over salads. Sprinkle with pine nuts and savory. **Yield:** 6 servings.

Nutrition Facts: 1 serving equals 138 calories, 8 g fat (2 g saturated fat), 7 mg cholesterol, 201 mg sodium, 15 g carbohydrate, 5 g fiber, 5 g protein. **Diabetic Exchanges:** 3 vegetable, 1-1/2 fat.

Raspberry-Turkey Spinach Salad

Prep/Total Time: 20 min.

This fruity main-dish medley is a lunchtime favorite on hot, lazy summer days. If you like, try substituting cooked chicken for the turkey...or replace the raspberry flavors by using strawberries and strawberry preserves.
—Priscilla Gilbert, Indian Harbour Beach, Florida

✓ This recipe includes Nutrition Facts and Diabetic Exchanges.

- **4 cups fresh baby spinach**
- **2 cups cubed cooked smoked turkey**
- **1 small red onion, thinly sliced and separated into rings**
- **1-1/2 cups fresh raspberries**
- **1 can (11 ounces) mandarin oranges, drained**
- **1/2 cup red raspberry preserves**
- **2 tablespoons red wine vinegar**
- **1 teaspoon grated lemon peel**

Divide the spinach, turkey, onion, raspberries and oranges among four serving plates. In a microwave-safe bowl, heat the preserves, vinegar and peel until preserves are melted, stirring once; cool slightly. Drizzle over salads. **Yield:** 4 servings.

Nutrition Facts: 1 serving equals 259 calories, 2 g fat (trace saturated fat), 30 mg cholesterol, 666 mg sodium, 42 g carbohydrate, 5 g fiber, 20 g protein. **Diabetic Exchanges:** 3 very lean meat, 2 starch, 1/2 fruit.

Layered Italian Chicken Salad

Prep/Total Time: 30 min.

Want a new way to use up hard-cooked eggs? This hearty salad from our Test Kitchen staff will help you do just that. And if you don't have any in the fridge, you may want to cook some especially for this recipe!

- **1 medium head iceberg lettuce, torn**
- **1 medium red onion, chopped**
- **1 jar (12 ounces) roasted sweet red peppers, sliced**
- **3 hard-cooked eggs, sliced**
- **1 can (15 ounces) white kidney *or* cannellini beans, rinsed and drained**
- **1 can (3.8 ounces) sliced ripe olives, drained**
- **3 cups cubed cooked chicken breast**
- **1 cup halved grape tomatoes**
- **1 cup (4 ounces) shredded Italian cheese blend**
- **1/4 cup pine nuts, toasted**
- **Italian salad dressing of your choice**

In a 3-1/2-qt. bowl, layer the first 10 ingredients in the order listed. Pour dressing over salad; toss to coat. **Yield:** 8 servings.

Picnic Vegetable Salad

(Pictured below)

Prep/Total Time: 30 min.

When I take this dish to my husband's company picnic, I never have any leftovers—just a lot of requests for the recipe! To save time, fix it a day in advance. You could also add diced cooked chicken and pasta to turn it into a meal.
—Diana Porter, Pelion, South Carolina

- **3 cups fresh broccoli florets**
- **3 cups fresh cauliflowerets**
- **2 cups cherry tomatoes, halved**
- **2 medium cucumbers, cut into chunks**
- **1 *each* medium green, sweet yellow and red pepper, cut into chunks**
- **6 green onions, thinly sliced**
- **1 can (6 ounces) pitted ripe olives, drained and halved**
- **1 bottle (16 ounces) Greek vinaigrette**
- **1 cup (4 ounces) crumbled feta cheese**

In a large bowl, combine the broccoli, cauliflowerets, tomatoes, cucumbers, peppers, green onions and ripe olives. Drizzle with salad dressing; toss to coat. Chill until serving. Just before serving, sprinkle with cheese. **Yield:** 18 servings.

Picnic Vegetable Salad

Hot Chicken Salad

Hot Chicken Salad

(Pictured above)

Prep: 15 min. **Bake:** 30 min.

This creamy mix of veggies and chicken is topped with crispy potato chips. The whole family will love this comforting dish—and you'll love its oh-so-fast preparation!
—Bernice Knutson, Danbury, Iowa

- **1 package (9 ounces) frozen diced cooked chicken breast, thawed**
- **2 cups thinly sliced celery**
- **1 can (8 ounces) sliced water chestnuts, drained**
- **1/2 cup chopped almonds**
- **1/3 cup chopped green pepper**
- **1 jar (2 ounces) diced pimientos, drained**
- **2 tablespoons finely chopped onion**
- **2/3 cup shredded Swiss cheese, *divided***
- **1 cup mayonnaise**
- **2 tablespoons lemon juice**
- **1/2 teaspoon salt**
- **2 cups crushed potato chips**

In a large bowl, combine the chicken, celery, water chestnuts, almonds, green pepper, pimientos, onion and 1/3 cup cheese. In a small bowl, combine the mayonnaise, lemon juice and salt. Stir into chicken mixture until blended.

Transfer to a greased 8-in. square baking dish. Bake, uncovered, at 350° for 20 minutes.

Sprinkle with potato chips and remaining cheese. Bake 10-15 minutes longer or until heated through and cheese is melted. **Yield:** 4 servings.

Mandarin Romaine Salad

Prep/Total Time: 15 min.

Give tossed greens luscious flavor, a touch of heat, plenty of crunch and a citrus sparkle with this recipe. When I need an impressive but family-pleasing salad for Christmas dinner or another special occasion, this is the one I turn to.
—Barbara Carlucci, Orange Park, Florida

- **9 cups torn romaine**
- **1 can (11 ounces) mandarin oranges, drained**
- **1 can (8 ounces) sliced water chestnuts, drained**
- **1 cup finely chopped celery**
- **2 green onions, thinly sliced**
- **6 tablespoons vegetable oil**
- **3 tablespoons sugar**
- **3 tablespoons raspberry vinegar**
- **1-1/2 teaspoons dried parsley flakes**
- **3/4 teaspoon salt**
- **3/4 teaspoon pepper**
- **1/4 to 1/2 teaspoon hot pepper sauce**
- **1/2 cup chopped pecans**

In a large bowl, combine the first five ingredients. In a jar with a tight-fitting lid, combine the oil, sugar, raspberry vinegar, parsley, salt, pepper and pepper sauce; shake well.

Just before serving, sprinkle the salad with pecans. Shake dressing and pour over salad; toss to coat. **Yield:** 12 servings.

Zucchini Parmesan

Prep/Total Time: 25 min.

Here's an easy-to-assemble side that's absolutely delicious. I think it's best when the zucchini comes fresh out of the garden.
—Sandi Guettler, Bay City, Michigan

- **1/2 to 1 teaspoon minced garlic**
- **1 tablespoon olive oil**
- **4 medium zucchini, cut into 1/4-inch slices**
- **1 can (14-1/2 ounces) Italian diced tomatoes, undrained**
- **1 teaspoon seasoned salt**
- **1/4 teaspoon pepper**
- **1/4 cup grated Parmesan cheese**

In a large skillet, saute garlic in oil. Add zucchini; cook and stir for 4-5 minutes or until crisp-tender.

Stir in the tomatoes, seasoned salt and pepper. Simmer, uncovered, for 9-10 minutes or until the liquid is absorbed and the mixture is heated through. Sprinkle with the Parmesan cheese. Serve with a slotted spoon. **Yield:** 6 servings.

Chicken Caesar Salad

(Pictured below)

Prep/Total Time: 30 min.

A homemade dressing sets this hard-to-resist Caesar salad apart from other versions—but doesn't make it time-consuming to prepare. With Parmesan cheese, romaine and chicken strips, it's a true classic...only better!
—Rebecca Porter, Yigo, Guam

4 boneless skinless chicken breast halves (about 1 pound)
1/2 cup shredded Parmesan cheese, *divided*
1 tablespoon lemon juice
1 teaspoon minced garlic
1 teaspoon Worcestershire sauce
1/4 teaspoon ground mustard
1/8 teaspoon pepper
1/4 cup olive oil
8 cups hearts of romaine salad mix
2 hard-cooked eggs, sliced
1 cup Caesar salad croutons

Place chicken on a greased broiler pan. Broil 6 in. from the heat for 7-8 minutes on each side or until juices run clear. Cut chicken into strips; set aside.

Meanwhile, in a blender, combine 1/4 cup Parmesan cheese, lemon juice, garlic, Worcestershire sauce, mustard and pepper. Cover and process until blended. While processing, gradually add oil in a steady stream.

Place romaine in a large salad bowl. Add Parmesan cheese mixture; toss to coat. Top with chicken strips, eggs, croutons and remaining Parmesan cheese. **Yield:** 4 servings.

Chicken Caesar Salad

Salami Pasta Salad

Salami Pasta Salad

(Pictured above)

Prep/Total Time: 20 min.

The first time I tasted this wonderful medley was at my wedding. I still recall that I noticed—even in the blur of that day—that the salad was in high demand. Now, years later, I'm still asked to bring it to backyard cookouts and parties. I usually double the recipe to keep some for us.
—Sarah Ryan, Geneva, Ohio

2 cups uncooked small pasta shells
3/4 cup chopped green pepper
3/4 cup chopped fresh tomatoes
1/2 cup chopped pepperoni
1/2 cup cubed hard salami
1/2 cup whole ripe olives, quartered
2 ounces provolone cheese, cubed
1/3 cup chopped onion
DRESSING:
1/3 cup vegetable oil
1/4 cup red wine vinegar
2 tablespoons sugar
1-1/2 teaspoons salt
1-1/2 teaspoons dried oregano
1/2 teaspoon pepper

Cook the pasta according to the package directions; drain and rinse in cold water. Place in a large bowl; add the green pepper, tomatoes, pepperoni, salami, olives, cheese and onion.

In a jar with a tight-fitting lid, combine the dressing ingredients; shake well. Pour over the pasta mixture; toss to coat. Cover salad and refrigerate until serving. **Yield:** 9 servings.

Apple Stuffing

Apple Stuffing

(Pictured above)

Prep/Total Time: 15 min.

I add fruit and veggies to give stuffing mix a flavor that's anything but ordinary. It's a simple alternative to from-scratch versions. —Terri McKitrick, Delafield, Wisconsin

1 medium tart apple, chopped
1/2 cup chopped onion
1/4 cup chopped celery
1 tablespoon butter
1 package (6 ounces) stuffing mix

In a large skillet, saute the apple, onion and celery in butter until tender. Prepare the mix according to package directions. Stir in apple mixture. **Yield:** 5 servings.

Layered Southwestern Chicken Salad

Prep/Total Time: 30 min.

This beautiful salad is pretty enough to be a centerpiece and goes together in a snap. Guests will think you spent hours on it! —Marci Dietrich, Fairfax Station, Virginia

1/2 cup lime juice
1/2 cup sour cream
1/3 cup fresh cilantro leaves
2 tablespoons sugar
1/2 teaspoon salt
1/2 teaspoon pepper
1/2 cup olive oil
1 package (10 ounces) hearts of romaine salad mix
1 medium tomato, chopped
1 can (15 ounces) black beans, rinsed and drained
1 small red onion, chopped
2 packages (6 ounces *each*) ready-to-use Southwestern chicken strips
2 cups (8 ounces) shredded Mexican cheese blend
1 can (11 ounces) Mexicorn, drained
1 can (6 ounces) sliced ripe olives, drained
2 cups coarsely crushed tortilla chips
Additional fresh cilantro leaves

For the dressing, combine the first six ingredients in a blender; cover and process until smooth. While processing, gradually add oil in a steady stream. Transfer to a small bowl; cover and refrigerate until serving.

In a 4-qt. glass salad bowl, layer the remaining ingredients in the order listed. Serve with dressing. **Yield:** 8 servings.

Mashed Potatoes with a Kick

(Pictured below)

Prep/Total Time: 30 min.

These are absolutely my favorite potatoes. A handful of ingredients, a pot and a bowl are all you need to fix this home-style side. —Valerie Belley, St. Louis, Missouri

10 medium potatoes (3 pounds), peeled and cubed
1 cup heavy whipping cream
1/4 cup butter, cubed
2 tablespoons prepared horseradish
1 teaspoon salt
1 teaspoon pepper

Place potatoes in a Dutch oven and cover with water. Bring to a boil. Reduce heat; cover and cook for 15-20 minutes or until tender. Drain.

In a large mixing bowl, mash potatoes with remaining ingredients. **Yield:** 8 servings.

Mashed Potatoes with a Kick

Orange-Glazed Beets

Orange-Glazed Beets

(Pictured above)

Prep/Total Time: 25 min.

Beets were a popular vegetable in our house when I was growing up, and this side-dish recipe is one of the best we ever had. It's very easy to prepare in less than half an hour, and the tangy citrus glaze delights everyone who tastes it.
—Susan Punzal, Orchard Park, New York

✓ This recipe includes Nutrition Facts and Diabetic Exchanges.

3/4 cup orange marmalade
6 tablespoons orange juice
1/3 cup butter, cubed
1/4 teaspoon salt
1/4 teaspoon pepper
3 cans (14-1/2 ounces *each*) sliced beets, drained

In a large skillet, combine the first five ingredients. Bring to a boil; cook and stir for 3-4 minutes or until thickened. Add the beets; cook and stir 6-8 minutes longer or until most of the liquid is absorbed. **Yield:** 8 servings.

Nutrition Facts: 1/2 cup equals 194 calories, 8 g fat (5 g saturated fat), 20 mg cholesterol, 443 mg sodium, 32 g carbohydrate, 3 g fiber, 2 g protein. **Diabetic Exchanges:** 1-1/2 fat, 1 vegetable, 1 fruit, 1/2 starch.

Honey-Pineapple Sweet Potatoes

(Pictured below)

Prep: 20 min. **Bake:** 25 min.

Pineapple chunks give an unexpected yet tongue-tingling burst of tartness to these sweet potatoes. If you like, add some pecans for another layer of flavor people will love.
—Paula Mayo, Feedings Hills, Massachusetts

✓ This recipe includes Nutrition Facts and Diabetic Exchanges.

3 pounds sweet potatoes, peeled and cut into 3/4-inch cubes
1 cup water
1 can (8 ounces) crushed pineapple
1 can (8 ounces) pineapple chunks, drained
1/4 cup honey
1/2 cup coarsely chopped pecans, optional

Place sweet potatoes and water in a 2-qt. microwave-safe dish. Cover and microwave on high for 8-10 minutes or until potatoes are tender; drain.

Drain crushed pineapple, reserving juice. In a large bowl, combine the crushed pineapple, pineapple chunks and sweet potatoes. Transfer to a 2-1/2-qt. baking dish coated with cooking spray. In a small bowl, combine honey and reserved juice; pour over sweet potatoes.

Bake, uncovered, at 350° for 10 minutes. Stir; sprinkle with pecans if desired. Bake 15-20 minutes longer or until heated through. **Yield:** 13 servings.

Editor's Note: This recipe was tested in a 1,100-watt microwave.

Nutrition Facts: 3/4 cup (calculated without pecans) equals 105 calories, trace fat (trace saturated fat), 0 cholesterol, 7 mg sodium, 26 g carbohydrate, 2 g fiber, 1 g protein. **Diabetic Exchange:** 2 starch.

Honey-Pineapple Sweet Potatoes

Chapter 9

Breads in a Jiffy

WHO SAYS today's busy cooks don't have the time to prepare their own golden, homemade baked goods? You'll see those mouth-watering treats are well within reach when you page through this chapter!

Turn your kitchen into an aromatic bakery in a snap with delights such as Cranberry Banana Bread, Rhubarb Lemon Muffins and Pull-Apart Caramel Coffee Cake. And don't forget savory favorites such as Garlic-Cheese Crescent Rolls and Fresh Herb Flat Bread.

Most of the recipes are either ready to eat or ready to bake in under 30 minutes. Choose one for your next family meal...and watch eyes light up!

FRESH FROM THE OVEN. Peach Cobbler Coffee Cake (p. 154).

Surprise Monkey Bread

Surprise Monkey Bread

(Pictured above)

Prep: 25 min. **Bake:** 40 min.

This recipe is really just a glorified monkey bread, but it's so good! When my neighbor has her Christmas brunch, this is always her request. I've also made it with garlic and cheese for dinner. —*Lois Rutherford, Elkton, Florida*

1 cup packed brown sugar
1/2 cup butter, cubed
2 tubes (12 ounces *each*) refrigerated flaky buttermilk biscuits
1/2 cup sugar
1 tablespoon ground cinnamon
1 package (8 ounces) cream cheese, cut into 20 cubes
1-1/2 cups chopped walnuts

In a small microwave-safe bowl, heat the brown sugar and butter on high for 1 minute or until the sugar is dissolved; set aside.

Flatten each biscuit into a 3-in. circle. Combine the sugar and cinnamon; sprinkle 1/2 teaspoon in the center of each biscuit. Top with a cream cheese cube. Fold dough over filling; pinch the edges to seal tightly.

Sprinkle 1/2 cup walnuts into a greased 10-in. fluted tube pan. Layer with half of the biscuits, cinnamon-sugar and butter mixture and 1/2 cup walnuts. Repeat the layers.

Bake at 350° for 40-45 minutes or until golden brown. Immediately invert onto a serving platter. Serve warm. Refrigerate leftovers. **Yield:** 1 loaf.

Creamy Pumpkin-Filled Biscuits

(Pictured below)

Prep/Total Time: 30 min.

Refrigerator biscuits are the speedy key to these fried, pie-inspired goodies. With their warm and creamy pumpkin filling, they'll invite you to take bite after bite. —*Michelle Kester, Cleveland, Ohio*

1 package (8 ounces) cream cheese, softened
1 cup canned pumpkin
1/2 cup cold milk
1/2 cup whipped topping
1 package (3.4 ounces) instant vanilla pudding mix
1/2 teaspoon pumpkin pie spice
1 tube (17.3 ounces) large refrigerated flaky biscuits
Oil for deep-fat frying
Confectioners' sugar, optional

In a small mixing bowl, beat the first six ingredients until smooth; set aside. On a lightly floured surface, roll out each biscuit into a 6-in. circle. Spread 1/3 cup cream cheese mixture on half of each biscuit. Bring dough from opposite side over filling just until edges meet; pinch seams to seal.

In a deep-fat fryer, heat oil to 375°. Fry biscuits, a few at a time, for 1-2 minutes on each side or until golden brown. Drain on paper towels. Dust with confectioners' sugar while warm if desired. Serve immediately. **Yield:** 8 servings.

Creamy Pumpkin-Filled Biscuits

Caraway Beer Bread

Prep: 10 min. **Bake:** 40 min. + cooling

This tender loaf boasts a mild beer-and-caraway taste that holds its own alongside soups and hearty main dishes. It's also delicious with ham salad or cream cheese.
—Janet Newmyer, Wilber, Nebraska

2-1/2 cups biscuit/baking mix
2 tablespoons sugar
1 teaspoon caraway seeds
2 eggs
1 cup beer *or* nonalcoholic beer
3 tablespoons butter, melted

In a large bowl, combine the biscuit mix, sugar and caraway seeds. In a small bowl, whisk the eggs, beer and butter until smooth. Stir into the dry ingredients just until moistened.

Pour into a greased 9-in. x 5-in. x 3-in. loaf pan. Bake at 350° for 40-45 minutes or until a toothpick inserted near the center comes out clean. Cool for 10 minutes before removing to a wire rack. **Yield:** 1 loaf.

Cinnamon Raisin Coffee Cake

Prep/Total Time: 30 min.

When you want a nice sweet bread to serve at brunch or bring to friends, this is it. No one believes it's a 30-minute recipe—but it is, thanks to the refrigerated dough.
—Bev Credle, Hampton, Virginia

1/4 cup sugar
2 teaspoons ground cinnamon
2 tubes (12.4 ounces *each*) refrigerated cinnamon roll dough
1/2 cup chopped pecans
3 to 4 tablespoons raisins

In a small bowl, combine sugar and cinnamon. Set aside icing packet from cinnamon rolls.

Separate the cinnamon roll dough into 16 rolls; cut each roll into quarters. Place half of the roll pieces, cinnamon side up, in a lightly greased 11-in. x 7-in. x 2-in. baking dish. Sprinkle with the chopped pecans, raisins and half of the cinnamon-sugar mixture. Top with remaining roll pieces. Sprinkle with remaining cinnamon-sugar mixture.

Bake at 375° for 25-30 minutes or until golden brown. Spread with the reserved icing; serve warm. **Yield:** 8 servings.

Speedy Softening

To soften cold sticks of butter quickly for use in baked goods or other recipes, I microwave the sticks at 70 percent power in 10-second intervals from two to four times. The butter is softened and ready to use.
—Patricia Winn, Freeville, New York

Mini Toffee Rolls

Mini Toffee Rolls

(Pictured above)

Prep: 20 min. **Bake:** 15 min.

I discovered this in a magazine years ago and adapted the original recipe to make it my own. The bite-sized treats are full of cinnamon flavor and terrific with coffee.
—Carol Gillespie, Chambersburg, Pennsylvania

6 tablespoons butter, softened
1/2 cup packed brown sugar
1 teaspoon ground cinnamon
1/3 cup English toffee bits *or* almond brickle chips
2 tubes (8 ounces *each*) refrigerated crescent rolls
1 cup confectioners' sugar
4-1/2 teaspoons milk
1/4 teaspoon vanilla extract

In a small mixing bowl, cream the butter, brown sugar and cinnamon until light and fluffy. Stir in toffee bits.

Separate each tube of crescent dough into four rectangles; seal perforations. Spread evenly with the butter mixture. Roll up each rectangle jelly-roll style, starting with a long side.

Cut each into six 1-in. slices; place cut side down into two greased 8-in. square baking dishes. Bake at 375° for 14-16 minutes or until golden brown.

In a small bowl, combine the confectioners' sugar, milk and vanilla until smooth. Drizzle over warm rolls. **Yield:** 4 dozen.

Pumpkin Oat Muffins

(Pictured below)

Prep: 15 min. **Bake:** 20 min.

With this mouth-watering recipe, you can enjoy the taste of classic pumpkin pie in easy-to-eat muffins. At my house, it just isn't "officially" considered Thanksgiving or Christmas until these fresh-from-the-oven goodies are on the table!
—Carol Hale, Sarver, Pennsylvania

1 cup all-purpose flour
1/2 cup packed brown sugar
2 teaspoons baking powder
1 teaspoon pumpkin pie spice
1/2 teaspoon salt
1/4 teaspoon baking soda
1 egg, lightly beaten
3/4 cup canned pumpkin
1/4 cup milk
1/4 cup vegetable oil
1 cup old-fashioned oats
1/2 cup raisins
TOPPING:
1/3 cup packed brown sugar
1 tablespoon all-purpose flour
3/4 teaspoon pumpkin pie spice
1 tablespoon cold butter

In a large bowl, combine the first six ingredients. Combine the egg, pumpkin, milk and oil; add to the dry ingredients just until moistened. Stir in oats and raisins.

Pumpkin Oat Muffins

Fill greased or paper-lined muffin cups two-thirds full. In a small bowl, combine the brown sugar, flour and pie spice; cut in butter until crumbly. Sprinkle 1 rounded teaspoonful over each muffin. Bake at 375° for 15-20 minutes or until a toothpick comes out clean.

Cool for 5 minutes before removing from pan to a wire rack. Serve warm. **Yield:** 1 dozen.

Pesto Parmesan Bread

Prep: 15 min. + rising **Bake:** 20 min. + cooling

This large, round bread has a mild Parmesan-pesto flavor and a light texture. Try a loaf to round out your next Italian meal. *—Michele Burns, St. Albert, Alberta*

✓ This recipe includes Nutrition Facts and Diabetic Exchanges.

1-1/3 cups water (70° to 80°)
2 tablespoons butter, softened
4-1/2 teaspoons sugar
1-1/2 teaspoons salt
4 cups bread flour
2 tablespoons nonfat dry milk powder
3 teaspoons active dry yeast
1/4 cup grated Parmesan cheese
2 tablespoons prepared pesto
2 teaspoons olive oil

In bread machine pan, place the first seven ingredients in order suggested by manufacturer. Select dough setting (check dough after 5 minutes of mixing; add 1 to 2 tablespoons of water or flour if needed). Just before the final kneading (your machine may audibly signal this), add the Parmesan and pesto.

When the cycle is completed, turn the dough onto a lightly floured surface. Shape into a ball. Place on a baking sheet coated with cooking spray; brush with oil. Cover and let rise in a warm place until doubled, about 30 minutes.

Bake at 375° for 20-25 minutes or until golden brown. Remove bread to a wire rack to cool. **Yield:** 1 loaf (2 pounds, 16 slices).

Editor's Note: If your bread machine has a time-delay feature, we recommend you do not use it for this recipe.

Nutrition Facts: 1 slice equals 143 calories, 3 g fat (1 g saturated fat), 6 mg cholesterol, 279 mg sodium, 24 g carbohydrate, 1 g fiber, 6 g protein. **Diabetic Exchanges:** 1-1/2 starch, 1/2 fat.

Fast and Fresh

WHEN YOU WANT fresh muffins in the morning, do some of the prep work the night before, combining dry ingredients in a plastic bag and measuring any other ingredients that will hold. The following morning, you can quickly stir together the batter, pop the muffins in the oven and enjoy a just-baked treat.

Garlic-Cheese Crescent Rolls

Onion Cheese Biscuits

(Pictured below)

Prep/Total Time: 30 min.

Our Test Kitchen cooks whipped up these made-from-scratch buttermilk biscuits in a mere 30 minutes. With two kinds of cheese, the melt-in-your-mouth bites are simple enough for weekdays but special enough for guests.

2 cups all-purpose flour
1 tablespoon sugar
2 teaspoons baking powder
1 teaspoon onion powder
1 teaspoon garlic powder
1/4 teaspoon salt
1/4 teaspoon baking soda
1/4 cup cold butter
2 cups (8 ounces) shredded cheddar-Monterey Jack cheese, *divided*
1/2 cup grated Parmesan cheese
1 cup buttermilk

In a large bowl, combine the flour, sugar, baking powder, onion powder, garlic powder, salt and baking soda. Cut in butter until mixture resembles coarse crumbs. Stir in 1-1/4 cups cheddar-Monterey Jack cheese and the Parmesan cheese. Stir in buttermilk just until moistened.

Turn onto a lightly floured surface; knead 6-8 times. Pat or roll out to 1/2-in. thickness; cut with a floured 2-1/2-in. biscuit cutter. Place 2 in. apart on a greased baking sheet. Sprinkle with remaining cheddar-Monterey Jack cheese. Bake at 400° for 10-15 minutes or until golden brown. Serve warm. **Yield:** 1 dozen.

Garlic-Cheese Crescent Rolls

(Pictured above)

Prep/Total Time: 20 min.

Roll recipes just don't get much quicker or simpler than this version. Garlic powder, oregano and Parmesan cheese really jazz up the refrigerated dough and create a tasty accompaniment for any main course. You may want to double the batch because they get snatched up fast!

—Lori Abad, East Haven, Connecticut

1 tube (8 ounces) refrigerated crescent rolls
3 tablespoons butter, melted
1-1/2 teaspoons garlic powder
1 teaspoon dried oregano
2 tablespoons grated Parmesan cheese

Separate the crescent dough into eight triangles. Roll up each from the wide end and place point side down 2 in. apart on an ungreased baking sheet. Curve the ends to form crescents.

Combine the melted butter, garlic powder and oregano; brush over the crescent rolls. Sprinkle with Parmesan cheese.

Bake at 375° for 10-12 minutes or until golden brown. Serve warm. **Yield:** 8 servings.

Onion Cheese Biscuits

Cranberry Banana Bread

Pour into a greased 8-in. x 4-in. x 2-in. loaf pan.

Bake at 350° for 50-55 minutes or until a toothpick inserted near the center comes out clean. Cool for 10 minutes before removing from pan to a wire rack. **Yield:** 1 loaf (12 slices).

Pull-Apart Caramel Coffee Cake

(Pictured below)

Prep: 10 min. **Bake:** 25 min.

The first time I made this gooey treat for a brunch, it was a huge hit. Now I get requests every time family or friends do anything around the breakfast hour!
—Jaime Keeling, Keizer, Oregon

✓ This recipe includes Nutrition Facts.

- **2 tubes (12 ounces *each*) refrigerated flaky buttermilk biscuits**
- **1 cup packed brown sugar**
- **1/2 cup heavy whipping cream**
- **1 teaspoon ground cinnamon**

Cut each biscuit into four pieces; arrange evenly in a 10-in. fluted tube pan coated with cooking spray. Combine the brown sugar, cream and cinnamon; pour over the biscuits.

Bake at 350° for 25-30 minutes or until golden brown. Cool for 5 minutes before inverting onto a serving platter. **Yield:** 12 servings.

Nutrition Facts: 1 slice equals 240 calories, 5 g fat (3 g saturated fat), 14 mg cholesterol, 496 mg sodium, 45 g carbohydrate, trace fiber, 5 g protein.

Cranberry Banana Bread

(Pictured above)

Prep: 25 min. **Bake:** 50 min. + cooling

Dotted with dried cranberries and walnuts, these moist, golden loaves make wonderful breakfast treats and gifts for friends. *—Eva Rider, Montgomery, Alabama*

- **1/3 cup shortening**
- **2/3 cup sugar**
- **2 eggs**
- **1 cup mashed ripe bananas (about 2 medium)**
- **1-1/2 cups all-purpose flour**
- **1/3 cup cinnamon graham cracker crumbs (about 2 whole crackers)**
- **1-1/2 teaspoons baking powder**
- **1/2 teaspoon baking soda**
- **1/2 teaspoon salt**
- **1/2 cup chopped walnuts *or* pecans**
- **1/2 cup dried cranberries**

In a large mixing bowl, cream the shortening and sugar until light and fluffy. Add the eggs, one at a time, beating well after each addition. Stir in the bananas. Combine the flour, graham cracker crumbs, baking powder, baking soda and salt; gradually add to the creamed mixture. Fold in the nuts and cranberries.

Pull-Apart Caramel Coffee Cake

Fresh Herb Flat Bread

Fresh Herb Flat Bread

(Pictured above)

Prep/Total Time: 25 min.

There's no mistaking the piney aroma of rosemary—a little of this potent herb goes a long way! Although there's much more basil in this recipe, you'll taste a strong rosemary flavor in this delicious bread that's sprinkled with Parmesan cheese.
—Bev Credle, Hampton, Virginia

☑ This recipe includes Nutrition Facts and Diabetic Exchanges.

1 tube (8 ounces) refrigerated crescent rolls
1/4 cup fresh basil leaves, thinly sliced
1-1/2 teaspoons minced fresh rosemary
1 egg, beaten
1 tablespoon grated Parmesan cheese

Unroll crescent dough and separate into two rectangles. On a lightly floured surface, roll each into a 10-in. x 7-in. rectangle, sealing seams and perforations.

Place one rectangle on an ungreased baking sheet. Sprinkle basil and rosemary to within 1/2 in. of edges. Top with remaining dough; pinch edges to seal. Brush with egg; sprinkle with Parmesan cheese.

Bake at 375° for 10-12 minutes or until golden brown. Cut into slices. Serve warm. **Yield:** 10 servings.

Nutrition Facts: 1 slice equals 99 calories, 6 g fat (1 g saturated fat), 22 mg cholesterol, 193 mg sodium, 9 g carbohydrate, trace fiber, 2 g protein. **Diabetic Exchanges:** 1 fat, 1/2 starch.

Cinnamon Raisin Bread

(Pictured below)

Prep: 15 min. **Bake:** 55 min. + cooling

Plenty of cinnamon and raisins bring heartwarming, homey flavor to this mildly sweet loaf. It's ideal anytime you need an on-the-go breakfast or a fast snack before dinnertime. You'll want to bake it for holidays, too—the swirled slices are so pretty and special-looking.
—Flo Burtnett, Gage, Oklahoma

4 cups all-purpose flour
2 teaspoons baking soda
1 teaspoon salt
2 cups sugar, *divided*
1/2 cup vegetable oil
2 eggs
2 cups buttermilk
1/2 cup raisins
3 teaspoons ground cinnamon

In a large bowl, combine the flour, baking soda and salt. In a mixing bowl, beat 1-1/2 cups sugar and oil. Beat in the eggs and buttermilk until combined. Stir egg mixture into the dry ingredients just until moistened. Fold in the raisins. Combine the cinnamon and remaining sugar; set aside.

Spoon half of the bread batter into two greased 8-in. x 4-in. x 2-in. loaf pans. Sprinkle with half of the reserved cinnamon-sugar; repeat layers. Cut through batter with a knife to swirl.

Bake at 350° for 55-60 minutes or until a toothpick inserted near the center comes out clean. Cool in pans for 10 minutes before removing from pans to wire racks. **Yield:** 2 loaves (12 slices each).

Cinnamon Raisin Bread

Peach Cobbler Coffee Cake

(Pictured above and on page 146)

Prep: 25 min. **Bake:** 70 min. + cooling

"Absolutely delicious" is how people describe this coffee cake, which has the yummy flavor of a peach cobbler. Served warm, the crumb-topped and drizzled cake is an extra-special treat. —Virginia Krites, Cridersville, Ohio

1 cup butter, softened
1 cup sugar
2 eggs
3 teaspoons vanilla extract
3 cups all-purpose flour
1 teaspoon baking powder
1 teaspoon baking soda
1/2 teaspoon salt
1-1/4 cups sour cream
1 can (21 ounces) peach pie filling
1 can (15-1/4 ounces) sliced peaches, drained

TOPPING:

1 cup packed brown sugar
1 cup all-purpose flour
1/2 cup quick-cooking oats
1/4 teaspoon ground cinnamon
1/2 cup cold butter, cubed

GLAZE:

1 cup confectioners' sugar
1 to 2 tablespoons milk

In a large mixing bowl, cream the butter and sugar until light and fluffy. Add the eggs, one at a time, beating well after each addition. Beat in the vanilla. Combine the flour, baking powder, baking soda and salt; add to the creamed mixture alternately with sour cream. Beat just until combined.

Pour half of the batter into a greased 13-in. x 9-in. x 2-in. baking dish. Combine the pie filling and peaches; spread over batter. Drop remaining batter by tablespoonfuls over filling.

For topping, combine the brown sugar, flour, oats and cinnamon in a bowl. Cut in butter until mixture is crumbly. Sprinkle over batter.

Bake at 350° for 70-75 minutes or until a toothpick inserted near the center comes out clean. Cool on a wire rack. Combine glaze ingredients; drizzle over coffee cake. **Yield:** 12 servings.

Sour Cream & Chive Biscuits

Prep/Total Time: 20 min.

Chives add a mild onion taste to just about any recipe—including these tender biscuits, which go together quickly thanks to a baking mix. I think they're especially good fresh from the oven with a little butter or honey.
—Priscilla Gilbert, Indian Harbour Beach, Florida

✓ This recipe includes Nutrition Facts and Diabetic Exchanges.

3 cups biscuit/baking mix
3 tablespoons snipped chives
2/3 cup water
2/3 cup sour cream

In a large bowl, combine biscuit mix and chives. Stir in water and sour cream just until moistened.

Drop by heaping tablespoonfuls onto a baking sheet coated with cooking spray. Bake at 450° for 8-10 minutes or until lightly browned. Serve biscuits warm. **Yield:** 16 biscuits.

Nutrition Facts: 1 biscuit equals 112 calories, 5 g fat (2 g saturated fat), 7 mg cholesterol, 287 mg sodium, 14 g carbohydrate, trace fiber, 2 g protein. **Diabetic Exchanges:** 1 starch, 1 fat.

Bacon Spinach Muffins

Prep: 20 min. **Bake:** 20 min.

A new addition to my cooking "repertoire," these rustic muffins with a touch of feta cheese have already proven popular. They make a fabulous accompaniment to soups and salads...and are ready to bake in just 20 minutes.
—Rebecca Lindamood, Belfast, New York

6 bacon strips, diced
1/2 cup butter, softened
2 tablespoons sugar
1 egg
1/2 cup sour cream
1/2 cup milk
2 cups all-purpose flour
1/2 teaspoon baking powder
1/2 teaspoon baking soda
1/2 teaspoon salt
1/2 cup crumbled feta cheese
1/4 cup finely chopped onion
1 package (10 ounces) frozen chopped spinach, thawed and squeezed dry

In a small skillet, cook the bacon over medium heat until crisp. Remove to paper towels to drain. Meanwhile, in a small mixing bowl, cream the butter and sugar until light and fluffy; beat in the egg.

Combine sour cream and milk. Combine the flour, baking powder, baking soda and salt; add to creamed mixture alternately with the sour cream mixture just until moistened. Fold in the bacon, feta cheese, onion and 1/4 cup spinach (save the remaining spinach for another use).

Fill greased or paper-lined muffin cups three-fourths full. Bake at 375° for 18-22 minutes or until a toothpick comes out clean. Cool for 5 minutes before removing from pan to a wire rack. Serve warm. **Yield:** 1 dozen.

Rhubarb Lemon Muffins

(Pictured below)

Prep: 15 min. **Bake:** 20 min.

My father has a rhubarb plant and gives me part of his bounty every spring. I always save some of it to use in a new recipe, and this is one of the best I've ever tried.
—Kathleen Smith, Pittsburgh, Pennsylvania

2 cups all-purpose flour
1 cup plus 1-1/2 teaspoons sugar, *divided*
3 teaspoons baking powder
1/2 teaspoon salt
1/2 teaspoon ground ginger
2 eggs
1/2 cup buttermilk
1/4 cup vegetable oil
1 tablespoon grated lemon peel
1-3/4 cups sliced fresh *or* frozen rhubarb

In a large bowl, combine the flour, 1 cup sugar, baking powder, salt and ginger. In a small bowl, combine the eggs, buttermilk, oil and lemon peel. Stir into dry ingredients just until moistened. Fold in the rhubarb.

Fill paper-lined muffin cups two-thirds full. Sprinkle with remaining sugar. Bake at 375° for 20-25 minutes or until a toothpick comes out clean. Cool for 5 minutes before removing from pan to a wire rack. **Yield:** 1 dozen.

Editor's Note: If using frozen rhubarb, measure rhubarb while still frozen, then thaw completely. Drain in a colander, but do not press liquid out.

Rhubarb Lemon Muffins

Chapter 10

Slow-Cooked Sensations

FOR FAST SOLUTIONS to the "What's for dinner?" dilemma on weekdays, just take things slow—as in slow-cooked!

When it comes to convenient appliances, the slow cooker is hard to beat. It'll serve up a hot supper with minimal effort on your part. And when you arrive home at the end of a busy day, you'll have a just-cooked meal that's ready to enjoy.

So relax and sit down to terrific dinners such as Brisket 'n' Bean Burritos, Chicken Merlot with Mushrooms, Country Pork Chop Supper and Veggie Meatball Soup. These recipes are so delicious and schedule-friendly, you'll wonder what you ever did without them!

RIGHT ON TIME. Chunky Pasta Sauce (p. 161).

Italian Chicken

(Pictured below)

Prep: 20 min. **Cook:** 3 hours

A friend shared this simple dinner recipe with me years ago, and I've tweaked the spices a bit to suit my family's tastes. Now, I'm asked to make it at least twice a month. During the 3-hour cooking time, I can easily find a few minutes to fix some rice to go along with the chicken.
—Judi Guizado, Rancho Cucamonga, California

6 boneless skinless chicken breast halves (about 8 ounces *each*)
1 can (14-1/2 ounces) Italian stewed tomatoes
3/4 cup plus 3 tablespoons water, *divided*
2 tablespoons dried minced onion
2 teaspoons chicken bouillon granules
2 teaspoons chili powder
1/2 teaspoon dried tarragon
1/2 teaspoon Italian seasoning
1/4 teaspoon garlic powder
3 tablespoons cornstarch
Hot cooked rice

Place chicken in a 5-qt. slow cooker. Combine the tomatoes, 3/4 cup water, onion, bouillon and seasonings; pour over chicken.

Cover and cook on low for 3-4 hours or until a meat thermometer inserted into the chicken reads 170°.

Transfer chicken to a serving platter; keep warm. Pour cooking juices into a small saucepan. Combine cornstarch and remaining water until smooth; stir into cooking juices. Bring to a boil. Cook and stir for 2 minutes or until thickened. Serve with chicken and rice. **Yield:** 6 servings.

Italian Chicken

Pepper Jack Chicken

Pepper Jack Chicken

(Pictured above)

Prep: 20 min. **Cook:** 5 hours

With this no-fuss recipe, you can simmer up a lighter yet delicious meal using just a few basic ingredients. Your family is sure to love this colorful medley featuring tender chicken, peppers and a taste-tempting sauce.
—Linda Foreman, Locust Grove, Oklahoma

✓ This recipe includes Nutrition Facts and Diabetic Exchanges.

6 boneless skinless chicken breast halves (5 ounces *each*), cut into chunks
1 *each* small green, sweet red and orange pepper, cut into thin strips
1 can (10-3/4 ounces) condensed Southwest-style pepper Jack soup, undiluted
1/2 cup chunky salsa
1/8 teaspoon chili powder
4-1/2 cups hot cooked rice

In a 3-qt. slow cooker, combine the chicken, peppers, soup, salsa and chili powder. Cover and cook on low for 5-6 hours or until chicken juices run clear. Serve with rice. **Yield:** 6 servings.

Nutrition Facts: 1 cup chicken mixture with 3/4 cup rice equals 360 calories, 7 g fat (2 g saturated fat), 84 mg cholesterol, 553 mg sodium, 41 g carbohydrate, 2 g fiber, 34 g protein. **Diabetic Exchanges:** 4 very lean meat, 2-1/2 starch, 1/2 fat.

Cider-Glazed Ham

Prep: 15 min. **Cook:** 4 hours

We raise our own pork, and I'm always looking for new ways to prepare it. This flavorful glazed ham satisfies everyone's appetite at the end of a long day.
—Jennifer Foos-Furer, Marysville, Ohio

1 boneless fully cooked ham (3 pounds)
1-3/4 cups apple cider *or* juice
1/4 cup packed brown sugar
1/4 cup Dijon mustard
1/4 cup honey
2 tablespoons cornstarch
2 tablespoons cold water

Place the ham in a 5-qt. slow cooker. In a bowl, combine the apple cider, brown sugar, mustard and honey; pour over the ham. Cover and cook on low for 4-5 hours or until a meat thermometer reads 140° and the ham is heated through.

Remove ham and keep warm. Pour cooking juices into a small saucepan. Combine cornstarch and water until smooth; stir into cooking juices. Bring to a boil; cook and stir for 2 minutes or until thickened. Serve with ham. **Yield:** 8 servings.

Slow Cooker Chuck Roast

Prep: 20 min. **Cook:** 4 hours

This home-style roast served with a lip-smacking gravy can be prepared and cooked during an afternoon—offering busy cooks plenty of downtime and a terrific supper, too!
—Linnea Rein, Topeka, Kansas

1 boneless beef chuck roast (4 pounds), trimmed and cut in half
1 can (8 ounces) tomato sauce
1/2 cup chopped onion
1/4 cup water
1/4 cup cider vinegar
1/4 cup ketchup
2 teaspoons Worcestershire sauce
1 teaspoon paprika
1 teaspoon prepared mustard
1/2 teaspoon beef bouillon granules
1/4 teaspoon garlic powder
1/4 cup cornstarch
6 tablespoons cold water
Dash salt and pepper

Place roast in a 5-qt. slow cooker. Combine tomato sauce, onion, water, vinegar, ketchup, Worcestershire sauce, paprika, mustard, bouillon and garlic powder; pour over meat. Cover and cook on low for 4-5 hours or until the meat is tender.

Remove meat and keep warm. Skim fat from cooking juices if necessary; transfer to a large saucepan. Combine cornstarch and cold water until smooth; stir into cooking juices. Bring to a boil; cook and stir for 2 minutes or until thickened. Season with salt and pepper. Serve with roast. **Yield:** 10 servings.

Veggie Meatball Soup

(Pictured below)

Prep: 20 min. **Cook:** 6 hours

Loaded with vegetables and Italian meatballs, this meal-in-one soup is hearty enough to warm up any cold fall or winter day. It's a recipe you'll rely on time and again.
—Penny Fagan, Mobile, Alabama

25 frozen cooked Italian meatballs (1/2 ounce *each*)
1 can (28 ounces) diced tomatoes, undrained
3 cups beef broth
2 cups shredded cabbage
1 can (16 ounces) kidney beans, rinsed and drained
1 medium zucchini, sliced
1 cup fresh green beans, cut into 1-inch pieces
1 cup water
2 medium carrots, sliced
1 teaspoon dried basil
1/2 teaspoon minced garlic
1/4 teaspoon salt
1/8 teaspoon dried oregano
1/8 teaspoon pepper
1 cup uncooked elbow macaroni
1/4 cup minced fresh parsley
Grated Parmesan cheese, optional

In a 5-qt. slow cooker, combine the first 14 ingredients. Cover and cook on low for 5-1/2 to 6 hours or until vegetables are almost tender.

Stir in the macaroni and parsley; cook 30 minutes longer or until macaroni is tender. Serve with Parmesan cheese if desired. **Yield:** 6 servings (2-1/2 quarts).

Veggie Meatball Soup

Lemon Chicken

(Pictured above)

Prep: 20 min. **Cook:** 4-1/4 hours

This saucy chicken is bound to become a staple for anyone who tries it. With everyday ingredients, it's fuss-free yet delicious. —Elizabeth Hokanson, Arborg, Manitoba

1 teaspoon dried oregano
1/2 teaspoon seasoned salt
1/4 teaspoon pepper
6 boneless skinless chicken breast halves (6 ounces *each*)
2 teaspoons chicken bouillon granules
1/4 cup boiling water
3 tablespoons lemon juice
1-1/2 teaspoons minced garlic
1-1/2 cups (12 ounces) sour cream
2 teaspoons minced fresh parsley
Hot cooked brown rice, optional

Combine the oregano, seasoned salt and pepper; rub over chicken. Place in a 3-qt. slow cooker. In a small bowl, dissolve bouillon in boiling water. Stir in lemon juice and garlic. Pour over chicken. Cover and cook on low for 4 hours or until a meat thermometer reads 170°.

Remove chicken and keep warm. Stir in sour cream and parsley; cover and cook for 15 minutes or until heated through. Serve chicken with sauce and rice if desired. **Yield:** 6 servings.

Burgundy Beef

Prep: 10 min. **Cook:** 8-1/4 hours

When my adult children are coming over for dinner, this is what they request. All three of them—and their significant others—love it! —Urilla Cheverie, Alfred, Maine

4 pounds beef sirloin tips, cut into 1-inch cubes
3 large onions, sliced
1 cup water
1 cup burgundy wine *or* beef broth
1 cup ketchup
1/4 cup quick-cooking tapioca
1/4 cup packed brown sugar
1/4 cup Worcestershire sauce
4 teaspoons paprika
1-1/2 teaspoons salt
1 teaspoon minced garlic
1 teaspoon ground mustard
2 tablespoons cornstarch
3 tablespoons cold water
Hot cooked noodles

In a 5-qt. slow cooker, combine the first 12 ingredients. Cover and cook on low for 8-9 hours or until the meat is tender.

Combine the cornstarch and cold water until smooth; stir into pan juices. Cover and cook on high for 15 minutes or until the gravy is thickened. Serve with noodles. **Yield:** 10 servings.

Beef and Three-Bean Chili

Prep: 20 min. **Cook:** 5-1/2 hours

On football Sundays, cool nights or any time you're craving chili, consider this flavor-packed recipe. It's chock-full of beef stew meat and three kinds of beans. We like it best served with slices of homemade corn bread.
—Nancy Whitford, Edwards, New York

✓ This recipe includes Nutrition Facts and Diabetic Exchanges.

1-1/2 pounds beef stew meat, cut into 1-inch pieces
2 teaspoons chili powder
1-1/3 cups chopped onion
2 tablespoons canola oil
1 can (16 ounces) kidney beans, rinsed and drained
1 can (15 ounces) cannellini *or* white kidney beans, rinsed and drained
1 can (15 ounces) black beans, rinsed and drained
2 cans (14-1/2 ounces *each*) diced tomatoes, undrained
1 cup beef broth
1 can (6 ounces) tomato paste
2 jalapeno peppers, seeded and chopped
1 tablespoon brown sugar
2 teaspoons minced garlic
1/2 teaspoon salt
1/2 teaspoon pepper
1/4 teaspoon ground cumin
Sour cream, optional

Place beef in a large resealable plastic bag; add chili powder and toss to coat. In a large skillet over medium heat, brown beef and onion in oil.

Meanwhile, in a greased 5-qt. slow cooker, combine the beans, tomatoes, broth, tomato paste, jalapenos, brown sugar, garlic, salt, pepper and cumin. Stir in beef, onion and drippings.

Cover and cook on low for 5-1/2 to 6-1/2 hours or until meat is tender. Serve with sour cream if desired. **Yield:** 9 servings.

Editor's Note: When cutting hot peppers, disposable gloves are recommended. Avoid touching your face.

Nutrition Facts: 1 cup (calculated without sour cream) equals 309 calories, 9 g fat (2 g saturated fat), 47 mg cholesterol, 620 mg sodium, 34 g carbohydrate, 9 g fiber, 24 g protein. **Diabetic Exchanges:** 3 lean meat, 2 vegetable, 1 starch, 1/2 fat.

Tomato Paste Tip

Here's an easy way to get all of the tomato paste out of those small cans. Simply open the can at both ends, then remove the lid and push the other end all the way through the can. There's no mess and less waste.
—Julie Wan Wyk, Sully, Iowa

Chunky Pasta Sauce

(Pictured below and on page 156)

Prep: 15 min. **Cook:** 6 hours

Your kitchen will smell heavenly while this is cooking. Add the extra 1/2 cup of water if you'd prefer your sauce a bit thinner.
—Christy Hinrichs, Parkville, Missouri

✓ This recipe includes Nutrition Facts.

1 pound ground beef
1/2 pound ground pork
2 cans (28 ounces *each*) diced tomatoes
1/2 to 1 cup water
1 can (6 ounces) tomato paste
1 medium onion, cut into wedges
1 medium sweet red pepper, cut into 1-inch pieces
1 cup chopped carrots
2 tablespoons sugar
2 teaspoons minced garlic
1 teaspoon salt
1 teaspoon dried basil
1 teaspoon dried oregano
1 teaspoon pepper
6 cups cooked bow tie pasta

In a large skillet, cook beef and pork over medium heat until no longer pink; drain.

Transfer to a 3-qt. slow cooker. Stir in tomatoes, water, tomato paste, vegetables, sugar, garlic and seasonings. Cover and cook on low for 6-7 hours or until vegetables are tender. Serve with pasta. **Yield:** 8 servings.

Nutrition Facts: 1-1/4 cups sauce with 3/4 cup pasta equals 366 calories, 10 g fat (4 g saturated fat), 47 mg cholesterol, 735 mg sodium, 46 g carbohydrate, 5 g fiber, 23 g protein.

Chunky Pasta Sauce

Slow Cooker Sloppy Joes

Glazed Corned Beef Dinner

Prep: 20 min. **Cook:** 8 hours 20 min.

This recipe is so good, my family won't eat corned beef any other way. The glaze is the kicker—it combines orange juice, honey and mustard for a real taste sensation.
—Shannon Strate, Salt Lake City, Utah

8 medium red potatoes, quartered
2 medium carrots, sliced
1 medium onion, sliced
1 corned beef brisket with spice packet (3 pounds)
1-1/2 cups water
4 orange peel strips (3 inches)
3 tablespoons orange juice concentrate
3 tablespoons honey
1 tablespoon Dijon mustard

Place the potatoes, carrots and onion in a 5-qt. slow cooker. Cut brisket in half; place over vegetables. Add the water, orange peel and contents of spice packet. Cover and cook on low for 8-9 hours or until meat and vegetables are tender.

Using a slotted spoon, transfer corned beef and vegetables to a 13-in. x 9-in. x 2-in. baking dish. Discard orange peel.

Combine the orange juice concentrate, honey and mustard; pour over meat. Bake, uncovered, at 375° for 20 minutes, basting occasionally. **Yield:** 8 servings.

Slow Cooker Sloppy Joes

(Pictured above)

Prep: 20 min. **Cook:** 3 hours

These sloppy joes are my favorites for hot summer days because they cook without heating up the kitchen. Plus, it's easy to double or triple the recipe when you're serving a crowd, and you can freeze any leftovers to enjoy another time.
—Carol Losier, Baldwinsville, New York

1-1/2 pounds ground beef
1 cup chopped celery
1/2 cup chopped onion
1 bottle (12 ounces) chili sauce
2 tablespoons brown sugar
2 tablespoons sweet pickle relish
1 tablespoon Worcestershire sauce
1 teaspoon salt
1/8 teaspoon pepper
8 hamburger buns, split

In a large skillet, cook the beef, celery and onion over medium heat until meat is no longer pink; drain. Transfer to a 3-qt. slow cooker.

Stir in the chili sauce, brown sugar, sweet pickle relish, Worcestershire sauce, salt and pepper. Cover and cook on low for 3-4 hours or until the flavors are combined. Spoon 1/2 cup beef mixture onto each hamburger bun. **Yield:** 8 servings.

Pulled Pork Sandwiches

Prep: 15 min. **Cook:** 7 hours

You'll love the ease of these saucy sandwiches. You can throw everything in the slow cooker, then get out of the kitchen and go about the rest of your busy day.
—Terri McKitrick, Delafield, Wisconsin

✓ This recipe includes Nutrition Facts and Diabetic Exchanges.

1 can (8 ounces) tomato sauce
1 cup chopped onion
1 cup barbecue sauce
3 teaspoons chili powder
1 teaspoon ground cumin
1/2 teaspoon ground cinnamon
1 boneless pork sirloin roast (2 pounds), trimmed
8 seeded hamburger buns, split

In a 3-qt. slow cooker, combine the first six ingredients; add the pork roast. Spoon some of the sauce over the roast. Cover and cook on low for 7 hours or until the meat is tender.

Remove meat; shred with two forks. Return to slow cooker and heat through. Spoon 1/2 cup onto each bun. **Yield:** 8 servings.

Nutrition Facts: 1 sandwich equals 322 calories, 10 g fat (3 g saturated fat), 68 mg cholesterol, 681 mg sodium, 29 g carbohydrate, 3 g fiber, 28 g protein. **Diabetic Exchanges:** 3 lean meat, 2 starch.

Vegetable Lentil Soup

Prep: 15 min. **Cook:** 4-1/2 hours

Created by the home economists in our Test Kitchen, this better-for-you soup is ideal for vegetarians and those who are watching their weight. Squash and lentils make it filling, while herbs add a medley of flavors.

- **4 cups vegetable broth**
- **3 cups cubed peeled butternut squash**
- **1 cup dried lentils, rinsed**
- **1 cup chopped carrot**
- **1 cup chopped onion**
- **2 teaspoons minced garlic**
- **1 teaspoon dried oregano**
- **1 teaspoon dried basil**
- **1 can (14-1/2 ounces) Italian diced tomatoes, undrained**
- **1 package (9 ounces) frozen cut green beans**

In a 5-qt. slow cooker, combine the first eight ingredients. Cover and cook on low for 4 hours or until the lentils are tender.

Stir in the tomatoes and beans. Cover and cook on high for 30 minutes or until beans are heated through. **Yield:** 6 servings.

Greek Chicken Dinner

Prep: 20 min. **Cook:** 5 hours

I received this recipe from my sister, and everyone in my family really likes it—not only the taste, but also the aroma that wafts through the house as it cooks! The amount of garlic may seem high enough to overpower the other ingredients, but we think it's just right.

—Terri Christensen, Montague, Michigan

- **6 medium Yukon Gold potatoes, quartered**
- **1 broiler/fryer chicken (3-1/2 pounds), cut up and skin removed**
- **2 large onions, quartered**
- **1 whole garlic bulb, separated and peeled**
- **3 teaspoons dried oregano**
- **1 teaspoon salt**
- **3/4 teaspoon pepper**
- **1/2 cup plus 1 tablespoon water, *divided***
- **1 tablespoon olive oil**
- **4 teaspoons cornstarch**

Place potatoes in a 5-qt. slow cooker. Add the chicken, onions and garlic. In a small bowl, combine the oregano, salt, pepper and 1/2 cup water; pour over chicken and vegetables. Drizzle with oil. Cover and cook on low for 5-6 hours or until chicken juices run clear and vegetables are tender.

Remove chicken and vegetables to a serving platter and keep warm. Strain the cooking juices and skim the fat; transfer to a small saucepan. Combine the cornstarch and remaining water until smooth; stir into the cooking juices. Bring to a boil; cook and stir for 2 minutes or until thickened. Serve with chicken and vegetables. **Yield:** 6 servings.

Hawaiian Pork Roast

(Pictured below)

Prep: 30 min. **Cook:** 3 hours + standing

This sweet-tangy pork is one of my favorite slow cooker dishes. It's great with rice or potatoes and any vegetables. Plus, leftovers reheat well for lunch the next day.

—Ruth Chiarenza, La Vale, Maryland

- **1 boneless whole pork loin roast (3 pounds)**
- **1/2 teaspoon salt**
- **1/4 teaspoon pepper**
- **3 tablespoons vegetable oil**
- **2 cups unsweetened pineapple juice**
- **1 can (8 ounces) unsweetened crushed pineapple, undrained**
- **1/2 cup packed brown sugar**
- **1/2 cup sliced celery**
- **1/2 cup cider vinegar**
- **1/2 cup soy sauce**
- **1/4 cup cornstarch**
- **1/3 cup cold water**

Cut pork roast in half. Sprinkle with salt and pepper. In a large skillet, brown roast in oil on all sides; drain. Place in a 5-qt. slow cooker.

In a large bowl, combine the pineapple juice, pineapple, brown sugar, celery, vinegar and soy sauce. Pour over the roast. Cover and cook on low for 3 to 3-1/2 hours or until a meat thermometer reads 160°.

Remove roast and keep warm. Let stand for 10 minutes before slicing. Meanwhile, strain cooking juices; transfer to a large saucepan. Combine cornstarch and water until smooth; stir into cooking juices. Bring to a boil; cook and stir for 2 minutes or until thickened. Serve with pork. **Yield:** 8 servings.

Hawaiian Pork Roast

Hearty Short Ribs

Hearty Short Ribs

(Pictured above)

Prep: 15 min. **Cook:** 6 hours

With a side of mashed potatoes or even rice, these short ribs make a great sit-down dinner for your family. The meat is so tender that it falls off the bone, and the gravy is lip-smacking good. —Helena Ivy, St. Louis, Missouri

1 large onion, sliced
4 pounds bone-in beef short ribs
1/2 pound sliced fresh mushrooms
1 can (10-3/4 ounces) condensed cream of mushroom soup, undiluted
1/2 cup water
1 envelope brown gravy mix
1 teaspoon minced garlic
1/2 teaspoon dried thyme
1 tablespoon cornstarch
2 tablespoons cold water
Hot mashed potatoes

Place onion in a 5-qt. slow cooker; top with ribs. Combine the mushrooms, soup, 1/2 cup water, gravy mix, garlic and thyme; pour over ribs. Cover and cook on low for 6 to 6-1/2 hours or until meat is tender.

Remove meat to serving platter; keep warm. Skim fat from cooking juices; transfer to a small saucepan. Bring to a boil. Combine cornstarch and cold water until smooth. Gradually stir into pan. Bring to a boil. Cook and stir for 2 minutes or until thickened. Serve with meat and mashed potatoes. **Yield:** 6 servings.

Brisket 'n' Bean Burritos

(Pictured below)

Prep: 20 min. **Cook:** 4-1/2 hours

Slow-cook your way to a terrific Mexican meal with this easy recipe. The shredded beef brisket is perfect for burritos. With refried beans, cheese and your favorite salsa, these wraps beat the drive-thru kind hands down! —Ruth Weatherford, Huntington Beach, California

1 fresh beef brisket (2 pounds)
1 cup chopped onion
3 bacon strips, diced
1 can (8 ounces) tomato sauce
3/4 teaspoon pepper
1/4 teaspoon salt
1 can (16 ounces) refried beans
1/2 cup salsa
1 can (4 ounces) chopped green chilies
1-1/2 cups (6 ounces) shredded Monterey Jack cheese
10 flour tortillas (10 inches), warmed

Place brisket in a 5-qt. slow cooker; top with onion and bacon. Combine the tomato sauce, pepper and salt; pour over meat. Cover and cook on low for 4-1/2 to 5 hours or until tender.

In a microwave-safe bowl, combine the refried beans, salsa and chilies. Cover and microwave on high for 2-3 minutes or until heated through. Remove meat from slow cooker; shred with two forks. Layer the bean mixture, meat and cheese off-center on each tortilla. Fold sides and ends over filling and roll up. **Yield:** 10 servings.

Editor's Note: This is a fresh beef brisket, not corned beef. The meat comes from the first cut of the brisket.

Brisket 'n' Bean Burritos

Pork Roast with Twist of Orange

Prep: 25 min. **Cook:** 4-1/2 hours

The citrus flavor of this pork roast with gravy really sets it apart from other roasts. It's one of my family's favorite main courses...and it takes less than half an hour to get in the slow cooker. —Janie Canals, West Jordan, Utah

☑ This recipe includes Nutrition Facts.

4 bacon strips, diced
1 boneless pork shoulder roast (3 to 4 pounds), trimmed
1 large onion, thinly sliced
1-1/2 teaspoons minced garlic
1 jalapeno pepper, seeded and finely chopped
4-1/2 teaspoons chili powder
1 teaspoon salt
1 teaspoon pepper
1 cup chicken broth, *divided*
2/3 cup orange juice
1/4 cup all-purpose flour
Hot mashed potatoes, optional

In a large skillet, cook the bacon over medium heat until crisp. Remove to paper towels to drain; set aside. Cut the pork roast in half. Brown the meat in the drippings on all sides. Transfer to a 5-qt. slow cooker, reserving 1 tablespoon drippings.

Brown the onion and garlic in drippings. Add the jalapeno, chili powder, salt and pepper. Gradually stir in 1/2 cup chicken broth, orange juice and bacon; pour over roast. Cover and cook on low for 4-1/2 to 5 hours or until a meat thermometer reads 160°.

Remove pork and onion; keep warm. Pour cooking juices into a small saucepan and skim fat. Combine flour and remaining broth until smooth; stir into cooking juices. Bring to a boil; cook and stir for 2 minutes or until thickened. Serve with pork and mashed potatoes if desired. **Yield:** 8 servings.

Editor's Note: When cutting hot peppers, disposable gloves are recommended. Avoid touching your face.

Nutrition Facts: 5 ounces cooked meat with 1/4 cup gravy (calculated without mashed potatoes) equals 514 calories, 26 g fat (9 g saturated fat), 202 mg cholesterol, 701 mg sodium, 9 g carbohydrate, 1 g fiber, 57 g protein.

Sweet 'n' Tangy Chicken Wings

(Pictured above right)

Prep: 20 min. **Cook:** 3-1/4 hours

Try these saucy wings for your next Super Bowl party or other casual get-together. With hardly any work, you'll have winning appetizers. —Ida Tuey, Kokomo, Indiana

3 pounds chicken wingettes (about 30)
1/2 teaspoon salt, *divided*
Dash pepper
1-1/2 cups ketchup

Sweet 'n' Tangy Chicken Wings

1/4 cup packed brown sugar
1/4 cup red wine vinegar
2 tablespoons Worcestershire sauce
1 tablespoon Dijon mustard
1 teaspoon minced garlic
1 teaspoon Liquid Smoke, optional
Sesame seeds, optional

Sprinkle the chicken wings with a dash of salt and pepper. Broil 4-6 in. from the heat for 5-10 minutes on each side or until golden brown. Transfer to a greased 5-qt. slow cooker.

Combine the ketchup, brown sugar, vinegar, Worcestershire sauce, mustard, garlic, Liquid Smoke if desired and remaining salt; pour over wings. Toss to coat. Cover and cook on low for 3-1/4 to 3-3/4 hours or until chicken juices run clear. Sprinkle with sesame seeds if desired. **Yield:** about 2-1/2 dozen.

Pork Spareribs

Prep: 5 min. **Cook:** 6 hours

Who would have guessed that just five ingredients could taste so good? You'll be amazed when you sample these delicious ribs. —Shari Sieg, Silver Springs, Florida

3 pounds pork spareribs
2 cans (28 ounces *each*) diced tomatoes, undrained
2 cups barbecue sauce
1/4 cup packed brown sugar
1/4 cup white wine vinegar

Place ribs in a 5-qt. slow cooker. Combine the remaining ingredients; pour over ribs. Cover and cook on low for 6-7 hours or until meat is tender. Serve with a slotted spoon. **Yield:** 6 servings.

Smothered Round Steak

(Pictured below)

Prep: 20 min. **Cook:** 7 hours

For a satisfying but budget-friendly meal, try less-expensive round steak and gravy served over egg noodles. Chock-full of veggies, this slow-cooked creation is a complete dinner and will solve your "What's for supper?" dilemma on weeknights.
—Kathy Garrett, Camden, West Virginia

1/3 cup all-purpose flour
1 teaspoon salt
1/4 teaspoon pepper
1-1/2 pounds boneless beef top round steak, cut into 1-1/2-inch strips
1 large onion, sliced
1 large green pepper, sliced
1 can (14-1/2 ounces) diced tomatoes, undrained
1 jar (4 ounces) sliced mushrooms, drained
3 tablespoons soy sauce
2 tablespoons molasses
Hot cooked egg noodles, optional

In a large resealable plastic bag, combine the flour, salt and pepper. Add beef and shake to coat. Transfer to a 3-qt. slow cooker. Add the onion, green pepper, tomatoes, mushrooms, soy sauce and molasses.

Cover and cook on low for 7-8 hours or until meat is tender. Serve with noodles if desired. **Yield:** 4 servings.

Smothered Round Steak

Chicken Merlot with Mushrooms

Prep: 10 min. **Cook:** 5 hours

This elegant recipe was shared by a friend who enjoyed cooking as much as I do. I still think of her whenever I prepare it, and my family and friends request it often.
—Shelli McWilliam, Salem, Oregon

5-1/4 cups sliced fresh mushrooms
1 cup chopped onion
2 teaspoons minced garlic
3 pounds boneless skinless chicken thighs
1 can (6 ounces) tomato paste
3/4 cup chicken broth
1/4 cup Merlot wine *or* additional chicken broth
2 tablespoons quick-cooking tapioca
2 teaspoons sugar
1-1/2 teaspoons dried basil
1/2 teaspoon salt
1/4 teaspoon pepper
2 tablespoons grated Parmesan cheese
Hot cooked pasta, optional

Place the mushrooms, onion and garlic in a 5-qt. slow cooker. Top with chicken.

In a small bowl, combine the tomato paste, broth, wine or additional broth, tapioca, sugar, basil, salt and pepper. Pour over chicken. Cover and cook on low for 5-6 hours or until the chicken is tender.

Sprinkle with Parmesan cheese. Serve with pasta if desired. **Yield:** 5 servings.

Slow Cooker Pork Chops

Prep: 15 min. **Cook:** 3 hours

Everyone likes the flavor of these fork-tender chops featuring a creamy, light gravy. The recipe jazzes up the meat using basic ingredients, which I usually have on hand in my pantry. I like to round out this meal with a side of mashed potatoes and either coleslaw or a green salad.
—Sue Bingham, Madisonville, Tennessee

3/4 cup all-purpose flour, *divided*
1/2 teaspoon ground mustard
1/2 teaspoon garlic pepper blend
1/4 teaspoon seasoned salt
4 boneless pork loin chops (1/2 inch thick and 4 ounces *each*)
2 tablespoons vegetable oil
1 can (14-1/2 ounces) chicken broth

In a large resealable plastic bag, combine 1/2 cup flour, mustard, pepper blend and seasoned salt. Add pork chops, one at a time, and shake to coat. In a large skillet, brown the meat in oil on each side.

Transfer to a 5-qt. slow cooker. Place remaining flour in a small bowl; whisk in broth until smooth. Pour over chops. Cover and cook on low for 3 to 3-1/2 hours or until meat is tender.

Remove pork to a serving plate and keep warm. Whisk pan juices until smooth; serve with pork. **Yield:** 4 servings.

Slow Cooker Beef Brisket

Prep: 20 min. **Cook:** 6 hours

This fuss-free brisket has been a favorite in our family for years. I added the fresh mushrooms to "beef up" the flavor! To cut down on prep, buy mushrooms that are already sliced. —Mary Ann Lee, Clifton Park, New York

1 fresh beef brisket (3 to 4 pounds)
1/2 pound sliced fresh mushrooms
2 bay leaves
2 cups crushed tomatoes
1 cup chopped onion
1/2 cup packed brown sugar
1/2 cup balsamic vinegar
1/2 cup ketchup
1/4 cup cornstarch
1/4 cup cold water

Cut brisket in half; place in a 5-qt. slow cooker. Add mushrooms and bay leaves. Combine the tomatoes, onion, brown sugar, vinegar and ketchup; pour over beef. Cover and cook on low for 6-7 hours or until meat is tender.

Remove the beef and keep warm. Discard the bay leaves. In a large saucepan, combine the cornstarch and water until smooth. Gradually stir in the cooking liquid. Bring to a boil; cook and stir for 2 minutes or until thickened. Slice meat across the grain; serve with gravy. **Yield:** 6-8 servings.

Editor's Note: This is a fresh beef brisket, not corned beef. The meat comes from the first cut of the brisket.

Country Pork Chop Supper

Prep: 10 min. **Cook:** 6 hours

Dinner doesn't get much easier or more delicious than this hearty meal-in-one. There's no pre-cooking involved—everything goes right into the slow cooker. You'll love it! —Sandy Mullen, Gage, Oklahoma

6 boneless pork loin chops (1/2 inch thick and 4 ounces *each*)
2 jars (12 ounces *each*) pork gravy
1 can (10-3/4 ounces) condensed cream of mushroom soup, undiluted
2 tablespoons ketchup
1 tablespoon minced chives
1 teaspoon pepper
1 teaspoon soy sauce
1/2 teaspoon seasoned salt
3 medium potatoes, peeled and quartered
1 package (16 ounces) frozen mixed vegetables

Place the pork chops in a greased 5-qt. slow cooker. Combine the gravy, cream of mushroom soup, ketchup, chives, pepper, soy sauce and seasoned salt; pour over pork chops.

Stir in potatoes and vegetables. Cover and cook on low for 6-7 hours or until meat and potatoes are tender. **Yield:** 6 servings.

Mushroom 'n' Steak Sroganoff

Mushroom 'n' Steak Stroganoff

(Pictured above)

Prep: 15 min. **Cook:** 6-1/4 hours

This main dish is one of my top choices for guests. The Stroganoff is comforting and pleasing to most everyone. —Marilyn Shehane, Colorado Springs, Colorado

2 tablespoons all-purpose flour
1/2 teaspoon garlic powder
1/2 teaspoon pepper
1/4 teaspoon paprika
1-3/4 pounds boneless beef top round steak, cut into 1-1/2-inch strips
1 can (10-3/4 ounces) condensed cream of mushroom soup, undiluted
1/2 cup water
1/4 cup onion mushroom soup mix
2 jars (4-1/2 ounces *each*) sliced mushrooms, drained
1/2 cup sour cream
1 tablespoon minced fresh parsley
Hot cooked egg noodles, optional

In a large resealable plastic bag, combine the flour, garlic powder, pepper and paprika. Add beef strips and shake to coat. Transfer to a 3-qt. slow cooker.

Combine the soup, water and soup mix; pour over beef. Cover and cook on low for 6-7 hours or until the meat is tender.

Stir in the mushrooms, sour cream and parsley. Cover and cook 15 minutes longer or until sauce is thickened. Serve with noodles if desired. **Yield:** 6 servings.

Chapter 11

Breakfast & Brunch Favorites

WAKE UP to more than just a cup of coffee or food from the drive-thru. Get your day started off right with recipes such as Breakfast Pizza, Walnut Fruit Salad, Andouille Egg Burritos, Baked Apple French Toast and Chai Tea Lattes.

Think it's impossible to fix such scrumptious, homemade fare on busy weekdays? You'll be surprised at just how quickly these daybreak delights get on the table. Even on your most time-crunched mornings, you and your family will be able to enjoy a wholesome meal.

In this chapter, you'll also see fast but fancy dishes for a holiday or weekend brunch. They'll make it easy to rise and shine!

SUNRISE SENSATIONS. Pumpkin Waffles with Orange Walnut Butter and Nutmeg Syrup (both recipes on p. 175).

Brunch Egg Burritos

Brunch Egg Burritos

(Pictured above)

Prep/Total Time: 30 min.

Besides being delicious, these hearty wraps are so quick and easy to prepare—and that's the best part when you're in a hurry in the morning. They're great for lunch and dinner, too. —*Jenny Flake, Gilbert, Arizona*

2 cups refrigerated shredded hash brown potatoes
3 tablespoons butter, *divided*
6 eggs
1/2 cup milk
1 can (4 ounces) chopped green chilies
1/4 teaspoon salt
1/4 teaspoon salt-free garlic seasoning blend
1/4 teaspoon pepper
4 to 6 drops Louisiana-style hot sauce
12 slices ready-to-serve fully cooked bacon, crumbled
2 cups (8 ounces) shredded Monterey Jack cheese
1 cup salsa
4 flour tortillas (10 inches), warmed

In a large skillet, cook potatoes in 2 tablespoons butter over medium heat for 6-7 minutes or until golden brown, stirring occasionally.

Meanwhile, in a small bowl, whisk the eggs, milk, chilies, seasonings and hot sauce. In another large skillet, heat remaining butter until hot. Add egg mixture; cook and stir over medium heat until eggs are completely set.

Layer 1/3 cup potatoes, about 1/2 cup egg mixture, 1/4 cup bacon, 1/2 cup cheese and 1/4 cup salsa off center on each tortilla. Fold sides and ends over filling and roll up. Serve immediately. **Yield:** 4 servings.

Walnut Fruit Salad

Prep/Total Time: 15 min.

My co-worker is always asked to bring this yummy dish to work parties. Fresh fruit and a homemade honey dressing lend a burst of flavor, and walnuts add a nice crunch. —*Diane Cohen, St. Louis, Missouri*

2 medium apples, chopped
2 medium bananas, sliced
1 can (11 ounces) mandarin oranges, drained
1 cup seedless red grapes
1 cup shredded lettuce
1 tablespoon lemon juice
1/3 cup mayonnaise
1/4 cup honey
1/2 cup chopped walnuts

In a large salad bowl, combine the apples, bananas, oranges, grapes, lettuce and lemon juice. In a small bowl, combine mayonnaise and honey. Pour over salad and toss to coat. Sprinkle with walnuts. Serve immediately. **Yield:** 6 servings.

Apple Butter Mix

(Pictured below)

Prep/Total Time: 25 min.

I've received so many requests for this special fruit spread over the years that I started assembling homemade mixes and giving them away as gifts. The wonderfully spiced apple butter is a snap to prepare and turns your plain toast, bagel or English muffin into a morning treat.
—Jessica Willhite, Cusseta, Georgia

✓ This recipe includes Nutrition Facts and Diabetic Exchanges.

1 cup packed brown sugar
2 teaspoons ground cinnamon
1/2 teaspoon salt
1/2 teaspoon ground cloves
1/4 teaspoon ground allspice
ADDITIONAL INGREDIENTS (for each batch):
4 large tart apples, peeled and chopped
1 cup unsweetened apple juice

In a small bowl, combine the first five ingredients. Store in an airtight container in a cool dry place for up to 4 months. **Yield:** 4 batches (about 1 cup total).

To prepare apple butter: In a large saucepan, bring apples and apple juice to a boil. Reduce heat; cover and simmer for 5-7 minutes or until apples are tender. Drain; mash with a potato masher. Stir in 1/4 cup mix until sugar is dissolved. Cover and refrigerate for up to 5 days. **Yield:** about 1-1/4 cups.

Nutrition Facts: 1 tablespoon equals 38 calories, trace fat (trace saturated fat), 0 cholesterol, 17 mg sodium, 10 g carbohydrate, 1 g fiber, trace protein. **Diabetic Exchange:** 1/2 starch.

Apple Butter Mix

Apple Cherry Punch

Apple Cherry Punch

(Pictured above)

Prep/Total Time: 25 min.

Try this cheery beverage to give the holidays a festive touch or to warm up your family anytime. It fills the house with a lovely aroma. *—Joslyn Stock, Hampton, Iowa*

✓ This recipe includes Nutrition Facts.

4 cups water
4 cups unsweetened apple juice
1 cup sugar
1 envelope unsweetened cherry soft drink mix
1/4 teaspoon ground cinnamon
1/8 teaspoon ground nutmeg
1/8 teaspoon ground cloves

In a large saucepan, combine all ingredients. Bring to a boil over medium heat. Reduce heat; simmer, uncovered, for 15 minutes. **Yield:** about 7 cups.

Nutrition Facts: 1 cup equals 178 calories, trace fat (trace saturated fat), 0 cholesterol, 10 mg sodium, 45 g carbohydrate, trace fiber, trace protein.

Spread the Flavor

PLAN TO GIVE Apple Butter Mix (recipe above left) to someone who has a sweet tooth? The spread created from the mix could also be delicious as a dessert topping. Suggest spooning the spiced apple mixture over vanilla ice cream or slices of pound cake.

Breakfast Pizza

Breakfast Pizza

(Pictured above)

Prep/Total Time: 25 min.

I used to bake this for my morning drivers when I worked at a pizza-delivery place, and they just loved it. It's a fast, simple eye-opener that appeals to all ages.
—Cathy Shortall, Easton, Maryland

1 tube (13.8 ounces) refrigerated pizza crust
2 tablespoons olive oil, *divided*
6 eggs
2 tablespoons water
1 package (3 ounces) real bacon bits
1 cup (4 ounces) shredded Monterey Jack cheese
1 cup (4 ounces) shredded cheddar cheese

Unroll the pizza crust into a greased 15-in. x 10-in. x 1-in. baking pan; flatten the dough and build up the edges slightly. Brush with 1 tablespoon oil. Prick dough thoroughly with a fork. Bake at 400° for 7-8 minutes or until lightly browned.

Meanwhile, in a small bowl, whisk the eggs and water. In a small skillet, heat the remaining oil until hot. Add the eggs; cook and stir over medium heat until completely set.

Spoon eggs over crust. Sprinkle with bacon and cheeses. Bake 5-7 minutes longer or until cheese is melted. **Yield:** 8 slices.

Blueberry-Poppy Seed Brunch Cake

(Pictured below)

Prep: 15 min. **Bake:** 50 min. + cooling

This cake is so yummy! For an alternate glaze, I sometimes substitute 1 teaspoon each of lemon juice and milk for the 1 tablespoon of milk and add a little fresh lemon peel. *—Ruth Gruchow, Yorba Linda, California*

1/2 cup butter, softened
2/3 cup sugar
1 egg
2 teaspoons grated lemon peel
1-1/2 cups all-purpose flour
2 tablespoons poppy seeds
1/2 teaspoon baking powder
1/4 teaspoon baking soda
1/4 teaspoon salt
1/2 cup sour cream
TOPPING:
1/3 cup sugar
2 teaspoons all-purpose flour
1/4 teaspoon ground nutmeg
2 cups fresh *or* frozen unsweetened blueberries
GLAZE:
1/2 cup confectioners' sugar
1 tablespoon milk

In a small mixing bowl, cream butter and sugar until light and fluffy. Add egg; beat well. Stir in lemon peel. Combine the flour, poppy seeds, baking powder, baking soda and salt; add to the creamed mixture alternately with sour cream. Beat just until combined. Spread into a greased 9-in. springform pan.

For topping, in a small bowl, combine the sugar, flour and nutmeg; gently stir in berries until coated. Sprinkle over batter. Bake at 350° for 50-55 minutes or until a toothpick inserted near the center comes out clean. Cool for 10 minutes on a wire rack; remove sides of pan.

Blueberry-Poppy Seed Brunch Cake

Meanwhile, in a small bowl, whisk confectioners' sugar and milk until smooth; drizzle over cake. Refrigerate leftovers. **Yield:** 8 servings.

Editor's Note: If using frozen blueberries, do not thaw before adding to batter.

Maple Oatmeal with Dried Fruit

Prep/Total Time: 15 min.

Find oatmeal boring? In this recipe, cranberries, raisins, maple syrup and cinnamon turn a bowlful into a real treat. —Carrie Sandblom, Concord, New Hampshire

3 cups milk *or* water
1/4 teaspoon salt
1-1/2 cups quick-cooking oats
1/3 cup dried cranberries
1/3 cup golden raisins
3 tablespoons maple syrup
1-1/2 teaspoons ground cinnamon

In a large saucepan, bring milk and salt to a boil. Stir in oats; cook for 1-2 minutes or until thickened, stirring occasionally. Remove from the heat. Stir in the cranberries, raisins, syrup and cinnamon. **Yield:** 4 servings.

Rosy Rhubarb Punch

Prep: 30 min. + chilling

My friend Elsie serves this refreshing beverage at special events and shared the recipe with me. It's a great way to use up rhubarb. —Shirley Hochstedler, Kalona, Iowa

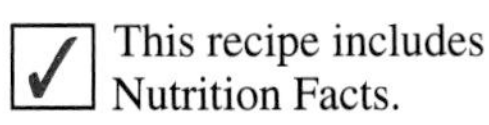
This recipe includes Nutrition Facts.

2 quarts water
4 cups chopped fresh *or* frozen rhubarb
2 cans (6 ounces *each*) unsweetened pineapple juice
1 cup sugar
2 tablespoons orange *or* cherry gelatin powder

In a Dutch oven, combine water and rhubarb; bring to a boil. Reduce heat; cover and simmer for 10 minutes or until rhubarb is tender.

Strain, reserving liquid; return to the pan. Stir in the pineapple juice, sugar and gelatin powder; heat until sugar is dissolved. Cool. Transfer to a punch bowl or pitcher; cover and refrigerate until chilled. **Yield:** 10 servings (2-1/2 quarts).

Nutrition Facts: 1 cup equals 116 calories, trace fat (trace saturated fat), 0 cholesterol, 9 mg sodium, 29 g carbohydrate, 1 g fiber, 1 g protein.

Peanut Butter Banana Oatmeal

Prep/Total Time: 15 min.

If your kids like the combination of peanut butter and bananas, brighten up their morning with this easy and yummy oatmeal. —Debbie Purdue, Westland, Michigan

Weekend Breakfast Bake

3 cups milk *or* water
1/4 teaspoon salt
1-1/2 cups quick-cooking oats
2 large bananas, sliced
2 tablespoons peanut butter
1/2 teaspoon vanilla extract

In a large saucepan, bring milk and salt to a boil. Stir in oats; cook for 1-2 minutes or until thickened, stirring occasionally. Remove from the heat. Stir in the bananas, peanut butter and vanilla. **Yield:** 4 servings.

Weekend Breakfast Bake

(Pictured above)

Prep: 15 min. **Bake:** 30 min.

My family really enjoys this sausage casserole on weekends and holidays. With five ingredients, it's so quick to prepare and a very satisfying way to start the day. —Melissa Ball, Pearisburg, Virginia

1 pound bulk pork sausage
1/3 cup chopped onion
4 cups (16 ounces) shredded Monterey Jack *or* cheddar cheese
8 eggs, lightly beaten
1 can (10-3/4 ounces) condensed cream of mushroom soup, undiluted

In a large skillet, cook sausage and onion over medium heat until meat is no longer pink; drain. Transfer to a greased 13-in. x 9-in. x 2-in. baking dish. Sprinkle with cheese. Combine eggs and cream of mushroom soup; pour over cheese.

Bake, uncovered, at 400° for 30-35 minutes or until a knife inserted near the center comes out clean. Let stand for 5 minutes before cutting. **Yield:** 8 servings.

Baked Apple French Toast

(Pictured below)

Prep: 20 min. + chilling **Bake:** 35 min.

This is a wonderful brunch recipe you start the night before and quickly get in the oven the next morning. I serve it with whipped topping, maple syrup and additional pecans. Guests say it could even make a great dessert.
—Beverly Johnston, Rubicon, Wisconsin

20 slices French bread (1 inch thick)
1 can (21 ounces) apple pie filling
8 eggs
2 cups milk
2 teaspoons vanilla extract
1/2 teaspoon ground cinnamon
1/2 teaspoon ground nutmeg
TOPPING:
1 cup packed brown sugar
1/2 cup cold butter, cubed
1 cup chopped pecans
2 tablespoons corn syrup

Arrange 10 slices of bread in a greased 13-in. x 9-in. x 2-in. baking dish. Spread with pie filling; top with remaining bread. In a large bowl, combine the eggs, milk, vanilla, cinnamon and nutmeg. Pour over bread. Cover and refrigerate overnight.

Remove from the refrigerator 30 minutes before baking. Meanwhile, place brown sugar in a small bowl. Cut in butter until mixture resembles coarse crumbs. Stir in pecans and corn syrup. Sprinkle over French toast.

Bake, uncovered, at 350° for 35-40 minutes or until a knife inserted near the center comes out clean. **Yield:** 10 servings.

Baked Apple French Toast

Amaretto Peach Oatmeal

Prep/Total Time: 15 min.

Plain oatmeal gets dressed up with diced peaches and Amaretto creamer in this 15-minute recipe. Your family is sure to be thrilled with the interesting blend of flavors—and to request the same breakfast the next day!
—Renee Endress, Galva, Illinois

3 cups milk *or* water
1/4 teaspoon salt
1-1/2 cups quick-cooking oats
2 snack-size cups (4 ounces *each*) diced peaches
1/4 cup sugar
2 tablespoons refrigerated Amaretto nondairy creamer

In a large saucepan, bring milk and salt to a boil. Stir in oats; cook for 1-2 minutes or until thickened, stirring occasionally. Remove from the heat. Stir in the peaches, sugar and creamer. **Yield:** 4 servings.

Green Bean Ham Quiche

Prep: 20 min. **Bake:** 35 min.

If you're lucky enough to have leftover ham from a holiday dinner or other special occasion, put those extras to good use in this hearty, simple-as-can-be quiche. It goes together especially fast because there's no crust.
—Sandy Flick, Toledo, Ohio

✓ This recipe includes Nutrition Facts and Diabetic Exchanges.

1/2 pound fresh green beans, trimmed and cut into 1-inch pieces
1 cup cubed fully cooked ham
1 jar (6 ounces) sliced mushrooms, drained
1 cup (4 ounces) shredded Swiss cheese
1/2 cup finely chopped onion
1/8 teaspoon garlic powder
3 eggs, beaten
1-1/2 cups milk
3/4 cup biscuit/baking mix
1/2 teaspoon salt
1/4 teaspoon pepper

Place the beans in a large saucepan and cover with water. Bring to a boil; cook, uncovered, for 5 minutes or until crisp-tender.

Meanwhile, in a large bowl, combine the ham, mushrooms, cheese, onion and garlic powder. Drain beans; stir into ham mixture. Transfer to a 9-in. deep-dish pie plate coated with cooking spray.

In a small bowl, combine eggs, milk, biscuit mix, salt and pepper just until blended; pour over ham mixture.

Bake at 400° for 35-40 minutes or until a knife inserted near the center comes out clean. Let stand for 5 minutes before cutting. **Yield:** 8 servings.

Nutrition Facts: 1 slice equals 198 calories, 10 g fat (5 g saturated fat), 108 mg cholesterol, 686 mg sodium, 14 g carbohydrate, 2 g fiber, 13 g protein. **Diabetic Exchanges:** 1-1/2 lean meat, 1 starch, 1 fat.

Pumpkin Waffles with Orange Walnut Butter
Nutmeg Syrup

Pumpkin Waffles with Orange Walnut Butter

(Pictured above and on page 168)

Prep/Total Time: 30 min.

Crave the taste of pumpkin during fall? Treat yourself to these yummy waffles. I like them best with the accompanying butter. —Brandi Davis, Pullman, Washington

1 cup plus 2 tablespoons all-purpose flour
2 tablespoons brown sugar
1 teaspoon ground cinnamon
1/2 teaspoon salt
1/2 teaspoon baking powder
1/4 teaspoon baking soda
2 eggs
1 cup milk
1/2 cup canned pumpkin
2 tablespoons butter, melted
ORANGE WALNUT BUTTER:
1/2 cup butter, softened
1/4 cup chopped walnuts
1 tablespoon grated orange peel
Maple syrup

In a large bowl, combine the first six ingredients. In another bowl, combine the eggs, milk, pumpkin and butter; stir into dry ingredients just until combined.

Bake in a preheated waffle iron according to manufacturer's directions until golden brown.

Meanwhile, for orange walnut butter, in a small bowl, combine the butter, walnuts and orange peel until blended. Serve waffles with butter mixture and maple syrup. **Yield:** 4 servings.

Nutmeg Syrup

(Pictured above and on page 168)

Prep/Total Time: 15 min.

I'm a music teacher, and I served this spiced syrup one morning at a teachers' breakfast—to rave reviews! The nutmeg adds a rich, homey touch everyone loves.
—Rochelle Felsburg, Fredericksburg, Virginia

1 cup sugar
2 tablespoons all-purpose flour
1 teaspoon ground cinnamon
1/2 teaspoon ground nutmeg
2 cups cold water
2 tablespoons butter
1 teaspoon vanilla extract
1/4 teaspoon rum extract, optional

In a large saucepan, combine the sugar, flour, cinnamon, nutmeg and water until smooth. Bring to a boil; cook and stir for 2 minutes or until thickened. Remove from the heat; stir in butter, vanilla and rum extract if desired. **Yield:** 2-1/3 cups.

Strawberry Bruschetta

Prep/Total Time: 25 min.

Plain toast just can't compare to these slices of French bread topped with sweetened cream cheese, strawberries and jelly. —*Bob Knobel, Granger, Indiana*

☑ This recipe includes Nutrition Facts and Diabetic Exchanges.

1 loaf (8 ounces) French bread, cut into 24 slices
1 carton (8 ounces) spreadable cream cheese
1 tablespoon honey
1 pint strawberries, sliced
1/4 cup strawberry jelly, warmed

Arrange bread slices in a single layer on an ungreased baking sheet. Bake at 375° for 4-5 minutes on each side or until lightly crisp.

In a small mixing bowl, beat cream cheese and honey until smooth; spread over one side of each slice of bread. Top with berries; brush with jelly. **Yield:** 2 dozen.

Nutrition Facts: 1 appetizer equals 74 calories, 3 g fat (2 g saturated fat), 9 mg cholesterol, 93 mg sodium, 9 g carbohydrate, trace fiber, 2 g protein. **Diabetic Exchanges:** 1/2 starch, 1/2 fat.

Andouille Egg Burritos

(Pictured above)

Prep/Total Time: 30 min.

Give yourself a morning wake-up call with these spicy burritos. They make a terrific on-the-go breakfast, but you'll also want to try them on weeknights for a filling dinner. —*Frank Millard, Janesville, Wisconsin*

1/4 cup chopped onion
1 tablespoon butter
3/4 pound fully cooked andouille sausage links, sliced
1 tablespoon chopped green chilies
1 jalapeno pepper, seeded and chopped
8 eggs, lightly beaten
1/8 teaspoon salt
1/8 teaspoon pepper
Dash cayenne pepper
6 flour tortillas (8 inches), warmed
3 ounces pepper Jack cheese, shredded
Taco sauce, optional

In a large skillet over medium heat, cook onion in butter until tender. Add the sausage, chilies and jalapeno; cook 4-5 minutes longer or until heated through. Add the eggs, salt, pepper and cayenne; cook and stir until the eggs are completely set.

Spoon filling off center on each tortilla. Sprinkle each with 2 tablespoons cheese. Fold sides and ends over filling and roll up. Serve with taco sauce if desired. **Yield:** 6 servings.

Editor's Note: When cutting hot peppers, disposable gloves are recommended. Avoid touching your face.

Colorful Bacon & Egg Bake

Prep: 20 min. + chilling **Bake:** 50 min.

With this recipe from our Test Kitchen, you can whip up a tasty morning casserole the night before. Lots of peppers, bacon and cheese give it home-style appeal.

1 pound sliced bacon, diced
1/2 cup julienned sweet orange pepper
1/2 cup julienned sweet red pepper
6 cups cubed day-old bread
1-1/2 cups shredded Mexican cheese blend
9 eggs, beaten
2 cups milk
1 can (4 ounces) chopped green chilies
1-1/2 teaspoons chili powder
1 teaspoon ground cumin
Salsa and sour cream, optional

In a large skillet, cook the bacon over medium heat until crisp. Using a slotted spoon, remove to paper towels. Drain, reserving 1 tablespoon bacon drippings. In the same skillet, saute the sweet peppers in drippings until tender; transfer to a large bowl. Stir in the bacon, bread and cheese.

In another large bowl, combine eggs, milk, chilies, chili powder and cumin. Pour over bread mixture; gently stir to combine. Transfer to a greased 13-in. x 9-in. x 2-in. baking dish. Cover and refrigerate overnight.

Remove from the refrigerator 30 minutes before baking. Bake, uncovered, at 350° for 50-55 minutes or until a knife inserted near the center comes out clean. Let stand for 5 minutes before serving. Serve with salsa and sour cream if desired. **Yield:** 12 servings.

Chai Tea Latte

(Pictured below)

Prep/Total Time: 15 min.

My family loves this comforting tea, especially on cold days in place of hot chocolate...or when they're feeling under the weather. I simplified the recipe by using the filter basket of our coffeepot. Top each mug with a dollop of whipped topping and a sprinkling of ground nutmeg.
—Julie Plummer, Sykesville, Maryland

2 individual tea bags
1 teaspoon ground cinnamon
1/2 teaspoon ground ginger
1/4 teaspoon ground allspice
1 cup water
1 cup milk
1/4 cup packed brown sugar
2 tablespoons refrigerated French vanilla nondairy creamer
Whipped topping and ground nutmeg, optional

Place the tea bags, cinnamon, ginger and allspice in the coffee filter of a drip coffeemaker. Add water; brew according to manufacturer's directions.

Meanwhile, in a small saucepan, combine the milk, brown sugar and creamer. Cook and stir over medium heat until heated through and sugar is dissolved.

Pour milk mixture into mugs; stir in tea. Dollop with whipped topping and sprinkle with nutmeg if desired. **Yield:** 2 servings.

Chai Tea Latte

Mushroom Quiche Lorraine

Mushroom Quiche Lorraine

(Pictured above)

Prep: 15 min. **Bake:** 30 min.

Everyone at your breakfast table will delight in this savory quiche featuring mushrooms and green onions. Cheese and bacon lend a touch of decadence.—Michelle Fincher
Lyman, South Carolina

1 unbaked pastry shell (9 inches)
1 cup sliced fresh mushrooms
1/2 cup chopped green onions
2 tablespoons butter
4 eggs
1-1/4 cups half-and-half cream
1/8 teaspoon pepper
1 cup (4 ounces) shredded Swiss cheese
4 bacon strips, cooked and crumbled

Line unpricked pastry shell with a double thickness of heavy-duty foil. Bake at 450° for 8 minutes. Remove foil; bake 5 minutes longer. Remove from the oven; reduce heat to 375°.

Meanwhile, in a small skillet, saute mushrooms and onions in butter until tender. In a large bowl, beat eggs, cream and pepper. Using a slotted spoon, transfer mushrooms and onions to egg mixture. Stir in cheese and bacon.

Pour into crust. Cover edges loosely with foil. Bake for 30-35 minutes or until a knife inserted near the center comes out clean. Let stand for 5 minutes before cutting. **Yield:** 6 servings.

Chapter 12

Snappy Soups & Sandwiches

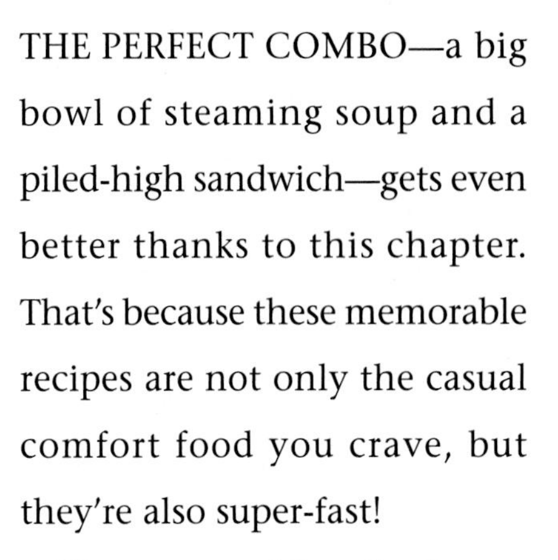

THE PERFECT COMBO—a big bowl of steaming soup and a piled-high sandwich—gets even better thanks to this chapter. That's because these memorable recipes are not only the casual comfort food you crave, but they're also super-fast!

No more waiting for hours for a simmering pot of soup—or needing too much time to fix a simple sandwich. You'll be eating in a snap when you choose favorites such as Stovetop Beef Stew, Mushroom Corn Chowder, Grilled Bacon Burgers and Chicken Pesto Wraps.

Whether you need a quick lunch or a satisfying dinner for your family, these recipes are guaranteed to please.

TASTY TWOSOME. Turkey Salad Sandwiches (p. 184) and Sausage and Bean Soup (p. 187).

Mushroom Corn Chowder

Hearty Open-Faced Sandwiches

Prep/Total Time: 25 min.

I discovered this quick-to-fix recipe a long time ago, and it's really good. With three kinds of meat and two bold sauces, the sandwiches pack a flavorful punch. And because they're oven-baked, they're great when your family craves a hot meal.
—Beverly McClure, Ames, Iowa

6 English muffins, split
3 tablespoons butter, melted
1 teaspoon garlic powder
1/2 cup Thousand Island salad dressing
12 bacon strips, halved and cooked
12 ounces thinly sliced deli pastrami
6 ounces thinly sliced deli ham
1/2 cup horseradish sauce
6 slices Swiss cheese, halved
1/4 to 1/2 teaspoon dill weed
Dill pickle slices, optional

Arrange the English muffin halves, cut side up, on a baking sheet. Broil 4-6 in. from the heat for 2-3 minutes or until golden brown.

Combine the butter and garlic powder; brush over the muffin halves. Spread with salad dressing. Layer with bacon, pastrami, ham, horseradish and Swiss cheese; sprinkle with dill.

Broil 4-6 in. from the heat for 3-4 minutes or until the cheese is melted. Serve sandwiches with pickles if desired. **Yield:** 6 servings.

Mushroom Corn Chowder

(Pictured above)

Prep/Total Time: 30 min.

Chock-full of vegetables, ham and cheese, this thick and creamy chowder will take the chill off even the nippiest of fall or winter evenings. Serve it with slices of crusty French bread. *—Elaine Krupsky, Las Vegas, Nevada*

1-1/4 cups sliced fresh carrots
1 cup chopped celery with leaves
3/4 cup sliced fresh mushrooms
3 green onions, sliced
1/4 cup butter, cubed
1 can (10-3/4 ounces) condensed cream of mushroom soup, undiluted
1-1/3 cups milk
1-1/2 cups frozen corn, thawed
1/2 cup cubed fully cooked ham
1/2 teaspoon seasoned salt
1/2 cup cubed process cheese (Velveeta)

In a large saucepan, saute the carrots, celery, mushrooms and onions in butter until tender. Stir in the soup, milk, corn, ham and seasoned salt. Bring to a boil. Reduce heat; stir in cheese. Cook and stir 3-5 minutes longer or until cheese is melted. **Yield:** 8 servings.

Toasted PB & Banana Sandwiches

Prep/Total Time: 20 min.

When I first came across this unusual recipe, I thought, "No way!" But the grilled peanut butter and banana sandwiches are a surprisingly delicious, finger-licking treat. Try them for yourself—you'll be as amazed as I was!
—Marian Pickett, Argyle, Wisconsin

✓ This recipe includes Nutrition Facts.

2 large ripe bananas
6 tablespoons reduced-fat peanut butter
8 slices whole wheat bread
2 tablespoons honey
Refrigerated butter-flavored spray

Cut each banana in half widthwise, then cut each half lengthwise into four pieces. Spread peanut butter on each slice of bread. Place the banana slices on four slices of bread; drizzle with honey. Top with the remaining bread slices.

Spritz the outsides of sandwiches with butter-flavored spray. In a large nonstick skillet, toast the sandwiches over medium heat until golden brown. **Yield:** 4 servings.

Nutrition Facts: 1 sandwich equals 358 calories, 11 g fat (2 g saturated fat), 0 cholesterol, 433 mg sodium, 58 g carbohydrate, 7 g fiber, 13 g protein.

Grilled Bacon Burgers

(Pictured below)

Prep/Total Time: 20 min.

I really enjoy cooking and having guests over for meals. These juicy burgers are always a hit at get-togethers.
—Wanda Holoubek, Omaha, Nebraska

1 egg
1/2 cup shredded cheddar cheese
2 tablespoons chopped onion
2 tablespoons soy sauce
2 tablespoons ketchup
1/4 teaspoon pepper
1 pound ground beef
5 bacon strips
5 hamburger buns, split
Leaf lettuce, tomato slices and onion slices, optional

In a small bowl, combine the egg, cheese, onion, soy sauce, ketchup and pepper. Crumble beef over mixture and mix well. Shape into five patties. Wrap a bacon strip around each; secure with a toothpick.

Grill patties, uncovered, over medium-hot heat for 5-6 minutes on each side or until meat is no longer pink. Discard toothpicks. Serve on buns with lettuce, tomato and onion if desired. **Yield:** 5 servings.

Grilled Bacon Burgers

Tomato Seafood Soup

Tomato Seafood Soup

(Pictured above)

Prep: 10 min. **Cook:** 35 min.

We like to make this chunky soup on Sundays during football season. For a little extra zip, we sometimes add red pepper flakes or use jalapeno-flavored tomatoes.
—Mary Adams, Fairport, New York

1/2 cup chopped onion
1/2 cup chopped green pepper
1/2 teaspoon minced garlic
1 tablespoon olive oil
1 can (14 ounces) diced tomatoes, undrained
1 jar (14 ounces) spaghetti sauce
1 cup salsa
3/4 cup chicken broth
1/2 cup white wine *or* additional chicken broth
3 teaspoons dried parsley flakes
1/4 teaspoon dried oregano
1/4 teaspoon dried basil
1/8 to 1/4 teaspoon pepper
1 package (12 ounces) frozen uncooked shrimp, thawed, peeled and deveined
1 package (8 ounces) imitation crabmeat, chopped *or* 2 cans (6 ounces *each*) crabmeat, drained, flaked and cartilage removed
1 can (6-1/2 ounces) minced clams, undrained

In a Dutch oven, saute the onion, green pepper and garlic in oil until onion is tender. Stir in the tomatoes, spaghetti sauce, salsa, broth, wine or additional broth and seasonings. Bring to a boil. Reduce heat; cover and simmer for 20 minutes.

Add the shrimp, crab and clams. Cover and simmer for 5-7 minutes or until shrimp turn pink. **Yield:** 8 servings (2 quarts).

Stovetop Beef Stew

(Pictured below)

Prep/Total Time: 30 min.

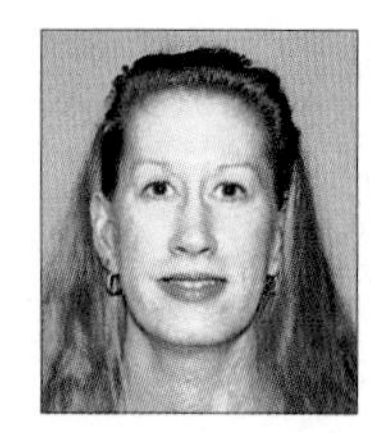

Homemade beef stew in 30 minutes? It's possible with this recipe. The secret is using convenience items—a frozen dinner, canned tomatoes and packaged veggies. Serve bowlfuls with a tossed salad and dinner rolls for a complete meal.
—Mitzi Sentiff, Alexandria, Virginia

- **1 package (24 ounces) frozen Yankee pot roast skillet dinner**
- **1 can (14-1/2 ounces) diced tomatoes with roasted garlic, undrained**
- **1 cup reduced-sodium beef broth**
- **1/2 cup dry red wine *or* additional reduced-sodium beef broth**
- **1/2 cup sliced celery**
- **1/2 teaspoon pepper**
- **1/8 to 1/4 teaspoon dried marjoram**
- **1 package (9 ounces) frozen peas and pearl onions**
- **2 tablespoons minced fresh parsley**

In a large saucepan, combine the pot roast dinner, tomatoes, broth, wine or additional broth, celery, pepper and marjoram. Bring to a boil. Reduce heat; cover and simmer for 8 minutes.

Stir in the peas and onions; cook 7-9 minutes longer or until onions are tender. Sprinkle with parsley. **Yield:** 4 servings.

Editor's Note: This recipe was tested with Stouffer's Skillets Yankee Pot Roast.

Stovetop Beef Stew

Chicken Pesto Wraps

Chicken Pesto Wraps

(Pictured above)

Prep/Total Time: 20 min.

This makes a really speedy lunch or supper for us. The wraps are so simple to prepare—and cleanup is just as easy. My wife likes to add a dollop of sour cream to hers.
—Gary Phile, Ravenna, Ohio

- **1/2 pound ground chicken**
- **1 tablespoon vegetable oil**
- **1/4 cup sun-dried tomato pesto**
- **4 flour tortillas (8 inches), warmed**
- **1/2 cup shredded part-skim mozzarella cheese**
- **8 grape tomatoes, cut in half**
- **4 slices red onion, separated into rings**
- **1 cup shredded lettuce**

In a large skillet, cook chicken in oil over medium heat for 5-6 minutes or until juices run clear; drain.

Spread pesto over each tortilla; spoon chicken down the center. Layer with cheese, tomatoes, onion and lettuce; roll up. **Yield:** 4 servings.

Seconds on Stew

When I fix beef stew, I usually make extra so I'm sure to have some left over. I reheat it another night and add a pastry crust on top. My family looks forward to this "potpie" just as much as the original stew.
—Amelia Law, Ardmore, Pennsylvania

Hearty Sausage Stromboli

Prep: 25 min. **Bake:** 15 min.

Serve slices of this meaty stromboli, and you're sure to get raves from the whole gang. With a deliciously seasoned filling and tender Italian bread, what's not to love?
—Debbie Brunssen, Randolph, Nebraska

1/2 pound bulk Italian sausage
1/4 pound ground beef
1/2 cup chopped onion
1/2 cup sliced fresh mushrooms
1/4 cup chopped green pepper
1/2 cup water
1/3 cup tomato paste
2 tablespoons grated Parmesan cheese
1/2 teaspoon salt
1/4 teaspoon dried oregano
1/4 teaspoon minced garlic
1/8 teaspoon dried rosemary, crushed
1 loaf (1 pound) Italian bread
6 slices part-skim mozzarella cheese

In a large skillet, cook the sausage, beef, onion, mushrooms and green pepper over medium heat until meat is no longer pink; drain. Stir in the water, tomato paste, Parmesan cheese, salt, oregano, garlic and rosemary. Bring to a boil. Reduce the heat; simmer, uncovered, for 5 minutes or until thickened.

Meanwhile, cut top third off loaf of bread; carefully hollow out bottom, leaving a 1/2-in. shell (discard removed bread or save for another use).

Line bottom half with three mozzarella cheese slices; top with sausage mixture and remaining cheese. Replace the bread top. Wrap sandwich loaf in foil. Bake at 400° for 15-20 minutes or until cheese is melted. Let stand for 5 minutes before slicing. **Yield:** 6 servings.

Baked Ham Salad Sandwiches

Prep/Total Time: 30 min.

When something hot is the order of the day, you can still enjoy ham salad sandwiches—thanks to this oven-baked version. *—Nancy Cornelius, Mercer, Pennsylvania*

3 tablespoons mayonnaise
1-1/2 teaspoons cider vinegar
3/4 teaspoon sugar
6 ounces shaved fully cooked ham, chopped
3 ounces process cheese (Velveeta), cubed
1 hard-cooked egg, chopped
1/4 cup chopped celery
2 tablespoons chopped onion
2 tablespoons chopped green pepper
4 onion rolls, split

In a large bowl, combine the mayonnaise, vinegar and sugar. Stir in the ham, cheese, egg, celery, onion and green pepper. Spoon about 1/2 cup onto each roll bottom; replace tops.

Wrap individually in heavy-duty foil. Place on a baking sheet. Bake at 350° for 15-20 minutes or until heated through. **Yield:** 4 servings.

Spicy Chicken Bundles

(Pictured below)

Prep: 25 min. **Bake:** 15 min.

A friend introduced me to these popovers, and I altered the recipe a bit by adding jalapeno peppers. With that added "kick," my family has enjoyed these for many years.
—Vicki Bluemner, Collinsville, Illinois

1 package (3 ounces) cream cheese, softened
2 tablespoons milk
1 tablespoon pickled jalapeno slices, chopped
1/4 teaspoon pepper
2 cups cubed cooked chicken
1/2 cup chopped onion
2 tubes (8 ounces *each*) refrigerated crescent rolls
1 tablespoon butter, melted
4 teaspoons seasoned bread crumbs
MUSHROOM SAUCE:
1 can (10-3/4 ounces) condensed cream of mushroom soup, undiluted
1/2 cup milk

In a large mixing bowl, beat the cream cheese, milk, jalapenos and pepper until blended. Stir in the chicken and onion.

Separate crescent dough into eight rectangles; seal perforations. Spoon 1/4 cup chicken mixture onto the center of each rectangle; bring corners up to the center and pinch edges to seal.

Place on an ungreased baking sheet. Brush with butter; sprinkle with bread crumbs. Bake at 375° for 15-20 minutes or until golden brown.

Meanwhile, in a small saucepan, combine soup and milk. Cook and stir over medium heat until heated through. Serve with bundles. **Yield:** 8 servings.

Editor's Note: When cutting hot peppers, disposable gloves are recommended. Avoid touching your face.

Spicy Chicken Bundles

Wedding Soup

Wedding Soup

(Pictured above)

Prep: 20 min. **Cook:** 25 min.

We love this simplified version of classic Italian wedding soup. My son requests it often—and begs me to put leftovers in his lunch box! —Kimberly Parker, Elyria, Ohio

- **1 egg, beaten**
- **3/4 cup chopped onion, *divided***
- **1/3 cup dry bread crumbs**
- **1/2 pound ground turkey**
- **1-1/2 teaspoons vegetable oil**
- **2 cups sliced fresh carrots**
- **1-1/2 cups chopped celery**
- **1 tablespoon butter**
- **4 cups fresh baby spinach**
- **3 cans (14-1/2 ounces *each*) chicken broth**
- **1 cup cubed cooked chicken breast**
- **2 tablespoons minced fresh parsley**
- **1/2 teaspoon dried thyme**
- **1/8 teaspoon salt**
- **1/8 teaspoon pepper**
- **1-1/4 cups acini di pepe pasta *or* small pasta shells**

In a large bowl, combine the egg, 1/4 cup onion and bread crumbs. Crumble turkey over mixture and mix well. Shape into 1-in. balls. In a large skillet, brown meatballs in oil until no longer pink; drain and set aside.

Meanwhile, in a large saucepan, saute the carrots, celery and remaining onion in butter until crisp-tender. Add the spinach, broth, chicken, parsley, thyme, salt, pepper and reserved meatballs. Cook, uncovered, over medium heat for 10 minutes.

Bring to a boil. Add pasta; cook, uncovered, for 6-7 minutes or until pasta is tender, stirring occasionally. **Yield:** 6 servings.

Turkey Salad Sandwiches

(Pictured on page 178)

Prep/Total Time: 15 min.

Inspired by a terrific turkey salad sandwich on the menu at a local deli, I developed a version to suit my family's tastes. Serve it on croissants for an elegant luncheon...or on hearty whole-grain bread for a filling meal.
—Merrijane Rice, Bountiful, Utah

- **10 ounces deli turkey, cubed**
- **2 cups torn romaine**
- **6 bacon strips, cooked and crumbled**
- **1/2 cup shredded Swiss cheese**
- **1/2 cup mayonnaise**
- **1/3 cup frozen peas, thawed**
- **2 green onions, thinly sliced**
- **1/4 teaspoon pepper**
- **12 slices whole wheat bread**

In a large bowl, combine the first eight ingredients. Spoon 2/3 cup mixture on each of six bread slices. Top with remaining bread slices. **Yield:** 6 servings.

Herbed Tomato Soup

Prep: 15 min. **Cook:** 30 min.

This wonderful, comforting recipe may appear complicated at first glance, but it actually goes together in only 15 minutes—and is well worth the effort!
—Bev Hatfield, Arlington, Washington

1-1/4 cups chopped celery
1/2 cup chopped onion
1-1/2 teaspoons minced garlic
2 tablespoons butter
2 medium carrots, grated
1 medium potato, peeled and chopped
1 cup water
2 cups tomato juice
1 can (10-3/4 ounces) condensed tomato soup, undiluted
1 can (14-1/2 ounces) diced tomatoes, undrained
1 tablespoon minced fresh parsley *or* 1 teaspoon dried parsley flakes
1 bay leaf
1 teaspoon dried oregano
1 teaspoon dried basil
1/2 teaspoon salt
1/4 teaspoon pepper
1 cup milk
1 cup salad croutons
1/2 cup shredded Parmesan cheese

In a large saucepan, saute the celery, onion and garlic in butter until tender. Stir in the carrots, potato and water. Bring to a boil. Reduce heat; cover and simmer for 10 minutes.

Stir in the tomato juice, soup, tomatoes, parsley, bay leaf, oregano, basil, salt and pepper. Bring to a boil. Reduce heat; simmer, uncovered, for 5-10 minutes or until vegetables are tender.

Stir in the milk; heat through. Discard bay leaf. Top each serving with croutons and Parmesan cheese. **Yield:** 5 servings.

Ham and Cheese Loaf

Prep: 15 min. **Bake:** 30 min.

Convenient refrigerated dough makes it easy to prepare this golden bread stuffed with ham and cheese. I created the recipe by experimenting with a few ingredients my family likes. It's a hot, satisfying sandwich anytime.
—Gloria Lindell, Welcome, Minnesota

1 tube (13.8 ounces) refrigerated pizza crust
10 slices deli ham
1/4 cup sliced green onions
1 cup (4 ounces) shredded part-skim mozzarella cheese
1 cup (4 ounces) shredded cheddar cheese
4 slices provolone cheese
1 tablespoon butter, melted

Unroll dough onto a greased baking sheet; top with ham, onions and cheeses. Roll up tightly jelly-roll style, starting with a long side; pinch seam to seal and tuck ends under. Brush with butter.

Bake at 350° for 30-35 minutes or until golden brown. Let stand for 5 minutes; cut into 1-in. slices. **Yield:** 6 servings.

Easy Chicken Melts

(Pictured below)

Prep/Total Time: 30 min.

These cheesy, Cajun-flavored sandwiches are delicious right out of the oven. When I have leftover baked chicken breasts, I cut them up to use instead of canned chicken.
—Jessi Holland, Pensacola, Florida

1 can (9-3/4 ounces) chunk white chicken, drained and flaked
1 cup (4 ounces) shredded cheddar cheese, *divided*
1/2 cup finely chopped onion
1/2 cup diced green pepper
1/4 cup mayonnaise
3/4 teaspoon Cajun seasoning
1/2 teaspoon minced garlic
10 slices Italian bread (1/2 inch thick)
2 plum tomatoes, sliced

In a small bowl, combine the chicken, 1/2 cup cheese, onion, green pepper, mayonnaise, Cajun seasoning and garlic. Spread over bread slices. Top each with a tomato slice; sprinkle with remaining cheese.

Place on an ungreased baking sheet. Bake at 375° for 10-12 minutes or until bread is toasted and golden brown. **Yield:** 5 servings.

Easy Chicken Melts

Mushroom Swiss Burgers

(Pictured below)

Prep/Total Time: 30 min.

Heaped with slices of fresh mushrooms and Swiss cheese, these saucy skillet sandwiches are fantastic when you're craving a juicy burger but don't want to fire up the grill. Add fries and shakes for a winning, all-American meal.
—Mrs. James Bowles, Ironton, Ohio

- **1-1/2 pounds ground beef**
- **1 pound sliced fresh mushrooms**
- **1 can (10-3/4 ounces) condensed cream of mushroom soup, undiluted**
- **1 cup water**
- **6 slices Swiss cheese**
- **6 hamburger buns, split**

Shape the ground beef into six patties. In a large skillet, cook the beef patties over medium-high heat for 5-7 minutes on each side or until the meat is no longer pink. Remove to paper towels; drain, reserving 2 tablespoons drippings. Saute the fresh mushrooms in the drippings until tender.

Meanwhile, in a microwave-safe bowl, combine the soup and water. Cover and microwave on high for 2-1/2 to 3-1/2 minutes or until heated through. Return patties to the skillet. Stir in soup. Bring to a boil. Reduce heat; simmer, uncovered, for 3 minutes.

Top each patty with cheese. Remove from the heat; cover and let stand until cheese is melted. Serve on buns with mushrooms. **Yield:** 6 servings.

Mushroom Swiss Burgers

Tarragon Crab Sandwiches

Prep/Total Time: 20 min.

With a flavor similar to that of anise, tarragon adds its own distinct flair to these crab salad sandwiches from our Test Kitchen home economists. They added even more of a kick with hot pepper sauce. Using packaged precooked bacon shortens the preparation time.

- **1 package (16 ounces) imitation crabmeat, chopped**
- **1/3 cup chopped celery**
- **1/3 cup mayonnaise**
- **1 tablespoon chopped green onion**
- **2 teaspoons minced fresh tarragon**
- **2 to 3 drops hot pepper sauce**
- **1/8 teaspoon salt**
- **1/8 teaspoon pepper**
- **12 ready-to-serve fully cooked bacon strips**
- **12 slices sourdough bread, toasted**
- **6 lettuce leaves**
- **6 slices tomato**

In a small bowl, combine the first eight ingredients. Cook the bacon according to the package directions. On six slices of bread, layer the lettuce, tomato, bacon and crab mixture. Top with the remaining bread slices. **Yield:** 6 servings.

Creamy Turkey Vegetable Soup

Prep: 15 min. **Cook:** 30 min.

Have leftover cooked turkey from a holiday dinner or other special meal? Here's the solution: Dice up the extras and put them in this wonderful soup. It also features plenty of vegetables and is especially good on chilly nights.
—Stephanie Moon, Silverdale, Washington

- **1 cup diced fresh carrots**
- **1/2 cup chopped celery**
- **1/3 cup chopped onion**
- **2 tablespoons butter**
- **2 cups diced cooked turkey**
- **2 cups water**
- **1-1/2 cups diced peeled potatoes**
- **2 teaspoons chicken bouillon granules**
- **1/2 teaspoon salt**
- **1/2 teaspoon pepper**
- **2-1/2 cups milk, *divided***
- **3 tablespoons all-purpose flour**

In a large saucepan, saute the carrots, celery and onion in butter until tender. Stir in the turkey, water, potatoes, bouillon, salt and pepper. Bring to a boil. Reduce heat; cover and simmer for 10-12 minutes or until vegetables are tender.

Stir in 2 cups milk. Combine flour and remaining milk until smooth. Stir into soup. Bring to a boil; cook and stir for 2 minutes or until thickened. **Yield:** 4 servings.

Sausage and Bean Soup

Sausage and Bean Soup

(Pictured above and on page 178)

Prep: 15 min. **Cook:** 25 min.

I love to prepare this recipe when the weather turns crisp. The meaty, filling soup tastes like it has simmered all day on the stove, but it's actually ready to enjoy in less than an hour. It's become a real family favorite.
—Joan Hallford, North Richland Hills, Texas

2 bacon strips, diced
1/2 cup chopped onion
1 cup thinly sliced halved fresh carrots
1 cup cubed peeled potatoes
3 cups water
8 ounces smoked Polish sausage, halved and thinly sliced
2 cups frozen cut green beans, thawed
1 can (15 ounces) white kidney *or* cannellini beans, rinsed and drained
1/2 cup minced fresh parsley
3/4 teaspoon salt
1/2 teaspoon pepper
1/2 teaspoon minced fresh marjoram *or* 1/8 teaspoon dried marjoram

In a large saucepan, cook bacon over medium heat until crisp. Using a slotted spoon, remove to paper towels to drain. Saute onion in drippings until tender. Stir in carrots and potatoes; cook for 2 minutes. Add the water; bring to a boil. Reduce the heat; cover and simmer for 9-12 minutes or until vegetables are tender.

Stir in the sausage, green beans, kidney beans, parsley, salt, pepper and marjoram; heat through. Sprinkle with reserved bacon. **Yield:** 5 servings.

Barbecued Ham Sandwiches

(Pictured below)

Prep/Total Time: 25 min.

I came up with this recipe one day when I was trying to use up food in the refrigerator. You won't need a side of coleslaw with these because the coleslaw is part of the sandwich! Try it when you need a hurry-up meal.
—Mary Ann Lee, Clifton Park, New York

1/4 cup butter, softened
1 tablespoon Dijon mustard
2 teaspoons minced fresh thyme *or* 1/2 teaspoon dried thyme
2 teaspoons minced fresh parsley
1/2 teaspoon minced garlic
1/8 teaspoon pepper
3/4 pound fully cooked ham, thinly sliced
3/4 cup barbecue sauce
1 cup deli coleslaw
8 slices white bread

In a small bowl, combine the butter, mustard, thyme, parsley, garlic and pepper; set aside.

In a large saucepan, cook the ham and barbecue sauce over medium heat for 3-4 minutes or until heated through.

Place the ham and coleslaw on four bread slices; top with the remaining bread. Spread the outsides of the sandwiches with butter mixture. In a large skillet, toast sandwiches for 1-2 minutes on each side or until golden brown. **Yield:** 4 servings.

Barbecued Ham Sandwiches

Chicken Alfredo Sandwiches

Chicken Alfredo Sandwiches

(Pictured above)

Prep/Total Time: 30 min.

Everyone raves over this deliciously different meal-in-a-sandwich. Prepared Alfredo sauce makes it a cinch to put together. —Bernice Janowski, Stevens Point, Wisconsin

1/2 teaspoon Italian seasoning
1/4 teaspoon salt
1/4 teaspoon pepper
4 boneless skinless chicken breast halves (4 ounces *each*)
1 tablespoon vegetable oil
1 jar (7 ounces) roasted sweet red peppers, drained and cut into strips
1/4 cup butter, melted
2 tablespoons minced fresh parsley
1/2 teaspoon onion powder
1/2 teaspoon garlic powder
4 Italian rolls (6 inches), split
1 cup fresh baby spinach
1/2 cup Alfredo sauce, warmed

Combine the Italian seasoning, salt and pepper; sprinkle over chicken. In a large skillet, cook chicken in oil over medium heat for 8-10 minutes on each side or until juices run clear, topping with red pepper strips during the last 3 minutes.

Meanwhile, in a small bowl, combine the butter, parsley, onion powder and garlic powder; brush over cut sides of rolls. Place cut side up on an ungreased baking sheet. Broil 4 in. from the heat for 2-3 minutes or until lightly browned.

On each roll bottom, layer 1/4 cup spinach, 1 tablespoon Alfredo sauce, a chicken breast half and another tablespoon of Alfredo sauce. Replace tops of rolls. **Yield:** 4 servings.

Farmhouse Ham Chowder

(Pictured below)

Prep: 10 min. **Cook:** 30 min.

This chowder is full-flavored and so comforting. Pair big bowlfuls with crusty rolls, biscuits or thick slices of bread on the side. —Lisa Renshaw, Kansas City, Missouri

1/2 cup finely chopped onion
1/2 cup finely chopped celery
1/2 cup chopped sweet red pepper
2 tablespoons butter
1/4 cup all-purpose flour
1 envelope ranch salad dressing mix
4-1/4 cups milk
2 cups frozen cubed hash brown potatoes, thawed
2 cups frozen corn, thawed
2 cups cubed fully cooked ham
1 teaspoon minced fresh thyme *or* 1/4 teaspoon dried thyme
2 ounces smoked Gouda cheese, shredded

In a large saucepan, saute the onion, celery and red pepper in butter until vegetables are crisp-tender. Stir in flour and dressing mix until smooth; gradually stir in milk. Bring to a boil; cook and stir for 2 minutes or until thickened.

Add the potatoes, corn, ham and thyme. Bring to a boil. Reduce heat; simmer, uncovered, for 8-10 minutes or until heated through. Sprinkle with the cheese before serving. **Yield:** 8 servings (2 quarts).

Farmhouse Ham Chowder

Cashew Chicken Salad Sandwiches

(Pictured at right)

Prep/Total Time: 15 min.

I think this is the best chicken salad recipe around! It's wholesome, has wonderful flavor and gets a nice crunch from the cashews. —Peggi Kelly, Fairbury, Nebraska

2 cups diced cooked chicken
1/2 cup chopped salted cashews
1/2 cup chopped red apple
1/2 cup chopped peeled cucumber
1/2 cup mayonnaise
1/2 teaspoon sugar
1/2 teaspoon salt
Dash pepper
6 lettuce leaves, optional
6 kaiser rolls *or* croissants, split

In a large bowl, combine the chicken, cashews, apple and cucumber. In a small bowl, combine the mayonnaise, sugar, salt and pepper. Add to chicken mixture and toss to coat.

Place a lettuce leaf if desired and 1/2 cup chicken salad on each roll bottom; replace the roll tops. **Yield:** 6 servings.

Cashew Chicken Salad Sandwiches

Flank Steak Sandwiches

Prep: 25 min. + marinating **Grill:** 25 min.

My sister and I found this recipe 15 years ago, changed a few ingredients and made it our own. When family and friends hear we're serving these sandwiches, they come running! —Elizabeth Hiner, Chico, California

1 cup chopped onion
1 cup dry red wine *or* beef broth
3/4 cup soy sauce
1/2 cup olive oil, *divided*
4-1/2 teaspoons minced garlic, *divided*
1-1/2 teaspoons ground mustard
1-1/2 teaspoons ground ginger
1 beef flank steak (1-1/2 pounds)
1 medium sweet red pepper, cut into 1-inch strips
1 medium sweet yellow pepper, cut into 1-inch strips
1 medium red onion, thickly sliced
1/4 teaspoon pepper
6 French rolls, split

In a small bowl, combine the onion, wine or broth, soy sauce, 1/4 cup olive oil, 2-1/2 teaspoons garlic, mustard and ginger. Pour 1-3/4 cups into a large resealable plastic bag; add steak. Pour remaining marinade into another resealable plastic bag; add the peppers and onion. Seal bags and turn to coat; refrigerate for 3 hours or overnight, turning occasionally.

Drain and discard the marinade from the steak. Grill, covered, over medium heat for 6-7 minutes on each side or until the meat reaches the desired doneness (for medium-rare, a meat thermometer should read 145°; medium, 160°; well-done, 170°).

Drain and discard marinade from vegetables. Place in a grill basket or disposable foil pan with slits cut in the bottom. Grill, uncovered, over medium-hot heat for 9-11 minutes or until tender, stirring frequently.

In a small bowl, combine the pepper and the remaining oil and garlic; brush over the cut sides of rolls. Place cut side down on grill for 2-3 minutes or until golden brown.

Thinly slice steak across the grain; place on bun bottoms. Top with vegetables and bun tops. Serve immediately. **Yield:** 6 servings.

Taco Avocado Wraps

Prep/Total Time: 30 min.

I came up with these one night when we wanted a light meal but didn't want to heat the oven. The taco-flavored wraps make a great lunch, too...or even a filling snack. —Renee Rutherford, Andover, Minnesota

1 package (8 ounces) cream cheese, softened
1/2 cup sour cream
1 can (4 ounces) chopped green chilies, drained
1 tablespoon taco seasoning
4 flour tortillas (10 inches), room temperature
2 medium ripe avocados, peeled and sliced
2 plum tomatoes, thinly sliced
5 green onions, sliced
1 can (4 ounces) sliced ripe olives, drained

In a small bowl, combine the cream cheese, sour cream, chilies and taco seasoning. Spread about 1/2 cup over each tortilla. Top with the avocados, tomatoes, onions and olives; roll up. **Yield:** 4 servings.

Chapter 13

Easy Half-Hour Entrees

AFTER A BUSY DAY at work, running errands or doing other activities, the last thing you want to do is spend lots of time in the kitchen making supper. After all, you're tired, and your family's hungry!

The good news is, a mere 30 minutes is all you'll ever need to put a hearty, home-cooked meal on the dinner table. This chapter proves it's true with quick but delicious entrees, including Barbecued Pork Chops, Tomato Cheese Pizza and Pita Fajitas.

You'll even find satisfying main dishes you can fix in just 15 minutes, such as Vegetable Fish Dinner. With all of these time-saving meals, you'll always have plenty of time to relax.

30-MINUTE MAINSTAY. Curry Chicken (p. 199).

Southwest Smothered Chicken

Herbed Artichoke Cheese Tortellini

(Pictured below)

Prep/Total Time: 30 min.

Parsley can accent nearly anything with its slightly peppery taste and vibrant color. It also enhances other herbs—like the ones in this delicious meatless pasta dish. It looks and tastes like a specialty you'd find at an Italian restaurant.
—Karen Anzelc, Peoria, Arizona

2 cans (14-1/2 ounces *each*) Italian diced tomatoes
2 jars (6-1/2 ounces *each*) marinated quartered artichoke hearts
2 packages (9 ounces *each*) refrigerated cheese tortellini
2 cups chopped onions
1/2 cup minced fresh parsley
2 to 4 tablespoons minced fresh *or* 2 to 4 teaspoons dried basil
2 teaspoons minced garlic
1/2 teaspoon dried oregano
1/8 teaspoon crushed red pepper flakes
1/2 cup olive oil
1 can (2-1/4 ounces) sliced ripe olives, drained
1/2 teaspoon salt
1/4 cup grated Parmesan cheese

Drain tomatoes, reserving 2/3 cup juice; set aside. Drain artichokes, reserving 3/4 cup liquid; chop and set aside.

Cook tortellini according to package directions. Meanwhile, in a large skillet, saute the onions, parsley, basil, garlic, oregano and pepper flakes in oil for 4-5 minutes or until onions are tender. Add the reserved tomatoes, tomato juice and artichoke liquid.

Bring to a boil. Reduce heat; simmer, uncovered, for 10-12 minutes or until slightly thickened. Drain tortellini; add to tomato mixture. Stir in the olives, salt and reserved artichokes; heat through. Sprinkle with Parmesan cheese. **Yield:** 8 servings.

Herbed Artichoke Cheese Tortellini

Southwest Smothered Chicken

(Pictured above)

Prep/Total Time: 30 min.

Get ready to hear "Wow" from your family! There's a fiesta in every bite of this chicken entree, which is guaranteed to spice up and speed up your dinnertime routine. If you're concerned about the heat level, simply reduce the amount of jalapenos or eliminate them altogether.
—Debbie Schaefer, Durand, Michigan

4 boneless skinless chicken breast halves (6 ounces *each*)
1/2 teaspoon ground cumin
1/2 teaspoon cayenne pepper
1 tablespoon vegetable oil
1 cup fresh *or* frozen corn
1 cup salsa
1 cup (4 ounces) shredded pepper Jack cheese
1/4 cup pickled jalapeno slices
1/4 cup sour cream

Flatten the chicken breast halves to 1/2-in. thickness. Sprinkle both sides of chicken with cumin and cayenne pepper. In a large skillet, cook chicken in oil over medium heat for 4-5 minutes on each side or until the juices run clear.

Meanwhile, combine corn and salsa; spoon over chicken. Top with cheese and jalapenos. Cover and cook for 3-5 minutes or until heated through and cheese is melted. Top each chicken breast with sour cream. **Yield:** 4 servings.

Burritos Made Easy

Burritos Made Easy

(Pictured above)

Prep/Total Time: 30 min.

These big burritos are packed with a hearty bean-and-beef filling and Southwestern flavor. No one will leave the table hungry! —*Jennifer McKinney, Washington, Illinois*

1 pound ground beef
1/4 cup chopped onion
1 can (15 ounces) chili with beans
1-1/4 cups chunky salsa
1/4 cup chopped green chilies
8 flour tortillas (8 inches), warmed
8 slices process American cheese
Taco sauce and shredded lettuce, optional

In a large skillet, cook beef and onion over medium heat until meat is no longer pink; drain. Stir in the chili, salsa and chilies. Bring to a boil. Reduce heat; simmer, uncovered, for 5 minutes.

Spoon about 1/2 cupful beef mixture off center on each tortilla. Top each with a cheese slice; roll up. Serve with taco sauce and lettuce if desired. **Yield:** 8 burritos.

Tuna-Stuffed Tomatoes

Prep/Total Time: 15 min.

I consider this recipe an old standby. It's always a good choice for a satisfying lunch, and I usually have the ingredients handy. —*Molly Seidel, Edgewood, New Mexico*

2 large tomatoes
1 can (6 ounces) solid white tuna, drained
1 whole dill pickle, chopped
1/4 cup mayonnaise
2 tablespoons finely chopped onion
1 tablespoon prepared mustard
1/8 teaspoon salt
1/8 teaspoon pepper
1 hard-cooked egg, chopped

Cut a thin slice off the top of each tomato. Scoop out the pulp, leaving 1/2-in. shells. Invert onto paper towels to drain.

In a small bowl, combine the tuna, pickle, mayonnaise, onion, mustard, salt and pepper. Gently stir in egg; spoon into tomato shells. **Yield:** 2 servings.

Vegetable Fish Dinner

(Pictured below)

Prep/Total Time: 15 min.

Everyone in our family loves fish. I like to fix it in the microwave because it doesn't dry out, and it's easier than frying. —*Paula Marches, Lenhartsville, Pennsylvania*

✓ This recipe includes Nutrition Facts and Diabetic Exchanges.

2 fresh *or* frozen orange roughy fillets (6 ounces *each*)
2 tablespoons minced chives
2 teaspoons minced fresh thyme
1 medium lime, thinly sliced
3 cups frozen Italian vegetables, thawed
2 teaspoons butter, melted
1/4 teaspoon salt
1/8 teaspoon pepper

Place fish in an 8-in. square microwave-safe dish. Sprinkle with chives and thyme. Top with lime and vegetables. Drizzle with butter; sprinkle with salt and pepper.

Cover and microwave on high for 5-7 minutes or until fish flakes easily with a fork and vegetables are heated through. **Yield:** 2 servings.

Editor's Note: This recipe was tested in a 1,100-watt microwave.

Nutrition Facts: 1 fillet with 1-1/2 cups vegetables equals 247 calories, 5 g fat (2 g saturated fat), 112 mg cholesterol, 517 mg sodium, 16 g carbohydrate, 6 g fiber, 31 g protein. **Diabetic Exchanges:** 5 very lean meat, 2 vegetable, 1 fat.

Vegetable Fish Dinner

Scallops with Thai Sauce

(Pictured below)

Prep/Total Time: 30 min.

Tender scallops and crunchy cashews are the stars of this restaurant-quality dinner. The recipe calls for sea scallops, which are about 1-1/2 inches in diameter. You could also use their sweeter, smaller relative, the bay scallop.
—Joe Hable, Madison, Wisconsin

1 tablespoon cornstarch
1 can (14-1/2 ounces) vegetable broth
2 tablespoons creamy peanut butter
1 to 2 tablespoons Thai chili sauce
1 pound sea scallops
2 tablespoons vegetable oil, *divided*
1 small onion, sliced
1 large sweet red pepper, julienned
1/2 cup salted cashews
2 teaspoons minced garlic
1 can (8-3/4 ounces) whole baby corn, drained
Hot cooked angel hair pasta, optional

In a small bowl, combine the cornstarch, broth, peanut butter and chili sauce until smooth; set aside.

In a large skillet, saute the scallops in 1 tablespoon oil for 2-3 minutes on each side or until opaque. Remove with a slotted spoon and keep warm. In the same pan, saute the onion, red pepper, cashews and garlic in the remaining oil for 3-5 minutes or until the vegetables are crisp-tender.

Stir peanut butter mixture and add to pan. Bring to a boil; cook and stir for 1-2 minutes or until thickened. Add the scallops and corn; heat through. Serve over pasta if desired. **Yield:** 5 servings.

Scallops with Thai Sauce

Barbecued Pork Chops

Barbecued Pork Chops

(Pictured above)

Prep/Total Time: 20 min.

Sherry, honey and two sauces combine to give these pork chops a beautiful, flavorful glaze. It's good on chicken breasts, too. *—LaJuana Kay Holland, Amarillo, Texas*

1/2 cup hickory smoke-flavored barbecue sauce
1/2 cup A.1. steak sauce
1/2 cup sherry *or* unsweetened apple juice
3 tablespoons honey
6 bone-in pork loin chops (3/4 inch thick and 8 ounces *each*)
3/4 teaspoon salt
1/2 teaspoon pepper

Coat grill rack with cooking spray before starting grill. In a small bowl, combine barbecue sauce, steak sauce, sherry or apple juice and honey. Transfer 1/3 cup sauce to another bowl; set aside.

Sprinkle pork chops with salt and pepper. Grill, covered, over medium heat for 4-5 minutes on each side or until a meat thermometer reads 160°, basting frequently with the remaining sauce. Serve with reserved sauce. **Yield:** 6 servings.

Creamy Shrimp 'n' Spaghetti

Prep/Total Time: 25 min.

As a single parent, I rely on quick-and-easy meals. This fast-to-fix entree is a definite favorite and special enough to serve guests. *—David Burgess, Olympia, Washington*

1 package (7 ounces) spaghetti
1 cup sliced fresh mushrooms
1/2 cup julienned green pepper
2 tablespoons butter, *divided*
1 envelope (1.6 ounces) garlic-herb pasta sauce mix
2 tablespoons all-purpose flour

2-1/2 cups milk
1/4 cup water
3/4 pound frozen cooked small shrimp, thawed
1/4 teaspoon white pepper
1/2 cup grated Parmesan cheese

Cook spaghetti according to package directions. Meanwhile, in a large skillet, saute the mushrooms and green pepper in 1 tablespoon butter for 3-4 minutes or until crisp-tender.

In a small bowl, whisk pasta sauce mix, flour, milk and water until blended. Stir into skillet. Bring to a boil; cook and stir for 2 minutes or until thickened. Add the shrimp, white pepper and remaining butter; cook 2-3 minutes longer or until heated through.

Drain spaghetti; toss with shrimp mixture. Sprinkle with Parmesan cheese. **Yield:** 3 servings.

Avocado Chicken Pitas

(Pictured below)

Prep/Total Time: 30 min.

I used to fix these with chicken breasts. Recently, I began using store-bought rotisserie chicken cut into strips. It's nice and quick! —*Barbara Hunt, Nipomo, California*

4 whole pita breads
2 tablespoons olive oil
1 medium ripe avocado, peeled and pitted
1 tablespoon lemon juice
1/4 teaspoon salt
1/4 teaspoon garlic powder
1/8 teaspoon hot pepper sauce
3/4 pound cooked rotisserie chicken (skin removed), cut into strips
1 medium tomato, chopped
2 cups (8 ounces) shredded Monterey Jack cheese

Brush one side of each pita bread with oil. Place on an ungreased baking sheet. Bake at 350° for 12-15 minutes or until browned and crisp.

Avocado Chicken Pitas

Steak with Orange-Thyme Sauce

Meanwhile, in a small bowl, mash the avocado with lemon juice, salt, garlic powder and hot pepper sauce. Spread over pitas. Layer with the chicken, tomato and cheese. Bake for 5-6 minutes or until cheese is melted. **Yield:** 4 servings.

Steak with Orange-Thyme Sauce

(Pictured above)

Prep/Total Time: 25 min.

Thyme is such a versatile herb, you can use it just about anywhere. It's a wonderful addition to the sauce of this main course. —*Mitzi Sentiff, Annapolis, Maryland*

✓ This recipe includes Nutrition Facts and Diabetic Exchanges.

1/2 cup orange marmalade
2 teaspoons minced fresh thyme *or* 1/2 teaspoon dried thyme
1-1/2 teaspoons grated orange peel
1 teaspoon soy sauce
3/4 teaspoon seasoned salt
1/2 teaspoon garlic powder
1/8 teaspoon cayenne pepper
1-1/4 pounds boneless beef top sirloin steak

In a small bowl, combine the first seven ingredients; set aside 1/3 cup for basting.

Broil steak 4-6 in. from the heat for 8-10 minutes on each side or until meat reaches desired doneness (for medium-rare, a meat thermometer should read 145°; medium, 160°; well-done, 170°), basting with some of the reserved sauce. Let stand for 5 minutes before slicing. Serve with the remaining sauce. **Yield:** 4 servings.

Nutrition Facts: 4 ounces cooked beef with 4 teaspoons sauce equals 339 calories, 12 g fat (5 g saturated fat), 92 mg cholesterol, 450 mg sodium, 27 g carbohydrate, trace fiber, 31 g protein. **Diabetic Exchanges:** 4 lean meat, 2 starch.

Apple-Spiced Pork

Apple-Spiced Pork

(Pictured above)

Prep/Total Time: 30 min.

I've passed on copies of this recipe so many times. It also works well with ground pork or cubed leftover pork roast.
—Linda Murray, Allenstown, New Hampshire

2 cups uncooked yolk-free noodles
1 pork tenderloin (1 pound), halved lengthwise and cut into 1/2-inch slices
1/4 cup chopped celery
2 tablespoons chopped onion
1 tablespoon canola oil
2 medium tart apples, chopped
1/3 cup raisins
1 tablespoon brown sugar
1/2 teaspoon seasoned salt
1/4 to 1/2 teaspoon ground cinnamon
4-1/2 teaspoons cornstarch
1 can (14-1/2 ounces) reduced-sodium beef broth
2 tablespoons chopped walnuts

Cook noodles according to package directions; drain. Meanwhile, in a large skillet, brown pork with celery and onion in oil; drain. Add apples, raisins, brown sugar, seasoned salt and cinnamon. Cook and stir over medium heat for 8-10 minutes or until pork is no longer pink and vegetables are tender.

In a small bowl, combine cornstarch and broth until smooth; gradually add to the pork mixture. Bring to a boil; cook and stir for 2 minutes or until thickened. Serve with noodles. Sprinkle with walnuts. **Yield:** 4 servings.

Almond-Crusted Salmon

Prep/Total Time: 20 min.

This two-serving salmon entree is a great one to share with someone special. I like to pair the crunchy fish with lots of mango salsa. *—Marc Nadeau, Wanship, Utah*

2 egg whites
1 tablespoon dried cilantro flakes
1 teaspoon lemon juice
1/2 teaspoon ground ginger
1/2 teaspoon cayenne pepper
1/2 cup ground almonds
2 salmon fillets (6 ounces *each*)

In a shallow bowl, beat egg whites, cilantro, lemon juice, ginger and cayenne. Place almonds in another shallow bowl. Dip salmon in egg mixture, then coat with almonds. Place on a greased baking sheet. Bake at 450° for 10-15 minutes or until fish flakes easily with a fork. **Yield:** 2 servings.

Broiled Pork Chops with Mango Sauce

(Pictured below)

Prep/Total Time: 30 min.

Surprise your family tonight with our Test Kitchen's pork chop dinner. You won't believe how much taste-tempting flavor you get from just six ingredients.

3 medium mangoes, peeled, pitted and cut into chunks
1/4 cup chicken broth
2 tablespoons apricot preserves
1/2 teaspoon ground coriander
4 boneless butterflied pork chops (8 ounces *each*)
2 teaspoons lemon-pepper seasoning

In a blender, combine the mangoes and broth; cover and process until smooth. In a small saucepan, combine the mango puree, preserves and coriander. Bring to a boil; cook and stir for 2 minutes. Reduce heat; simmer, uncovered, for 10 minutes.

Meanwhile, sprinkle pork chops with lemon-pepper. Broil chops 3-4 in. from the heat for 5-6 minutes on each side or until meat juices run clear. Serve with mango sauce. **Yield:** 4 servings.

Broiled Pork Chops with Mango Sauce

Beef Fettuccine Dinner

Beef Fettuccine Dinner

(Pictured above)

Prep/Total Time: 20 min.

This cheesy, beefy pasta is a big hit with my husband and children. We have it twice a month and eat up every last bite! —*Barbara Spohn, Broken Arrow, Oklahoma*

1 pound ground beef
1-1/2 cups water
1 package (4.3 ounces) fettuccine and beef-flavored sauce mix
1 can (8 ounces) tomato sauce
2 teaspoons chili powder
1 can (11 ounces) whole kernel corn, drained
1 cup (4 ounces) shredded cheddar cheese, *divided*

In a large skillet, cook beef over medium heat until no longer pink; drain. Add water; bring to a boil. Stir in the fettuccine mix, tomato sauce and chili powder. Return to a boil. Reduce the heat; simmer, uncovered, for 7 minutes or until thickened.

Stir in corn and 2/3 cup cheese; heat through. Sprinkle with remaining cheese. **Yield:** 4 servings.

Flat-Out Fast

TO EASILY flatten boneless chicken breasts, start by placing them in a resealable plastic bag or between two pieces of waxed paper or plastic wrap. Beginning in the center and working out to the edges, pound lightly with the flat side of a meat mallet until the chicken is even in thickness.

Chicken Marsala with Pasta

(Pictured below)

Prep/Total Time: 30 min.

Here's an elegant entree that's quick enough for a weekday. If you have leftover broiled chicken breasts, feel free to use those to save time. —*Trisha Kruse, Eagle, Idaho*

2 cups sliced fresh mushrooms
2 teaspoons minced garlic
1/4 cup butter, *divided*
2-1/4 cups hot water
1/4 cup marsala wine *or* chicken broth
1 envelope (4.3 ounces) fettuccine and chicken-flavored sauce mix
4 boneless skinless chicken breast halves (4 ounces *each*)
1/4 cup all-purpose flour
1/4 teaspoon salt
1/4 teaspoon pepper
1 tablespoon vegetable oil
2 tablespoons sour cream

In a large saucepan, saute mushrooms and garlic in 2 tablespoons butter for 4-5 minutes or until tender. Add water and wine or broth. Bring to a boil; stir in pasta mix. Reduce heat; simmer, uncovered, for 10 minutes or until pasta is tender.

Meanwhile, flatten chicken to 1/2-in. thickness. In a large resealable plastic bag, combine the flour, salt and pepper. Add chicken, a few pieces at a time, and shake to coat.

In a large skillet, cook chicken in oil and remaining butter over medium heat for 4-5 minutes on each side or until juices run clear. Remove the pasta mixture from the heat. Stir in sour cream. Serve with chicken. **Yield:** 4 servings.

Chicken Marsala with Pasta

Sausage Pierogi Skillet

(Pictured below)

Prep/Total Time: 30 min.

I made this speedy recipe one night when I hadn't planned anything for dinner. It's convenient because it uses items I usually have on hand, and there's hardly any cleanup.
—Susan Held, Cooksville, Maryland

- **1 package (16.9 ounces) frozen potato and onion pierogies**
- **2 tablespoons butter, *divided***
- **2 tablespoons vegetable oil, *divided***
- **1 package (16 ounces) smoked turkey sausage, cut in half lengthwise and sliced into 1/2-inch pieces**
- **1 medium onion, sliced**
- **1 package (16 ounces) coleslaw mix**
- **1/2 teaspoon garlic powder**
- **1/4 teaspoon celery salt**
- **1/4 teaspoon pepper**
- **1 bay leaf**

Cook pierogies according to package directions. Meanwhile, in a large skillet over medium heat, melt 1 tablespoon butter with 1 tablespoon oil. Add sausage and onion; cook and stir for 2 minutes. Add the remaining ingredients; cook and stir for 1-2 minutes longer or until coleslaw is wilted. Remove from heat; keep warm.

In another large skillet, heat remaining butter and oil. Drain pierogies; add to skillet. Cook and stir until browned; add the sausage mixture and toss to coat. Discard bay leaf. **Yield:** 5 servings.

Sausage Pierogi Skillet

Creole Pork Chops

Creole Pork Chops

(Pictured above)

Prep/Total Time: 30 min.

This flavor-packed skillet supper has been a favorite in our household for over 20 years. Now that our children are grown, I've discovered how versatile the recipe is. I can easily cut it down and cook just half for my husband and me.
—Ann Rogers, Ocala, Florida

- **1/2 teaspoon salt**
- **1/2 teaspoon dried basil**
- **1/2 teaspoon paprika**
- **1/2 teaspoon pepper**
- **1/4 teaspoon ground cumin**
- **1/8 to 1/4 teaspoon cayenne pepper**
- **4 boneless pork loin chops (4 ounces *each*)**
- **2 tablespoons vegetable oil**
- **1 can (8 ounces) tomato sauce**
- **1/2 cup chopped onion**
- **1/2 cup chopped green pepper**
- **1/4 cup chopped celery**
- **1 tablespoon Worcestershire sauce**
- **1/2 teaspoon minced garlic**

In a small bowl, combine the first six ingredients; rub over both sides of pork.

In a large skillet, brown pork chops in oil over medium heat. Add the remaining ingredients. Cover and cook 15-20 minutes longer or until the meat is tender. **Yield:** 4 servings.

Black Bean Burritos

(Pictured below)

Prep/Total Time: 25 min.

I came across this zesty recipe while searching for a new quick-and-easy dish. After making it just once, we were hooked! —Amy Chop, Eufaula, Alabama

1 can (15 ounces) black beans, rinsed and drained
1 can (4 ounces) chopped green chilies
1/4 cup chopped onion
1/4 cup chopped green pepper
1/4 cup chopped sweet red pepper
1 tablespoon vegetable oil
3 teaspoons chili powder
1/2 teaspoon minced garlic
1/4 teaspoon dried oregano
1/4 teaspoon ground cumin
1/8 teaspoon salt
8 flour tortillas (8 inches), warmed
1 cup (4 ounces) shredded Monterey Jack cheese
Salsa and sour cream

Place the beans in a large microwave-safe bowl; mash lightly. Stir in the green chilies, onion, peppers, oil, chili powder, garlic, oregano, cumin and salt. Cover and microwave on high for 2-3 minutes or until heated through, stirring once.

Spread about 1/4 cup bean mixture down the center of each tortilla. Top each with 2 tablespoons of the cheese; roll up. Place seam side down in an ungreased 11-in. x 7-in. x 2-in. microwave-safe dish. Cover with a damp microwave-safe paper towel. Microwave on high for 25-40 seconds or until heated through. Serve with salsa and sour cream. **Yield:** 4 servings.

Editor's Note: This recipe was tested in a 1,100-watt microwave.

Black Bean Burritos

Curry Chicken

Curry Chicken

(Pictured above and on page 190)

Prep/Total Time: 30 min.

This is a dinnertime winner in our home. Even my kids gobble up the curry-spiced chicken and vegetables served over rice. —Tracy Simiele, Chardon, Ohio

1-1/2 cups uncooked instant rice
1 pound boneless skinless chicken breasts, cut into 1-inch cubes
2 teaspoons curry powder
3/4 teaspoon salt
1/4 teaspoon pepper
1/2 cup chopped onion
1 tablespoon vegetable oil
1 can (13-1/2 ounces) coconut milk
2 tablespoons tomato paste
3 cups fresh baby spinach
1 cup chopped tomato

Cook the rice according to package directions. Meanwhile, sprinkle the chicken with curry, salt and pepper. In a large skillet, saute chicken and onion in oil until the chicken is no longer pink.

Stir in the coconut milk and tomato paste. Bring to a boil. Reduce the heat; simmer, uncovered, for 5 minutes or until thickened. Add spinach and tomato; cook 2-3 minutes longer or until spinach is wilted. Serve with rice. **Yield:** 4 servings.

Editor's Note: You may substitute 1/4 teaspoon coconut extract and 1 cup milk, cream or other dairy product for each cup of coconut milk.

Mexican Chicken Penne

Mexican Chicken Penne

(Pictured above)

Prep/Total Time: 25 min.

This cheesy dinner can easily be adjusted for kids. If they want just the pasta and chicken, fix their portions without the veggies. —*Marti Gutwein, Rensselaer, Indiana*

1 package (16 ounces) penne pasta
2 cups cubed cooked chicken
1-1/4 cups salsa con queso dip
1/2 cup milk
1/4 teaspoon salt
1 can (15 ounces) black beans, rinsed and drained
1 large tomato, chopped
3 green onions, sliced
1/4 cup shredded cheddar cheese

Cook the pasta according to the package directions. Meanwhile, in a large bowl, combine the chicken, dip, milk and salt.

Drain pasta; return to pan. Stir in chicken mixture and toss to coat. Top with black beans, tomato, onions and cheese; heat through. **Yield:** 6 servings.

Mozzarella Chicken with Veggies

Prep/Total Time: 30 min.

I often serve this moist chicken dish with a green salad and Italian bread. It's a complete, satisfying meal in half an hour. —*Danielle Williams, Westville, Oklahoma*

4 boneless skinless chicken breast halves (5 ounces *each*)
2 tablespoons olive oil
1 pound sliced fresh mushrooms
1 medium sweet orange pepper, julienned
1 medium sweet red pepper, julienned
1 teaspoon minced garlic
1/2 teaspoon salt
1/4 teaspoon pepper
4 slices part-skim mozzarella cheese

In a large skillet, cook chicken in oil over medium heat for 5-7 minutes on each side or until juices run clear. Remove and keep warm.

In the same skillet, saute the mushrooms, peppers, garlic, salt and pepper until vegetables are tender. Return chicken to the pan; top with cheese. Cover and cook until cheese is melted. **Yield:** 4 servings.

Saucy Pork Chops

(Pictured below)

Prep/Total Time: 30 min.

Balsamic vinaigrette really perks up these skillet chops. I like that all of the ingredients are cooked together in one pan. —*Sherry Thompson, Seneca, South Carolina*

4 boneless pork loin chops (1 inch thick and 6 ounces *each*)
1 tablespoon vegetable oil
4 ounces cream cheese, cubed
1/2 cup chicken broth
1/4 cup grated Parmesan cheese
1/4 cup balsamic vinaigrette
1 tablespoon lemon juice

In a large skillet, cook pork chops in oil over medium heat for 8-10 minutes on each side or until a meat thermometer reads 160°. Remove and keep warm.

Add cream cheese, broth, Parmesan, vinaigrette and lemon juice to the skillet; cook and stir until blended. Return chops to pan; heat through. **Yield:** 4 servings.

Saucy Pork Chops

Tomato Cheese Pizza

Tomato Cheese Pizza

(Pictured above)

Prep/Total Time: 30 min.

This pizza not only makes a great meatless main course, but it can also be used as an appetizer—just cut smaller slices. —Greta Sawyers, Mt. Airy, North Carolina

- **1 tube (13.8 ounces) refrigerated pizza crust**
- **1 teaspoon minced garlic**
- **2 cups (8 ounces) shredded part-skim mozzarella cheese**
- **2/3 cup grated Romano cheese**
- **2 teaspoons dried oregano**
- **2 plum tomatoes, thinly sliced**

Unroll pizza dough onto a greased 12-in. pizza pan; flatten dough and build up the edges slightly. Spread garlic over crust. Bake at 375° for 7 minutes.

Sprinkle half of the cheeses and oregano over crust. Arrange tomatoes on top. Sprinkle with remaining cheeses and oregano. Bake for 15-17 minutes or until crust is golden brown and the cheese is melted. **Yield:** 8 slices.

Tilapia Wraps

Prep/Total Time: 15 min.

For a terrific seafood supper in 15 minutes, try this recipe that wraps up seasoned fillets, cheese and salsa in flour tortillas. —Michelle Williams, Fort Worth, Texas

- **3/4 cup salsa**
- **1 can (4 ounces) chopped green chilies**
- **6 tilapia fillets (6 ounces *each*)**
- **2 tablespoons olive oil**
- **2 tablespoons steak seasoning**
- **12 flour tortillas (6 inches), warmed**
- **3/4 cup shredded cheddar cheese**

In a small bowl, combine the salsa and green chilies; set aside. Drizzle the fillets with oil; sprinkle both sides with steak seasoning. Transfer to a large skillet. Cook, uncovered, over medium heat for 5-8 minutes or until the fish flakes easily with a fork. Add reserved salsa mixture, stirring gently.

Spoon a heaping 1/3 cupful onto each flour tortilla; top with cheddar cheese. Roll up; serve immediately. **Yield:** 6 servings.

Editor's Note: This recipe was tested with McCormick's Montreal Steak Seasoning. Look for it in the spice aisle.

Beefed Up

I've discovered that pizza is a great way to use up leftover taco meat. I sprinkle the seasoned ground beef on a homemade pizza crust, then add chopped green peppers and cheese. It's a tasty Southwestern dinner that offers a change of pace from the tacos.
—Tina Boyer, Lynchburg, Virginia

Fruit-Topped Pork Chops and Rice

(Pictured below)

Prep/Total Time: 30 min.

Dried fruit gives these pork chops a different but special look and taste. I often serve this hearty entree to guests.
—Priscilla Gilbert, Indian Harbour Beach, Florida

- **4 bone-in center-cut pork loin chops (6 ounces *each*)**
- **1/4 teaspoon pepper**
- **2 tablespoons plus 1 teaspoon vegetable oil, *divided***
- **1/3 cup chopped shallots**
- **1 package (7 ounces) dried fruit bits**
- **1 cup chicken broth**
- **1 package (8.8 ounces) ready-to-serve long grain rice**
- **4 teaspoons butter**
- **4 teaspoons minced fresh parsley**

Sprinkle pork chops with pepper. In a large skillet, cook pork chops in 2 tablespoons oil over medium-high heat for 7-8 minutes on each side or until juices run clear. Remove and keep warm.

In the the same skillet, saute the shallots in the remaining oil for 1 minute. Add the dried fruit and chicken broth. Bring to a boil. Reduce the heat; cover and simmer for 3-5 minutes or until mixture is slightly thickened. Return chops to the pan; cook for 1-2 minutes or until heated through.

Meanwhile, microwave rice according to package directions. Divide rice among serving plates; dot with butter and sprinkle with parsley. Serve with the pork chops and fruit. **Yield:** 4 servings.

Editor's Note: This recipe was tested in a 1,100-watt microwave.

Fruit-Topped Pork Chops and Rice

Saucy Chicken and Florets

Saucy Chicken and Florets

(Pictured above)

Prep/Total Time: 25 min.

This meal-in-one is so good! Sometimes I make it lighter using the reduced-fat versions of sour cream and cream soup. *—Ruth Stallings, Spokane, Washington*

- **1 package (16 ounces) frozen cauliflower and broccoli florets**
- **4 boneless skinless chicken breast halves (5 ounces *each*)**
- **1 can (10-3/4 ounces) condensed cream of mushroom soup, undiluted**
- **1/2 cup sour cream**
- **1/4 teaspoon garlic salt**
- **1/4 teaspoon onion powder**
- **1/4 teaspoon dried thyme**
- **1/3 cup dry bread crumbs**
- **1/4 cup shredded Colby cheese**
- **1 tablespoon butter, melted**

Place cauliflower and broccoli in a 2-1/2-qt. microwave-safe dish. Top with chicken. Cover and microwave on high for 10-14 minutes or until chicken juices run clear.

Meanwhile, in a small bowl, combine the soup, sour cream, garlic salt, onion powder and thyme. Drain chicken and vegetables; add soup mixture and stir to coat. Cover and microwave on high for 2-3 minutes or until heated through.

Toss the crumbs, cheese and butter; sprinkle over chicken. Microwave, uncovered, on high for 45-60 seconds or until cheese is melted. **Yield:** 4 servings.

Editor's Note: This recipe was tested in a 1,100-watt microwave.

Chicken-Bow Tie Primavera

Prep/Total Time: 30 min.

When you don't have time to fix a side dish, choose this sure-to-please supper. It offers cheesy pasta, chicken and veggies. *—Mary Thomas, North Lewisburg, Ohio*

3-1/2 cups uncooked bow tie pasta
1 pound boneless skinless chicken breasts, cut into 1-inch cubes
2/3 cup sliced fresh carrot
1 tablespoon olive oil
1 medium zucchini, halved lengthwise and sliced
1 medium yellow summer squash, quartered and sliced
1/2 teaspoon seasoned salt
1/4 teaspoon pepper
2 cups heavy whipping cream
1-1/2 cups shredded Parmesan cheese
Additional shredded Parmesan cheese, optional

Cook pasta according to package directions. Meanwhile, in a large skillet, saute chicken and carrot in oil for 5-6 minutes or until chicken juices run clear; drain.

Add the zucchini, squash, seasoned salt and pepper. Cook, uncovered, until the vegetables are tender, stirring occasionally.

Drain pasta. Add the pasta, cream and Parmesan cheese to the chicken mixture; stir to combine. Cook, uncovered, until cheese is melted. Sprinkle with additional cheese if desired. **Yield:** 6 servings.

Hearty Chicken Pesto Pizzas

(Pictured below)

Prep/Total Time: 30 min.

Brimming with tasty toppings, these loaded personal pizzas are best served with a knife and fork. They're always a big hit. —Joanna Burke, Culpeper, Virginia

4 whole pita breads
1 small onion, thinly sliced
1 teaspoon minced garlic
1 tablespoon olive oil
1/4 cup sour cream
1/4 cup prepared pesto
2 packages (6 ounces *each*) ready-to-use Southwestern chicken strips
2 medium tomatoes, coarsely chopped
1 cup (4 ounces) shredded part-skim mozzarella cheese

Place pita breads on an ungreased baking sheet. Bake at 400° for 5-7 minutes or until lightly browned.

Meanwhile, in a small skillet, saute onion and garlic in oil until tender. In a small bowl, combine sour cream and pesto. Top each pita with onion mixture; spread pesto mixture evenly over onion layer.

Top with the chicken strips, tomatoes and mozzarella cheese. Bake for 7-9 minutes or until cheese is melted. **Yield:** 4 servings.

Hearty Chicken Pesto Pizzas

Tuna Veggie Macaroni

(Pictured above)

Prep/Total Time: 25 min.

After a lot of experimenting with various versions of this recipe, I came up with one my family loves. They can't get enough of it! —Al Robbins, Chandler, Arizona

1-1/4 cups uncooked elbow macaroni
5 ounces process cheese (Velveeta), cubed
1/2 cup milk
2 cups frozen peas and carrots, thawed
1 can (6 ounces) solid white tuna, drained
1/4 teaspoon dill weed

Cook the macaroni according to package directions; drain. Add cheese and milk; stir until cheese is melted. Stir in the vegetables, tuna and dill; heat through. **Yield:** 3 servings.

Tuna Veggie Macaroni

Ham Fettuccine

Ham Fettuccine

(Pictured above)

Prep/Total Time: 25 min.

After one taste, you'll be craving this quick-to-fix pasta. It's a terrific choice when you have leftover cooked ham from a holiday. —*Trish Moore, Toledo, Ohio*

- **12 ounces uncooked fettuccine**
- **1/4 cup chopped onion**
- **1 teaspoon minced garlic**
- **3 tablespoons butter**
- **3 cups cubed fully cooked ham**
- **1/2 pound sliced fresh mushrooms, optional**
- **1-1/4 teaspoons dried oregano**
- **1-1/4 teaspoons dried basil**
- **1-1/4 teaspoons dried parsley flakes**
- **1/2 teaspoon crushed red pepper flakes**
- **1 cup meatless spaghetti sauce**
- **3/4 cup heavy whipping cream**

Cook the fettuccine according to package directions. Meanwhile, in a large skillet, saute onion and garlic in butter until tender. Add the ham, mushrooms if desired, oregano, basil, parsley and pepper flakes. Cook and stir for 4-5 minutes or until mushrooms are tender.

Stir in spaghetti sauce. Bring to a boil; cook for 2 minutes. Remove from heat; stir in cream. Drain fettuccine; toss with ham mixture. **Yield:** 6 servings.

Ramen Chicken 'n' Vegetables

Prep/Total Time: 25 min.

I found this recipe years ago in a magazine. It looked so good, I tried it that very same night! It's been a standby ever since. —*Buffy Sias, Whitehorse, Yukon Territory*

- **2 cups water**
- **2 packages (3 ounces *each*) chicken ramen noodles**
- **2 cans (8-3/4 ounces *each*) whole baby corn, drained**
- **1 small zucchini, sliced**
- **1 cup fresh sugar snap peas**
- **1 jar (6 ounces) sliced mushrooms, drained**
- **2 tablespoons soy sauce**
- **1/4 to 1/2 teaspoon crushed red pepper flakes**
- **3 cups cubed cooked chicken**

In a large saucepan, bring water to a boil. Stir in ramen noodles with contents of seasoning packets. Add the vegetables, soy sauce and pepper flakes.

Reduce heat; cover and simmer for 3-4 minutes or until noodles and vegetables are tender, stirring occasionally. Stir in chicken; heat through. **Yield:** 6 servings.

Broccoli Cheese Tortellini

(Pictured below)

Prep/Total Time: 25 min.

When we lived in Seattle, my favorite restaurant served a wonderful dish I ordered every time I ate there. When we moved away, I created this homemade version. —*Darlene Brenden, Salem, Oregon*

- **2 packages (9 ounces *each*) refrigerated cheese tortellini**
- **2 cups heavy whipping cream**
- **1 cup fresh broccoli florets**
- **2-1/2 cups shredded Parmesan cheese, *divided***
- **1/4 teaspoon coarsely ground pepper**
- **2 teaspoons minced fresh parsley**

Cook tortellini according to package directions. Meanwhile, in a large saucepan, cook cream and broccoli, uncovered, over medium-low heat for 5-6 minutes or until broccoli is crisp-tender.

Broccoli Cheese Tortellini

Lemon Shrimp with Parmesan Rice

Stir in 2 cups Parmesan cheese and pepper. Bring to a boil. Reduce heat; simmer, uncovered, for 10-12 minutes or until cheese is melted and mixture is thickened, stirring occasionally.

Drain tortellini; add to sauce and toss to coat. Sprinkle with parsley and remaining cheese. **Yield:** 6 servings.

Lemon Shrimp with Parmesan Rice

(Pictured above)

Prep/Total Time: 20 min.

I grew up in Biloxi, Mississippi, where seafood, rice and garlic are staples. This lemony dish is one we enjoyed time and time again. —*Amie Overby, Reno, Nevada*

2 cups chicken broth
2 cups uncooked instant rice
1 pound uncooked medium shrimp, peeled and deveined
1/2 cup chopped green onions
2 teaspoons minced garlic
2 tablespoons butter
2 tablespoons olive oil
3 tablespoons lemon juice
1/4 teaspoon pepper
1/2 cup grated Parmesan cheese
2 tablespoons minced fresh parsley

In a small saucepan, bring the broth to a boil. Stir in the rice; cover and remove from the heat. Let stand for 5 minutes.

Meanwhile, in a large skillet, cook the shrimp, onions and garlic in butter and oil over medium heat for 5-6 minutes or until the shrimp turn pink. Stir in the lemon juice and pepper.

Stir the Parmesan cheese and parsley into the rice; serve with shrimp. **Yield:** 4 servings.

Pork Chops with Apple Dressing

Prep/Total Time: 25 min.

Years ago when we got our microwave, I was dying to cook with it. This is the first recipe I tried, and it's still tops with my husband. —*Donna Garvin, Glens Falls, New York*

1-1/2 cups crushed seasoned stuffing
1 medium tart apple, peeled and chopped
3 tablespoons butter, melted
2 tablespoons chopped onion
1 tablespoon sugar
1/4 teaspoon rubbed sage
1/4 teaspoon salt
1/4 cup raisins
4 boneless pork loin chops (1/2 inch thick and 6 ounces *each*)
1 envelope pork gravy mix

In a small bowl, combine the first eight ingredients. Place in a greased 11-in. x 7-in. x 2-in. microwave-safe dish. Top with pork chops; sprinkle with gravy mix.

Cover and microwave on high for 8-10 minutes or until meat is tender. **Yield:** 4 servings.

Editor's Note: This recipe was tested in a 1,100-watt microwave.

Artichoke Chicken Fettuccine

(Pictured below)

Prep/Total Time: 30 min.

A medley of artichokes, red pepper and chicken creates a lovely entree when paired with fettuccine and a creamy sauce. It's the kind of all-purpose dinner that will dazzle guests but also save time in the kitchen on weeknights.
—Winnie Struse, Hereford, Arizona

8 ounces uncooked fettuccine
1 pound boneless skinless chicken breasts, cut into 1-inch strips
4 bacon strips, diced
1/4 cup chopped onion
2 tablespoons chopped sweet red pepper
2 tablespoons butter
2 tablespoons all-purpose flour
1 cup chicken broth
1/2 cup milk
1 teaspoon Dijon mustard
2 tablespoons grated Parmesan cheese
1 can (14 ounces) water-packed artichoke hearts, rinsed and drained
2 tablespoons mayonnaise

Cook fettuccine according to package directions. Meanwhile, in a large skillet, saute the chicken, bacon, onion and red pepper until chicken juices run clear and vegetables are tender; drain and keep warm.

In a large saucepan, melt the butter; stir in the flour until smooth. Gradually add the chicken broth, milk and mustard. Bring to a boil; cook and stir for 2 minutes or until thickened.

Stir in the Parmesan cheese and artichokes. Remove from the heat; stir in the mayonnaise and chicken mixture. Drain the fettuccine; serve with chicken mixture. **Yield:** 4 servings.

Artichoke Chicken Fettuccine

Pork Chops with Sour Cream Sauce

Prep/Total Time: 30 min.

This is one of my favorite main dishes. It's easy, fast and gives you that home-style comfort food families crave.
—Norma Bursick, Sioux City, Iowa

6 boneless pork loin chops (5 ounces *each*)
1 tablespoon vegetable oil
1/2 cup water
2 tablespoons brown sugar
2 tablespoons chopped onion
2 tablespoons ketchup
1 teaspoon beef bouillon granules
1 teaspoon minced garlic
2 tablespoons all-purpose flour
1/4 cup cold water
1/2 cup sour cream

In a large skillet, brown pork chops in oil on both sides. Combine the water, brown sugar, onion, ketchup, bouillon and garlic; add to skillet. Bring to a boil. Reduce heat; cover and simmer for 15-20 minutes or until the meat juices run clear.

Remove chops and keep warm. Combine flour and cold water until smooth; stir into skillet. Bring to a boil; cook and stir for 2 minutes or until thickened. Remove from the heat; stir in sour cream. Serve with pork chops. **Yield:** 6 servings.

Pita Fajitas

Prep/Total Time: 30 min.

Fajitas are always popular, and these are a breeze to prepare. They go together with pantry ingredients, barbecue sauce and salsa. —Meredyth Crofton, Oak Grove, Oregon

1 boneless beef top round steak (1 pound), cut into thin strips
1 cup sliced onion
1/3 cup julienned sweet red pepper
1/3 cup julienned green pepper
2 tablespoons vegetable oil
1/2 cup salsa
1/2 cup barbecue sauce
1/2 teaspoon ground cumin
4 pita breads (6 inches), halved
Shredded cheddar cheese

In a large skillet, cook the round steak, onion and peppers in oil over medium heat until the meat is no longer pink; drain.

Add the salsa, barbecue sauce and cumin. Bring to a boil. Remove from the heat. Spoon about 1/2 cup into each pita half. Sprinkle with cheese. **Yield:** 4 servings.

Soft Vegetable Tacos

Soft Vegetable Tacos

(Pictured above)

Prep/Total Time: 25 min.

In the mood for Mexican? Here's a wholesome but delicious choice—meatless tacos featuring corn, black beans and cheese. —Leona Strait, Colorado Springs, Colorado

1-2/3 cups fresh *or* frozen corn, thawed
1 small zucchini, finely chopped
1 small onion, finely chopped
1 tablespoon vegetable oil
1 can (15 ounces) black beans, rinsed and drained
1/4 cup salsa
8 flour tortillas (6 inches), warmed
1/2 cup sour cream
1 cup (4 ounces) shredded cheddar cheese

In a large skillet, saute the corn, zucchini and onion in oil until tender.

Stir in the black beans and salsa. Cook, uncovered, over medium heat for 3-4 minutes or until heated through, stirring occasionally.

Spoon a heaping 1/3 cupful onto half of each tortilla; top with sour cream and cheese. Fold tortillas over filling; serve immediately. **Yield:** 4 servings.

Tuna Crescent Ring

(Pictured below)

Prep/Total Time: 30 min.

I came up with this foolproof recipe one day using items I had in the pantry. The tuna-stuffed ring was so good, now I always make sure to have the ingredients handy. —Julia Bivens, Martinsburg, West Virginia

1 tube (8 ounces) refrigerated crescent rolls
1 can (12 ounces) solid white tuna, drained and flaked
1 cup frozen peas and carrots
1/2 cup shredded cheddar cheese
1/4 cup mayonnaise
1 tablespoon Dijon mustard
1-1/2 teaspoons dried minced onion
1 teaspoon Italian seasoning

Unroll the crescent roll dough and separate into triangles. Place on an ungreased 12-in. pizza pan, forming a ring with the pointed ends facing the outer edge of pan and the wide ends overlapping. Lightly press wide ends together.

In a small bowl, combine the remaining ingredients. Spoon over wide ends of ring. Fold points over filling and tuck under wide ends (filling will be visible).

Bake at 375° for 15-20 minutes or until golden brown and filling is hot. **Yield:** 4 servings.

Tuna Crescent Ring

Taco Takeoff

My daughter loves the taco roll-ups in frozen dinners. To make those roll-ups myself for a lot less, I brown ground beef and add taco seasoning. I put a small amount of meat on warm corn tortillas, roll them up tightly and secure them with toothpicks. Then I freeze them on a cookie sheet before storing them in a freezer bag in the freezer. The individual roll-ups can be microwaved for 30 seconds to reheat them.
—Stefanie Healey, Alpine, Utah

Chapter 14

Delectable Desserts

HERE'S A TREAT busy cooks are sure to appreciate—a chapter full of fast-to-fix, sweet sensations for every occasion.

Want an impressive, elegant finale to a holiday dinner? Cinnamon Pumpkin Pie gets into the oven in a mere 10 minutes. Need a contribution for a bake sale? Chocolate-Mallow Peanut Candy will come together—and then disappear—in a flash!

You'll even find desserts you can enjoy on hectic weeknights. Frozen Banana Split Pie is perfect to fix ahead of time, then keep in the freezer for those especially time-crunched days. Or dress up a boxed mix and enjoy a freshly baked Chocolate Peanut Butter Cake. Yum!

SWEET TEMPTATION. Deep-Dish Apple Pie (p. 224).

Chocolate Silk Pie

Chocolate Silk Pie

(Pictured above)

Prep: 30 min. + chilling

This creamy, smooth chocolate pie not only melts in your mouth, it melts any resistance to dessert! What a wonderful, simple way to make loved ones feel special.
—Mary Relyea, Canastota, New York

1 unbaked pastry shell (9 inches)
1 jar (7 ounces) marshmallow creme
1 cup (6 ounces) semisweet chocolate chips
1/4 cup butter, cubed
2 squares (1 ounce *each*) unsweetened chocolate
2 tablespoons strong brewed coffee
1 cup heavy whipping cream, whipped
TOPPING:
1 cup heavy whipping cream
2 tablespoons confectioners' sugar
Chocolate curls, optional

Line unpricked pastry shell with a double thickness of heavy-duty foil. Bake at 450° for 8 minutes. Remove foil; bake 5 minutes longer. Cool on a wire rack.

Meanwhile, in a heavy saucepan, combine the marshmallow creme, chocolate chips, butter, unsweetened chocolate and coffee; cook and stir over low heat until the chocolate is melted and the mixture is smooth. Cool. Fold in the whipped cream; pour into the crust.

For topping, in a large mixing bowl, beat cream until it begins to thicken. Add confectioners' sugar; beat until stiff peaks form. Spread over filling. Refrigerate for at least 3 hours before serving. Garnish with chocolate curls if desired. **Yield:** 6-8 servings.

Frozen Raspberry Cheesecake

(Pictured below)

Prep: 20 min. + freezing

I got this recipe from my sister years ago and often rely on it when I'm rushed. It's fancy enough for special occasions but so easy to fix. For a change of pace, try varying the juices and fruits. *—Donna Rear, Red Deer, Alberta*

1-1/2 cups cream-filled chocolate sandwich cookie crumbs (about 15 cookies)
1/4 cup butter, melted
1 package (8 ounces) cream cheese, softened
3/4 cup confectioners' sugar
1 package (10 ounces) frozen sweetened raspberries, thawed
3/4 cup cranberry-raspberry juice, *divided*
1 teaspoon lemon juice
2 cups heavy whipping cream, whipped

Combine cookie crumbs and butter; press onto the bottom of an ungreased 9-in. springform pan. In a large mixing bowl, beat cream cheese and confectioners' sugar until combined. Beat in berries, 1/2 cup cranberry-raspberry juice and lemon juice until blended. Fold in whipped cream. Pour onto crust.

Spoon remaining juice over cheesecake; cut through batter with a knife to swirl. Cover and freeze overnight. Remove from the freezer 15 minutes before serving. **Yield:** 12 servings.

Frozen Raspberry Cheesecake

Minty Cream Cheese Bars

Minty Cream Cheese Bars

(Pictured above)

Prep: 25 min. **Bake:** 25 min. + cooling

There's so much to love about these treats! The decadent squares not only offer the popular combination of mint and chocolate, but they also have a hint of mocha.
—Paula Marchesi, Lenhartsville, Pennsylvania

2 cups (12 ounces) semisweet chocolate chips
6 tablespoons butter, cubed
3/4 teaspoon mint extract
2 cups crushed cream-filled chocolate sandwich cookies (about 20 cookies)
2 cups chopped walnuts
2 packages (8 ounces *each*) cream cheese, softened
1/2 cup sugar
4 eggs
1/4 cup all-purpose flour
2 tablespoons cold brewed coffee

In a large microwave-safe bowl, combine chocolate chips and butter. Microwave, uncovered, on high for 1-2 minutes or until melted. Add extract; stir until smooth. Stir in cookie crumbs and walnuts (mixture will be very moist).

Set aside 2 cups for topping. Press remaining crumb mixture onto the bottom of an ungreased 13-in. x 9-in. x 2-in. baking pan. Bake at 350° for 10-12 minutes or until lightly browned.

Meanwhile, in a large mixing bowl, beat cream cheese and sugar until smooth. Add eggs, one at a time, beating well after each addition. Gradually add the flour and coffee. Beat until combined.

Spread over crust. Sprinkle with reserved crumb mixture. Bake for 25-27 minutes or until set. Cool on a wire rack. Cut into bars. **Yield:** about 2-1/2 dozen.

Chocolate Chip Strawberry Shortcakes

(Pictured below)

Prep: 20 min. **Bake:** 20 min. + cooling

What goes better with juicy strawberries than whipped cream and chocolate? Our Test Kitchen cooks put it all together for this takeoff on the classic shortcake dessert. Luscious and fun, it's a hit with kids and adults alike.

3 cups sliced fresh strawberries
1/4 cup sugar
BISCUITS:
2 cups all-purpose flour
3 tablespoons sugar, *divided*
3 teaspoons baking powder
1/2 teaspoon salt
1 cup heavy whipping cream
1/2 cup plus 1 tablespoon butter, melted, *divided*
1/2 cup miniature semisweet chocolate chips
Whipped cream, optional

In a small bowl, combine strawberries and sugar; cover and refrigerate until serving.

In a large bowl, combine the flour, 2 tablespoons sugar, baking powder and salt. In a small bowl, combine cream and 1/2 cup butter; stir into dry ingredients until a thick batter forms. Gently stir in chocolate chips.

Drop by 1/3 cupfuls onto a greased baking sheet. Brush with remaining butter; sprinkle with remaining sugar. Bake at 375° for 18-20 minutes or until golden brown. Remove to wire racks to cool.

Cut the biscuits in half horizontally. Spoon strawberries onto the bottom halves. Top with whipped cream if desired; replace the biscuit tops. Serve immediately. **Yield:** 8 servings.

Chocolate Chip Strawberry Shortcakes

Watermelon Bombe

(Pictured below)

Prep: 25 min. + freezing

I've lost count of the number of times I've prepared this wonderful treat, which is a must-have at our summer barbecues. The dessert gets its watermelon look from layers of tinted ice cream and chocolate chip "seeds."
—Mary Ann Dell, Phoenixville, Pennsylvania

1 pint pistachio ice cream, softened
6 drops green food coloring
1 pint vanilla ice cream, softened
1 pint strawberry ice cream, softened
6 drops red food coloring
1/2 cup miniature semisweet chocolate chips

Line a 2-qt. freezer-safe bowl with plastic wrap. Place in the freezer for 30 minutes. In a small bowl, combine the pistachio ice cream and green food coloring. Quickly spread pistachio ice cream over the bottom and up the sides to within 1/2 in. of the top of bowl. Freeze for 1 hour or until firm. Repeat with vanilla ice cream. Freeze for 2 hours or until firm.

In a small bowl, combine strawberry ice cream and red food coloring; stir in chocolate chips. Spoon into ice cream shell. Cover and freeze overnight.

Remove from the freezer and invert onto a serving plate. Remove bowl and plastic wrap. Cut into wedges. **Yield:** 8 servings.

Watermelon Bombe

Coconut Pistachio Pie

Coconut Pistachio Pie

(Pictured above)

Prep: 20 min. + chilling

Our Test Kitchen quickly gave this a special touch with a crust of lightly toasted coconut. You'll need just 20 minutes to assemble the pistachio-topped pie.

2-1/2 cups flaked coconut, lightly toasted
1/3 cup butter, melted
2 cups cold milk
2 packages (3.4 ounces *each*) instant pistachio pudding mix
1 cup whipped topping
2 tablespoons chopped pistachios, optional

In a small bowl, combine coconut and butter. Press onto the bottom and up the sides of a greased 9-in. pie plate. Refrigerate for at least 30 minutes or until firm.

In a small bowl, whisk the milk and pudding mixes for 2 minutes. Spread 1-1/2 cups over crust. Fold whipped topping into remaining pudding; spread over pie. Sprinkle with pistachios if desired. Cover and refrigerate for at least 2 hours. **Yield:** 8 servings.

Toasting Technique

PLAN ON MAKING luscious Coconut Pistachio Pie (recipe above)? To toast the flaked coconut for the crust, spread the coconut in a 15-in. x 10-in. x 1-in. baking pan. Bake at 350° for 5-10 minutes or until lightly browned, stirring occasionally.

Mint Sundae Brownie Squares

(Pictured below)

Prep: 20 min. + freezing **Bake:** 25 min. + cooling

Brownies are a weakness of mine, and this dressed-up version turns an everyday treat into a luscious after-dinner delight. It looks fancy drizzled with hot fudge and sprinkled with peanuts. Get ready for lots of compliments!
—Edie DeSpain, Logan, Utah

- **1 package fudge brownie mix (13-inch x 9-inch pan size)**
- **3/4 cup chopped walnuts**
- **1 can (14 ounces) sweetened condensed milk**
- **2 teaspoons peppermint extract**
- **4 drops green food coloring, optional**
- **2 cups heavy whipping cream, whipped**
- **1/2 cup miniature semisweet chocolate chips**
- **1 jar (16 ounces) hot fudge ice cream topping, warmed**
- **1/3 cup chopped salted peanuts**

Prepare brownie mix according to package directions. Stir in walnuts. Pour into a greased 13-in. x 9-in. x 2-in. baking pan. Bake at 325° for 23-27 minutes or until a toothpick inserted in the center comes out clean (do not overbake). Cool on a wire rack.

Meanwhile, in a large bowl, combine the sweetened condensed milk, peppermint extract and food coloring if desired. Fold in whipped cream and chocolate chips. Spread over brownie layer. Cover and freeze for several hours or overnight.

Let stand at room temperature for 10 minutes before cutting. Drizzle with ice cream topping; sprinkle with peanuts. **Yield:** 15 servings.

Mint Brownie Sundae Squares

Rainbow Sherbet Dessert

Rainbow Sherbet Dessert

(Pictured above)

Prep: 30 min. + freezing

You'll hear oohs and aahs when you serve this unusual, refreshing dessert. Crunchy pecans and macaroon cookies contrast wonderfully with the smooth sherbet...and colorful layers create an eye-catching look. For even more flair, try adding a garnish of fresh strawberries.
—Kathryn Dunn, Cumberland, Virginia

- **12 macaroon cookies, crumbled**
- **2 cups heavy whipping cream**
- **3 tablespoons confectioners' sugar**
- **1 teaspoon vanilla extract**
- **3/4 cup chopped pecans, toasted**
- **1 pint *each* raspberry, lime and orange sherbet, softened**

Sprinkle cookie crumbs onto an ungreased baking sheet. Bake at 350° for 5-8 minutes or until golden brown. Cool completely.

In a large mixing bowl, beat cream until it begins to thicken. Add confectioners' sugar and vanilla; beat until stiff peaks form. Combine cookie crumbs and pecans; fold in whipped cream. Spread half of cream mixture onto the bottom of an ungreased 9-in. springform pan. Freeze for 30 minutes.

Gently spread raspberry sherbet over cream layer. Layer with lime and orange sherbets; spread with remaining cream mixture. Cover and freeze until firm. Remove from the freezer 10 minutes before serving. Remove sides of pan. **Yield:** 12 servings.

Apple Blueberry Crisp

Apple Blueberry Crisp

(Pictured above)

Prep: 20 min. **Bake:** 30 min.

This warm, homey crisp is so comforting on a cool afternoon or evening. You could even serve it as part of Sunday brunch. —*Margaret Wilson, Hemet, California*

✓ This recipe includes Nutrition Facts.

4 cups sliced peeled tart apples
2 cups fresh *or* frozen blueberries
1/4 cup packed brown sugar
1/4 cup orange juice concentrate
2 tablespoons all-purpose flour
1 teaspoon ground cinnamon
TOPPING:
1 cup old-fashioned oats
1/2 cup packed brown sugar
2 tablespoons all-purpose flour
1/2 teaspoon ground cinnamon
1/3 cup cold butter, cubed
Vanilla ice cream

In a large bowl, combine the first six ingredients. Transfer to a greased 9-in. square baking dish. For topping, combine oats, brown sugar, flour and cinnamon. Cut in butter until mixture is crumbly; sprinkle over fruit.

Bake at 350° for 30-35 minutes or until the topping is golden and the fruit is tender. Serve warm with vanilla ice cream. **Yield:** 8 servings.

Nutrition Facts: 1 serving (calculated without ice cream) equals 258 calories, 9 g fat (5 g saturated fat), 20 mg cholesterol, 63 mg sodium, 46 g carbohydrate, 3 g fiber, 3 g protein.

Strawberry Trifle

Prep/Total Time: 30 min.

Here's a scrumptious way to use fresh-picked summer strawberries. Layered in a glass bowl and sprinkled with toasted nuts, the trifle makes any meal seem special. Plus, you can fix it in advance—just store it in the fridge.
—*Crystal Edwards, Van Alstyne, Texas*

1 package (8 ounces) cream cheese, softened
2 cups cold milk
2 teaspoons almond extract
1 package (3.4 ounces) instant cheesecake *or* vanilla pudding mix
1 carton (8 ounces) frozen whipped topping, thawed, *divided*
2 cups sliced fresh strawberries
1 carton (13-1/2 ounces) strawberry glaze
1 loaf (10-3/4 ounces) frozen pound cake, thawed and cubed
1/4 cup slivered almonds, toasted

In a large mixing bowl, beat cream cheese until smooth. Gradually beat in milk and extract. Whisk in pudding mix. Fold in 2 cups whipped topping.

In a small bowl, gently combine strawberries and glaze. In a 3-qt. trifle bowl, layer half of the cake cubes, pudding mixture and strawberry mixture. Repeat layers. Garnish with remaining whipped topping. Refrigerate until serving. Sprinkle with almonds just before serving. **Yield:** 12 servings.

Pecan Chocolate Candies

Prep: 30 min. + chilling

Whether you're looking for a new candy recipe for Christmas or just want to treat a sweet tooth, look no further! These rich, pecan-coated balls from our Test Kitchen cooks are irresistible and require no baking.

✓ This recipe includes Nutrition Facts and Diabetic Exchanges.

1 can (5 ounces) evaporated milk
1/2 cup sugar
1 cup (6 ounces) semisweet chocolate chips
2 teaspoons vanilla extract
2-1/2 cups crushed vanilla wafers (about 70 wafers)
1-1/2 cups chopped pecans, *divided*

In a large saucepan over medium heat, bring the evaporated milk and sugar to a boil; remove from the heat. Stir in the chocolate chips and vanilla until smooth.

Add the crushed vanilla wafers and 1/3 cup pecans; stir until well combined. Transfer to a bowl. Refrigerate for 30 minutes or until set.

Shape into 3/4-in. balls. Roll in remaining pecans to

coat. Place on waxed paper-lined baking sheets. Refrigerate until set. **Yield:** 3 dozen.

Nutrition Facts: 1 piece equals 108 calories, 6 g fat (2 g saturated fat), 2 mg cholesterol, 29 mg sodium, 13 g carbohydrate, 1 g fiber, 1 g protein. **Diabetic Exchanges:** 1 starch, 1 fat.

Apricot Bars

(Pictured below)

Prep: 25 min. **Bake:** 25 min. + cooling

I created these last winter...and have been pleasantly surprised by all of the favorable reviews they've received. The apricot flavor really comes through, and a sprinkling of almonds and coconut gives them a pretty touch.
—Barbara Rohlf, Spirit Lake, Iowa

- **1 package (16 ounces) pound cake mix**
- **4 eggs**
- **1/2 cup butter, melted**
- **2 teaspoons vanilla extract, *divided***
- **1 cup chopped dried apricots**
- **1 package (8 ounces) cream cheese, softened**
- **2 cups confectioners' sugar**
- **1/2 cup apricot preserves**
- **3/4 cup flaked coconut**
- **3/4 cup sliced almonds**

In a large bowl, combine the pound cake mix, 2 eggs, butter and 1 teaspoon vanilla; beat until well blended. Fold in the dried apricots. Spread into a greased 15-in. x 10-in. x 1-in. baking pan; set aside.

Apricot Bars

Nutty Cookies & Cream Dessert

In another bowl, beat the cream cheese, confectioners' sugar, preserves and remaining vanilla. Add remaining eggs; beat on low speed just until combined. Gently spread over cake batter. Sprinkle with coconut and almonds.

Bake at 350° for 25-30 minutes or until golden brown. Cool on a wire rack. Cut into bars. Refrigerate leftovers. **Yield:** 2 dozen.

Nutty Cookies & Cream Dessert

(Pictured above)

Prep: 25 min. + freezing

You'll get hot fudge, caramel, chocolate cookies and ice cream in every bite of this fabulous frozen delight. No matter how stuffed everyone is after a big meal, they always manage to find room for a piece of this treat!
—Cheryl Melerski, Harborcreek, Pennsylvania

- **1 package (18 ounces) cream-filled chocolate sandwich cookies, crushed**
- **1/2 cup butter, melted**
- **1/2 gallon cookies and cream ice cream, softened**
- **1-1/2 cups salted peanuts, coarsely chopped**
- **2/3 cup hot fudge ice cream topping**
- **2/3 cup caramel ice cream topping**
- **1 carton (8 ounces) frozen whipped topping, thawed**

In a large bowl, combine the cookie crumbs and butter; set aside 1 cup. Press the remaining crumbs into an ungreased 13-in. x 9-in. x 2-in. dish. Spread with ice cream. Layer with peanuts, ice cream toppings and whipped topping; sprinkle with reserved crumbs. Cover and freeze until firm.

Remove from the freezer 15 minutes before serving. **Yield:** 15 servings.

Pecan Pear Torte

Pecan Pear Torte

(Pictured above)

Prep: 25 min. **Bake:** 20 min. + cooling

I layer my pear-flavored cake with a creamy, butterscotch-flavored whipped topping and top it off with a butterscotch drizzle. It's a real showstopper at holiday dinners.
—Jeanne Holt, Mendota Heights, Minnesota

1 can (15 ounces) pear halves
1 package (18-1/4 ounces) butter recipe golden cake mix
1/2 cup butter, softened
3 eggs
1 teaspoon vanilla extract
1/2 cup chopped pecans, toasted

TOPPING:

1 carton (8 ounces) frozen whipped topping, thawed
2/3 cup butterscotch ice cream topping, *divided*
2 cups chopped peeled ripe pears
1/3 cup pecan halves, toasted

Drain pears, reserving liquid. Puree the pears in a blender; add enough of the reserved liquid to measure 1 cup. In a large mixing bowl, combine the cake mix, butter, eggs, vanilla, chopped pecans and pear puree; beat on low speed for 30 seconds. Beat on medium for 2 minutes. Pour into two greased and floured 9-in. round baking pans.

Bake at 375° for 20-25 minutes or until a toothpick inserted near the center comes out clean. Cool for 10 minutes before removing from the pans to wire racks to cool completely.

In a small mixing bowl, fold whipped topping into 1/3 cup butterscotch topping. Place one cake layer on a serving plate. Spread with half of the filling; top with half of the chopped pears. Drizzle with 2 tablespoons butterscotch topping. Repeat layers.

Arrange pecan halves on top of cake. Drizzle with the remaining butterscotch topping. Refrigerate until serving. **Yield:** 10 servings.

Editor's Note: Butterscotch topping should be at room temperature.

Chocolate Peanut Butter Cake

(Pictured below)

Prep: 10 min. **Bake:** 30 min. + cooling

The ever-popular flavors of chocolate and peanut butter come together in this moist, delicious cake. Try it, and you'll see—kids of every age will be all over this one!
—Brenda Melancon, Port Allen, Louisiana

2 cups miniature marshmallows
1 package (18-1/4 ounces) chocolate cake mix
1-1/4 cups water
3/4 cup peanut butter
1/3 cup vegetable oil
3 eggs
1 cup (6 ounces) semisweet chocolate chips

Sprinkle marshmallows into a greased 13-in. x 9-in. x 2-in. baking pan. In a large mixing bowl, combine the cake mix, water, peanut butter, oil and eggs; beat on low speed for 30 seconds. Beat on medium for 2 minutes or until smooth. Pour over marshmallows; sprinkle with chocolate chips.

Bake at 350° for 30-35 minutes or until a toothpick inserted near the center comes out clean. Cool on a wire rack. **Yield:** 12-15 servings.

Chocolate Peanut Butter Cake

Pecan Toffee Fudge

Pecan Toffee Fudge

(Pictured above)

Prep: 20 min. + chilling

Packed in a festive tin, this tantalizing fudge can make a yummy gift for family, friends and neighbors during the Christmas holiday season. The simple recipe goes together so quickly, you'll want to make a batch for your next bake sale, too! People love the creaminess and toffee bits.
—Diane Willey, Bozman, Maryland

✓ This recipe includes Nutrition Facts and Diabetic Exchanges.

1 teaspoon butter
1 package (8 ounces) cream cheese, softened
3-3/4 cups confectioners' sugar
6 squares (1 ounce *each*) unsweetened chocolate, melted and cooled
1/4 teaspoon almond extract
Dash salt
1/4 cup coarsely chopped pecans
1/4 cup English toffee bits

Line a 9-in. square pan with foil and grease the foil with butter; set aside. In a large bowl, beat cream cheese until fluffy. Gradually beat in confectioners' sugar. Add the melted chocolate, extract and salt; mix well. Stir in the pecans and toffee bits.

Spread into the prepared pan. Cover and refrigerate overnight or until firm. Using foil, lift the fudge out of the pan. Gently peel off the foil; cut the fudge into 1-in. squares. Store in an airtight container in the refrigerator. **Yield:** 2-1/2 pounds.

Nutrition Facts: 1 piece equals 49 calories, 3 g fat (1 g saturated fat), 3 mg cholesterol, 15 mg sodium, 7 g carbohydrate, trace fiber, 1 g protein. **Diabetic Exchanges:** 1/2 starch, 1/2 fat.

Swirled Sherbet Dessert

(Pictured below)

Prep: 25 min. + freezing

Lemon and orange sherbet are swirled over a coconut-and-pecan crust in this bright, refreshing dessert. It has a tropical kind of appeal, especially during summer. Just prepare it the day before, then pop it in the freezer.
—Agnes Ward, Stratford, Ontario

1 cup crushed vanilla wafers (about 30 wafers)
1/3 cup flaked coconut
1/3 cup chopped pecans
1/4 cup butter, melted
1 pint lemon sherbet, softened
1 pint orange sherbet, softened

In a small bowl, combine the wafer crumbs, coconut, pecans and butter; press onto the bottom of an ungreased 9-in. springform pan. Bake at 350° for 10-12 minutes or until lightly browned. Cool for 10 minutes on a wire rack.

Arrange scoops of sherbet over crust, alternating flavors. Cut through sherbet with a knife to swirl. Cover and freeze overnight. Remove from the freezer 15 minutes before serving. **Yield:** 12 servings.

Swirled Sherbet Dessert

Fruit Pizza

Fruit Pizza

(Pictured above)

Prep: 30 min. + chilling

Here's my all-time favorite fruit pizza. The sugar cookie crust is a snap to create using refrigerated dough, and the simple citrus glaze gives the fruit a pretty sheen.
—Gaynelle Henry, Newland, North Carolina

1 tube (16-1/2 ounces) refrigerated sugar cookie dough
1 cup sugar, *divided*
2 tablespoons cornstarch
1/2 cup orange juice
1/4 cup lemon juice
1 package (8 ounces) cream cheese, softened
1 tablespoon milk
1 teaspoon grated orange peel
2/3 cup heavy whipping cream
1-1/2 cups halved fresh strawberries
1 medium peach, thinly sliced
1 small banana, sliced
1 small apple, thinly sliced
1/2 cup fresh blueberries

Let dough stand at room temperature for 5-10 minutes to soften. Press onto an ungreased 14-in. pizza pan. Bake at 350° for 13-16 minutes or until golden brown. Cool on a wire rack.

In a small saucepan, combine 1/2 cup sugar, cornstarch and juices. Bring to a boil; cook and stir for 2 minutes or until thickened. Remove from the heat; set aside to cool.

In a large mixing bowl, beat the cream cheese, milk, orange peel and remaining sugar until blended. In a small mixing bowl, beat cream until soft peaks form; fold into cream cheese mixture. Spread over crust. Arrange fruit over filling; spread with reserved glaze. Refrigerate until chilled. **Yield:** 12 servings.

Poppy Seed Citrus Cake

(Pictured below)

Prep: 15 min. **Bake:** 40 min. + cooling

My youngest daughter is a fan of anything with lemon, and this refreshing cake always makes her eyes light up. It's perfect for Easter and easy to pack for picnics, too.
—Charolette Westfall, Houston, Texas

1 package (18-1/4 ounces) lemon cake mix
3 eggs
1-1/3 cups orange juice
1/2 cup vegetable oil
1 to 2 tablespoons poppy seeds
1 teaspoon grated lemon peel
1 teaspoon grated orange peel

GLAZE:
2 cups confectioners' sugar
3 to 4 tablespoons orange juice
1/2 teaspoon grated lemon peel
1/2 teaspoon grated orange peel

In a large mixing bowl, combine the lemon cake mix, eggs, orange juice and oil. Beat on medium speed for 2 minutes. Fold in the poppy seeds and the lemon and orange peels.

Pour into a well-greased and floured 10-in. fluted tube pan. Bake at 350° for 40-45 minutes or until a toothpick inserted near the center comes out clean. Cool for 10 minutes before removing from pan to a wire rack to cool completely.

In a small bowl, combine the confectioners' sugar and orange juice until smooth. Drizzle over the cake. Sprinkle with lemon and orange peels. **Yield:** 12 servings.

Poppy Seed Citrus Cake

Cinnamon Pumpkin Pie

Cinnamon Pumpkin Pie

(Pictured above)

Prep: 10 min. **Bake:** 55 min. + cooling

Looking to simplify your Thanksgiving dinner menu? Consider the fuss-free recipe here. You'll need just 10 minutes to get this smooth, cinnamon-spiced pie into the oven. And it won't disappoint your family. My daughter, Jessica, says it's the best pumpkin pie she's ever eaten!
—Jacqueline Deibert, Klingerstown, Pennsylvania

1 cup sugar
4 teaspoons cornstarch
1/2 teaspoon salt
1/2 teaspoon ground cinnamon
2 eggs
1 can (15 ounces) solid-pack pumpkin
1 cup milk
1 unbaked pastry shell (9 inches)
Whipped cream in a can, optional

In a small bowl, combine the sugar, cornstarch, salt and cinnamon. In a large mixing bowl, beat eggs. Stir in pumpkin and sugar mixture. Gradually stir in milk. Pour into pastry shell.

Bake at 400° for 10 minutes. Reduce heat to 350°; bake 45-50 minutes longer or until a knife inserted near the center comes out clean. Cool on a wire rack. Top with whipped cream if desired. Refrigerate leftovers. **Yield:** 6 servings.

Pumpkin for Pie

In fall, I like to buy a large pumpkin, cut it up, cook it and freeze it. It's a wonderful treat to have pumpkin pie made from cooked fresh pumpkin. It can be used cup-for-cup in place of canned pumpkin.
—Jacqueline Deibert, Klingerstown, Pennsylvania

Chocolate Cherry Cheesecake

(Pictured below)

Prep: 15 min. **Bake:** 30 min. + cooling

I started cooking when I was 11 years old and have enjoyed creating and modifying recipes ever since. This cheesecake has always been a big hit. Everyone agrees the chocolate and cherries are a winning combination.
—Shelly Klingler, Bloomington, Illinois

1 jar (12 ounces) maraschino cherries
2 packages (8 ounces *each*) cream cheese, softened
1/2 cup sugar
2 eggs
1/2 cup miniature semisweet chocolate chips
1 chocolate cookie crust (9 inches)
6 chocolate-covered cherries

Drain the maraschino cherries, reserving 2 teaspoons cherry juice. Cut maraschino cherries into quarters; set aside. In a small mixing bowl, beat the cream cheese, sugar and reserved cherry juice. Add the eggs; beat just until combined. Fold in the chocolate chips and reserved cherries.

Pour into the crust (crust will be full). Bake at 350° for 30-35 minutes or until the center is almost set. Cool on a wire rack. Serve with chocolate-covered cherries. **Yield:** 6 servings.

Chocolate Cherry Cheesecake

Coffee Ice Cream Pie

(Pictured below)

Prep: 30 min. + freezing

If you're a fan of coffee flavor, you're sure to find this pie irresistible. Serve it at your next "girls' get-together" or luncheon for friends—and be prepared for recipe requests from fellow mocha lovers! When you're in the mood for a change of pace, just try a different kind of ice cream.
—Velma Jo Brown, Turner Station, Kentucky

2 squares (1 ounce *each*) unsweetened chocolate
1/4 cup butter, cubed
1 can (5 ounces) evaporated milk
1/2 cup sugar
1 pint coffee ice cream, softened
1 chocolate crumb crust (8 inches)
1 carton (8 ounces) frozen whipped topping, thawed
1/4 cup chopped pecans

In a heavy saucepan, melt the chocolate and butter over low heat. Stir in the evaporated milk and sugar. Bring to a boil over medium heat, stirring constantly. Cook and stir for 3-4 minutes or until thickened. Remove from heat; cool completely.

Spoon coffee ice cream into the chocolate crumb crust. Stir the sauce; spread over the ice cream. Top with whipped topping; sprinkle with pecans. Freeze until firm. Remove from the freezer 15 minutes before serving. **Yield:** 8 servings.

Coffee Ice Cream Pie

Fresh Blackberry Cobbler

Prep: 20 min. **Bake:** 25 min.

I'm not that confident about making pies, but cobblers are simple enough for anyone. This blackberry version is absolutely heavenly. —Tonda Powell, McGehee, Arkansas

✓ This recipe includes Nutrition Facts.

1/2 cup plus 1 tablespoon sugar, *divided*
1 tablespoon cornstarch
4 cups fresh blackberries
1 teaspoon lemon juice
1 cup all-purpose flour
1-1/2 teaspoons baking powder
1/2 teaspoon salt
3 tablespoons shortening
1/2 cup milk
Vanilla ice cream, optional

In a large saucepan, combine 1/2 cup sugar and cornstarch. Stir in berries and lemon juice. Bring to a boil; cook and stir for 2 minutes or until thickened. Pour into a 1-1/2-qt. baking dish coated with cooking spray.

In a small bowl, combine flour, baking powder, salt and remaining sugar; cut in shortening until crumbly. Add milk; stir into flour mixture just until moistened. Drop by tablespoonfuls onto hot fruit. Bake at 400° for 25-30 minutes or until topping is golden brown. Serve warm with ice cream if desired. **Yield:** 6 servings.

Nutrition Facts: 1 serving (calculated without ice cream) equals 262 calories, 7 g fat (2 g saturated fat), 2 mg cholesterol, 306 mg sodium, 46 g carbohydrate, 6 g fiber, 4 g protein.

Sweetened Whipped Cream

Prep/Total Time: 10 min.

Homemade whipped cream is easier to make than you may think. Our Test Kitchen shares this recipe that'll have you whipping up your own in no time.

1 cup heavy whipping cream
3 tablespoons confectioners' sugar
1/2 teaspoon vanilla extract

In a chilled small glass mixing bowl and using chilled beaters, beat cream until it begins to thicken. Add confectioners' sugar and vanilla; beat until soft peaks form. Store in the refrigerator. **Yield:** 2 cups.

Convenient Cream

THE RECIPE for whipped cream (above) can be used for a number of the desserts in this chapter, whether as an optional topping or as part of the recipe. For example, you can use the whipped cream recipe to prepare Chocolate Chip Strawberry Shortcakes (p. 211) and Citrus Raspberry Shortcakes (p. 223).

Apricot Cheesecake Tarts

Apricot Cheesecake Tarts

(Pictured above)

Prep: 30 min. + chilling

Dark chocolate and apricots make these bite-size cheesecakes something special for a springtime buffet, bridal shower or other event. It's hard to stop at just one!
—Alicia Montalvo Pagan, New Bedford, Massachusetts

☑ This recipe includes Nutrition Facts and Diabetic Exchanges.

3 squares (1 ounce *each*) bittersweet chocolate
1/2 teaspoon shortening
1 package (2.1 ounces) frozen miniature phyllo tart shells
1 package (3 ounces) cream cheese, softened
2 tablespoons sour cream
2 tablespoons confectioners' sugar
2 teaspoons apricot nectar
3 dried apricots, cut into thin strips
1 to 1-1/2 teaspoons grated chocolate

In a small microwave-safe bowl, melt bittersweet chocolate and shortening; stir until smooth. Brush over the bottom and up the sides of tart shells. Refrigerate for 15 minutes or until chocolate is set.

Meanwhile, in a small mixing bowl, beat the cream cheese, sour cream and confectioners' sugar until smooth. Beat in nectar. Spoon into shells. Cover and chill for at least 20 minutes. Just before serving, top with apricot strips and grated chocolate. **Yield:** 15 tarts.

Nutrition Facts: 1 tart equals 83 calories, 6 g fat (3 g saturated fat), 8 mg cholesterol, 28 mg sodium, 7 g carbohydrate, 1 g fiber, 1 g protein. **Diabetic Exchanges:** 1 fat, 1/2 starch.

Frosty Mallow Fruit Dessert

(Pictured below)

Prep: 10 min. + freezing

This recipe originated with my husband's relatives in Holland and has been a family favorite for many years. It's frosty and pretty as a picture—each slice reveals colorful chunks of fruit. Plus, it goes together in 10 minutes.
—Patricia Swart, Bridgeton, New Jersey

1 package (8 ounces) cream cheese, softened
1 cup (8 ounces) sour cream
1/4 cup sugar
1 can (15 ounces) apricot halves, drained and coarsely chopped
1 can (8 ounces) crushed pineapple, drained
1 cup miniature marshmallows
1 can (15 ounces) pitted dark sweet cherries, drained

In a large mixing bowl, beat the cream cheese, sour cream and sugar until smooth. Fold in the apricots, pineapple and miniature marshmallows. Gently fold in the cherries. Spoon into a 5-cup ring mold coated with cooking spray.

Cover and freeze for 4 hours or until firm. Just before serving, invert onto a platter. **Yield:** 8 servings.

Frosty Mallow Fruit Dessert

Crescent Apple Dessert

Crescent Apple Dessert

(Pictured above)

Prep: 25 min. **Bake:** 20 min. + cooling

My family loves good old-fashioned apple pie—and any dessert that tastes like it! Here's one that's so simple, even children can help make it. My grandkids like to lend a hand when I'm preparing treats such as this.
—Judy Taylor, Kenna, West Virginia

1 tube (8 ounces) refrigerated crescent rolls
1 cup chopped walnuts
3/4 cup sugar
1/2 teaspoon ground cinnamon
1/4 teaspoon ground nutmeg
1 can (21 ounces) apple pie filling, chopped
TOPPING:
1/2 cup all-purpose flour
1/2 cup packed brown sugar
1/4 cup cold butter
1 cup flaked coconut
1/4 cup chopped walnuts

Unroll crescent dough into an ungreased 13-in. x 9-in. x 2-in. baking pan; seal seams and perforations. Bake at 375° for 10 minutes.

Combine the walnuts, sugar, cinnamon and nutmeg; sprinkle over crust. Spread with pie filling. In a small bowl, combine the flour and brown sugar; cut in butter until mixture resembles coarse crumbs. Stir in coconut and walnuts. Sprinkle over the filling.

Bake at 375° for 18-22 minutes or until golden brown. Cool on a wire rack. **Yield:** 12 servings.

Chocolate-Filled Crescents

(Pictured below)

Prep: 25 min. **Bake:** 15 min.

I get compliments and recipe requests whenever I bake a batch of these rich, flaky rolls drizzled with chocolate. They're wonderful for dessert, brunch or your midday coffee break. *—Carol Formholtz, Deltona, Florida*

3 tablespoons butter, softened
1 cup confectioners' sugar
1 tablespoon milk
1 teaspoon vanilla extract
1/4 cup baking cocoa
3 tablespoons finely chopped pecans
2 tubes (8 ounces *each*) refrigerated crescent rolls
CHOCOLATE GLAZE:
1 cup confectioners' sugar
2 tablespoons baking cocoa
2 tablespoons plus 1 teaspoon water
2 tablespoons butter, melted
1/2 teaspoon vanilla extract

In a small mixing bowl, cream butter and confectioners' sugar. Beat in milk and vanilla. Gradually add cocoa; mix well. Stir in pecans.

Unroll the crescent roll dough and separate into triangles. Spread about 2 rounded teaspoons of filling over each triangle to within 1/4 in. of the edges. Roll up each from the wide end. Place point side down 2 in. apart on ungreased baking sheets. Curve the ends to form crescent shapes.

Bake at 375° for 12-15 minutes or until golden brown. Remove to wire racks; cool slightly. In a small bowl, whisk glaze ingredients until smooth; drizzle over crescents. **Yield:** 16 servings.

Chocolate-Filled Crescents

Citrus Raspberry Shortcakes

Prep: 20 min. **Bake:** 20 min. + cooling

Lightly flavored with orange and pecans, these tender biscuits from our Test Kitchen are the perfect base for a spoonful of fresh raspberries and whipped cream. It's a delightful twist on the usual strawberry shortcake.

3 cups fresh raspberries
3 tablespoons sugar
BISCUITS:
2 cups all-purpose flour
1/4 cup plus 1 tablespoon sugar, *divided*
3 teaspoons baking powder
1 teaspoon grated lemon peel
1 teaspoon grated orange peel
1/2 teaspoon salt
1 cup heavy whipping cream
1/2 cup plus 1 tablespoon butter, melted, *divided*
1/4 cup finely chopped pecans
Whipped cream, optional

In a small bowl, combine raspberries and sugar; cover and refrigerate until serving.

In a large bowl, combine the flour, 1/4 cup sugar, baking powder, lemon peel, orange peel and salt. In a small bowl, combine whipping cream and 1/2 cup butter; stir into dry ingredients until a thick batter forms. Gently stir in pecans.

Drop by 1/3 cupfuls onto a greased baking sheet. Brush with remaining butter; sprinkle with remaining sugar. Bake at 375° for 18-20 minutes or until golden brown. Remove to wire racks to cool.

Cut the biscuits in half horizontally. Spoon the raspberries onto the bottom halves. Top with whipped cream if desired; replace biscuit tops. Serve immediately. **Yield:** 8 servings.

Chocolate-Mallow Peanut Candy

Prep: 10 min. + chilling

Pastel marshmallows give a pretty springtime touch to these bars, which taste just like candy. I've contributed them to countless bake sales, and they disappear from the table in a flash. —*Karen Perry, Askov, Minnesota*

✓ This recipe includes Nutrition Facts and Diabetic Exchanges.

1 package (11-1/2 ounces) milk chocolate chips
1 package (10 ounces) butterscotch chips
1 cup creamy peanut butter
1 package (10-1/2 ounces) pastel miniature marshmallows
1-3/4 cups salted peanuts
1 cup crisp rice cereal

In a large microwave-safe bowl, melt chips and peanut butter; stir until smooth. Add the marshmallows, peanuts and cereal; mix well.

Transfer to a 13-in. x 9-in. x 2-in. dish coated with cooking spray. Refrigerate for 2 hours or until firm before cutting. **Yield:** 5 dozen.

Nutrition Facts: 1 piece equals 121 calories, 7 g fat (3 g saturated fat), 1 mg cholesterol, 53 mg sodium, 12 g carbohydrate, 1 g fiber, 3 g protein. **Diabetic Exchanges:** 1 starch, 1 fat.

Strawberry Sundae Sauce

Strawberry Sundae Sauce

(Pictured above)

Prep: 25 min. + standing

My husband and kids are always thrilled when I pour this yummy sauce over their bowlfuls of vanilla ice cream. If you choose to prepare this recipe without using the raspberry liqueur, simply replace 1-1/2 cups of the mashed strawberries with 1-1/2 cups mashed raspberries instead. —*Peggy Townsend, Florence, Colorado*

2 quarts fresh strawberries
6 cups sugar
1 pouch (3 ounces) liquid fruit pectin
1/3 cup chocolate syrup
1/3 cup raspberry liqueur, optional
Vanilla ice cream

Wash and mash strawberries, measuring out enough mashed berries to make 4 cups. In a Dutch oven, combine berries and sugar. Bring to a full rolling boil over high heat, stirring constantly. Stir in pectin. Boil 1 minute longer, stirring constantly. Remove from the heat. Stir in syrup and liqueur if desired. Skim off foam.

Pour into jars or freezer containers, leaving a 1/2-in. headspace. Cool to room temperature, about 1 hour. Cover and let stand overnight or until set. Refrigerate for up to 3 weeks or freeze for up to 1 year. Serve with ice cream. **Yield:** 8 cups.

Deep-Dish Apple Pie

(Pictured below and on page 208)

Prep: 50 min. **Bake:** 40 min. + cooling

Our Test Kitchen cooks love this recipe from the Salem Cross Inn of West Brookfield, Massachusetts. The classic apple pie baked in a 13-in. x 9-in. pan will feed a crowd.

2 cups all-purpose flour
1/2 cup shortening
1 egg
1/4 cup cold water
2 tablespoons white vinegar
FILLING:
10 cups sliced peeled tart apples
1 teaspoon lemon juice
1/4 cup sugar
1/4 cup packed brown sugar
3 tablespoons all-purpose flour
1 teaspoon ground cinnamon
1/2 teaspoon ground nutmeg
1 tablespoon butter
1 egg
1 tablespoon milk

Place flour in a large bowl; cut in shortening until mixture resembles coarse crumbs. In a small bowl, combine the egg, water and vinegar; gradually add to crumb mixture, tossing with a fork until a ball forms. Cover and refrigerate for 20 minutes or until easy to handle.

Meanwhile, in a large bowl, toss apples with lemon juice. In a small bowl, combine sugars, flour, cinnamon and nutmeg; add to apple mixture and toss to coat. Pour into a 13-in. x 9-in. x 2-in. baking dish; dot with butter.

Roll out the dough to fit the top of pie. Flute edges. Beat egg with milk; brush over pastry. Bake at 375° for 40-50 minutes or until crust is golden brown and apples are tender. Cool on a wire rack. **Yield:** 15 servings.

Lime Poppy Seed Shortcakes

Prep: 20 min. **Bake:** 20 min. + cooling

Tropical flavor gives a burst of refreshment to this dessert, created by our home economists. The cakes make an elegant finale to a summer meal or even brunch.

3 cups fresh blueberries
1 cup chopped peeled mango
2 tablespoons brown sugar
BISCUITS:
2 cups all-purpose flour
1/4 cup plus 1 tablespoon sugar, *divided*
4 teaspoons poppy seeds
3 teaspoons baking powder
1-1/2 teaspoons grated lime peel
1/2 teaspoon salt
1 cup heavy whipping cream
1/2 cup plus 1 tablespoon butter, melted, *divided*
TOPPING:
1 cup (8 ounces) sour cream
1/4 cup packed brown sugar

In a small bowl, combine the blueberries, mango and brown sugar; cover and refrigerate until serving.

In a large bowl, combine flour, 1/4 cup sugar, poppy seeds, baking powder, lime peel and salt. In a small bowl, combine cream and 1/2 cup butter; stir into dry ingredients until a thick batter forms.

Drop by 1/3 cupfuls onto a greased baking sheet. Brush with remaining butter; sprinkle with remaining sugar. Bake at 375° for 18-20 minutes or until golden brown. Remove to wire racks to cool.

In a small bowl, combine the topping ingredients. Cut the biscuits in half horizontally. Spoon about 1/3 cup fruit mixture and 2 tablespoons topping onto the biscuit bottoms; replace biscuit tops. Serve immediately. **Yield:** 8 servings.

Deep-Dish Apple Pie

Pecan Shortbread Diamonds

Pecan Shortbread Diamonds

(Pictured above)

Prep: 40 min. **Bake:** 20 min. + cooling

My mom and I made these shortbread cookies every year for the holiday season. They have a chewy filling and a hint of chocolate. —Jane Ellen Benroth, Bluffton, Ohio

✓ This recipe includes Nutrition Facts and Diabetic Exchanges.

3/4 cup butter, softened
1/2 cup confectioners' sugar
2 cups all-purpose flour
1/2 teaspoon salt
FILLING:
2 squares (1 ounce *each*) unsweetened chocolate
4 eggs
1-1/2 cups packed brown sugar
2 teaspoons vanilla extract
1/2 teaspoon salt
3 cups chopped pecans

In a large mixing bowl, cream butter and confectioners' sugar until light and fluffy. Combine flour and salt; gradually add to creamed mixture and mix well. Press into an ungreased 15-in. x 10-in. x 1-in. baking pan. Bake at 375° for 12-15 minutes or until lightly browned. Cool for 5 minutes on a wire rack. Reduce temperature to 350°.

For filling, in a microwave-safe bowl, melt chocolate; stir until smooth. Cool. In a large bowl, combine eggs, brown sugar, vanilla, salt and melted chocolate; fold in pecans. Pour filling over crust. Bake for 18-20 minutes or until filling is set. Cool completely on a wire rack. Cut into diamond-shaped bars. **Yield:** 5 dozen.

Nutrition Facts: 1 piece equals 111 calories, 7 g fat (2 g saturated fat), 20 mg cholesterol, 63 mg sodium, 11 g carbohydrate, 1 g fiber, 2 g protein. **Diabetic Exchanges:** 1 starch, 1 fat.

Apple Bread Pudding

(Pictured below)

Prep: 20 min. **Bake:** 40 min.

With lots of walnuts, cinnamon and butterscotch chips, this bread pudding is a comforting treat—perfect for chilly days. —Sally Sibthorpe, Shelby Township, Michigan

1/4 cup butter
2 cups chopped peeled tart apples
1/3 cup packed brown sugar
8 cups cubed French bread
1/2 cup butterscotch chips
1/2 cup cinnamon baking chips
1/2 cup chopped walnuts
4 eggs
3 cups half-and-half cream
1 teaspoon vanilla extract
Additional cinnamon baking chips, melted, optional

In a large skillet, melt butter. Stir in apples and brown sugar. Cook over medium heat for 6-7 minutes or until apples are tender, stirring occasionally.

Place bread cubes in a greased 13-in. x 9-in. x 2-in. baking dish. Add the apple mixture, chips and walnuts; toss to coat. In a large bowl, whisk the eggs, cream and vanilla; pour over bread mixture.

Bake at 350° for 40-45 minutes or until a knife inserted near the center comes out clean. Drizzle with melted cinnamon chips if desired. Serve warm. Refrigerate leftovers. **Yield:** 12 servings.

Apple Bread Pudding

Chocolate Berry Freeze

Chocolate Berry Freeze

(Pictured above)

Prep: 20 min. + freezing

This make-ahead dessert is so tempting and tastes just as good as it looks. Keep one handy in the freezer for drop-in guests. —*Lisa Ruehlow, Blaine, Minnesota*

- **2 cups cream-filled chocolate sandwich cookie crumbs**
- **1/2 cup butter, melted**
- **3/4 cup sweetened condensed milk, *divided***
- **1/3 cup frozen unsweetened strawberries, thawed and chopped**
- **2 tablespoons strawberry ice cream topping**
- **1-1/4 cups heavy whipping cream, whipped, *divided***
- **1/3 cup slivered almonds, toasted**
- **2 tablespoons chocolate syrup**

Line the bottom and sides of a 9-in. x 5-in. x 3-in. loaf pan with heavy-duty foil. Combine cookie crumbs and butter; press half of the mixture into prepared pan. Freeze for 15 minutes.

Pour half of the milk into a small bowl; stir in strawberries and strawberry topping. Fold in half of whipped cream. Spread over crust. Sprinkle with remaining crumb mixture. Freeze for 45-60 minutes or until firm.

In a small bowl, combine the almonds, chocolate syrup and remaining milk. Fold in remaining whipped cream. Spread over crumb layer (pan will be full). Cover and freeze for several hours or overnight. May be frozen for up to 2 months.

Remove from the freezer 10 minutes before serving. Using foil, lift dessert out of pan. Invert onto a serving platter; discard foil. Cut into slices. **Yield:** 10 servings.

Peaches with Lemon Cream

Prep/Total Time: 30 min.

Love to grill? Why stop at the main course? This wonderful grilled dessert makes a memorable ending to any fresh-air feast. My family looks forward to it all summer long. —*Carole Fraser, North York, Ontario*

☑ This recipe includes Nutrition Facts and Diabetic Exchanges.

- **1/4 cup heavy whipping cream**
- **1 tablespoon brown sugar**
- **1 teaspoon vanilla extract**
- **1/2 teaspoon grated lemon peel**
- **3 medium peaches, halved**
- **2 tablespoons canola oil**

In a small mixing bowl, beat cream until it begins to thicken. Add brown sugar, vanilla and lemon peel; beat until stiff peaks form. Cover and refrigerate until serving.

Brush cut sides of peaches with oil; place cut side down on grill rack. Grill, covered, over medium heat for 10-12 minutes or until peaches are tender and begin to caramelize.

Place peaches on dessert plates; fill with lemon cream mixture. **Yield:** 6 servings.

Nutrition Facts: 1 peach half with 4 teaspoons cream equals 104 calories, 8 g fat (3 g saturated fat), 14 mg cholesterol, 5 mg sodium, 7 g carbohydrate, 1 g fiber, 1 g protein. **Diabetic Exchanges:** 1-1/2 fat, 1/2 fruit.

Easy Cherry Strudels

Prep: 15 min. **Bake:** 20 min.

These simplified strudels with a ruby-red cherry filling are on the table every Christmas morning at our house. It's a must! —*Susan Dancy, Tallahassee, Florida*

- **1 can (14-1/2 ounces) pitted tart cherries**
- **1 cup sugar**
- **1/2 cup dried cranberries *or* raisins**
- **1 tablespoon butter**
- **3 tablespoons cornstarch**
- **1-1/2 cups chopped walnuts**
- **1 package (17.3 ounces) frozen puff pastry, thawed**
- **1 egg, beaten**

Drain the cherries, reserving 1/3 cup juice. In a large saucepan, combine the cherries, sugar, cranberries and butter. Cook and stir over medium heat until heated through. Combine cornstarch and reserved juice and add to the pan. Bring to a boil. Cook and stir 2 minutes longer or until thickened. Remove from heat; stir in nuts.

Unfold one pastry sheet and cut in half. Mound half of the cherry mixture on one pastry half to within 1/2 in. of edges. Top with remaining half; pinch edges to seal. Repeat with remaining pastry and filling.

Place on a greased foil-lined baking sheet. With a sharp knife, cut diagonal slits into tops of strudels; brush with egg. Bake at 400° for 20-25 minutes or until golden brown. **Yield:** 2 strudels (5 slices each).

Blueberry Peach Fool

(Pictured below)

Prep: 25 min. + chilling

When you're in the mood for something creamy and refreshing, you can't go wrong with this layered whipped dessert from our Test Kitchen home economists. Blueberries and peaches make a delightful combination.

1-1/2 cups chopped peeled fresh *or* frozen peaches
1/4 cup sugar
1/4 cup unsweetened apple juice
1/2 teaspoon ground cinnamon
Dash salt
1 cup heavy whipping cream
1/4 teaspoon vanilla extract
1-1/2 cups fresh *or* frozen blueberries, thawed

In a small saucepan, combine the peaches, sugar, apple juice, cinnamon and salt. Bring to a boil. Reduce heat; cover and simmer for 6-8 minutes or until peaches are tender. Cool slightly.

In a blender, process the peach mixture until smooth. Transfer the mixture to a small bowl; cover and refrigerate until chilled.

Just before serving, whip cream until it begins to thicken. Add vanilla; beat until soft peaks form. Fold into the peach mixture. In parfait glasses, alternately layer blueberries and cream mixture. **Yield:** 2 servings.

Frozen Banana Split Pie

Blueberry Peach Fool

Frozen Banana Split Pie

(Pictured above)

Prep: 25 min. + freezing

Planning an all-American menu of hamburgers and fries? Add this make-ahead dessert, and you'll have a meal to remember! The pie is tall and impressive—sure to make eyes light up—and tastes just like a frozen banana split.
—Joy Collins, Birmingham, Alabama

3 tablespoons chocolate hard-shell ice cream topping
1 graham cracker crust (9 inches)
2 medium bananas, sliced
1/2 teaspoon lemon juice
1/2 cup pineapple ice cream topping
1 quart strawberry ice cream, softened
2 cups whipped topping
1/2 cup chopped walnuts, toasted
Chocolate syrup
8 maraschino cherries with stems

Pour the chocolate ice cream topping into the graham cracker crust; freeze for 5 minutes or until the chocolate is firm.

Meanwhile, place bananas in a small bowl; toss with lemon juice. Arrange bananas over chocolate topping. Layer with pineapple topping, ice cream, whipped topping and walnuts.

Cover and freeze until firm. Remove from the freezer 15 minutes before cutting. Garnish with chocolate syrup and cherries. **Yield:** 8 servings.

Chapter 15

Make-Ahead Marvels

WHAT a great feeling—you arrive home after a hectic day, and there's a delicious homemade casserole in the freezer, waiting to go in the oven. And just like that, dinner's done!

This chapter is chock-full of family-pleasing recipes you can assemble ahead of time, then enjoy later with a minimum of fuss. From overnight breakfast bakes to marinated main courses for the grill, you'll find a sensational selection of fixed-in-advance fare.

When you have a few spare moments, take advantage of it by putting together dishes such as Three-Cheese Lasagna, Beef Potato Bake and Chicken Potpies. You'll be glad you did!

CONVENIENT CUISINE. Sweet 'n' Spicy Country Ribs (p. 234).

Chicken Taco Quiche

Chicken Taco Quiche

(Pictured above)

Prep: 20 min. **Bake:** 35 min. + standing

When I was craving quiche but not the usual ingredients for it, I tried using items on hand. This was the tasty result!
—Tamie Bradford, Grand Forks AFB, North Dakota

2 unbaked pastry shells (9 inches)
2 cups cubed cooked chicken
2 envelopes taco seasoning, *divided*
2/3 cup salsa
2 cups (8 ounces) shredded cheddar cheese
8 eggs
2 cups half-and-half cream
2 tablespoons butter, melted
1 can (4 ounces) chopped green chilies
1/2 cup sliced ripe olives

Line unpricked pastry shells with a double thickness of heavy-duty foil. Bake at 400° for 4 minutes. Remove foil; bake 4 minutes longer.

In a small bowl, combine chicken and one envelope taco seasoning; spoon into pastry shells. Top with salsa and cheese. In a large bowl, whisk the eggs, cream, butter and remaining taco seasoning. Stir in chilies and olives. Pour over cheese.

Cover and freeze one quiche for up to 3 months. Cover edges of remaining quiche loosely with foil; place on a baking sheet. Bake at 400° for 33-35 minutes or until a knife inserted near the center comes out clean. Let stand for 10 minutes before cutting.

To use frozen quiche: Remove from freezer 30 minutes before baking (do not thaw). Cover edges of crust loosely with foil; place on a baking sheet. Bake at 400° for 70-75 minutes or until a knife inserted near the center comes out clean. Let stand for 10 minutes before cutting. **Yield:** 2 quiches (6 servings each).

Ground Beef Spiral Bake

Prep: 40 min. **Bake:** 25 min.

We got this recipe from my mother-in-law's neighbor, who also happened to be a restaurant cook. It's a great weeknight dinner. —Monika Rahn, Dillsburg, Pennsylvania

1 package (16 ounces) spiral pasta
2 pounds ground beef
2/3 cup chopped onion
1 teaspoon minced garlic
2 jars (28 ounces *each*) spaghetti sauce
2 tablespoons tomato paste
1 teaspoon dried basil
1 teaspoon dried oregano
4 cups (16 ounces) shredded part-skim mozzarella cheese

Cook the pasta according to package directions; drain. Meanwhile, in a Dutch oven, cook the beef, onion and garlic over medium heat until meat is no longer pink; drain. Stir in the spaghetti sauce, tomato paste, basil and oregano. Bring to a boil. Reduce heat; simmer, uncovered, for 5-10 minutes.

Stir pasta into meat mixture. Transfer to two greased 13-in. x 9-in. x 2-in. baking dishes. Sprinkle each with 2 cups cheese. Cover and freeze one casserole for up to 3 months. Bake second casserole, uncovered, at 350° for 25-30 minutes or until heated through.

To use frozen casserole: Thaw casserole in refrigerator overnight. Bake, uncovered, at 350° for 35-40 minutes or until heated through. **Yield:** 2 casseroles (8-10 servings each).

Bacon Potato Salad

Prep: 10 min. **Cook:** 25 min. + chilling

My family requests this dish whenever we have a picnic. The salad is well seasoned and gets a lot of flavor from the bacon. —Charlotte McDaniel, Williamsville, Illinois

2-1/4 pounds red potatoes (about 8 medium)
1/2 pound sliced bacon, diced
1/2 cup chopped onion
2 teaspoons cider vinegar
1 teaspoon celery seed
3/4 teaspoon salt
1/4 teaspoon pepper
1 cup mayonnaise

Place potatoes in a Dutch oven and cover with water. Bring to a boil. Reduce heat; cover and cook for 20-25 minutes or until tender.

Meanwhile, in a large skillet, cook the bacon over medium heat until crisp. Using a slotted spoon, remove the bacon to paper towels. Drain, reserving 2 tablespoons drippings.

Drain potatoes. When cool enough to handle, peel and cut into cubes. Place in a large bowl. Add the onion, vinegar, celery seed, salt, pepper, bacon and reserved drippings; toss gently. Cool to room temperature. Fold in mayonnaise. Cover and refrigerate overnight. **Yield:** 8 servings.

Hearty Minestrone

(Pictured below)

Prep: 20 min. **Cook:** 45 min.

This meaty minestrone is my all-time favorite soup. The taste reminds me of spaghetti and sauce—only eaten with a spoon! —Katie Koziolek, Hartland, Minnesota

- **1 pound ground pork**
- **1/2 cup chopped celery**
- **1/2 cup chopped onion**
- **1/2 teaspoon minced garlic**
- **1 can (28 ounces) crushed tomatoes**
- **1 can (16 ounces) kidney beans, rinsed and drained**
- **1 can (15 ounces) garbanzo beans *or* peas, rinsed and drained**
- **2 cups tomato juice**
- **1 can (15 ounces) tomato sauce**
- **1 can (14-1/2 ounces) beef broth**
- **3 medium carrots, chopped**
- **1 medium zucchini, halved lengthwise and thinly sliced**
- **1 tablespoon Italian seasoning**
- **1 to 1-1/2 teaspoons salt**
- **1/2 teaspoon sugar, optional**
- **1/8 teaspoon pepper**

Hearty Minestrone

ADDITIONAL INGREDIENTS (for each batch):

- **1/2 cup water**
- **1 cup uncooked ziti *or* small tube pasta**

In a Dutch oven, cook the pork, celery, onion and garlic over medium heat until meat is no longer pink; drain.

Stir in tomatoes, beans, tomato juice, tomato sauce, beef broth, carrots, zucchini, Italian seasoning, salt, sugar if desired and pepper. Bring to a boil. Reduce heat; cover and simmer for 30-35 minutes or until the carrots are tender.

Transfer 6 cups of soup to a freezer container; freeze for up to 3 months. Add water and pasta to remaining soup; bring to a boil. Cover; cook until pasta is tender.

To use frozen soup: Thaw in the refrigerator; transfer to a large saucepan. Stir in the water. Bring to a boil; reduce heat. Add pasta; cover and cook until tender. **Yield:** 2 batches (6 servings each).

Three-Cheese Lasagna

Prep: 25 min. **Bake:** 15 min.

With all of the flavor of lasagna but none of the work to layer the ingredients, this recipe is as easy as it is delicious. Everything is stirred together in a skillet, then put in two baking dishes to give you one meal now and one later. —Del Mason, Martensville, Saskatchewan

- **2 pounds ground beef**
- **1/2 cup chopped onion**
- **1 package (6.4 ounces) lasagna dinner mix**
- **2-1/4 cups hot water**
- **2 cans (14-1/2 ounces *each*) diced tomatoes, undrained**
- **1 package (10 ounces) frozen chopped spinach, thawed and squeezed dry**
- **1 cup sliced fresh mushrooms**
- **1/2 cup chopped green onions**
- **1 cup (8 ounces) 4% cottage cheese**
- **1/4 cup grated Parmesan cheese**
- **1-1/2 cups (6 ounces) shredded part-skim mozzarella cheese**

In a large skillet, cook the ground beef and onion over medium heat for 10-12 minutes or until the meat is no longer pink; drain.

Stir in pasta from the dinner mix, contents of seasoning mix, water, tomatoes, spinach, mushrooms and onions. Bring to a boil. Reduce heat; cover and simmer for 10-13 minutes or until pasta is tender. Stir in cottage cheese and Parmesan cheese.

Transfer to two greased 8-in. square baking dishes. Sprinkle with mozzarella cheese.

Cover and freeze one casserole for up to 3 months. Cover and bake remaining casserole at 350° for 15-20 minutes or until bubbly and cheese is melted.

To use frozen casserole: Remove casserole from the freezer 30 minutes before baking (do not thaw). Cover and bake at 350° for 1 hour. Uncover; bake 15-20 minutes longer or until heated through. **Yield:** 2 casseroles (4 servings each).

Editor's Note: This recipe was tested with Hamburger Helper Lasagna Dinner Mix.

Chicken Potpies

Chicken Potpies

(Pictured above)

Prep: 20 min. **Bake:** 35 min.

The flaky, golden-brown crust and creamy sauce make these veggie-packed pies a sure hit. Our Test Kitchen cut down the preparation time using convenience items.

4 cups cubed cooked chicken
4 cups frozen Southern-style hash brown potatoes, thawed
1 package (16 ounces) frozen mixed vegetables, thawed and drained
1 can (10-3/4 ounces) condensed cream of chicken soup, undiluted
1 can (10-3/4 ounces) condensed cream of onion soup, undiluted
1 cup milk
1 cup (8 ounces) sour cream
2 tablespoons all-purpose flour
1/2 teaspoon salt
1/2 teaspoon pepper
1/4 teaspoon garlic powder
1 package (15 ounces) refrigerated pie pastry

In a large bowl, combine the first 11 ingredients. Divide between two 9-in. deep-dish pie plates. Roll out the pastry to fit the top of each pie. Cut slits in pastry. Place over filling; trim, seal and flute the edges.

Cover and freeze one potpie for up to 3 months. Bake the remaining potpie at 400° for 35-40 minutes or until golden brown.

To use frozen potpie: Remove from freezer 30 minutes before baking. Cover edges loosely with foil; place on a baking sheet. Bake at 425° for 30 minutes. Reduce heat to 350°; remove foil and bake 50-55 minutes longer or until golden brown. **Yield:** 2 potpies (6 servings each).

Bow Tie Ham Bake

Prep: 20 min. **Bake:** 25 min.

This comes from our family cookbook, which is filled with longtime favorites from generations of women. And one thing we loved was casseroles...as shown by all of those recipes in the book! —*Suzette Jury, Keene, California*

4 cups uncooked bow tie pasta
6 cups frozen broccoli florets
4 cups cubed fully cooked ham
2 cartons (10 ounces *each*) refrigerated Alfredo sauce
2 cups (8 ounces) shredded Swiss cheese
1 can (8 ounces) mushroom stems and pieces, drained

Cook the bow tie pasta according to the package directions, adding the broccoli during the last 5 minutes of cooking.

Meanwhile, in a large bowl, combine the ham, Alfredo sauce, cheese and mushrooms. Drain pasta mixture; add to ham mixture and toss to coat. Transfer to two greased 11-in. x 7-in. x 2-in. baking dishes.

Cover and freeze one casserole for up to 3 months. Cover and bake the remaining casserole at 375° for 20 minutes. Uncover and bake 5-10 minutes longer or until bubbly.

To use frozen casserole: Thaw the casserole in the refrigerator overnight. Remove from refrigerator 30 minutes before heating. Cover and microwave on high for 8-10 minutes or until heated through, stirring once. **Yield:** 2 casseroles (6 servings each).

Editor's Note: This recipe was tested in a 1,100-watt microwave.

Overnight Raisin French Toast

Prep: 15 min. + chilling **Bake:** 45 min.

I received this yummy recipe from a colleague years ago. I really like the convenience of assembling it the day before, then just popping it into the oven in the morning.
—*Stephanie Weaver, Sligo, Pennsylvania*

1 loaf (1 pound) cinnamon-raisin bread, cubed
1 package (8 ounces) cream cheese, cubed
8 eggs
1-1/2 cups half-and-half cream
1/2 cup sugar
1/2 cup maple syrup
2 tablespoons vanilla extract
1 tablespoon ground cinnamon
1/8 teaspoon ground nutmeg

Place half of the bread cubes in a greased 13-in. x 9-in. x 2-in. baking dish. Top with the cream cheese and remaining bread. In a large bowl, combine the remaining ingredients. Pour over the top. Cover and refrigerate overnight.

Remove from the refrigerator 30 minutes before baking. Cover and bake at 350° for 30 minutes. Uncover; bake 15-20 minutes longer or until a knife inserted near the center comes out clean. **Yield:** 12 servings.

Chicken Tater Bake

Prep: 20 min. **Bake:** 40 min.

You'll please everyone in the family with this warm and comforting main dish. It tastes just like a chicken potpie with a Tater-Tot crust. —Fran Allen, St. Louis, Missouri

- **2 cans (10-3/4 ounces *each*) condensed cream of chicken soup, undiluted**
- **1/2 cup milk**
- **1/4 cup butter, cubed**
- **3 cups cubed cooked chicken**
- **1 package (16 ounces) frozen peas and carrots, thawed**
- **1-1/2 cups (6 ounces) shredded cheddar cheese, *divided***
- **1 package (32 ounces) frozen Tater Tots**

In a large saucepan, combine soup, milk and butter. Cook and stir over medium heat until heated through. Remove from heat; stir in chicken, vegetables and 1 cup cheese. Transfer to two greased 8-in. square baking dishes. Top with Tater Tots; sprinkle with remaining cheese.

Cover and freeze one casserole for up to 3 months. Cover and bake remaining casserole at 350° for 35 minutes. Uncover and bake 5-10 minutes longer or until heated through.

To use frozen casserole: Remove from the freezer 30 minutes before baking (do not thaw). Cover and bake at 350° for 1-1/2 to 1-3/4 hours or until heated through. **Yield:** 2 casseroles (6 servings each).

Ham & Cheese Casseroles

Prep: 20 min. **Bake:** 25 min.

This recipe came from my mother, and I really appreciate its simplicity. Plus, it's handy to keep in the freezer for unexpected guests. —Jan Schoshke, Brookville, Kansas

- **1-1/2 pounds uncooked egg noodles**
- **3 pounds cubed fully cooked ham**
- **4 cans (10-3/4 ounces *each*) condensed cream of chicken soup, undiluted**
- **4 cups frozen cut green beans, thawed**
- **1 cup milk**
- **1/4 cup butter, melted**
- **2 cups (8 ounces) shredded Colby-Monterey Jack cheese**

Cook pasta according to package directions. Meanwhile, in a large bowl, combine the ham, soup, beans and milk. Drain the pasta; pour over the ham mixture and toss to coat. Transfer to two greased 13-in. x 9-in. x 2-in. baking dishes.

Drizzle each with butter; sprinkle with cheese. Cover and freeze one casserole for up to 3 months. Bake the remaining casserole, uncovered, at 350° for 25-30 minutes or until heated through.

To use frozen casserole: Thaw the casserole in the refrigerator overnight. Remove from refrigerator 30 minutes before baking. Bake, uncovered, at 350° for 40-45 minutes or until heated through. **Yield:** 2 casseroles (8 servings each).

Squash Corn Bread

(Pictured below)

Prep: 15 min. **Bake:** 20 min.

Enjoy the fresh flavor of summer squash with this moist and hearty corn bread. It's good enough to eat by itself! —Marlene Huffstetler, Chapin, South Carolina

☑ This recipe includes Nutrition Facts and Diabetic Exchanges.

- **5 medium yellow summer squash (about 2 pounds), chopped**
- **2 packages (8-1/2 ounces *each*) corn bread/muffin mix**
- **4 eggs, lightly beaten**
- **2/3 cup 4% cottage cheese**
- **1/2 cup shredded cheddar cheese**
- **1/2 cup chopped onion**
- **1/4 teaspoon salt**
- **1/4 teaspoon pepper**

Place squash in a steamer basket; place in a large saucepan over 1 in. of water. Bring to a boil; cover and steam for 3-5 minutes or until tender. Drain and squeeze dry.

In a large bowl, combine corn bread mixes and eggs. Fold in squash, cheeses, onion, salt and pepper.

Pour into two 8-in. square baking pans coated with cooking spray. Bake at 400° for 20-25 minutes or until a toothpick inserted near the center comes out clean.

Serve warm or cool for 10 minutes before removing from pan to a wire rack to cool completely. Wrap in foil and freeze for up to 3 months.

To use frozen bread: Thaw at room temperature. Serve warm. **Yield:** 2 dozen.

Nutrition Facts: 1 piece equals 116 calories, 4 g fat (2 g saturated fat), 44 mg cholesterol, 242 mg sodium, 17 g carbohydrate, 1 g fiber, 4 g protein. **Diabetic Exchanges:** 1 starch, 1 fat.

Squash Corn Bread

Sweet 'n' Spicy Country Ribs

Sweet 'n' Spicy Country Ribs

(Pictured above and on page 228)

Prep: 15 min. + marinating **Grill:** 40 min.

Through the years, family members and friends have asked me to bottle my barbecue sauce, rubs and marinades. My favorite saying is, "You cook it, and they will come." And they sure will come for these tender ribs! —Allan Stackhouse, Jr. Jennings, Louisiana

3/4 cup unsweetened apple juice
1/2 cup vegetable oil
1/2 cup cola
1/4 cup packed brown sugar
1/4 cup honey
1 tablespoon minced garlic
1 tablespoon Worcestershire sauce
2 teaspoons Liquid Smoke, optional
1 teaspoon salt
1 teaspoon dried thyme
1 teaspoon pepper
1/2 teaspoon cayenne pepper
1/2 teaspoon ground nutmeg
3 to 4 pounds boneless country-style pork ribs

In a small bowl, combine the apple juice, oil, cola, brown sugar, honey, garlic, Worcestershire sauce, Liquid Smoke if desired and seasonings. Pour 1-1/2 cups marinade into a large resealable plastic bag; add the ribs. Seal the the bag and turn to coat; refrigerate for 5 hours or overnight, turning once. Cover and refrigerate remaining marinade for basting.

Coat grill rack with cooking spray before starting the grill. Prepare grill for indirect heat. Drain and discard marinade. Grill ribs, covered, over indirect medium heat for 10 minutes on each side, basting occasionally. Grill 20-25 minutes longer or until juices run clear and meat is tender, turning and basting occasionally with remaining marinade. **Yield:** 12 servings.

Hearty Breakfast Egg Bake

Prep: 10 min. + chilling **Bake:** 45 min. + standing

I always fix this when I have overnight guests. I just add toast or biscuits and fresh fruit for a complete breakfast everyone loves. —Pamela Norris, Fenton, Missouri

1-1/2 pounds bulk pork sausage
3 cups frozen shredded hash brown potatoes, thawed
2 cups (8 ounces) shredded cheddar cheese
8 eggs
1 can (10-3/4 ounces) condensed cream of mushroom soup, undiluted
3/4 cup evaporated milk

Crumble sausage into a large skillet. Cook over medium heat until no longer pink; drain. Transfer to a greased 13-in. x 9-in. x 2-in. baking dish. Sprinkle with hash browns and cheese. In a large bowl, whisk remaining ingredients; pour over top. Cover; refrigerate overnight.

Remove from refrigerator 30 minutes before baking. Bake, uncovered, at 350° for 45-50 minutes or until a knife inserted near the center comes out clean. Let stand for 10 minutes before cutting. **Yield:** 8 servings.

Spaghetti Beef Casserole

Prep: 25 min. **Bake:** 20 min.

For me—a mom of three active boys—this casserole has been a lifesaver! Fast and hearty, it's a reliable choice for pregame meals. —Jane Radtke, Griffith, Indiana

1-1/2 pounds uncooked spaghetti
3 pounds ground beef
1 cup chopped onion
2/3 cup chopped green pepper
1 teaspoon minced garlic
2 cans (10-3/4 ounces *each*) condensed cream of mushroom soup, undiluted
2 cans (10-3/4 ounces *each*) condensed tomato soup, undiluted
1-1/3 cups water
1 can (8 ounces) mushroom stems and pieces, drained
3 cups (12 ounces) shredded cheddar cheese, *divided*

Cook spaghetti according to package directions. Meanwhile, in a large skillet, cook the beef, onion, green pepper and garlic over medium heat until meat is no longer pink; drain. Stir in the soups, water and mushrooms.

Drain spaghetti. Add spaghetti and 1 cup cheese to beef mixture. Transfer to two greased 13-in. x 9-in. x 2-in. baking dishes. Sprinkle with remaining cheese. Cover and freeze one casserole for up to 3 months. Bake remaining casserole, uncovered, at 350° for 20-25 minutes or until cheese is melted.

To use frozen casserole: Thaw in the refrigerator overnight. Remove from the refrigerator 30 minutes before baking. Cover and bake at 350° for 1 to 1-1/4 hours or until heated through and cheese is melted. **Yield:** 2 casseroles (8 servings each).

Bacon Spinach Strata

(Pictured below)

Prep: 30 min. + chilling **Bake:** 45 min. + standing

This make-ahead bake is pretty enough for any holiday brunch. And it disappears in a flash, thanks to the combination of eggs, bacon, spinach, mushrooms and cheese.
—Kris Kebisek, Brookfield, Wisconsin

1 package (8 ounces) sliced mushrooms
1 bunch green onions, sliced
2 teaspoons vegetable oil
1 loaf (1 pound) day old bread, cut into 3/4-inch cubes
1 cup (4 ounces) shredded Swiss cheese
1 package (1 pound) sliced bacon, cooked and crumbled
2 cups (8 ounces) shredded cheddar cheese
1 package (10 ounces) frozen chopped spinach, thawed and squeezed dry
9 eggs
3 cups milk
1/2 teaspoon *each* onion powder, garlic powder and ground mustard
1/4 teaspoon salt
1/4 teaspoon pepper

In a large skillet, saute mushrooms and onions in oil until tender. Place half of bread cubes and 1/2 cup Swiss cheese in a greased 13-in. x 9-in. x 2-in. baking dish. Layer with bacon, cheddar cheese, mushroom mixture, spinach and remaining Swiss cheese and bread cubes. In a large bowl, combine eggs, milk and seasonings. Pour over casserole. Cover and refrigerate overnight.

Remove from the refrigerator 30 minutes before baking. Bake, uncovered, at 375° for 45-55 minutes or until a knife inserted near the center comes out clean (cover loosely with foil if top browns too quickly). Let stand for 10 minutes before cutting. **Yield:** 12 servings.

Bacon Spinach Strata

Grilled Asian Flank Steak

Grilled Asian Flank Steak

(Pictured above)

Prep: 15 min. + marinating **Grill:** 15 min.

My mother's marinated ginger-sake flank steak was excellent. This is a lighter variation, and I think it measures up well. *—Shawn Solley, Morgantown, West Virginia*

✓ This recipe includes Nutrition Facts and Diabetic Exchanges.

1/4 cup Worcestershire sauce
1/4 cup reduced-sodium soy sauce
3 tablespoons honey
1 tablespoon sesame oil
1 teaspoon Chinese five-spice powder
1 teaspoon minced garlic
1/2 teaspoon minced fresh gingerroot
1 beef flank steak (1-1/2 pounds)
2 tablespoons hoisin sauce, warmed
3 green onions, thinly sliced
1 tablespoon sesame seeds, toasted, optional

In a large resealable plastic bag, combine the first seven ingredients; add steak. Seal bag and turn to coat; refrigerate overnight.

Drain and discard marinade. Grill steak, covered, over medium heat for 6-7 minutes on each side or until meat reaches desired doneness (for medium-rare, a meat thermometer should read 145°; medium, 160°; well-done, 170°). Let stand for 5 minutes.

Thinly slice steak across the grain. Drizzle with hoisin sauce; garnish with onions. Sprinkle with sesame seeds if desired. **Yield:** 6 servings.

Nutrition Facts: 3 ounces cooked beef (calculated without sesame seeds) equals 193 calories, 9 g fat (4 g saturated fat), 54 mg cholesterol, 241 mg sodium, 5 g carbohydrate, trace fiber, 22 g protein. **Diabetic Exchange:** 3 lean meat.

Peachy Barbecue Chicken

(Pictured below)

Prep: 10 min. **Cook:** 30 min.

Barbecue sauce and peach preserves bring the perfect combination of sweet and savory flavors to this tender chicken dinner. —Laura Mahaffey, Annapolis, Maryland

1/2 cup all-purpose flour
1 teaspoon salt
1/8 teaspoon pepper
8 boneless skinless chicken breast halves (5 ounces *each*)
1/4 cup vegetable oil
2 cups peach preserves
1 cup chopped onion
1 cup barbecue sauce
1/4 cup soy sauce
2 medium green peppers, julienned
2 cans (8 ounces *each*) sliced water chestnuts, drained
Hot cooked rice

In a shallow dish, combine flour, salt and pepper. Coat chicken in flour mixture. In a large skillet, brown chicken in oil in batches on both sides. Return all to skillet. In a large bowl, combine the preserves, onion, barbecue sauce and soy sauce; pour over chicken. Bring to a boil. Reduce heat; cover and simmer for 15 minutes.

Add green peppers and water chestnuts. Bring to a boil. Reduce heat; simmer, uncovered, for 5 minutes or until a meat thermometer reads 170°. Serve immediately with rice; or cool chicken and transfer to a freezer container and freeze for up to 3 months.

To use frozen chicken: Thaw in the refrigerator overnight. Remove from the refrigerator 30 minutes before reheating. Cover and bake at 350° for 50-60 minutes or until bubbly. Serve with rice. **Yield:** 8 servings.

Peachy Barbecue Chicken

Veggie Lasagna

Veggie Lasagna

(Pictured above)

Prep: 30 min. **Bake:** 40 min. + standing

With green beans and garden-style spaghetti sauce, this is a little different from the usual lasagna recipes. It's a nice meatless choice. —Alyce Wyman, Pembina, North Dakota

✓ This recipe includes Nutrition Facts and Diabetic Exchanges.

18 uncooked lasagna noodles
2 eggs
2 egg whites
2 cartons (15 ounces *each*) reduced-fat ricotta cheese
4 teaspoons dried parsley flakes
2 teaspoons dried basil
2 teaspoons dried oregano
1 teaspoon pepper
8 cups garden-style spaghetti sauce
4 cups (16 ounces) shredded part-skim mozzarella cheese
2 packages (16 ounces *each*) frozen cut green beans *or* 8 cups cut fresh green beans
2/3 cup grated Parmesan cheese

Cook the noodles according to the package directions. Meanwhile, in a small bowl, whisk the eggs, egg whites, ricotta cheese, parsley, basil, oregano and pepper; set aside. In each of two 13-in. x 9-in. x 2-in. baking dishes coated with cooking spray, spread 1 cup spaghetti sauce. Drain noodles; place three noodles over spaghetti sauce in each dish.

Layer each with a quarter of the ricotta mixture, 1 cup spaghetti sauce, 1 cup mozzarella cheese, three lasagna noodles and half of green beans. Top each with the remaining ricotta mixture, 1 cup spaghetti sauce, remaining lasagna noodles, spaghetti sauce and mozzarella cheese. Sprinkle Parmesan cheese over each.

Cover and freeze one casserole for up to 3 months. Bake remaining lasagna, uncovered, at 375° for 40-45 minutes or until bubbly and edges are lightly browned. Let stand for 10 minutes before serving.

To use frozen lasagna: Thaw in the refrigerator overnight. Remove from refrigerator 30 minutes before baking. Cover and bake at 375° for 1-1/4 to 1-1/2 hours or until bubbly. Let stand for 10 minutes before serving. **Yield:** 2 casseroles (9 servings each).

Nutrition Facts: 1 piece equals 320 calories, 10 g fat (5 g saturated fat), 56 mg cholesterol, 713 mg sodium, 38 g carbohydrate, 5 g fiber, 18 g protein. **Diabetic Exchanges:** 2 starch, 2 lean meat, 2 vegetable.

Beef Potato Bake

Prep: 10 min. **Bake:** 50 min.

For this hearty dish, you can use peas or green beans instead of mushrooms...or a different cream soup, such as celery. —Cathy Casement-McDowell, Tulsa, Oklahoma

- **2 pounds ground beef**
- **1 can (10-3/4 ounces) condensed cream of mushroom soup, undiluted**
- **1 can (10-3/4 ounces) condensed cream of celery soup, undiluted**
- **1-1/4 teaspoons dried parsley flakes**
- **1 teaspoon dried minced onion**
- **1/4 teaspoon pepper**
- **1 package (32 ounces) frozen cubed hash brown potatoes, thawed**
- **4 cups (16 ounces) shredded cheddar cheese, *divided***
- **1 can (8 ounces) mushroom stems and pieces, drained**

In a large skillet, cook beef over medium heat until no longer pink; drain.

Meanwhile, in a large bowl, combine the soups, parsley, onion and pepper. Add the potatoes, 2 cups cheese and mushrooms. Stir in beef.

Transfer to two greased 8-in. square baking dishes. Sprinkle each with 1 cup cheese. Cover and freeze one casserole for up to 3 months. Cover and bake the remaining casserole at 375° for 45-50 minutes or until potatoes are tender. Uncover and bake for 5-10 minutes or until the cheese is melted.

To use frozen casserole: Thaw the casserole in the refrigerator overnight. Remove from refrigerator 30 minutes before baking. Bake as directed. **Yield:** 2 casseroles (4 servings each).

Fresh from the Freezer

When I start getting peppers and onions in my garden, I save some for fresh use. Then I chop up the rest and store them in a freezer bag in the freezer. Later, when I'm rushed, I don't have to spend extra time chopping—I just take what I need from the freezer. The veggies keep their flavor for up to four months.

—Carol Schubert, Ellison Bay, Wisconsin

Garden Vegetable Soup

(Pictured below)

Prep: 25 min. **Cook:** 20 min.

I like cooking with vegetables to create a wholesome meal. This meatless soup makes a great dinner with a salad or bread. —Jennifer Black, San Jose, California

- **1-1/2 teaspoons minced garlic**
- **2 tablespoons olive oil**
- **1/4 cup uncooked long grain rice**
- **2 cans (14-1/2 ounces *each*) chicken broth**
- **1 cup chopped sweet red pepper**
- **1 cup chopped green pepper**
- **1/2 cup thinly sliced fresh carrots**
- **1 teaspoon salt**
- **1/2 teaspoon dried basil**
- **1/4 teaspoon dried rosemary, crushed**
- **Dash pepper**
- **2 medium zucchini, sliced**
- **6 plum tomatoes, chopped**

In a large saucepan, cook the garlic in oil for 1 minute. Stir in the rice; cook and stir for 1 minute. Add the chicken broth, peppers, carrots and seasonings. Bring to a boil. Reduce heat; cover and simmer for 15-20 minutes or until rice is tender.

Stir in zucchini and tomatoes; cook for 3 minutes. Cool. Transfer to freezer containers. May be frozen for up to 3 months.

To serve immediately, cook soup 3-5 minutes longer or until zucchini is tender.

To use frozen soup: Thaw the soup in the refrigerator overnight. Transfer to a saucepan. Cover and cook over medium heat until heated through. **Yield:** 8 servings (2 quarts).

Garden Vegetable Soup

Chapter 16

Casseroles and Oven Suppers

IT'S NOT a half-baked idea—relying on your oven to get a family dinner on the table on hectic weeknights.

When you have fast casseroles, pronto pizzas and other speedy oven suppers like the ones in this chapter, you'll need only minutes for the prep work. Then simply pop dinner in the oven, and you're done!

Your family is sure to enjoy main dishes such as Zucchini Crescent Pie, Garlic-Roasted Chicken and Potatoes, Tortilla Lasagna and Reuben Casserole.

While supper bakes, you'll have time to whip up a side dish or dessert to round out your menu...and likely even more time that you can spend relaxing with your family.

DELICIOUS HOT DISH. Sausage & Beans with Rice (p. 247).

Tasty Mozzarella Chicken

(Pictured above)

Prep: 15 min. **Bake:** 30 min.

This stress-free chicken dinner is guaranteed to become a family favorite. Use whatever variety of spaghetti sauce you prefer, such as tomato-and-basil or garlic-and-herb.
—Nancy Foust, Stoneboro, Pennsylvania

- **1 egg**
- **2 tablespoons water**
- **2/3 cup dry bread crumbs**
- **1 envelope onion soup mix**
- **1/8 teaspoon pepper**
- **6 boneless skinless chicken breast halves (5 ounces *each*)**
- **1-1/2 cups spaghetti sauce**
- **1 can (7 ounces) mushroom stems and pieces, drained**
- **1 cup (4 ounces) shredded part-skim mozzarella cheese**

In a shallow bowl, beat egg and water. In another shallow bowl, combine the bread crumbs, soup mix and pepper. Dip chicken in egg mixture, then coat with crumb mixture.

Place in a greased 13-in. x 9-in. x 2-in. baking dish. Bake, uncovered, at 400° for 22-25 minutes or until the juices run clear.

In a small bowl, combine spaghetti sauce and mushrooms; spoon over chicken. Sprinkle with cheese. Bake 5-7 minutes longer or until sauce is bubbly and cheese is melted. **Yield:** 6 servings.

Mostaccioli Beef Casserole

Prep: 35 min. **Bake:** 20 min.

What's not to love in this meaty bake? It's loaded with ground beef, noodles and cheddar cheese...and it's super-easy, too. *—Patty Hough, Sun City, Arizona*

- **8 ounces uncooked mostaccioli**
- **1-1/2 pounds ground beef**
- **1 cup chopped green pepper**
- **3/4 cup chopped onion**
- **2 cans (8 ounces *each*) tomato sauce**
- **1 jar (4-1/2 ounces) sliced mushrooms, drained**
- **3 teaspoons chili powder**
- **2 teaspoons sugar**
- **1 teaspoon salt**
- **1/4 teaspoon garlic powder**
- **1/4 teaspoon pepper**
- **2 tablespoons butter**
- **2 cups (8 ounces) shredded cheddar cheese**

Cook the mostaccioli according to package directions. Meanwhile, in a large skillet, cook the beef, green pepper and onion over medium heat until meat is no longer pink; drain.

Stir in the tomato sauce, mushrooms, chili powder, sugar, salt, garlic powder and pepper. Bring to a boil. Reduce heat; simmer, uncovered, for 5 minutes.

Drain pasta; toss with butter. Spread 1/2 cup meat sauce into a greased 2-1/2-qt. baking dish. Top with half of the pasta, meat sauce and cheese. Repeat layers.

Bake, uncovered, at 350° for 20-25 minutes or until heated through. **Yield:** 6 servings.

Zucchini Crescent Pie

(Pictured below)

Prep: 25 min. **Bake:** 20 min.

This is one of my mom's many recipes designed to use up a bounty of zucchini. Cooked ham and refrigerated dough cut the prep time. —Susan Davis, Ann Arbor, Michigan

- **1 package (8 ounces) refrigerated crescent rolls**
- **2 medium zucchini, sliced and quartered**
- **1/2 cup chopped onion**
- **1/4 cup butter, cubed**
- **2 teaspoons minced fresh parsley**
- **1/2 teaspoon salt**
- **1/2 teaspoon garlic powder**
- **1/2 teaspoon pepper**
- **1/4 teaspoon dried basil**
- **1/4 teaspoon dried oregano**
- **2 eggs, lightly beaten**
- **2 cups (8 ounces) shredded part-skim mozzarella cheese**
- **3/4 cup cubed fully cooked ham**
- **1 medium Roma tomato, thinly sliced**

Separate crescent dough into eight triangles; place in a greased 9-in. pie plate with points toward the center. Press onto the bottom and up the sides to form a crust; seal seams and perforations. Bake at 375° for 5-8 minutes or until lightly browned.

Meanwhile, in a large skillet, saute zucchini and onion in butter until tender; stir in seasonings. Spoon into crust. Combine eggs, cheese and ham; pour over zucchini mixture. Top with tomato slices.

Bake at 375° for 20-25 minutes or until a knife inserted near the center comes out clean. Let pie stand for 5 minutes before cutting. **Yield:** 6 servings.

Zucchini Crescent Pie

Sweet Potato Sausage Casserole

Sweet Potato Sausage Casserole

(Pictured above)

Prep: 20 min. **Bake:** 25 min.

Combining sweet potatoes, pasta and kielbasa may seem strange, but I gave it try and was really pleased with the results. —Rickey Madden, Clinton, South Carolina

- **8 ounces uncooked spiral pasta**
- **8 ounces smoked sausage, cut into 1/4-inch slices**
- **2 medium sweet potatoes, peeled and cut into 1/2-inch cubes**
- **1 cup chopped green pepper**
- **1/2 cup chopped onion**
- **1 teaspoon minced garlic**
- **2 tablespoons olive oil**
- **1 can (14-1/2 ounces) diced tomatoes, undrained**
- **1 cup heavy whipping cream**
- **1/4 teaspoon salt**
- **1/4 teaspoon pepper**
- **1 cup (4 ounces) shredded cheddar cheese**

Cook the pasta according to package directions. Meanwhile, in a large skillet, cook sausage, sweet potatoes, green pepper, onion and garlic in oil over medium heat for 5 minutes or until vegetables are tender; drain.

Add the tomatoes, cream, salt and pepper. Bring to a boil; remove from the heat. Drain the pasta; stir into sausage mixture. Transfer to a greased 13-in. x 9-in. x 2-in. baking dish. Sprinkle with cheese.

Bake, uncovered, at 350° for 25-30 minutes or until bubbly. Let casserole stand for 5 minutes before serving. **Yield:** 8 servings.

Marvelous Shells 'n' Cheese

(Pictured below)

Prep: 25 min. **Bake:** 30 min.

When you're craving comfort food, this pasta-and-cheese dish really fills the bill! I adapted the recipe from one my mother makes, and she agrees that my version is rich and delicious. Plus, it's easy to put together.
—Lauren Versweyveld, Delavan, Wisconsin

1 package (16 ounces) medium pasta shells
1 package (8 ounces) process cheese (Velveeta), cubed
1/3 cup milk
2 cups (16 ounces) 2% cottage cheese
1 can (10-3/4 ounces) condensed cream of onion soup, undiluted
3 cups (12 ounces) shredded Mexican cheese blend
2/3 cup dry bread crumbs
1/4 cup butter, melted

Cook the pasta according to package directions. Meanwhile, in a large saucepan, combine the process cheese and milk; cook and stir over low heat until melted. Remove from the heat. Stir in cottage cheese and cream of onion soup.

Drain pasta and add to cheese sauce; stir until coated. Transfer to a greased 13-in. x 9-in. x 2-in. baking dish. Sprinkle with Mexican cheese blend. Toss bread crumbs with butter; sprinkle over the top.

Bake, uncovered, at 350° for 30-35 minutes or until heated through. **Yield:** 6 servings.

Marvelous Shells 'n' Cheese

Chicken Penne Casserole

Chicken Penne Casserole

(Pictured above)

Prep: 35 min. **Bake:** 45 min.

Here is my family's absolute favorite casserole. We have this all-in-one dinner every week or two, and we never get tired of it. I like to assemble it in the early afternoon—that way, I can clean my kitchen and then relax while it bakes.
—Carmen Vanosch, Vernon, British Columbia

1-1/2 cups uncooked penne pasta
1 pound boneless skinless chicken thighs, cut into 1-inch pieces
1/2 cup *each* chopped onion, green pepper and sweet red pepper
1-1/2 teaspoons minced garlic
1 teaspoon *each* dried basil, oregano and parsley flakes
1/2 teaspoon salt
1/2 teaspoon crushed red pepper flakes
1 tablespoon vegetable oil
1 can (14-1/2 ounces) diced tomatoes, undrained
3 tablespoons tomato paste
3/4 cup chicken broth
2 cups (8 ounces) shredded part-skim mozzarella cheese
1/2 cup grated Romano cheese

Cook the penne pasta according to the package directions. Meanwhile, in a large saucepan, saute the chicken, onion, peppers, garlic and seasonings in oil until the chicken is no longer pink.

In a blender, combine tomatoes and tomato paste;

cover and process until blended. Add to the chicken mixture. Stir in chicken broth. Bring to a boil. Reduce heat; cover and simmer for 10-15 minutes or until slightly thickened.

Drain pasta; toss with chicken mixture. Spoon half of the mixture into a greased 11-in. x 7-in. x 2-in. baking dish. Sprinkle with half of the mozzarella and Romano. Repeat layers.

Cover and bake at 350° for 30 minutes. Uncover; bake 15-20 minutes longer or until heated through. **Yield:** 4 servings.

Reuben Casserole

Prep: 20 min. **Bake:** 40 min.

If you're a fan of classic Reuben sandwiches, you're sure to like this pasta bake. It gets its "deli" taste from the corned beef, Swiss cheese, sauerkraut and rye bread.
—Joy Hagen, Webster, South Dakota

- **5 cups uncooked egg noodles**
- **2 cans (14 ounces *each*) sauerkraut, rinsed and well drained**
- **2 cans (10-3/4 ounces *each*) condensed cream of chicken soup, undiluted**
- **3/4 cup milk**
- **1/2 cup chopped onion**
- **3 tablespoons prepared mustard**
- **3/4 pound sliced deli corned beef, chopped**
- **2 cups (8 ounces) shredded Swiss cheese**
- **2 slices day-old light rye bread**
- **2 tablespoons butter, melted**

Cook the noodles according to package directions. Meanwhile, in a large bowl, combine the sauerkraut, soup, milk, onion and mustard.

Drain noodles; stir into the sauerkraut mixture. Transfer to a greased 13-in. x 9-in. x 2-in. baking dish. Sprinkle with the corned beef and cheese.

Place bread in a food processor; cover and process until mixture resembles coarse crumbs. Toss crumbs with butter; sprinkle over the casserole.

Bake, uncovered, at 350° for 40-45 minutes or until bubbly. **Yield:** 5 servings.

Chicken Alfredo Pizza

(Pictured at right)

Prep: 25 min. + marinating **Bake:** 10 min.

Want a special pizza to serve guests? With Alfredo sauce, mushrooms and two kinds of cheese, the flavor of this pie is fantastic. —Kristin McPherson, Moultrie, Georgia

- **1 envelope zesty herb marinade mix**
- **1/3 cup water**
- **3 tablespoons cider vinegar**
- **3 tablespoons vegetable oil**
- **2 boneless skinless chicken breast halves (4 ounces *each*)**
- **1 prebaked Italian bread shell crust (14 ounces)**
- **1/2 cup prepared Alfredo sauce**
- **3 tablespoons grated Parmesan cheese**
- **3 teaspoons Italian seasoning**
- **1 teaspoon garlic powder**
- **1 cup (4 ounces) finely shredded pizza cheese blend**
- **1/2 medium green pepper, julienned**
- **1/2 small red onion, thinly sliced and separated into rings**
- **1/2 cup sliced fresh mushrooms**

In a small bowl, combine 2 tablespoons marinade mix, water, vinegar and oil. (Save remaining marinade mix for another use.) Pour 1/3 cup marinade into a large resealable plastic bag; add the chicken. Seal bag and turn to coat; refrigerate for 1 hour. Cover and refrigerate remaining marinade.

Drain and discard marinade from chicken. Grill chicken, covered, over medium heat or broil 4 in. from heat for 5-7 minutes on each side or until chicken juices run clear, basting occasionally with reserved marinade. Cool. Cube chicken and set aside.

Place crust on an ungreased 12-in. pizza pan. Spread with Alfredo sauce. Sprinkle with Parmesan cheese, Italian seasoning, garlic powder, 1/2 cup pizza blend cheese, green pepper, onion, mushrooms, cubed chicken and remaining cheese. Bake, uncovered, at 450° for 8-10 minutes or until cheese is melted. **Yield:** 6 slices.

Chicken Alfredo Pizza

Garlic-Roasted Chicken and Potatoes

Garlic-Roasted Chicken And Potatoes

(Pictured above)

Prep: 20 min. **Bake:** 1 hour

This time-saving recipe has been in my "favorites" file for almost 20 years. My husband and I enjoyed it before we had children, and now our kids like it, too.
—Beth Erbert, Livermore, California

1/4 cup maple syrup
1 teaspoon salt, *divided*
6 bone-in chicken thighs (4 ounces *each*)
6 chicken drumsticks
6 medium red potatoes (about 2 pounds), cut into 1-inch cubes
24 garlic cloves, peeled
1/4 cup butter, melted

In a small bowl, combine maple syrup and 1/4 teaspoon salt; set aside. Place the chicken, potatoes and garlic in a large roasting pan. Drizzle with butter; sprinkle with remaining salt. Toss to coat. Bake at 400° for 40 minutes.

Drizzle maple syrup mixture over chicken. Spoon pan juices over potatoes and garlic. Bake 20 minutes longer or until a meat thermometer reads 180° and potatoes are tender. **Yield:** 6 servings.

Ham Ravioli Bake

Prep: 20 min. **Bake:** 20 min.

When you have leftover ham from a holiday, turn those extras into a fast weekday dinner with this recipe. You'll need just five additional ingredients, plus convenient frozen ravioli. —Jennifer Berger, Eau Claire, Wisconsin

1 package (25 ounces) frozen cheese ravioli
1-1/2 cups cubed fully cooked ham
1-1/3 cups sliced fresh mushrooms
1/4 cup chopped onion
1/4 cup chopped green pepper
1 tablespoon vegetable oil
1 jar (17 ounces) Alfredo sauce

Cook ravioli according to package directions. Meanwhile, in a large skillet, cook ham, mushrooms, onion and green pepper in oil over medium heat for 4-5 minutes or until the vegetables are crisp-tender.

Spread 2 tablespoons Alfredo sauce into a greased 8-in. square baking dish. Stir remaining Alfredo sauce into the ham mixture; cook for 3-4 minutes or until heated through.

Drain ravioli; place half in the prepared baking dish. Top with half of the ham mixture. Repeat layers. Cover and bake at 375° for 20-25 minutes or until bubbly. **Yield:** 4 servings.

Tortilla Lasagna

(Pictured below)

Prep: 25 min. **Bake:** 50 min. + standing

I found a recipe similar to this one on-line, and when I finished adjusting it, this was the result. The Southwestern lasagna was an instant hit with the spicy-food fans in my house. —*Lynn Smith, Warrensburg, Missouri*

1 pound ground beef
1 cup water
1 envelope taco seasoning
1/2 teaspoon garlic powder
1/4 teaspoon cayenne pepper
1-1/2 cups (12 ounces) sour cream
1-1/2 teaspoons chili powder
2 cups (8 ounces) shredded Monterey Jack cheese
2 cups (8 ounces) shredded cheddar cheese
1 tablespoon cornmeal
10 flour tortillas (6 inches)
1 jar (8 ounces) salsa
1 small onion, sliced

In a large skillet, cook beef over medium heat until no longer pink; drain. Stir in the water, taco seasoning, garlic powder and cayenne. Bring to a boil. Reduce heat; simmer, uncovered, for 10 minutes.

Meanwhile, in a small bowl, combine sour cream and chili powder. In a large bowl, combine cheeses; set aside. Sprinkle cornmeal into a greased 13-in. x 9-in. x 2-in. baking dish. Arrange five tortillas, overlapping, in bottom of the dish; spread with 1/2 cup salsa. Layer with half of meat mixture, onion and sour cream mixture. Sprinkle with 1-1/2 cups cheese mixture. Repeat layers.

Bake, uncovered, at 375° for 40 minutes. Sprinkle with remaining cheese mixture. Bake 10 minutes longer or until cheese is melted. Let stand for 10 minutes before cutting. **Yield:** 8 servings.

Tortilla Lasagna

Nacho Cheese Beef Bake

Nacho Cheese Beef Bake

(Pictured above)

Prep: 25 min. **Bake:** 15 min.

My daughter created this hearty casserole when she was visiting her fiance's family. After her future father-in-law had a taste, he said she was a good cook! If you like, serve it with lettuce, sour cream and salsa as toppings.
—*Kendra McIntyre, Webster, South Dakota*

2 cups uncooked egg noodles
1 pound ground beef
1 can (14-1/2 ounces) diced tomatoes
1 can (10-3/4 ounces) condensed nacho cheese soup, undiluted
1 jar (5-3/4 ounces) sliced pimiento-stuffed olives, drained
1 can (4 ounces) chopped green chilies
1-1/2 cups (6 ounces) shredded cheddar cheese
2 cups crushed tortilla chips
1/3 cup prepared ranch salad dressing
Shredded lettuce, sour cream *and/or* salsa, optional

Cook noodles according to package directions; drain. Meanwhile, in a large saucepan, cook beef over medium heat until no longer pink; drain. Stir in the tomatoes, soup, olives and chilies. Bring to a boil. Reduce heat; simmer, uncovered, for 10 minutes. Stir in noodles.

Transfer to a greased 11-in. x 7-in. x 2-in. baking dish. Sprinkle with cheese. Bake at 350° for 15-20 minutes or until heated through. Top with tortilla chips; drizzle with salad dressing. Serve with lettuce, sour cream and/or salsa if desired. **Yield:** 4 servings.

Sneaky Lasagna

Sneaky Lasagna

(Pictured above)

Prep: 25 min. **Bake:** 55 min. + standing

My kids and husband don't like some veggies, so I sneak them into this recipe. The delicious lasagna is the perfect disguise! —*Catherine Yoder, New Paris, Indiana*

2 pounds ground beef
1 package (16 ounces) frozen California-blend vegetables
2 eggs
3 cups (24 ounces) 2% cottage cheese
2 jars (26 ounces *each*) spaghetti sauce
12 no-cook lasagna noodles
2 cups (8 ounces) shredded part-skim mozzarella cheese

In a Dutch oven, cook beef over medium heat until no longer pink. Meanwhile, cook vegetables according to package directions; drain. Finely chop vegetables; place in a bowl. Stir in eggs and cottage cheese; set aside.

Drain beef; stir in spaghetti sauce. Spread 2 cups meat mixture into a greased 13-in. x 9-in. x 2-in. baking dish. Top with four noodles. Spread half of the vegetable mixture to edges of noodles. Layer with 2 cups meat mixture and 1 cup mozzarella cheese. Top with four noodles, remaining vegetable mixture and 2 cups meat mixture. Layer with remaining noodles, meat mixture and mozzarella.

Cover and bake at 375° for 50 minutes. Uncover; bake 5-10 minutes longer or until the cheese is melted. Let lasagna stand for 15 minutes before cutting. **Yield:** 10-12 servings.

Meaty Corn Bread Casserole

(Pictured below)

Prep: 20 min. **Bake:** 15 min.

When it comes to stick-to-your-ribs, country-style food, this homey bake is tough to beat. You get two kinds of gravy, beef, sausage and corn bread. And the recipe is ideal for busy cooks because it calls for convenience items. —*Justina Wilson, West Salem, Wisconsin*

1/2 pound ground beef
1/2 pound bulk pork sausage
1-3/4 cups frozen corn, thawed
1 cup water
1 envelope brown gravy mix
1 package (8-1/2 ounces) corn bread/muffin mix
1 tablespoon real bacon bits
1-1/2 teaspoons pepper
1/8 teaspoon garlic powder
1 envelope country gravy mix

In a large skillet, cook beef and sausage over medium heat until no longer pink; drain. Stir in the corn, water and brown gravy mix. Bring to a boil; cook and stir for 1 minute or until thickened. Spoon into a greased 8-in. square baking dish.

Prepare corn bread batter according to package directions; stir in the bacon bits, pepper and garlic powder. Spread over meat mixture.

Bake, uncovered, at 400° for 15-20 minutes or until a toothpick inserted into the corn bread layer comes out clean. Meanwhile, prepare the country gravy mix according to the package directions; serve with casserole. **Yield:** 6 servings.

Meaty Corn Bread Casserole

Chicken Lasagna

Prep: 25 min. **Bake:** 30 min. + standing

A friend served this to us one night, and I just had to try it at home. Round out the meal with a Caesar salad and warm rolls. —Janelle Rutrough, Callaway, Virginia

- **2 cups (16 ounces) 2% cottage cheese**
- **1 package (3 ounces) cream cheese, softened**
- **4 cups cubed cooked chicken**
- **1 can (10-3/4 ounces) condensed cream of chicken soup, undiluted**
- **1 can (10-3/4 ounces) condensed cream of celery soup, undiluted**
- **2/3 cup milk**
- **1/2 cup chopped onion**
- **1/2 teaspoon salt**
- **6 lasagna noodles, cooked and drained**
- **1 package (6 ounces) stuffing mix**
- **1/2 cup butter, melted**

In a small bowl, combine cottage cheese and cream cheese. In a large bowl, combine chicken, soups, milk, onion and salt.

Spread half of the chicken mixture into a greased 13-in. x 9-in. x 2-in. baking dish. Top with three noodles. Spread with half of the cheese mixture. Repeat layers. Toss stuffing mix with butter; sprinkle over casserole.

Bake, uncovered, at 350° for 30-40 minutes or until golden brown. Let stand for 10 minutes before cutting. **Yield:** 8 servings.

Turkey Cabbage Bake

Prep: 30 min. **Bake:** 15 min.

I created this oven supper by revising an old recipe. I substituted ground turkey for the ground beef, added thyme and finely chopped the cabbage to improve the texture. —Irene Gutz, Fort Dodge, Iowa

- **2 tubes (8 ounces *each*) refrigerated crescent rolls**
- **1-1/2 pounds ground turkey**
- **1/2 cup chopped onion**
- **1/2 cup finely chopped carrot**
- **1 teaspoon minced garlic**
- **2 cups finely chopped cabbage**
- **1 can (10-3/4 ounces) condensed cream of mushroom soup, undiluted**
- **1/2 teaspoon dried thyme**
- **1 cup (4 ounces) shredded part-skim mozzarella cheese**

Unroll one tube of crescent dough into one long rectangle; seal seams and perforations. Press onto the bottom of a greased 13-in. x 9-in. x 2-in. baking dish. Bake at 425° for 6-8 minutes or until golden brown.

Meanwhile, in a large skillet, cook turkey, onion, carrot and garlic over medium heat until meat is no longer pink; drain. Add cabbage, soup and thyme. Pour over crust; sprinkle with cheese.

On a lightly floured surface, press second tube of crescent dough into a 13-in. x 9-in. rectangle, sealing seams and perforations. Place over the casserole.

Bake, uncovered, at 375° for 14-16 minutes or until crust is golden brown. **Yield:** 6 servings.

Sausage & Beans with Rice

(Pictured below and on page 238)

Prep: 15 min. **Bake:** 25 min.

This hearty casserole has a flavor combination the whole family will love. My husband is rather suspicious of new dishes—but he quickly became a fan of this one! —Beth Cholette, Penfield, New York

- **2/3 cup chopped onion**
- **1/2 cup chopped green pepper**
- **1 teaspoon minced garlic**
- **1 tablespoon vegetable oil**
- **1 pound smoked sausage, cut into 1/4-inch slices**
- **1 can (16 ounces) kidney beans, rinsed and drained**
- **1 can (15-1/2 ounces) great northern beans, rinsed and drained**
- **1 cup instant brown rice**
- **1 cup vegetable broth**
- **1/4 cup packed brown sugar**
- **1/4 cup ketchup**
- **3 tablespoons corn syrup**
- **1 tablespoon Dijon mustard**

In a large skillet, saute the onion, green pepper and garlic in oil until onion is crisp-tender. Stir in the remaining ingredients. Pour into a greased 13-in. x 9-in. x 2-in. baking dish.

Cover and bake at 350° for 15 minutes. Uncover; bake 10-15 minutes longer or until liquid is absorbed and the rice is tender. **Yield:** 6 servings.

Sausage & Beans with Rice

Penne Chicken with Sun-Dried Tomatoes

Penne Chicken with Sun-Dried Tomatoes

(Pictured above)

Prep: 20 min. **Bake:** 50 min.

Precooked chicken and Alfredo sauce from the store make this cheesy pasta casserole easy to prepare...and the sun-dried tomatoes give it a sophisticated, special feel.
—Robin Klawinski, Eagle, Idaho

3-3/4 cups uncooked penne pasta
1 jar (6 ounces) sliced mushrooms, drained
1 tablespoon butter
2 jars (16 ounces *each*) sun-dried tomato Alfredo sauce
2 packages (9 ounces *each*) ready-to-use Southwestern chicken strips
2 cups oil-packed sun-dried tomatoes, drained and chopped
4 green onions, sliced
1/8 teaspoon pepper
1-1/2 cups shredded Parmesan cheese

Cook pasta according to package directions. Meanwhile, in a small skillet, saute mushrooms in butter; set aside.

In a large bowl, combine the Alfredo sauce, chicken, tomatoes, green onions, pepper and reserved mushrooms. Drain the pasta; stir into the chicken mixture. Spoon into a greased 13-in. x 9-in. x 2-in. baking dish.

Cover and bake at 350° for 45-50 minutes or until heated through. Uncover; sprinkle with Parmesan cheese. Bake 5-8 minutes longer or until cheese is melted. **Yield:** 8 servings.

Company Swordfish

Prep: 10 min. **Bake:** 25 min.

This tender fish is dressed up with just five other ingredients. Pair it with a side of angel hair pasta for a terrific dinner. *—Callie Berger, Diamond Springs, California*

4 swordfish *or* halibut steaks (7 ounces *each*)
2 jars (7-1/2 ounces *each*) marinated artichoke hearts, drained and chopped
1/2 cup oil-packed sun-dried tomatoes, drained and chopped
4 shallots, chopped
2 tablespoons butter, melted
1 teaspoon lemon juice

Place the fish in a greased 13-in. x 9-in. x 2-in. baking dish. In a small bowl, combine the artichokes, tomatoes and shallots; spread over fish. Drizzle with butter and lemon juice.

Cover and bake at 425° for 20 minutes. Uncover; bake 5-7 minutes longer or until fish flakes easily with a fork. **Yield:** 4 servings.

Here's the Dish

IF YOU'RE not sure your baking dish is the right size for a casserole, remember that a dish that's too big is better than a smaller one that might run over. The cook time may be shorter with a shallow-filled dish, so check your casserole often.

Chicken Spinach Manicotti

(Pictured below)

Prep: 25 min. **Bake:** 50 min.

I made this when I misplaced a recipe for chicken-stuffed manicotti. Now I'm glad I couldn't find it—the results were delicious! —Melissa Holmquist, Pensacola, Florida

1 package (10 ounces) frozen chopped spinach, thawed
6 ounces frozen diced cooked chicken breast, thawed
3 tablespoons butter
3 tablespoons all-purpose flour
1 cup chicken broth
1/2 cup milk
3 cans (8 ounces *each*) tomato sauce
1 teaspoon dried basil
1 teaspoon dried oregano
3/4 teaspoon garlic powder
3/4 teaspoon brown sugar
6 uncooked manicotti shells
1 cup (4 ounces) shredded Monterey Jack cheese

Divide spinach in half; refrigerate one portion for another use. Squeeze the remaining spinach until dry; place in a small bowl. Add chicken; set aside.

In a large saucepan, melt butter. Stir in flour until smooth; gradually add broth and milk. Bring to a boil; cook and stir for 2 minutes or until thickened. Stir in the tomato sauce, basil, oregano, garlic powder and brown sugar; cook over medium heat for 3-4 minutes or until heated through.

Meanwhile, stuff 1/4 cup chicken mixture into each uncooked manicotti shell. Spread 1/2 cup sauce into a greased 11-in. x 7-in. x 2-in. baking dish. Arrange the manicotti over the sauce; top with the remaining sauce.

Cover and bake at 350° for 40-45 minutes or until bubbly. Uncover; sprinkle with cheese. Bake 8-10 minutes longer or until cheese is melted. Let stand for 5 minutes before serving. **Yield:** 3 servings.

Chicken Spinach Manicotti

Potluck Ham and Pasta

Potluck Ham and Pasta

(Pictured above)

Prep: 40 min. **Bake:** 25 min.

Because this dinner bakes in two pans, I often freeze one for later. It's creamy and filling, with wonderful ham-and-cheese flavor. —Nancy Foust, Stoneboro, Pennsylvania

1 package (16 ounces) elbow macaroni
4 cups fresh broccoli florets
1/2 cup finely chopped onion
1/2 cup butter, cubed
1/2 cup all-purpose flour
1 teaspoon ground mustard
1 teaspoon salt
1/4 teaspoon pepper
6 cups milk
1 jar (15 ounces) process cheese sauce
2 cups (8 ounces) shredded cheddar cheese, *divided*
4 cups cubed fully cooked ham

Cook macaroni according to package directions, adding broccoli during the last 3-4 minutes; drain.

In a Dutch oven, saute onion in butter for 2 minutes. Stir in the flour, mustard, salt and pepper until blended. Gradually stir in milk. Bring to a boil; cook and stir for 2 minutes or until thickened. Stir in cheese sauce and 1 cup cheddar cheese until blended.

Remove from the heat; stir in the ham, macaroni and broccoli. Divide between a greased 13-in. x 9-in. x 2-in. baking dish and a greased 8-in. square baking dish. Sprinkle with remaining cheese.

Bake, uncovered, at 350° for 25-35 minutes or until bubbly and heated through. **Yield:** 12 servings.

Meatless Spinach Lasagna

(Pictured below)

Prep: 45 min. **Bake:** 65 min. + standing

This rich crowd-pleaser is often my choice for our Christmas Eve meal. It's comforting, hearty and convenient for a group. —Barbara Carlucci, Orange Park, Florida

1/3 cup butter, cubed
1/3 cup all-purpose flour
3-3/4 cups half-and-half cream
1 cup heavy whipping cream
3/4 cup grated Parmesan cheese, *divided*
2 cartons (15 ounces *each*) ricotta cheese
1 package (10 ounces) frozen chopped spinach, thawed and squeezed dry
3/4 cup shredded carrot
12 no-cook lasagna noodles
2 cups (8 ounces) shredded part-skim mozzarella cheese
1/2 cup seasoned bread crumbs
1 tablespoon butter, melted

In a large saucepan, melt butter. Stir in flour until smooth; gradually add creams. Bring to a boil; cook and stir for 2 minutes or until thickened. Stir in 1/2 cup Parmesan cheese.

In a large bowl, combine ricotta cheese, spinach, carrot and remaining Parmesan cheese.

Spread 3/4 cup sauce mixture in a greased 13-in. x 9-in. x 2-in. baking dish. Layer with four noodles (noodles will overlap slightly), half of ricotta mixture, 1 cup sauce and 2/3 cup mozzarella cheese. Repeat layers. Top with remaining noodles, sauce and mozzarella cheese. Combine crumbs and butter; sprinkle over lasagna.

Cover and bake at 375° for 55 minutes. Uncover (dish will be full); bake 10-15 minutes longer or until bubbly. Let lasagna stand for 15 minutes before cutting. **Yield:** 12 servings.

Meatless Spinach Lasagna

Southwest Creamy Pasta Bake

Southwest Creamy Pasta Bake

(Pictured above)

Prep: 20 min. **Bake:** 30 min.

I like to cook boneless skinless chicken breasts in the microwave, then dice them up and store them in freezer bags. On hectic nights, it's a real time-saver for tasty recipes like this one. —Patty Putter, Marion, Kansas

12 ounces uncooked spiral pasta
3 cups cubed cooked chicken breast
2 cups (16 ounces) sour cream
2 cups (8 ounces) shredded Colby-Monterey Jack cheese
1 can (10-3/4 ounces) condensed cream of mushroom soup, undiluted
1 can (10-3/4 ounces) condensed cream of celery soup, undiluted
1 can (10 ounces) green chili salsa
1 cup chopped green onions
1 can (4-1/4 ounces) chopped ripe olives

Cook pasta according to package directions. Meanwhile, in a large bowl, combine the remaining ingredients. Drain pasta; stir into chicken mixture.

Transfer to a greased 13-in. x 9-in. x 2-in. baking dish. Bake, uncovered, at 350° for 30-35 minutes or until heated through. **Yield:** 8 servings.

Enchilada Chicken Pizza

Prep: 20 min. **Bake:** 20 min.

This pie has great south-of-the-border flavor without being too spicy. You'll love the "surprise"—a cheese-stuffed crust! —Erin Weyant, New Paris, Pennsylvania

1 loaf (1 pound) frozen bread dough, thawed
4 ounces string cheese

2/3 cup chopped onion
1 tablespoon vegetable oil
2 cups cubed cooked chicken
1 can (4 ounces) chopped green chilies
2 tablespoons taco seasoning
1/2 cup enchilada sauce
1 cup (4 ounces) shredded part-skim mozzarella cheese
1 cup (4 ounces) shredded Mexican cheese blend

On a lightly floured surface, roll the bread dough into a 15-in. circle. Transfer to a greased 14-in. pizza pan. Cut the string cheese in half lengthwise; place around the edge of pan. Fold the excess dough over string cheese; pinch to seal. Prick dough thoroughly with a fork. Bake at 350° for 5 minutes.

Meanwhile, in a large skillet, saute the onion in oil for 3-4 minutes or until tender. Add the chicken, green chilies and seasoning; cook 2-3 minutes longer or until heated through.

Spread sauce over crust. Sprinkle with mozzarella cheese and chicken mixture; top with Mexican cheese. Bake 18-20 minutes longer or until cheese is melted and crust is golden brown. **Yield:** 6 servings.

Ground Beef Noodle Bake

Prep: 35 min. **Bake:** 25 min.

When it's suppertime and your family's hungry, you just can't go wrong with this hearty casserole. Complete your meal with a side of hot vegetables and some Texas toast.
—Judy Taylor, Kenna, West Virginia

5 cups uncooked egg noodles
1-1/2 pounds ground beef
1 can (8 ounces) tomato sauce
1 teaspoon salt
1/4 teaspoon garlic salt
1/4 teaspoon pepper
2 teaspoons butter
1 cup (8 ounces) cream-style cottage cheese
1 cup (8 ounces) sour cream
4 green onions, chopped
1/2 cup minced fresh parsley
1 cup (4 ounces) shredded Swiss cheese

Cook noodles according to package directions. Meanwhile, in a large skillet, cook beef over medium heat until no longer pink; drain. Stir in the tomato sauce, salt, garlic salt and pepper. Bring to a boil. Reduce heat; simmer, uncovered, for 5 minutes.

Drain the noodles; toss with butter. Set aside. In a blender, process cottage cheese and sour cream until smooth. Transfer to a large bowl; stir in onions and parsley. Add noodles; toss to coat.

In a greased 11-in. x 7-in. x 2-in. baking dish, layer a third of the noodle mixture and half of the meat sauce. Repeat layers. Top with remaining noodle mixture; sprinkle with Swiss cheese.

Bake, uncovered, at 350° for 25-30 minutes or until bubbly and lightly browned. **Yield:** 6 servings.

Artichoke Shrimp Bake

(Pictured below)

Prep: 20 min. **Bake:** 20 min.

For this tasty dinner, you can use frozen asparagus cuts instead of artichokes...or a different cream soup, such as asparagus. —Jeanne Holt, Mendota Heights, Minnesota

1 pound cooked medium shrimp, peeled and deveined
1 can (14 ounces) water-packed quartered artichoke hearts, rinsed and drained
2/3 cup frozen pearl onions, thawed
2 cups sliced fresh mushrooms
1 small sweet red pepper, chopped
2 tablespoons butter
1 can (10-3/4 ounces) condensed cream of shrimp soup, undiluted
1/2 cup sour cream
1/4 cup sherry *or* chicken broth
2 teaspoons Worcestershire sauce
1 teaspoon grated lemon peel
1/8 teaspoon white pepper
TOPPING:
1/2 cup soft bread crumbs
1/3 cup grated Parmesan cheese
1 tablespoon minced fresh parsley
1 tablespoon butter, melted
Hot cooked rice, optional

Place the shrimp, artichokes and onions in a greased 11-in. x 7-in. x 2-in. baking dish; set aside. In a large skillet, saute mushrooms and red pepper in butter until tender. Stir in the soup, sour cream, sherry or chicken broth, Worcestershire sauce, lemon peel and white pepper; heat through. Pour over shrimp mixture.

In a small bowl, combine crumbs, cheese, parsley and butter; sprinkle over top. Bake, uncovered, at 375° for 20-25 minutes or until bubbly and topping is golden brown. Serve with rice if desired. **Yield:** 4 servings.

Artichoke Shrimp Bake

Chapter 17

Fast, Delicious...and Nutritious

IT CAN BE your little secret—these scrumptious, irresistible dishes are actually lightened-up recipes. When your family members and friends take a bite, they'll never guess!

In fact, they might feel like they're splurging when they sample taste-tempting specialties such as Beefy Tomato Rice Skillet, Garlic Pineapple Chicken and Fluffy Lemon Pie. Full of home-style flavor, they'll fool even the pickiest of palates.

Plus, each fast-to-fix favorite includes complete Nutrition Facts, and most have Diabetic Exchanges as well. (All recipes that have Nutrition Facts in this cookbook are flagged with a red checkmark in the indexes beginning on page 316).

THE LIGHTER SIDE. Gingered Green Bean Salad and Sweet 'n' Sour Pork Chops (both recipes on page 259).

✓ All recipes in this chapter include Nutrition Facts. Most include Diabetic Exchanges.

Tuna Veggie Kabobs

(Pictured above)

Prep: 30 min. + marinating **Grill:** 10 min.

This is such a quick, easy and fun-to-eat outdoor meal—perfect for summertime! My children like to help cut up the vegetables and thread everything onto the skewers.
—Lynn Caruso, San Jose, California

- **2 pounds tuna steaks, cut into 1-1/2-inch cubes**
- **16 large fresh mushrooms**
- **3 medium green peppers, seeded and cut into 2-inch pieces**
- **3 medium ears sweet corn, cut into 2-inch pieces**
- **3 medium zucchini, cut into 1-inch slices**
- **1/4 cup olive oil**
- **2 tablespoons lemon juice**
- **2 tablespoons finely chopped shallot**
- **1 tablespoon rice vinegar**
- **1 tablespoon minced garlic**
- **1 teaspoon salt**
- **1 teaspoon dried rosemary, crushed**
- **1 teaspoon dried thyme**
- **1/2 teaspoon pepper**

Place tuna pieces in a large resealable plastic bag; place the vegetables in another large resealable plastic bag. In a small bowl, combine the remaining ingredients. Place half of the marinade in each bag. Seal bags and turn to coat; refrigerate for 1 hour.

Drain and discard the marinade. On eight metal or soaked wooden skewers, alternately thread the tuna pieces and vegetables. Coat the grill rack with cooking spray before starting the grill. Grill, covered, over medium heat for 5-6 minutes on each side until the fish flakes easily with a fork and the vegetables are crisp-tender. **Yield:** 8 kabobs.

Nutrition Facts: 1 kabob equals 253 calories, 9 g fat (1 g saturated fat), 51 mg cholesterol, 348 mg sodium, 15 g carbohydrate, 3 g fiber, 30 g protein. **Diabetic Exchanges:** 4 very lean meat, 1 vegetable, 1 fat, 1/2 starch.

Creole Baked Tilapia

Prep/Total Time: 25 min.

I'm originally from Louisiana and love Creole cooking. This five-ingredient dish is great served alongside your favorite rice. —*Carolyn Collins, Freeport, Texas*

4 tilapia fillets (6 ounces *each*)
1 can (8 ounces) tomato sauce
1 small green pepper, thinly sliced
1/2 cup chopped red onion
1 teaspoon Creole seasoning

Place fish in an ungreased 13-in. x 9-in. x 2-in. baking dish. In a small bowl, combine remaining ingredients; pour over fish. Bake, uncovered, at 350° for 20-25 minutes or until fish flakes easily with a fork. **Yield:** 4 servings.

Editor's Note: The following spices may be substituted for 1 teaspoon Creole seasoning: 1/4 teaspoon each salt, garlic powder and paprika; and a pinch each of dried thyme, ground cumin and cayenne pepper.

Nutrition Facts: 1 fish fillet with 1/3 cup topping equals 166 calories, 2 g fat (1 g saturated fat), 83 mg cholesterol, 488 mg sodium, 6 g carbohydrate, 1 g fiber, 33 g protein. **Diabetic Exchanges:** 5 very lean meat, 1 vegetable.

Low-Fat Clam Chowder

Prep/Total Time: 30 min.

A bowl of this hearty soup tastes rich but has only 2 g of fat. Potatoes, turkey bacon and clams make each spoonful delicious. —*Linda Tindel, Avondale, Arizona*

2 turkey bacon strips, diced
1 cup chopped onion
2 cups cubed red potatoes
2 cans (6-1/2 ounces *each*) minced clams, undrained
1 cup reduced-sodium chicken broth
1 cup chopped celery
1/2 teaspoon dried basil
1/2 teaspoon dried thyme
1/2 teaspoon reduced-sodium seafood seasoning
1/2 teaspoon salt-free lemon-pepper seasoning
1/8 teaspoon white pepper
1 tablespoon all-purpose flour
1-1/2 cups fat-free half-and-half

In a large nonstick saucepan, cook bacon and onion over medium heat until onion is tender. Add the potatoes, clams, broth, celery and seasonings. Bring to a boil. Reduce heat; cover and simmer for 12-15 minutes or until vegetables are tender.

In a small bowl, combine the flour and half-and-half until smooth; stir into the potato mixture. Bring to a boil; cook and stir chowder for 2 minutes or until thickened. **Yield:** 4 servings.

Nutrition Facts: 1-1/4 cups equals 202 calories, 2 g fat (trace saturated fat), 22 mg cholesterol, 778 mg sodium, 31 g carbohydrate, 3 g fiber, 13 g protein. **Diabetic Exchanges:** 1-1/2 starch, 1 very lean meat, 1/2 fat-free milk.

Fresh Vegetable Salad

Fresh Vegetable Salad

(Pictured above)

Prep/Total Time: 15 min.

This crisp, colorful veggie salad is a terrific way to use up your excess garden produce in summer. I sometimes toss chopped zucchini into the mix for variety.
—*NanCee Maynard, Box Elder, South Dakota*

3 cups thinly sliced cucumbers
3/4 cup chopped red onion
1/2 cup *each* chopped green, sweet red and yellow peppers
1/2 cup cider vinegar
2 tablespoons sugar

In a large serving bowl, combine the cucumbers, onion and peppers. In a small bowl, whisk vinegar and sugar. Pour over vegetables; toss to coat. Chill until serving. Serve with a slotted spoon. **Yield:** 6 servings.

Nutrition Facts: 3/4 cup equals 43 calories, trace fat (trace saturated fat), 0 cholesterol, 3 mg sodium, 11 g carbohydrate, 1 g fiber, 1 g protein. **Diabetic Exchange:** 2 vegetable.

Nice Dicing

When you need diced bacon for a recipe or want to make bacon bits to sprinkle on a salad, use your kitchen shears to cut the uncooked bacon strips into small pieces. I've found it's quick and fuss-free.
—*Anna Mayer, Ft. Branch, Indiana*

Teriyaki Beef Tenderloin

Teriyaki Beef Tenderloin

(Pictured above)

Prep: 10 min. + marinating
Bake: 45 min. + standing

A beautiful oniony glaze coats this fantastic tenderloin. For convenience, start it the day before and let the meat marinate overnight. —Lillian Julow, Gainesville, Florida

- **1 cup sherry *or* reduced-sodium beef broth**
- **1/2 cup reduced-sodium soy sauce**
- **1 envelope onion soup mix**
- **1/4 cup packed brown sugar**
- **1 beef tenderloin (2 pounds), trimmed**
- **2 tablespoons water**

In a large bowl, combine the sherry or broth, soy sauce, soup mix and brown sugar. Pour 1 cup into a large resealable plastic bag; add tenderloin. Seal bag and turn to coat; refrigerate for 5 hours or overnight. Cover and refrigerate remaining marinade.

Drain and discard the marinade. Place the tenderloin on a rack in a shallow roasting pan. Bake, uncovered, at 425° for 45-50 minutes or until the meat reaches desired doneness (for medium-rare, a meat thermometer should read 145°; medium, 160°; well-done, 170°), basting often with 1/3 cup reserved marinade. Let stand for 10-15 minutes.

Meanwhile, in a small saucepan, bring the water and remaining marinade to a rolling boil for 1 minute or until the sauce is slightly reduced. Slice the beef; serve with the sauce. **Yield:** 8 servings.

Nutrition Facts: 3 ounces cooked beef with 1 tablespoon sauce equals 242 calories, 11 g fat (4 g saturated fat), 72 mg cholesterol, 695 mg sodium, 7 g carbohydrate, trace fiber, 24 g protein. **Diabetic Exchanges:** 3 lean meat, 1/2 starch.

Terrific Turkey Chili

(Pictured below)

Prep: 10 min. **Cook:** 35 min.

This chunky, satisfying chili is jam-packed with tomato flavor...and a good amount of fiber, too! If you like your bowl topped off with cheese and sour cream, keep things on the lighter side by choosing the reduced-fat versions.
—Kim Seeger, Brooklyn Park, Minnesota

- **1 pound lean ground turkey**
- **1 cup chopped onion**
- **1 cup chopped green pepper**
- **2 teaspoons minced garlic**
- **1 can (28 ounces) crushed tomatoes**
- **1 can (16 ounces) kidney beans, rinsed and drained**
- **1 can (11-1/2 ounces) tomato juice**
- **1 can (6 ounces) tomato paste**
- **1 can (4 ounces) chopped green chilies**
- **2 tablespoons brown sugar**
- **1 tablespoon dried parsley flakes**
- **1 tablespoon ground cumin**
- **3 teaspoons chili powder**
- **2 teaspoons dried oregano**
- **1-1/2 teaspoons pepper**

In a large saucepan, cook the ground turkey, onion, green pepper and garlic over medium heat until the meat is no longer pink; drain.

Stir in remaining ingredients. Bring to a boil. Reduce

Terrific Turkey Chili

heat; cover and simmer for 25 minutes. **Yield:** 6 servings (about 2 quarts).

Nutrition Facts: 1-1/3 cups chili equals 315 calories, 8 g fat (2 g saturated fat), 60 mg cholesterol, 706 mg sodium, 43 g carbohydrate, 11 g fiber, 23 g protein. **Diabetic Exchanges:** 3 vegetable, 2 lean meat, 1-1/2 starch.

Carrots and Snow Peas

Prep/Total Time: 25 min.

Without question, this is my favorite side dish—both for its taste and ease of preparation. Sherry adds an amazing spark to the fresh carrot slices and snow peas.
—Cheryl Donnelly, Arvada, Colorado

- **1-3/4 cups sliced fresh carrots**
- **2 tablespoons butter**
- **2-3/4 cups fresh snow peas**
- **1 shallot, minced**
- **1/4 teaspoon salt**
- **1 tablespoon sherry *or* chicken broth**

In a large skillet or wok, stir-fry the carrots in butter for 3 minutes. Add the snow peas, shallot and salt; stir-fry 2 minutes longer or until vegetables are crisp-tender.

Stir in sherry or chicken broth; heat through. **Yield:** 4 servings.

Nutrition Facts: 3/4 cup equals 129 calories, 6 g fat (4 g saturated fat), 15 mg cholesterol, 213 mg sodium, 15 g fiber, 4 g protein. **Diabetic Exchanges:** 2 vegetable, 1 fat.

Garlic Pineapple Chicken

Prep/Total Time: 25 min.

A stir-fry doesn't always have to feature Asian flavors—here's proof! Your family will love this delicious medley of chicken, pineapple and green pepper served over rice.
—Jayme Webb, Anderson, South Carolina

- **1-1/2 pounds boneless skinless chicken breasts, cut into 1-1/2-inch cubes**
- **2 cups uncooked instant rice**
- **1 can (20 ounces) unsweetened pineapple chunks, undrained**
- **1/2 cup fat-free French salad dressing**
- **1/3 cup chopped green pepper**
- **2 tablespoons salt-free garlic herb seasoning blend**

In a large skillet coated with cooking spray, cook and stir chicken over medium heat until juices run clear. Meanwhile, cook rice according to package directions.

Stir the pineapple chunks, French salad dressing, green pepper and garlic herb seasoning blend into the chicken. Bring to a boil. Reduce the heat; cook, uncovered, for 3-5 minutes or until heated through. Serve with rice. **Yield:** 5 servings.

Editor's Note: This recipe was prepared with McCormick Salt Free Garlic & Herb Seasoning.

Nutrition Facts: 1 cup chicken mixture with 3/4 cup rice equals 384 calories, 4 g fat (1 g saturated fat), 75 mg cholesterol, 319 mg sodium, 54 g carbohydrate, 3 g fiber, 30 g protein.

Fluffy Lemon Pie

Fluffy Lemon Pie

(Pictured above)

Prep: 15 min. + chilling

This smooth, tangy pie takes just minutes and is the perfect light dessert. I make it often because my husband likes it, and we both need to watch fat and cholesterol.
—Carolyn Bauers, Norfolk, Virginia

- **1 package (1 ounce) sugar-free instant vanilla pudding mix**
- **1 teaspoon sugar-free lemonade soft drink mix**
- **1 cup cold fat-free milk**
- **1 carton (8 ounces) frozen reduced-fat whipped topping, thawed, *divided***
- **1 reduced-fat graham cracker crust (8 inches)**

Combine pudding mix and soft drink mix. In a small bowl, whisk milk and pudding mixture for 2 minutes. Let stand for 2 minutes (pudding will be stiff).

Fold in half of the whipped topping. Spread into crust. Top with remaining whipped topping. Cover and chill for 2-3 hours or until set. **Yield:** 8 servings.

Editor's Note: This recipe was prepared with Crystal Light Drink Mix.

Nutrition Facts: 1 piece equals 189 calories, 6 g fat (4 g saturated fat), 1 mg cholesterol, 259 mg sodium, 27 g carbohydrate, trace fiber, 2 g protein. **Diabetic Exchanges:** 1-1/2 starch, 1-1/2 fat.

Angel Food Cake with Fruit

(Pictured above)

Prep/Total Time: 10 min.

I get so many compliments on this simple dessert. Fruit and peach pie filling create a lovely sauce for angel food cake, and no one guesses that it comes together in just 10 minutes. *—Jennifer Drake, Evans, Georgia*

1 can (21 ounces) peach pie filling
1 package (16 ounces) frozen unsweetened strawberries, thawed and drained *or* 1-1/2 cups fresh strawberries, halved
1 can (11 ounces) mandarin oranges, drained
2 medium apples, chopped
2 medium firm bananas, sliced
1 prepared angel food cake (8 inches), cut into 8 slices
Whipped topping, optional

In a large bowl, combine the pie filling, strawberries, oranges and apples. Fold in bananas. Spoon a heaping 1/2 cupful over each slice of cake. Garnish with whipped topping if desired. **Yield:** 8 servings.

Nutrition Facts: 1 serving equals 231 calories, 1 g fat (trace saturated fat), 0 cholesterol, 229 mg sodium, 56 g carbohydrate, 4 g fiber, 3 g protein.

Garbanzo Salad

Prep/Total Time: 25 min.

The garden-fresh flavors really shine through in this lightly dressed vegetable salad. It's perfect for warm-weather eating. The cubed mozzarella cheese is a must! *—Merwyn Garbini, Tucson, Arizona*

1 can (15 ounces) garbanzo beans *or* chickpeas, rinsed and drained
4 medium tomatoes, cut into wedges
2 cups thinly sliced celery
1 small red onion, halved and thinly sliced
4 ounces part-skim mozzarella cheese, cubed
DRESSING:
1/4 cup olive oil
1/3 cup red wine vinegar
1 tablespoon minced fresh basil
1/2 teaspoon salt
1/4 teaspoon pepper

In a large salad bowl, combine the beans, tomatoes, celery, onion and cheese.

In a small bowl, whisk dressing ingredients. Pour over bean mixture; toss to coat. Chill until serving. Serve with a slotted spoon. **Yield:** 12 servings.

Nutrition Facts: 3/4 cup equals 117 calories, 7 g fat (2 g saturated fat), 5 mg cholesterol, 216 mg sodium, 10 g carbohydrate, 2 g fiber, 5 g protein. **Diabetic Exchanges:** 1 vegetable, 1 fat, 1/2 starch.

Zucchini Saute

Prep/Total Time: 20 min.

My sister gave me this speedy recipe for a skillet side dish. It's a great way to use that end-of-summer zucchini...and it goes wonderfully with many different main courses. *—Colleen Harvel, Big Bear City, California*

4 medium zucchini, chopped
1-3/4 cups sliced fresh mushrooms
1/2 cup chopped onion
1 tablespoon canola oil
1 medium tomato, chopped
1/2 teaspoon salt
1/4 teaspoon garlic powder
1/4 teaspoon pepper
1/2 cup shredded cheddar cheese

In a large skillet, saute the zucchini, mushrooms and onion in oil until tender. Add the tomato, salt, garlic powder and pepper; cook for 1-2 minutes or until heated through. Sprinkle with cheese; let stand until melted. **Yield:** 4 servings.

Nutrition Facts: 3/4 cup equals 135 calories, 8 g fat (4 g saturated fat), 15 mg cholesterol, 404 mg sodium, 12 g carbohydrate, 3 g fiber, 7 g protein. **Diabetic Exchanges:** 2 vegetable, 1-1/2 fat.

Best Berries

THAWED frozen berries will always be softer and juicier than fresh berries. They're a good choice when you may want extra juice in a recipe, such as over shortcake or in a sauce for pound cake.

To defrost the berries, place the sealed bag in a large bowl of cold water for 10 to 15 minutes.

Sweet 'n' Sour Pork Chops

(Pictured below and on page 252)

Prep/Total Time: 25 min.

This recipe makes moist, tender pork chops your family is sure to love. My best friend shared the recipe, and I fix it all the time. —*Gina Young, Lamar, Colorado*

6 boneless pork loin chops (4 ounces *each*)
3/4 teaspoon pepper
1/2 cup water
1/3 cup cider vinegar
1/4 cup packed brown sugar
2 tablespoons reduced-sodium soy sauce
1 tablespoon Worcestershire sauce
1 tablespoon cornstarch
2 tablespoons cold water

Sprinkle pork chops with pepper. In a large nonstick skillet coated with cooking spray, cook the pork over medium heat for 4-6 minutes on each side or until lightly browned. Remove and keep warm.

Add the water, vinegar, brown sugar, soy sauce and Worcestershire sauce to skillet; stir to loosen browned bits. Bring to a boil. Combine cornstarch and cold water until smooth; stir into skillet. Bring to a boil; cook and stir for 2 minutes or until thickened.

Return chops to the pan. Reduce heat; cover and simmer for 4-5 minutes or until a meat thermometer reads 160°. **Yield:** 6 servings.

Nutrition Facts: 1 pork chop with 3 tablespoons sauce equals 198 calories, 6 g fat (2 g saturated fat), 55 mg cholesterol, 265 mg sodium, 12 g carbohydrate, trace fiber, 22 g protein. **Diabetic Exchanges:** 3 lean meat, 1/2 starch.

Gingered Green Bean Salad

(Pictured below and on page 252)

Prep/Total Time: 30 min.

With tangy sweetness and toasty flavor from the sesame vinaigrette, this crisp summer salad is hard to resist. It keeps well in the refrigerator...if it lasts that long! —*Trisha Kruse, Eagle, Idaho*

2 pounds fresh green beans, trimmed
1 cup thinly sliced red onion, separated into rings
1 cup canned bean sprouts, rinsed and drained

VINAIGRETTE:
1/4 cup rice vinegar
2 tablespoons sesame oil
1 tablespoon minced fresh gingerroot
1 tablespoon reduced-sodium soy sauce
2 teaspoons sesame seeds, toasted
1 teaspoon honey
1/2 teaspoon minced garlic

Place green beans in a large saucepan and cover with water. Bring to a boil. Cook, uncovered, for 4-7 minutes or until crisp-tender. Drain and immediately place in ice water; drain and pat dry.

In a large salad bowl, combine the green beans, red onion and bean sprouts. In a small bowl, whisk the vinaigrette ingredients. Pour vinaigrette over the green bean mixture; toss to coat. Serve salad immediately. **Yield:** 8 servings.

Nutrition Facts: 1 cup equals 88 calories, 4 g fat (1 g saturated fat), 0 cholesterol, 93 mg sodium, 12 g carbohydrate, 4 g fiber, 3 g protein. **Diabetic Exchanges:** 2 vegetable, 1 fat.

Gingered Green Bean Salad
Sweet 'n' Sour Pork Chops

Pear Chutney Chicken

(Pictured below)

Prep/Total Time: 30 min.

My freezer is hardly ever without servings of this fruity chicken. My grandson even has his own name for it—"pear chix!" —*Sheila Berg, Lucas Valley, California*

1 can (15-1/4 ounces) sliced pears
4 boneless skinless chicken breast halves (4 ounces *each*)
2 tablespoons all-purpose flour
1/4 teaspoon pepper
2 tablespoons olive oil
1/2 cup chopped onion
1/2 cup mango chutney
1 to 2 tablespoons lemon juice
3/4 to 1 teaspoon curry powder

Drain pears, reserving 1/4 cup juice; set pears and juice aside. Flatten chicken to 1/4-in. thickness. In a large resealable bag, combine flour and pepper. Add chicken in batches and shake to coat.

In a large skillet, cook chicken in oil over medium heat for 5-6 minutes on each side or until juices run clear. Remove and keep warm.

In the same skillet, combine the onion, chutney, lemon juice, curry powder and reserved pear juice. Bring to a boil. Add chicken and pears. Reduce heat; simmer, uncovered, for 3-5 minutes or until heated through. **Yield:** 4 servings.

Nutrition Facts: 1 serving equals 395 calories, 9 g fat (2 g saturated fat), 63 mg cholesterol, 404 mg sodium, 51 g carbohydrate, 1 g fiber, 24 g protein.

Pear Chutney Chicken

Citrus Spinach Salad

Prep/Total Time: 15 min.

Lime lovers will really appreciate the tangy homemade dressing that coats this colorful spinach salad. Orange sections add yet another burst of refreshing citrus flavor.
—*Edna Lee, Greeley, Colorado*

2 tablespoons olive oil
1 tablespoon lime juice
1 teaspoon sesame seeds, toasted
1/2 teaspoon sugar
1/2 teaspoon grated lime peel
1/4 teaspoon ground ginger
4 cups coarsely chopped fresh spinach
2 medium navel oranges, peeled and sectioned
1 cup sliced fresh mushrooms
1/2 small red onion, halved and thinly sliced

In a jar with a tight-fitting lid, combine the first six ingredients; shake well. In a large salad bowl, combine the remaining ingredients. Just before serving, shake the dressing and pour over the salad; toss to coat. **Yield:** 9 servings.

Nutrition Facts: 3/4 cup equals 52 calories, 3 g fat (trace saturated fat), 0 cholesterol, 13 mg sodium, 6 g carbohydrate, 1 g fiber, 1 g protein. **Diabetic Exchanges:** 1 vegetable, 1/2 fat.

Chili Rice Dinner

Prep/Total Time: 30 min.

I usually have the ingredients for this Southwestern beef supper on hand, making it ideal for busy weekdays when I don't know what to make. And it's so good, you'll even want to use this recipe when you have drop-in guests.
—*Ann Torrey, Brattleboro, Vermont*

3/4 pound ground beef
1 cup chopped green pepper
1/3 cup chopped onion
1 package (10 ounces) frozen corn
1 can (15 ounces) tomato sauce
1/2 cup water
3 teaspoons chili powder
1/2 teaspoon salt
1/2 teaspoon ground mustard
1 cup uncooked instant rice
1/2 cup shredded cheddar cheese

In a large skillet, cook the beef, green pepper and onion over medium heat until meat is no longer pink; drain. Stir in corn, tomato sauce, water, chili powder, salt and mustard. Bring to a boil.

Stir in rice. Remove from the heat; cover and let stand for 5 minutes or until rice is tender. Sprinkle with cheese. **Yield:** 5 servings.

Nutrition Facts: 1-1/3 cups equals 307 calories, 10 g fat (5 g saturated fat), 45 mg cholesterol, 759 mg sodium, 36 g carbohydrate, 4 g fiber, 20 g protein. **Diabetic Exchanges:** 3 vegetable, 2 lean meat, 1 starch, 1 fat.

Spinach Tortellini Soup

Prep/Total Time: 30 min.

Tortellini, spinach and tomatoes make a great combination in this tasty soup. The sprinkle of Parmesan adds a special touch. —Cindy Politowicz, Northville, Michigan

3/4 cup chopped onion
1 teaspoon minced garlic
1 tablespoon olive oil
2 cans (14-1/2 ounces *each*) reduced-sodium chicken broth
2 cups water
1 teaspoon sugar
1/4 teaspoon salt
1/4 teaspoon pepper
1 package (9 ounces) refrigerated cheese tortellini
1 can (14-1/2 ounces) diced tomatoes, undrained
1 package (10 ounces) frozen chopped spinach, thawed and squeezed dry
3 tablespoons shredded Parmesan cheese

In a large saucepan, saute onion and garlic in oil until tender. Add broth, water, sugar, salt and pepper. Bring to a boil. Add tortellini; cook for 5-8 minutes or until tender, stirring occasionally. Reduce heat. Stir in tomatoes and spinach; heat through. Just before serving, sprinkle with cheese. **Yield:** 6 servings (about 2 quarts).

Nutrition Facts: 1-1/2 cups equals 206 calories, 7 g fat (3 g saturated fat), 20 mg cholesterol, 782 mg sodium, 28 g carbohydrate, 4 g fiber, 11 g protein. **Diabetic Exchanges:** 2 vegetable, 1-1/2 lean meat, 1 starch.

Beefy Tomato Rice Skillet

Prep/Total Time: 25 min.

I put together this skillet supper one day using whatever items I could find. We enjoy it on weeknights and even when we go camping. —Ellyn Graebert, Yuma, Arizona

1 pound ground beef
1 cup chopped celery
2/3 cup chopped onion
1/2 cup chopped green pepper
1 can (11 ounces) whole kernel corn, drained
1 can (10-3/4 ounces) condensed tomato soup, undiluted
1 cup water
1 teaspoon Italian seasoning
1 cup uncooked instant rice

In a large skillet over medium heat, cook the beef, celery, onion and pepper until meat is no longer pink and vegetables are tender; drain.

Add corn, soup, water and seasoning; bring to a boil. Stir in rice; cover and remove from heat. Let stand for 10 minutes or until rice is tender. **Yield:** 6 servings.

Nutrition Facts: 1 cup equals 266 calories, 7 g fat (3 g saturated fat), 37 mg cholesterol, 506 mg sodium, 30 g carbohydrate, 2 g fiber, 17 g protein. **Diabetic Exchanges:** 2 lean meat, 2 vegetable, 1 starch, 1 fat.

Broccoli Cheese Soup

Broccoli Cheese Soup

(Pictured above)

Prep/Total Time: 15 min.

My husband is diabetic, and I'm watching my weight. This chunky, cheesy soup fits our diets and is done in just 15 minutes. —Carol Colvin, Derby, New York

1 can (10-3/4 ounces) reduced-fat reduced-sodium condensed cream of celery soup, undiluted
1 can (10-3/4 ounces) reduced-fat reduced-sodium condensed cream of chicken soup, undiluted
3 cups fat-free milk
1 tablespoon dried minced onion
1 teaspoon dried parsley flakes
1/2 teaspoon garlic powder
1/4 teaspoon pepper
3 cups frozen chopped broccoli, thawed
1 can (14-1/2 ounces) sliced potatoes, drained
1/2 cup shredded reduced-fat cheddar cheese

In a large saucepan, combine the soups, milk, onion, parsley, garlic powder and pepper. Stir in broccoli and potatoes; heat through. Just before serving, sprinkle with cheese. **Yield:** 8 servings.

Nutrition Facts: 1 cup equals 135 calories, 3 g fat (2 g saturated fat), 11 mg cholesterol, 521 mg sodium, 19 g carbohydrate, 3 g fiber, 8 g protein. **Diabetic Exchanges:** 1-1/2 starch, 1/2 fat.

Chapter 18

Plan an Instant Party

THINK you're just too busy to invite the whole gang over for a festive, home-cooked spread? You'll change your mind when you see the special but fast-to-fix recipes in this chapter!

Hosting a memorable bash is a snap when you rely on this fun fare for a sporting event... a summer bash on the patio... a family reunion...even a fall pumpkin-carving party. You get a complete menu of favorites for each get-together.

So go ahead—set a date and send out the invitations. Then get ready to amaze your guests with an impressive, delicious feast you whipped up yourself. They'll never guess how easy it was to prepare!

WOW THE CROWD. Turkey Brats with Slaw (p. 268).

Great Game-Day Munchies

A SUPER BOWL PARTY or other game-day event is extra fun when you have sensational snacks to serve your guests. So when the whole gang is gathered around the TV, offer these quick, casual munchies—from fun pizza-flavored fondue to always-popular nachos. They'll keep everyone cheering!

Pizza Fondue

(Pictured below)

Prep/Total Time: 25 min.

Served in a fondue pot with cubes of toasted bread, this warm dip is an eye-catching addition to any snack table. And the delicious pizza flavor has 'em coming back for more! —*Kristine Chayes, Smithtown, New York*

2 cans (10-3/4 ounces *each*) condensed cheddar cheese soup, undiluted
1 can (8 ounces) pizza sauce
1/2 cup milk
1/2 teaspoon dried basil
1/2 teaspoon dried oregano
1/4 teaspoon crushed red pepper flakes
1-1/2 cups (6 ounces) shredded pizza cheese blend
1/2 cup chopped pepperoni
Italian bread, cubed and toasted

In a large saucepan, combine the first six ingredients. Add the cheese and pepperoni; cook and stir over medium heat until the cheese is melted. Transfer to a fondue pot and keep warm. Serve with bread cubes. **Yield:** 4 cups.

Pizza Fondue

Dijon-Bacon Dip for Pretzels

Dijon-Bacon Dip for Pretzels

(Pictured above)

Prep/Total Time: 5 min.

With just a few kitchen staples, this winning appetizer goes together fast. If you like the zip of horseradish, start with 1 to 2 teaspoons and add more to suit your taste. —*Isabelle Rooney, Summerville, South Carolina*

1 cup mayonnaise
1/2 cup Dijon mustard
1/4 cup real bacon bits *or* crumbled cooked bacon
1 to 3 teaspoons prepared horseradish
Pretzels

In a small bowl, combine the mayonnaise, mustard, bacon and horseradish. Cover and chill until serving. Serve with pretzels. **Yield:** 1-1/2 cups.

Jalapeno Wontons

Prep: 20 min. **Cook:** 20 min.

My husband is a fan of jalapeno poppers, but they can be expensive. I created this economical, homemade version, and he loves them. He wishes I made them more often! —*Tina Heidler, Stinesville, Indiana*

✓ This recipe includes Nutrition Facts.

1 package (8 ounces) cream cheese, softened
3 tablespoons milk
1/2 teaspoon salt
3/4 cup pickled jalapeno slices, diced
1 package (12 ounces) wonton wrappers
Oil for deep-fat frying

In a small mixing bowl, beat the cream cheese, milk and salt. Stir in jalapenos. Place 1-1/2 teaspoons filling in the center of each wonton wrapper. Moisten the edges with water; fold the opposite corners together over filling and press to seal.

In an electric skillet, heat 1/4 in. of oil to 375°. Fry the wontons in batches for 1-2 minutes on each side or until golden brown. Drain wontons on paper towels. **Yield:** 2-1/2 dozen.

Editor's Note: When cutting hot peppers, disposable gloves are recommended. Avoid touching your face.

Nutrition Facts: 1 wonton equals 62 calories, 3 g fat (2 g saturated fat), 10 mg cholesterol, 207 mg sodium, 7 g carbohydrate, trace fiber, 2 g protein.

Sloppy Joe Nachos

(Pictured below)

Prep/Total Time: 15 min.

Kids and adults alike will dig right into these cheesy nachos. With ground beef, they could even make a quick meal. —*Janet Rhoden, Hortonville, Wisconsin*

1 pound ground beef
1 can (15-1/2 ounces) sloppy joe sauce
1 package (12 ounces) tortilla chips
3/4 cup shredded cheddar cheese
1/4 cup sliced ripe olives, optional

In a large skillet, cook beef over medium heat until no longer pink; drain. Add sloppy joe sauce; cook, uncovered, for 5 minutes or until heated through.

Arrange chips on a serving plate. Top with meat mixture, cheese and olives if desired. **Yield:** 6 servings.

Wontons Without Waiting

If you want to get some of your party preparations done ahead of time, make the jalapeno pepper filling for the wontons in advance—it'll keep for several days in the refrigerator. Keep in mind that the filling will become hotter the longer you store it.
—*Tina Heidler, Stinesville, Indiana*

Sloppy Joe Nachos

Summer Party on the Patio

THE SUNSHINE and warm weather of summertime—what more reason do you need to have a party? Kick off the season with these carefree but delicious appetizers, all perfect to enjoy in the fresh air.

Beer-Battered Potato Wedges

(Pictured below)

Prep: 25 min. **Cook:** 5 min./batch

These potatoes look and taste just like the ones served in restaurants. Pair the wedges with a bowl of sour cream for dipping. —Pat Miller, Lynnville, Tennessee

4 medium baking potatoes
1 cup all-purpose flour
1/4 cup milk
1 egg
1 tablespoon seasoned salt
1 tablespoon vegetable oil
1/2 teaspoon pepper
1/2 cup beer *or* nonalcoholic beer
Oil for deep-fat frying
Sour cream, optional

Scrub and pierce potatoes. Microwave, uncovered, on high for 10-12 minutes or just until tender, turning once.

Meanwhile, in a shallow bowl, whisk the flour, milk, egg, seasoned salt, oil and pepper until smooth. Stir in beer; set aside.

When potatoes are cool enough to handle, cut each into 12 wedges. In an electric skillet or deep-fat fryer,

Beer-Battered Potato Wedges

Smoked Salmon Pinwheels

heat oil to 375°. Dip potato wedges into batter. Fry in batches for 3-4 minutes or until golden brown, turning occasionally. Drain on paper towels. Serve with sour cream if desired. **Yield:** 4 dozen.

Editor's Note: This recipe was tested in a 1,100-watt microwave.

Smoked Salmon Pinwheels

(Pictured above)

Prep/Total Time: 20 min.

Inexpensive but impressive, this appetizer is ideal when you want to wow guests without spending all day in the kitchen. —Cristina Mathers, San Miguel, California

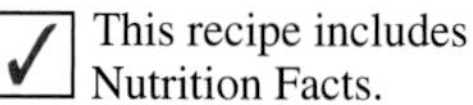

This recipe includes Nutrition Facts.

1 package (8 ounces) cream cheese, softened
1 tablespoon snipped fresh dill
1 tablespoon capers, drained
1/2 teaspoon garlic powder
1/2 teaspoon lemon juice
4 spinach tortillas (8 inches), room temperature
1/2 pound fully cooked smoked salmon fillets, flaked

In a small mixing bowl, combine the cream cheese, dill, capers, garlic powder and lemon juice. Spread over tortillas; top with salmon. Roll up tightly.

Cut into 1-in. pieces; secure with toothpicks. Chill until serving. Discard toothpicks before serving. Refrigerate leftovers. **Yield:** 32 appetizers.

Nutrition Facts: 1 appetizer equals 52 calories, 3 g fat (2 g saturated fat), 9 mg cholesterol, 116 mg sodium, 3 g carbohydrate, trace fiber, 2 g protein.

Patio Pizza

Patio Pizza

(Pictured above)

Prep/Total Time: 30 min.

Convenient refrigerated breadsticks form the crispy crust for this veggie-packed pizza. It's a cool choice for warm days. —Mary Ann Dell, Phoenixville, Pennsylvania

- **1 tube (11 ounces) refrigerated breadsticks**
- **1 teaspoon olive oil**
- **1/2 teaspoon minced garlic**
- **4 ounces cream cheese, softened**
- **1/2 teaspoon dried oregano**
- **1 can (14 ounces) water-packed artichoke hearts, rinsed, drained and chopped, *divided***
- **1 cup (4 ounces) crumbled feta cheese, *divided***
- **3/4 cup chopped tomato**
- **1/3 cup coarsely chopped peeled cucumber**
- **1/3 cup sliced ripe olives, drained**
- **1/3 cup sliced onion, halved**
- **2 tablespoons pine nuts, toasted**
- **1/4 cup balsamic vinaigrette**

Unroll the breadsticks. In the center of an ungreased 12-in. pizza pan, loosely wrap one breadstick around, forming a coil. Add another breadstick, pinching the ends to seal and continuing to coil. Repeat with the remaining breadsticks.

Roll or pat dough to within 1/2 in. of the edge of the pan. Brush with oil. Gently press garlic onto dough. Bake at 375° for 14-16 minutes or until golden brown. Cool on a wire rack.

In a small bowl, combine cream cheese and oregano. Stir in 1/4 cup artichokes and half of the feta cheese; spread over crust. Arrange remaining artichokes on top. Sprinkle with tomato, cucumber, olives, onion, pine nuts and remaining feta cheese. Drizzle with vinaigrette. **Yield:** 8 servings.

Editor's Note: This recipe was tested with Pillsbury refrigerated breadsticks.

Crab Cheese Fondue

Prep/Total Time: 25 min.

I received this recipe from a man who made it for hunting camp. After one taste of the rich fondue, it's hard to stop eating! —Kathy Brown, Lake Havasu City, Arizona

- **1 jar (15 ounces) process cheese sauce**
- **1/2 cup butter, cubed**
- **1/4 cup white wine *or* chicken broth**
- **1/8 teaspoon garlic powder**
- **3 pouches (3-1/2 ounces *each*) premium crabmeat, drained**
- **1 loaf (1 pound) French bread, cubed**

In a large saucepan, combine the cheese sauce, butter, wine or broth and garlic powder. Cook and stir over medium-low heat for 18-20 minutes or until cheese is melted. Stir in crab; cook 1-2 minutes longer or until heated through.

Transfer to a small fondue pot and keep warm. Serve with bread cubes. **Yield:** 3 cups.

Favorites for Family Reunions

WHEN THE WHOLE CLAN is getting together for a big feast and family fun, you can rely on the crowd-pleasing dishes here. They'll feed a bunch, get on the table fast and appeal to folks of all ages.

Turkey Brats with Slaw

(Pictured below and on page 262)

Prep: 15 min. **Cook:** 35 min.

The slaw-cranberry topping on these beer-boiled brats is good warm or cold. It's a nice change from kraut or other condiments. —Christy Hinrichs, Aarkville, Missouri

4 cups beer *or* nonalcoholic beer
3 teaspoons celery salt, *divided*
2 teaspoons minced garlic
2 packages (20 ounces *each*) turkey bratwurst
6 cups broccoli coleslaw mix
2/3 cup chopped red onion
4 teaspoons canola oil
2/3 cup dried cranberries
1/4 cup red wine vinegar
2 tablespoons honey
10 brat buns, split

In a Dutch oven, bring the beer, 2 teaspoons celery salt and garlic to a boil. Add the bratwurst. Reduce the heat; simmer, uncovered, for 20-25 minutes or until firm and cooked through.

Meanwhile, in a large skillet, saute coleslaw mix and onion in oil for 7-9 minutes or until tender. Stir in berries, vinegar, honey and remaining celery salt; heat through.

Drain bratwurst. Grill, covered, over medium heat or broil 4 in. from the heat for 2 to 2-1/2 minutes on each side or until browned. Serve on buns with coleslaw mixture. **Yield:** 10 servings.

Turkey Brats with Slaw

Chocolate Chip Cookie Delight

Chocolate Chip Cookie Delight

(Pictured above)

Prep: 35 min. + chilling

When I take this yummy layered dessert to potlucks, the pan always comes home empty. Everyone loves the chocolate chip cookie crust. —Diane Windley, Grace, Idaho

1 tube (16-1/2 ounces) refrigerated chocolate chip cookie dough
1 package (8 ounces) cream cheese, softened
1 cup confectioners' sugar
1 carton (12 ounces) frozen whipped topping, thawed, *divided*
3 cups cold milk
1 package (3.9 ounces) instant chocolate pudding mix
1 package (3.4 ounces) instant vanilla pudding mix
Chopped nuts and chocolate curls, optional

Let cookie dough stand at room temperature for 5-10 minutes to soften. Press into an ungreased 13-in. x 9-in. x 2-in. baking pan. Bake at 350° for 14-16 minutes or until golden brown. Cool on a wire rack.

In a large mixing bowl, beat cream cheese and confectioners' sugar until smooth. Fold in 1-3/4 cups whipped topping. Spread over crust.

In a large bowl, whisk the milk and pudding mixes for 2 minutes; let stand for 2 minutes or until soft-set.

Spread over the cream cheese layer. Top with the remaining whipped topping. Sprinkle with nuts and chocolate curls if desired.

Cover and refrigerate for 8 hours or overnight until firm. **Yield:** 15 servings.

Almond-Avocado Tossed Salad

(Pictured below)

Prep/Total Time: 30 min.

I received this recipe from a friend, and I added almonds for crunch. Fresh and colorful, the salad also travels well in warm weather. —*Suzanne Sager, Dallas, Texas*

✓ This recipe includes Nutrition Facts and Diabetic Exchanges.

- **3 cups torn iceberg lettuce**
- **3 cups torn leaf lettuce**
- **2-1/2 cups fresh baby spinach**
- **2 medium ripe avocados, peeled and chopped**
- **1 can (11 ounces) mandarin oranges, drained**
- **1 small cucumber, halved lengthwise, seeded and sliced**
- **1 small sweet red pepper, chopped**
- **1/2 cup honey roasted almonds**
- **1/2 cup red wine vinaigrette *or* vinaigrette of your choice**

In a large salad bowl, combine the first seven ingredients. Sprinkle with almonds. Drizzle with vinaigrette and toss to coat. Serve immediately. **Yield:** 14 servings.

Editor's Note: This recipe was tested with Almond Accents honey roasted almonds.

Nutrition Facts: 3/4 cup equals 105 calories, 8 g fat (1 g saturated fat), 0 cholesterol, 195 mg sodium, 7 g carbohydrate, 2 g fiber, 2 g protein. **Diabetic Exchanges:** 1-1/2 fat, 1 vegetable.

Hearty Tortellini Salad

Prep/Total Time: 20 min.

This pasta salad is a hit at summer picnics. Sometimes I'm embarrassed at how little effort it takes to get such rave reviews! —*Susan McCarthy, Old Lyme, Connecticut*

- **1 package (19 ounces) frozen cheese tortellini**
- **1 cup grape tomatoes, halved**
- **1 cup chopped zucchini**
- **1 cup chopped yellow summer squash**
- **4 ounces provolone cheese, cubed**
- **1 package (3-1/2 ounces) sliced pepperoni**
- **1/2 cup prepared pesto**
- **1/8 teaspoon salt**
- **1/8 teaspoon pepper**

Cook the cheese tortellini according to the package directions. Meanwhile, in a large bowl, combine the remaining ingredients.

Drain tortellini and rinse in cold water. Add to vegetable mixture and toss to coat. Cover and refrigerate until serving. **Yield:** 12 servings.

Almond-Avocado Tossed Salad

Carving Out a Pumpkin Party

LIGHT UP the fall season by gathering friends and family for a make-your-own jack-o'-lantern party. You'll see grins on your guests' faces as well as the pumpkins when you serve the tasty treats here!

Party Time Mini Cheeseburgers

(Pictured below)

Prep/Total Time: 30 min.

Jazzed up with dill pickle relish and topped with cheese slices in pumpkin shapes, these "sliders" from our Test Kitchen cooks are sure to disappear in no time flat.

1 egg, beaten
2 tablespoons dill pickle relish
2 tablespoons ketchup
2 teaspoons Worcestershire sauce
2 teaspoons prepared mustard
1/4 cup quick-cooking oats
1/4 teaspoon pepper
1/8 teaspoon garlic powder
1 pound ground beef
3 slices process American cheese
10 dinner rolls, split

In a large bowl, combine the first eight ingredients. Crumble beef over mixture and mix well. Shape into 10 patties. Broil 3-4 in. from the heat for 4-6 minutes on each side or until meat is no longer pink.

Meanwhile, using a 1-in. pumpkin-shaped cookie cutter, cut out 10 shapes from cheese slices. Immediately place on burgers; serve on rolls. **Yield:** 10 servings.

Party Time Mini Cheeseburgers

Cinnamon Orange Cider

Cinnamon Orange Cider

(Pictured above)

Prep/Total Time: 20 min.

You may want to double this recipe, then fill the punch bowl and keep more of the popular cider simmering during your party! —*Mark Morgan, Waterford, Wisconsin*

✓ This recipe includes Nutrition Facts.

4 cups apple cider *or* juice
2 cups orange juice
3 tablespoons red-hot candies
1-1/2 teaspoons whole allspice
4-1/2 teaspoons honey

In a large saucepan, combine cider, juice and candies. Place the allspice on a double thickness of cheesecloth; bring up corners of cloth and tie with string to form a bag. Add to pan. Bring to a boil. Reduce heat; cover and simmer for 5 minutes or until flavors are blended.

Discard bag; stir in honey. Transfer to a small slow cooker; keep warm over low heat. **Yield:** 1-1/2 quarts.

Nutrition Facts: 1 cup equals 161 calories, 0 fat (0 saturated fat), 0 cholesterol, 17 mg sodium, 40 g carbohydrate, trace fiber, trace protein.

Garlic Pumpkin Seeds

(Pictured below)

Prep/Total Time: 25 min.

What to do with all of those pumpkin seeds your guests will be scooping out of their jack-o'-lanterns? This microwave recipe will have folks eating 'em by the handful. Remember to save a few for yourself before they're gone!
—Iola Egle, Bella Vista, Arkansas

☑ This recipe includes Nutrition Facts and Diabetic Exchanges.

1 tablespoon canola oil
1/2 teaspoon celery salt
1/2 teaspoon garlic powder
1/2 teaspoon seasoned salt
2 cups fresh pumpkin seeds

In a small bowl, combine the oil, celery salt, garlic powder and seasoned salt. Add pumpkin seeds; toss to coat. Spread a quarter of the seeds in a single layer on a microwave-safe plate. Microwave, uncovered, on high for 1 minute; stir.

Microwave 2-3 minutes longer or until pumpkin seeds are crunchy and lightly browned, stirring after each minute. Repeat with remaining pumpkin seeds. Serve warm, or cool before storing in an airtight container. **Yield:** 2 cups.

Editor's Note: This recipe was tested in a 1,100-watt microwave.

Nutrition Facts: 1/4 cup equals 87 calories, 5 g fat (1 g saturated fat), 0 cholesterol, 191 mg sodium, 9 g carbohydrate, 1 g fiber, 3 g protein. **Diabetic Exchanges:** 1 fat, 1/2 starch.

Garlic Pumpkin Seeds

Gelatin Parfaits

Gelatin Parfaits

(Pictured above)

Prep: 15 min. + chilling

You can whip up this bright, airy dessert for almost any season or holiday you like—just switch up the colors of gelatin. *—Joyce Thompson, Bellingham, Washington*

☑ This recipe includes Nutrition Facts.

1 package (3 ounces) lemon gelatin
1 package (3 ounces) orange gelatin
3 cups cubed pound cake (1-inch cubes)
2-1/4 cups whipped topping
2 tablespoons sugar
1/8 teaspoon ground cinnamon
6 maraschino cherries with stems

Prepare gelatins separately according to package directions. Pour into separate ungreased 9-in. x 5-in. x 3-in. pans. Refrigerate until set. Cut into 1-in. cubes.

In each of six 1-1/2-cup parfait glasses or dessert dishes, layer 1/4 cup cake cubes, 1/3 cup cubed orange gelatin, 3 tablespoons whipped topping, 1/3 cup cubed lemon gelatin, 1/4 cup cake cubes and 3 tablespoons whipped topping. Combine sugar and cinnamon; sprinkle over topping. Top with a cherry. **Yield:** 6 servings.

Nutrition Facts: 1 parfait equals 299 calories, 9 g fat (7 g saturated fat), 36 mg cholesterol, 156 mg sodium, 50 g carbohydrate, trace fiber, 4 g protein.

Chapter 19

Swift Snacks & Easy Appetizers

CRAVING something tastier and more exciting than a bag of potato chips and store-bought dip? There's no need to go that routine route—even when your schedule is jam-packed. Just turn to the no-fuss munchies in this chapter!

You'll find special but speedy appetizers for dinner guests... wholesome homemade snacks you can whip for the kids after school...satisfying finger foods for your next Super Bowl party...and much more.

Try favorites such as Best Barbecue Wings, Caramel Apple Snack Mix, Delightful Deviled Eggs, Pepperoni Pizza Twists, Super Nacho Appetizer and Italian Egg Rolls. You'll never want store-bought snacks again!

QUICK FINGER FOOD. Fiesta Cream Cheese Spread (p. 279).

Delightful Deviled Eggs

Delightful Deviled Eggs

(Pictured above)

Prep/Total Time: 20 min.

Put leftover Easter eggs to good use with this simple recipe. Flavored with mustard, pickle relish and onion, it's sure to become a favorite. —*Kelly Alaniz, Eureka, California*

6 hard-cooked eggs
2 tablespoons mayonnaise
1-1/2 teaspoons grated onion
1-1/2 teaspoons sweet pickle relish
1/2 teaspoon spicy brown mustard
1/4 teaspoon salt
1/8 teaspoon crushed red pepper flakes
1/8 teaspoon pepper

Slice the eggs in half lengthwise. Remove yolks; set whites aside. In a small bowl, mash the yolks. Stir in the mayonnaise, onion, relish, mustard, salt, pepper flakes and pepper. Pipe or spoon into egg whites. Refrigerate until serving. **Yield:** 1 dozen.

Chunky Herbed Pizza Dip

Prep/Total Time: 20 min.

Oregano, basil and garlic give great flavor to this popular warm dip. I serve it with mozzarella sticks as dippers.
—*Clara Coulston, Washington Court House, Ohio*

✓ This recipe includes Nutrition Facts and Diabetic Exchanges.

1-1/2 teaspoons minced garlic
2 tablespoons olive oil
2 cans (14-1/2 ounces *each*) diced tomatoes
1 can (6 ounces) tomato paste
1 tablespoon minced fresh basil *or* 1 teaspoon dried basil
2-1/2 teaspoons minced fresh oregano *or* 3/4 teaspoon dried oregano
1-1/4 teaspoons sugar
Mozzarella sticks, optional

In a large saucepan, saute garlic in oil for 1-2 minutes or until tender. Drain one can of tomatoes; set aside. (Save tomato juice for another use.) Add the tomatoes, tomato paste, basil, oregano and sugar to the pan.

Bring to a boil. Reduce heat; simmer, uncovered, for 10-15 minutes or until thickened. Serve with mozzarella sticks if desired. **Yield:** 3-1/2 cups.

Nutrition Facts: 1/4 cup (calculated without mozzarella sticks) equals 42 calories, 2 g fat (trace saturated fat), 0 cholesterol, 84 mg sodium, 6 g carbohydrate, 2 g fiber, 1 g protein. **Diabetic Exchanges:** 1 vegetable, 1/2 fat.

Spinach Artichoke-Stuffed Mushrooms

(Pictured below)

Prep: 25 min. **Bake:** 20 min.

When your guests see these special-looking, savory mushrooms, they'll think you fussed. Only you will know the truth! —*Amy Gaisford, Salt Lake City, Utah*

1 package (3 ounces) cream cheese, softened
1/2 cup mayonnaise
1/2 cup sour cream
1 can (14 ounces) water-packed artichoke hearts, rinsed, drained and chopped
1 package (10 ounces) frozen chopped spinach, thawed and squeezed dry
1/3 cup shredded part-skim mozzarella cheese
4 tablespoons shredded Parmesan cheese, *divided*
3/4 teaspoon garlic salt
30 to 35 large fresh mushrooms

Spinach Artichoke-Stuffed Mushrooms

Pizza Loaf

In a small mixing bowl, beat cream cheese, mayonnaise and sour cream. Stir in artichokes, spinach, mozzarella cheese, 3 tablespoons Parmesan and garlic salt.

Remove stems from mushrooms (discard stems or save for another use). Fill each mushroom cap with about 1 tablespoon of filling. Sprinkle with remaining Parmesan cheese.

Place mushrooms on foil-lined baking sheets. Bake at 400° for 16-20 minutes or until mushrooms are tender. **Yield:** 30-35 appetizers.

Pizza Loaf

(Pictured above)

Prep: 25 min. **Bake:** 20 min.

With this fun recipe from my grandmother, refrigerated pizza crust wraps around the beef, mushrooms and other pizza "toppings." —*Amanda Wiersema, Archer, Iowa*

1 pound ground beef
1/2 cup chopped onion
1/2 cup chopped green pepper
1 cup Italian tomato sauce
1 can (4 ounces) mushroom stems and pieces, drained
1 teaspoon paprika
1/2 teaspoon garlic salt
1/2 teaspoon dried oregano
1/8 teaspoon pepper
1 tube (13.8 ounces) refrigerated pizza crust
1/2 cup shredded part-skim mozzarella cheese
1/2 cup shredded cheddar cheese

In a large skillet, cook the beef, onion and green pepper over medium heat until meat is no longer pink; drain. Stir in the tomato sauce, mushrooms, paprika, garlic salt, oregano and pepper.

Unroll pizza dough onto a greased baking sheet; roll into a 15-in. x 12-in. rectangle. Spoon meat mixture down the center of rectangle; sprinkle with cheeses. On each long side, cut 1-in.-wide strips about 2-1/2 in. into center. Starting at one end, fold alternating strips at an angle across filling. Pinch ends to seal.

Bake at 350° for 20-25 minutes or until golden brown. **Yield:** 6 servings.

Fresh Fruit Salsa

(Pictured below)

Prep/Total Time: 15 min.

Lots of fruits and veggies add nutrition to this delightful salsa. It has all the bright colors and refreshing flavors of summer. —*Mary Relyea, Canastota, New York*

✓ This recipe includes Nutrition Facts and Diabetic Exchanges.

1 cup chopped peeled mango
1 cup diced honeydew
1 cup unsweetened pineapple chunks
1 cup chopped sweet red pepper
2 large kiwifruit, peeled and chopped
1/2 cup chopped red onion
1/4 cup minced fresh cilantro
1 tablespoon cider vinegar
2 teaspoons lime juice
1 teaspoon chopped jalapeno pepper
1/2 teaspoon salt
1/4 teaspoon white pepper
Tortilla chips

In a large bowl, combine all ingredients. Refrigerate until serving. Serve with tortilla chips. **Yield:** 5 cups.

Editor's Note: When cutting hot peppers, disposable gloves are recommended. Avoid touching your face.

Nutrition Facts: 1/2 cup (calculated without tortilla chips) equals 47 calories, trace fat (trace saturated fat), 0 cholesterol, 122 mg sodium, 12 g carbohydrate, 2 g fiber, 1 g protein. **Diabetic Exchange:** 1 fruit.

Fresh Fruit Salsa

Mediterranean Dip with Pita Chips

(Pictured below)

Prep/Total Time: 30 min.

When I wanted a special appetizer to serve houseguests, I created this recipe. They loved it, and now it's one of my staples. —Denise Johanowicz, Madison, Wisconsin

- **6 pita breads (6 inches), halved**
- **1-3/4 teaspoons garlic powder, *divided***
- **12 ounces cream cheese, softened**
- **1 cup (8 ounces) plain yogurt**
- **1 teaspoon dried oregano**
- **3/4 teaspoon ground coriander**
- **1/4 teaspoon pepper**
- **1 large tomato, seeded and chopped**
- **5 pepperoncinis, sliced**
- **1/2 cup pitted Greek olives, sliced**
- **1 medium cucumber, seeded and diced**
- **1/3 cup crumbled feta cheese**
- **2 tablespoons minced fresh parsley**

Cut each pita half into six wedges; place on an ungreased baking sheet. Spritz both sides of wedges with cooking spray; sprinkle with 1 teaspoon garlic powder.

Bake at 350° for 5-6 minutes on each side or until golden brown. Cool on wire racks.

Meanwhile, in a small mixing bowl, beat the cream cheese, yogurt, oregano, coriander, pepper and remaining garlic powder. Spread into a 9-in. pie plate. Top with the tomato, pepperoncinis, olives, cucumber, feta cheese and parsley. Serve dip with the pita chips. **Yield:** 3-1/2 cups (6 dozen chips).

Editor's Note: Look for pepperoncinis (pickled peppers) in the pickle and olive section of your grocery store.

Mediterranean Dip with Pita Chips

Stromboli Slices

Stromboli Slices

(Pictured above)

Prep/Total Time: 25 min.

I've made this pizza-flavored stromboli for everyone from teens and college students to a women's group. It's always a hit. —Rachel Jackson, Pennsville, New Jersey

- **1 tube (11 ounces) refrigerated crusty French loaf**
- **2 tablespoons olive oil**
- **1/2 teaspoon dried basil**
- **1 package (3-1/2 ounces) sliced pepperoni**
- **2 cups (8 ounces) shredded part-skim mozzarella cheese**
- **1 cup meatless spaghetti sauce, warmed**

Unroll loaf of dough at the seam into a square; cut in half. Combine oil and basil; brush lengthwise down half of each rectangle to within 1/2 in. of edges. Layer brushed side with pepperoni and cheese. Fold plain dough over the filling and pinch the edges to seal. Place on greased baking sheets.

Bake at 350° for 10-15 minutes or until golden brown. Cut into slices. Serve warm with spaghetti sauce. **Yield:** 1-1/2 dozen.

Italian Egg Rolls

Prep: 25 min. **Cook:** 5 min./batch

Give Italian flavor to Asian egg rolls? You bet! The hearty, fried appetizers here are sure to surprise you with their terrific taste. —Shirley Intihar, Eveleth, Minnesota

- **1/2 pound bulk hot Italian sausage**
- **3/4 cup finely chopped green pepper**
- **1/2 cup finely chopped onion**
- **1 package (10 ounces) frozen chopped spinach, thawed and squeezed dry**
- **1-1/2 cups (6 ounces) shredded part-skim mozzarella cheese**
- **1/4 cup grated Parmesan cheese**

1/4 teaspoon garlic powder
14 egg roll wrappers
Oil for frying
Meatless spaghetti sauce, warmed, optional

In a large skillet, cook the sausage, pepper and onion over medium heat until meat is no longer pink; drain and cool. Stir in spinach, cheeses and garlic powder.

Place 1/3 cup sausage mixture in the center of each egg roll wrapper. Fold each bottom corner over filling; fold sides toward center over filling. Moisten remaining corner with water; roll up tightly to seal.

In an electric skillet or deep-fat fryer, heat 1 in. of oil to 375°. Fry rolls, in batches, for 2-4 minutes on each side or until golden brown. Drain on paper towels. Serve with spaghetti sauce if desired. **Yield:** 14 egg rolls.

Caramel Apple Snack Mix

(Pictured below)

Prep: 30 min. **Bake:** 45 min. + cooling

Favorite fall treats—caramel apples—become munchies in this fun recipe. It makes a party-sized portion of yummy snack mix. —Melody Michaelis, Sycamore, Illinois

7 cups popped popcorn
4 cups Crispix
4 cups Apple Jacks cereal
2 cups salted peanuts
1 cup packed brown sugar
1/2 cup butter, cubed
1/2 cup light corn syrup
2 teaspoons vanilla extract
1/2 teaspoon baking soda

In a large greased roasting pan, combine popcorn, cereals and peanuts; set aside. In a large saucepan, combine brown sugar, butter and corn syrup; bring to a rolling boil over medium-low heat, stirring constantly. Cook, without stirring, until mixture turns a medium amber color, about 8 minutes.

Caramel Apple Snack Mix

Veggie Ham Crescent Wreath

Remove from the heat; quickly stir in vanilla and baking soda until mixture is light and foamy. Immediately pour over cereal mixture; stir until evenly coated.

Bake at 250° for 45 minutes, stirring every 15 minutes. Spread mixture onto waxed paper-lined baking sheets. Cool completely. Store in airtight containers. **Yield:** 5 quarts.

Veggie Ham Crescent Wreath

(Pictured above)

Prep: 20 min. **Bake:** 15 min. + cooling

This Christmasy appetizer will bring extra cheer to holiday festivities. You can whip it up quickly using refrigerated dough. —Dixie Lundquist, Chandler, Arizona

2 tubes (8 ounces *each*) refrigerated crescent rolls
1/2 cup spreadable pineapple cream cheese
1/3 cup diced fully cooked ham
1/4 cup finely chopped sweet yellow pepper
1/4 cup finely chopped green pepper
1/2 cup chopped fresh broccoli florets
6 grape tomatoes, quartered
1 tablespoon chopped red onion

Remove crescent dough from tubes (do not unroll). Cut each roll into eight slices. Arrange in an 11-in. circle on an ungreased 14-in. pizza pan. Bake at 375° for 15-20 minutes or until golden brown. Cool 5 minutes before carefully removing to a platter; cool completely.

Spread cream cheese over wreath; top with ham, peppers, broccoli, tomatoes and onion. Store in the refrigerator. **Yield:** 16 appetizers.

Roasted Red Pepper Hummus

Roasted Red Pepper Hummus

(Pictured above)

Prep/Total Time: 20 min.

I didn't care for hummus until I discovered this recipe. Lemon juice and minced garlic create a fantastic burst of flavor. —*Heidi Pronk, Hudsonville, Michigan*

✓ This recipe includes Nutrition Facts and Diabetic Exchanges.

1/3 cup lemon juice
5 teaspoons olive oil
2 sprigs fresh parsley, stems removed
1 teaspoon minced garlic
1/2 teaspoon salt
1/2 teaspoon ground cumin
1/4 teaspoon cayenne pepper
1/4 teaspoon coarsely ground pepper
2 cans (15 ounces *each*) garbanzo beans *or* chickpeas, rinsed and drained
1 cup roasted sweet red peppers, drained
1/4 cup sesame seeds, toasted
Pita breads, warmed and cut into wedges

In a food processor, combine the first eight ingredients. Cover and process until blended. Add beans and peppers; cover and process until smooth. Transfer to a bowl; stir in seeds. Serve with pita wedges. **Yield:** 3 cups.

Nutrition Facts: 1/4 cup (calculated without pita wedges) equals 107 calories, 5 g fat (trace saturated fat), 0 cholesterol, 280 mg sodium, 13 g carbohydrate, 3 g fiber, 3 g protein. **Diabetic Exchanges:** 1 starch, 1 fat.

Hummus Hint

HUMMUS is a Middle Eastern sauce, often used as a dip. It tastes great with pita bread or fresh veggies and can even be used as a sandwich spread. If you don't have time to make the recipe above, look for prepared hummus in your supermarket's deli section.

Pepperoni Pizza Twists

(Pictured below)

Prep: 20 min. **Bake:** 30 min. + standing

My stepsister gave me this recipe, which I tweaked a bit to suit my taste. If you like, add diced green peppers and olives, too. —*Lisa Worley, Adairsville, Georgia*

2 packages (11 ounces *each*) refrigerated crusty French loaf
1 tablespoon all-purpose flour
1 cup (4 ounces) shredded part-skim mozzarella cheese
1 package (3-1/2 ounces) sliced pepperoni, finely chopped
1 jar (14 ounces) pizza sauce, *divided*
1 egg white, beaten
2 tablespoons grated Parmesan cheese
1/2 teaspoon Italian seasoning

Place one loaf on a lightly floured surface. With a sharp knife, make a lengthwise slit down the center of loaf to within 1/2 in. of bottom. Open dough so it lies flat; sprinkle with half of flour. Roll into a 14-in. x 5-in. rectangle. Repeat with the remaining loaf.

In a large bowl, combine mozzarella cheese and pepperoni. Spread half of mozzarella mixture down the center of each rectangle. Drizzle each with 3 tablespoons pizza sauce. Roll up jelly-roll style, starting from a long side; seal seams and ends. Place one loaf seam side down on a greased baking sheet. Place remaining loaf seam side down next to the first loaf. Twist loaves together three times.

With a sharp knife, make three shallow 3-in. slashes across top of each loaf; brush with egg white. Sprinkle with Parmesan cheese and Italian seasoning. Bake at 350° for 25 minutes. Cover loosely with foil. Bake 4 minutes longer or until golden brown. Let loaves stand for 10 minutes before slicing. Serve with remaining pizza sauce. **Yield:** 8 servings.

Pepperoni Pizza Twists

Fiesta Cream Cheese Spread

Fiesta Cream Cheese Spread

(Pictured above and on page 272)

Prep/Total Time: 15 min.

Salsa and apricot preserves may seem like a strange combination, but they actually create a very tasty appetizer! Give this one a try at your Super Bowl party this year.
—Sharyl Wolter, Rosenberg, Texas

1 package (8 ounces) cream cheese, softened
1/4 cup chunky salsa
1/4 cup apricot preserves *or* orange marmalade
2 tablespoons chopped avocado
1 tablespoon chopped ripe olives
1 tablespoon minced fresh cilantro
Assorted crackers

Place cream cheese on a serving plate. In a small bowl, combine salsa and preserves; spread over cream cheese. Sprinkle with avocado, olives and cilantro. Serve with crackers. **Yield:** 8 servings.

Chili Snack Mix

Prep: 20 min. **Bake:** 10 min./batch + cooling

I remember my mother making this mix instead of cookies for bake sales. It's a great take-along snack for road trips, too. *—Barb Gustison, Quincy, Illinois*

1 package (16 ounces) corn chips
1 can (11-1/2 ounces) mixed nuts
1 package (11 ounces) pretzel sticks
1 package (7.2 ounces) miniature cheddar cheese fish-shaped crackers
1 cup butter, cubed
1/2 cup packed brown sugar
1 tablespoon garlic powder
1 tablespoon chili powder
1/2 teaspoon baking soda

In a large bowl, combine the corn chips, nuts, pretzels and crackers. In a small saucepan, bring butter, brown sugar, garlic powder and chili powder to a boil. Remove from the heat; stir in baking soda. Pour over snack mixture and toss to coat.

Transfer to three greased 15-in. x 10-in. x 1-in. baking pans. Bake at 350° for 10-12 minutes or until lightly toasted. Cool completely on wire racks. Store in airtight containers. **Yield:** 6 quarts.

Beer Cheese in a Bread Bowl

(Pictured below)

Prep/Total Time: 15 min.

My family and friends are all fans of this cheese dip, especially when I serve it in a hollowed-out bread loaf. For extra flair, add a garnish of chopped green onions on top.
—Julie Koch, Delaware, Ohio

1 round loaf (1 pound) pumpernickel bread
2 jars (5 ounces *each*) sharp American cheese spread
1 package (8 ounces) cream cheese, softened
1/4 cup beer *or* nonalcoholic beer
1/2 cup real bacon bits

Cut the top fourth off the loaf of bread; carefully hollow out the bottom, leaving a 1/2-in. shell. Cube removed bread; set aside.

In a microwave-safe bowl, combine cheese spread and cream cheese. Microwave, uncovered, on high for 2 minutes, stirring every 30 seconds. Stir in beer. Microwave, uncovered, 20 seconds longer. Stir in bacon. Fill bread shell with cheese dip. Serve with reserved bread cubes. **Yield:** 2-1/2 cups.

Editor's Note: This recipe was tested in a 1,100-watt microwave.

Beer Cheese in a Bread Bowl

Szechwan Chicken Wings

(Pictured below)

Prep: 10 min. **Cook:** 10 min./batch

After sampling these fried wings flavored with Szechwan chili sauce, my friend begged for the recipe. It's not only a great snack, but it's also a satisfying main dish served over rice. —*Senon Ray Posadas, Chicago, Illinois*

1 cup soy sauce
1/3 cup sugar
1/3 cup water
3 tablespoons minced garlic
3 tablespoons lemon juice
2 teaspoons Szechwan chili sauce
2-1/2 pounds whole chicken wings
1 cup self-rising flour
Oil for deep-fat frying

In a large resealable plastic bag, combine the soy sauce, sugar, water, minced garlic, lemon juice and chili sauce; set aside.

Cut chicken wings into three sections; discard the wing tip sections. Place the flour in another large resealable plastic bag; add chicken wings, a few at a time, and shake to coat.

In an electric skillet or deep-fat fryer, heat oil to 375°. Fry chicken, a few pieces at a time, for 8 minutes or until golden brown and juices run clear, turning occasionally. Drain on paper towels. Add chicken to soy sauce mixture, a few pieces at a time, and shake to coat. **Yield:** 7 servings.

Editor's Note: As a substitute for 1 cup of self-rising flour, place 1-1/2 teaspoons baking powder and 1/2 teaspoon salt in a measuring cup. Add all-purpose flour to measure 1 cup. Uncooked chicken wing sections (wingettes) may be substituted for whole chicken wings.

Szechwan Chicken Wings

Festive Feta Cheese Ball

Festive Feta Cheese Ball

(Pictured above)

Prep: 10 min. + chilling

I created this when I was asked to bring an appetizer on Christmas Day. Rolling the ball in bacon and dill gives it a festive look. —*Cinde Ryan, Gig Harbor, Washington*

2 packages (8 ounces *each*) cream cheese, softened
1/2 cup crumbled feta cheese
2 teaspoons ranch salad dressing mix
1/4 cup shredded Parmesan cheese
1/4 cup crumbled cooked bacon
1/2 teaspoon dill weed
Assorted crackers

In a mixing bowl, beat cream cheese until fluffy. Add feta cheese and dressing mix; mix well. Shape into a ball. Combine the Parmesan cheese, bacon and dill weed; roll cheese ball in Parmesan mixture. Wrap tightly in plastic wrap. Refrigerate for at least 1 hour or until firm. Serve with crackers. **Yield:** 2 cups.

Best Barbecue Wings

Prep: 20 min. **Grill:** 20 min.

My husband always says these wings are "finger-licking good." The sweet-and-spicy sauce also pairs well with chicken breasts. —*Linda Gardner, Richmond, Virginia*

1/2 cup finely chopped onion
3 teaspoons minced garlic
1/4 cup vegetable oil
1-1/2 cups ketchup
1/2 cup cider vinegar
1/3 cup packed brown sugar
1/3 cup Worcestershire sauce
2 teaspoons chili powder
1/2 teaspoon cayenne pepper
1/2 teaspoon ground cumin
1/8 teaspoon hot pepper sauce
1/4 cup cider vinegar

1/4 cup olive oil
1/8 teaspoon salt
1/8 teaspoon pepper
30 frozen chicken wingettes, thawed

For barbecue sauce, in a large saucepan, saute onion and garlic in vegetable oil until tender. Stir in the ketchup, vinegar, brown sugar, Worcestershire sauce, chili powder, cayenne and cumin. Simmer, uncovered, for 8-10 minutes, stirring often. Remove from the heat; stir in hot pepper sauce. Set aside 2/3 cup for serving.

Coat grill rack with cooking spray before starting the grill. In a large resealable plastic bag, combine the vinegar, olive oil, salt and pepper; add chicken wings in batches and turn to coat.

Grill wings, covered, over medium heat for 12-16 minutes, turning occasionally. Brush with some of the remaining sauce. Grill, uncovered, 8-10 minutes longer or until juices run clear, basting and turning several times. Serve with reserved sauce. **Yield:** 2-1/2 dozen.

Editor's Note: This recipe was prepared with the first and second sections of the chicken wings.

Shrimp Appetizers with Seafood Sauce

Taco Dip

(Pictured below)

Prep/Total Time: 25 min.

This dip is one of my favorites, but I can't count on leftovers when I take it to parties. It seems to be a favorite of everyone elses, too! —Aleta Amick, Madison, Wisconsin

12 ounces cream cheese, softened
1/2 cup sour cream
1 teaspoon chili powder
1/2 cup salsa
2 cups shredded iceberg lettuce
1 cup (4 ounces) shredded cheddar cheese
1 cup (4 ounces) shredded Monterey Jack cheese
1/2 cup diced tomato
1 can (4-1/4 ounces) sliced ripe olives, drained, optional
Tortilla chips

Taco Dip

In a large mixing bowl, beat the cream cheese, sour cream and chili powder until smooth; stir in salsa. Spread cream cheese mixture over a large serving platter. Cover and refrigerate for 15 minutes.

Meanwhile, prepare toppings. Layer cream cheese mixture with lettuce, cheddar cheese, Monterey Jack cheese, tomato and olives if desired. Serve with chips. **Yield:** about 6-1/2 cups.

Shrimp Appetizers with Seafood Sauce

(Pictured above)

Prep/Total Time: 20 min.

My husband and I treat ourselves to these once or twice a month. The shrimp are delicious with the quick homemade sauce. —Alyce Wyman, Pembina, North Dakota

✓ This recipe includes Nutrition Facts and Diabetic Exchanges.

2 packages (9 ounces *each*) frozen breaded jumbo butterfly shrimp
1/2 cup ketchup
1/2 cup chili sauce
1 tablespoon lemon juice
1 tablespoon prepared horseradish
1/8 teaspoon hot pepper sauce

Bake shrimp according to package directions. Meanwhile, in a small bowl, combine remaining ingredients. Arrange shrimp on serving platter; serve with sauce. **Yield:** 26 appetizers.

Nutrition Facts: 1 shrimp with 1-1/2 teaspoons seafood sauce equals 59 calories, 2 g fat (trace saturated fat), 10 mg cholesterol, 233 mg sodium, 7 g carbohydrate, trace fiber, 2 g protein. **Diabetic Exchanges:** 1/2 starch, 1/2 fat.

Super Nacho Appetizer

Super Nacho Appetizer

(Pictured above)

Prep: 15 min. **Bake:** 20 min.

This appetizer truly is "super"—in more ways than one! Not only does it feed a crowd, but it's also a huge hit wherever I take it. —Connie Bolton San Antonio, Texas

1/2 pound ground beef
1/2 pound uncooked chorizo
2 cans (16 ounces *each*) refried beans
1 can (4 ounces) chopped green chilies
3 cups (12 ounces) shredded cheddar cheese
3/4 cup bottled taco sauce
3 large ripe avocados, peeled and pitted
1 tablespoon fresh lemon juice
1/4 teaspoon garlic salt
1 cup (8 ounces) sour cream
1 medium tomato, chopped
1/2 cup sliced pimiento-stuffed olives
Additional shredded cheddar cheese
Tortilla chips

In a large skillet, cook beef and chorizo over medium heat until no longer pink; drain well. In a greased 13-in. x 9-in. x 2-in. baking dish, layer the meat mixture, refried beans, chilies, cheese and taco sauce. Bake, uncovered, at 400° for 20 minutes.

For guacamole, in a small bowl, mash the avocados. Stir in lemon juice and garlic salt. Cool nacho mixture for 5 minutes. Top with guacamole, sour cream, tomato and olives. Garnish with additional cheese. Serve with tortilla chips. **Yield:** 30 servings.

Meatballs in Plum Sauce

Prep/Total Time: 15 min.

Using frozen meatballs really speeds up the prep for this microwave recipe, which features ginger, mustard and plum sauce. —Michael Compean, Valencia, California

✓ This recipe includes Nutrition Facts and Diabetic Exchanges.

3/4 cup plum sauce
2 tablespoons soy sauce
1 tablespoon Dijon mustard
2 teaspoons minced fresh gingerroot
36 frozen fully cooked meatballs (1/2 ounce *each*), thawed
1 green onion, chopped
1 tablespoon minced fresh cilantro

In a 2-qt. microwave-safe dish, combine the plum sauce, soy sauce, mustard and ginger. Add meatballs; stir gently to coat.

Cover and microwave on high for 5-6 minutes or until heated through, stirring once. Cool for 1 minute. Fold in onion and cilantro. **Yield:** 3 dozen.

Editor's Note: This recipe was tested in a 1,100-watt microwave.

Nutrition Facts: 1 meatball equals 42 calories, 2 g fat (1 g saturated fat), 12 mg cholesterol, 111 mg sodium, 3 g carbohydrate, trace fiber, 3 g protein. **Diabetic Exchange:** 1/2 lean meat.

Canadian Bacon-Stuffed Mushrooms

(Pictured below)

Prep: 30 min. **Bake:** 20 min.

I served these bites to guests during the holidays, and their response was great. The diced sweet red pepper gives the stuffing a festive look. —Joan Airey, Rivers, Manitoba

Canadian Bacon-Stuffed Mushrooms

Beef-Stuffed Crescents

30 to 35 large fresh mushrooms
1/4 pound Canadian bacon, diced
1/3 cup diced sweet red pepper
1/4 cup diced red onion
1 teaspoon minced garlic
1/2 teaspoon salt
1/2 teaspoon pepper
2 tablespoons vegetable oil
1/2 cup crumbled goat cheese *or* feta cheese
1/2 cup shredded cheddar cheese

Remove stems from mushrooms and finely chop; set caps aside. In a large skillet, saute the mushrooms, bacon, red pepper, onion, garlic, salt and pepper in oil until vegetables are crisp-tender.

Remove from the heat. Stir in cheeses. Fill each mushroom cap with about 1 tablespoon of filling.

Place mushrooms on foil-lined baking sheets. Bake at 400° for 16-20 minutes or until mushrooms are tender. **Yield:** 30-35 appetizers.

Beef-Stuffed Crescents

(Pictured above)

Prep: 25 min. **Bake:** 15 min.

My neighbor makes this recipe using jalapenos instead of green chilies—and calls it "rattlesnake bites!" I love that it's so easy and has so few ingredients. When I bring the little pockets to gatherings, I never have leftovers.
—Jennifer Bumgarner, Topeka, Kansas

1 pound ground beef
1 can (4 ounces) chopped green chilies
1 package (8 ounces) cream cheese, cubed
1/4 teaspoon ground cumin
1/4 teaspoon chili powder
3 tubes (8 ounces *each*) refrigerated crescent rolls

In a large skillet, cook beef and chilies over medium heat until meat is no longer pink; drain. Add cream cheese, cumin and chili powder; mix well. Cool slightly.

Separate crescent dough into 24 triangles. Place 1 tablespoon of beef mixture along the short end of each triangle; carefully roll up.

Place point side down 2 in. apart on ungreased baking sheets. Bake at 375° for 11-14 minutes or until golden brown. Serve warm. **Yield:** 2 dozen.

Spicy Crab Dip

(Pictured below)

Prep/Total Time: 15 min.

If you include the optional ingredients of cayenne pepper and hot sauce, you'll double up the heat for this delicious dip. It tastes special but takes only 15 minutes to prepare. *—Carol Forcum, Marion, Illinois*

1/3 cup mayonnaise
2 tablespoons dried minced onion
2 tablespoons lemon juice
2 tablespoons white wine *or* white grape juice
1 tablespoon minced garlic
1/2 teaspoon cayenne pepper, optional
1/2 teaspoon hot pepper sauce, optional
2 packages (8 ounces *each*) cream cheese, cubed
1 pound imitation crabmeat, chopped
Assorted crackers *or* fresh vegetables

In a food processor, combine the first eight ingredients. Cover and process until smooth. Transfer to a large microwave-safe bowl. Stir in crab; mix well.

Cover and microwave on high for 2-3 minutes or until bubbly. Serve warm with crackers or vegetables. **Yield:** 4 cups.

Editor's Note: This recipe was tested in a 1,100-watt microwave.

Spicy Crab Dip

Chapter 20

Test Kitchen Secrets

EVER WONDER how the pros create some of their impressive kitchen specialties? The ones that look so inviting and taste so scrumptious?

Now, you can learn some of those expert secrets—they're right here in this chapter! Our Test Kitchen home economists have revealed the keys to making standout stir-fries, baking from-scratch biscuits and preparing dishes that feature peppers and potatoes.

You'll also see how to quickly decorate Christmas cookies, roast a turkey for Thanksgiving and give classic recipes "makeovers" to cut prep time.

Try these simple techniques, and you'll be cooking like a pro before you know it!

IT'S ELEMENTARY. Golden Potato Soup (p. 295).

Chicken Lo Mein

Stir-Fries Simplified

ANCIENT Chinese secret? Not anymore! Here, our Test Kitchen shows how stir-frying can create delicious meals that are short on time, cost and cleanup. All you have to do is follow these easy recipes and how-tos. Whether you use a wok or skillet, give a stir-fry a try and enjoy some variety for dinner tonight.

Chicken Lo Mein

(Pictured at left)

Prep/Total Time: 30 min.

Get started with our Test Kitchen staff's time-saving but mouth-watering stir-fry supper, illustrated in the step-by-step photos and directions below.

4 ounces uncooked angel hair pasta
2 teaspoons cornstarch
1/4 cup reduced-sodium soy sauce
2 tablespoons rice wine vinegar
2 tablespoons hoisin sauce
1 tablespoon minced fresh gingerroot
1 teaspoon minced garlic
1 pound boneless skinless chicken breasts, cut into strips
2 tablespoons vegetable oil, *divided*
2 cups fresh broccoli florets
1 cup julienned carrots
1/4 cup salted peanuts, finely chopped

Cook pasta according to package directions. Meanwhile, in a small measuring cup or bowl, combine the cornstarch, soy sauce, vinegar, hoisin sauce, ginger and garlic until blended; set aside.

In a large skillet or wok, stir-fry chicken in 1 tablespoon oil for 5-8 minutes or until no longer pink. Remove with a slotted spoon. Drain pasta and set aside.

Stir-fry broccoli and carrots in remaining oil for 5-6 minutes or until crisp-tender. Stir cornstarch mixture and pour into the pan. Bring to a boil; cook and stir for 2 minutes or until thickened. Stir in chicken and pasta; heat through. Sprinkle with peanuts. **Yield:** 4 servings.

Method for Chicken Lo Mein

1. Chop and measure all of the ingredients, keeping them close at hand. Begin by stir-frying the chicken strips in a small amount of oil.

2. Remove the meat from the skillet when it is cooked through. Stir-fry the vegetables in the remaining oil.

3. Stir the soy sauce mixture and add to the pan. Bring to a boil; cook and stir for 2 minutes or until thickened. Add the chicken and pasta; heat through. Sprinkle with peanuts.

Nutty Pork Fried Rice

Prep/Total Time: 30 min.

This versatile recipe is so fast and tasty. It makes a great meal-in-one...or even a hearty side dish served as part of an Asian feast. —*Becky Reilly, Cheney, Washington*

1 package (6.2 ounces) fried rice mix
1 cup chopped walnuts, *divided*
1 tablespoon honey
2 boneless pork loin chops (4 ounces *each*), cut into strips
2 tablespoons vegetable oil
1 can (8 ounces) sliced water chestnuts, drained
1 cup sliced celery
1 cup chopped green onions
1/2 teaspoon minced garlic
1 cup coleslaw mix
2 tablespoons sesame seeds, toasted, *divided*
1 tablespoon lemon juice
1/2 teaspoon sesame oil

Prepare rice according to package directions. Meanwhile, in a small skillet over medium heat, cook and stir the walnuts and honey for 4 minutes or until coated. Spread on foil to cool.

In a large skillet or wok, stir-fry pork in oil for 3-4 minutes or until no longer pink. Remove with a slotted spoon. Stir-fry water chestnuts, celery, onions and garlic for 3-4 minutes or until vegetables are crisp-tender.

Add coleslaw mix, 1 tablespoon sesame seeds, lemon juice, sesame oil, rice and 1/2 cup walnuts. Cook and stir for 2 minutes. Add pork; heat through. Sprinkle with remaining sesame seeds and nuts. **Yield:** 4 servings.

Turkey Stir-Fry

(Pictured at far right)

Prep/Total Time: 20 min.

Need a nourishing meal in minutes? Packaged Oriental veggies make this entree super-quick. Your whole family will love it! —Mildred Sherrer, Fort Worth, Texas

1 pound turkey breast tenderloins, cubed
1 tablespoon vegetable oil
1 package (16 ounces) frozen Oriental mixed vegetables
1 medium onion, cut into wedges
1/2 cup stir-fry sauce
1/3 cup shredded carrot
Hot cooked rice

In a large skillet or wok, stir-fry the cubed turkey in oil for 3-4 minutes or until no longer pink. Remove with a slotted spoon.

Stir-fry the mixed vegetables, onion, stir-fry sauce and carrot for 4-6 minutes or until vegetables are tender. Add turkey; heat through. Serve with rice. **Yield:** 4 servings.

Soy Sauce Substitute

(Pictured below)

Prep/Total Time: 5 min.

Our Test Kitchen staff created this easy homemade sauce. It has authentic taste but is lower in sodium than both the regular and low-sodium soy sauces from the store.

Soy Sauce Substitute

3 tablespoons beef bouillon granules
1-1/2 cups boiling water
1/4 cup plus 1 teaspoon cider vinegar
2 tablespoons sesame oil
1 tablespoon dark molasses
Dash pepper

In a small bowl, dissolve bouillon in boiling water. Stir in the remaining ingredients. Pour into a jar with a tight-fitting lid. Store in the refrigerator. Shake well before using. **Yield:** about 2 cups.

Mandarin Chicken Stir-Fry

Prep: 10 min. + marinating **Cook:** 15 min.

My mother often made this dish when I was growing up, and now I make it. The oranges and dill really enhance the flavor. —Shari Magee, Spanaway, Washington

6 tablespoons soy sauce, *divided*
1/2 teaspoon salt
1/2 teaspoon dill weed
1 pound boneless skinless chicken breasts, cut into strips
2 cans (11 ounces *each*) mandarin oranges
2 tablespoons cornstarch
4 tablespoons vegetable oil, *divided*
2 cans (8 ounces *each*) sliced water chestnuts, drained
1-1/2 cups thinly sliced celery
Hot cooked rice

In a large resealable plastic bag, combine 4 tablespoons soy sauce, salt and dill. Add chicken. Seal bag and turn to coat; refrigerate for 20 minutes.

Meanwhile, drain mandarin oranges, reserving syrup; set oranges aside. In a small bowl, combine the cornstarch, remaining soy sauce and reserved syrup until smooth; set aside.

In a large skillet or wok, stir-fry chicken in 2 tablespoons oil for 6-7 minutes or until juices run clear. Remove with a slotted spoon. Stir-fry the water chestnuts and celery in remaining oil for 2-3 minutes or until lightly browned.

Stir cornstarch mixture and add to the pan. Bring to a boil; cook and stir for 2 minutes or until thickened. Add chicken; heat through. Gently stir in oranges. Serve with rice. **Yield:** 4 servings.

Nice Rice

FOR FLUFFY long grain white rice, combine 1 cup rice, 1 tablespoon butter or margarine, 1 teaspoon salt (if desired) and 2 cups water in a 2- to 3-quart saucepan. Heat to boiling, stirring once or twice. Reduce the heat; cover and simmer for 15 minutes.

It's best not to peek while the rice is cooking. If the water is not absorbed after 15 minutes, cover and continue to cook the rice for another 2-4 minutes. Fluff rice with a fork before serving.

Turkey Stir-Fry

Rapid Recipe Makeovers

THOSE CLASSIC, family-favorite, home-cooked foods that everyone loves require lots of time and effort in the kitchen, right? Not anymore! Here, the expert cooks in our Test Kitchen have taken ever-popular recipes and given them quick "makeovers," so they'll come together in a flash without sacrificing flavor.

Just follow these recipes and tips to create succulent stuffed pork chops, a sure-to-please homemade pizza...even meat loaf. You and your family will be sitting down to enjoy these specialties in no time!

Cherry-Stuffed Pork Chops

(Pictured below)

Prep: 35 min. **Cook:** 20 min.

The stuffed pork chops that Jim Korzenowski of Dearborn, Michigan made took over 2 hours to prepare. Here, our home economists share a speedier version of his recipe.

1/4 cup dried cherries
2 tablespoons water
3 tablespoons chopped onion
2 tablespoons chopped celery
1 tablespoon shredded carrot

Cherry-Stuffed Pork Chops

2 teaspoons dried parsley flakes
1 tablespoon butter
3/4 cup sage stuffing mix
1/3 cup reduced-sodium chicken broth
4 boneless pork loin chops (1 inch thick and 6 ounces *each*)
1/4 teaspoon pepper
2 tablespoons vegetable oil

GRAVY:

2 tablespoons all-purpose flour
1/4 teaspoon dried rosemary, crushed
1/8 teaspoon salt
3/4 cup plus 2 tablespoons reduced-sodium chicken broth
1/4 cup heavy whipping cream

In a small saucepan, bring cherries and water to a boil. Remove from the heat; set aside (do not drain).

In a small skillet, saute the onion, celery, carrot and parsley in butter until tender. Stir in the stuffing mix, broth and cherries. Remove from the heat; cover and let stand for 5 minutes or until moisture is absorbed. Then follow steps 1-3 below. **Yield:** 4 servings.

Steps of Stuffing

1. Cut a deep slit in each pork chop, forming a pocket for stuffing.

2. Stuff about 1/4 cup cherry mixture into each chop; secure with toothpicks. Sprinkle with pepper. In a large skillet, cook chops in oil for 8-10 minutes on each side or until a meat thermometer reads 160°. Remove and keep warm.

3. Add flour, rosemary and salt to the pan juices; stir until blended. Gradually stir in broth and cream. Bring to a boil; cook and stir for 2 minutes or until thickened. Serve the gravy with pork chops.

Pesto Sausage Pizza Makeover

Pesto Sausage Pizza Makeover

(Pictured above)

Prep: 20 min. **Bake:** 25 min.

Pizza at home that's better than delivery? You bet! Our Test Kitchen pros took a homemade recipe with over an hour of prep and cut it down to just 20 minutes.

1/2 pound bulk Italian sausage
1 cup chopped onion
1 loaf (1 pound) frozen bread dough, thawed
1 package (8 ounces) cream cheese, softened
1/4 cup prepared pesto
1 cup roasted garlic Parmesan spaghetti sauce
2 cups sliced fresh mushrooms
1 can (2-1/4 ounces) sliced ripe olives, drained
1-1/2 cups (6 ounces) shredded Monterey Jack cheese

In a large skillet, cook sausage and onion over medium heat until meat is no longer pink; drain.

On a lightly floured surface, roll dough into a 16-in. x 11-in. rectangle. Transfer to a greased 15-in. x 10-in. x 1-in. baking pan. Build up edges slightly.

In a small mixing bowl, beat cream cheese and pesto until blended. Spread over dough. Layer with spaghetti sauce, sausage mixture, mushrooms, olives and Monterey Jack cheese.

Bake at 400° for 25-30 minutes or until crust is golden brown and cheese is melted. **Yield:** 12 slices.

Meat Loaf Method

- When making the miniature meat loaves at right, try to form each loaf into a uniform size and shape to achieve even microwave cooking.
- After microwaving, be sure to drain any fat from the bowl before serving.
- Handle the mixture as little as possible when forming the loaves to keep them light in texture.
- Don't want to get your hands dirty while mixing things up? Try using a wooden spoon...or purchase a small box of plastic medical or food-service gloves to slip on. Look for the gloves at your local pharmacy or grocery store.
- When using a meat thermometer to test for doneness, be sure to test in the center of the meat. If needed, use tongs to pick up one of the loaves before inserting the thermometer.

South Dakota Meat Loaf Makeover

(Pictured below)

Prep/Total Time: 25 min.

Our cooks loved a meat loaf from Lauree Buus of Rapid City, South Dakota...but not the roughly 1-1/2 hours it took to make. To speed things up, they turned her large loaf into five mini loaves and used the microwave.

1 egg, lightly beaten
1/3 cup evaporated milk
2 tablespoons Worcestershire sauce
3/4 cup quick-cooking oats
1/4 cup chopped onion
1 teaspoon salt
1/2 teaspoon rubbed sage
1/8 teaspoon pepper
1-1/2 pounds ground beef
1/4 cup ketchup

In a large bowl, combine egg, milk, Worcestershire sauce, oats, onion, salt, sage and pepper. Crumble beef over mixture; mix well. Shape into five loaves; arrange around the edge of a microwave-safe deep-dish pie plate.

Cover and microwave on high for 5-6 minutes or until meat is no longer pink and a meat thermometer reads 160°. Let stand for 5 minutes. Spread ketchup over meat loaves. **Yield:** 5 servings.

Editor's Note: This recipe was tested in a 1,100-watt microwave.

South Dakota Meat Loaf Makeover

Baking Better Biscuits

WHIPPING up tender homemade biscuits like Mom used to make is easier than you may think. To guarantee success, just follow these simple recipes and tips from our Test Kitchen experts. Before you know it, you'll have a plate of warm, fluffy, from-scratch biscuits beckoning your gang to the table.

Iced Raisin Biscuits

(Pictured below)

Prep: 20 min. **Bake:** 15 min.

Believe it—you can bake these mouth-watering breakfast treats in a snap! Our Test Kitchen added sweet raisins, maple syrup and a heartwarming spice blend.

2 cups all-purpose flour
1 tablespoon sugar
1 tablespoon baking powder
1 teaspoon ground cinnamon

Iced Raisin Biscuits

1/2 teaspoon salt
1/8 teaspoon ground nutmeg
1/2 cup cold butter, cubed
1/3 cup raisins
1/2 cup milk
3 tablespoons maple syrup

ICING:

1/2 cup confectioners' sugar
2-1/4 teaspoons milk
1/8 teaspoon rum extract

In a large bowl, combine the first six ingredients. Cut in the butter until the mixture resembles coarse crumbs. Add the raisins. In a small bowl, combine the milk and maple syrup. Add to the crumb mixture; stir just until moistened.

Turn onto a lightly floured surface; knead 8-10 times. Pat or roll out to 1/2-in. thickness; cut with a floured 2-1/2-in. biscuit cutter. Place 1 in. apart on an ungreased baking sheet. Bake at 450° for 12-15 minutes or until golden brown.

Meanwhile, combine icing ingredients. Drizzle over warm biscuits. **Yield:** 10 biscuits.

Expert Advice

- Stir dry ingredients together to evenly distribute the baking powder and/or baking soda before cutting in the butter.
- The secret to flaky biscuits is to keep the butter cold. Pieces of cold butter create steam pockets as they melt, lofting the dough layers and helping to keep them tender.
- For tender biscuits, take care not to overmix or overknead the dough. Heat from your hands will melt the butter before baking.
- For cutout biscuits, use a lightly floured biscuit cutter. Make a straight downward motion—avoid twisting the cutter. Dip it in flour after each use to prevent sticking.
- To make biscuits in a hurry without reusing dough scraps, roll the dough into a larger rectangle and cut smaller rectangular biscuits with a sharp knife.
- Biscuits are done when they're golden brown on the top and bottom. The sides will always be a little light. Biscuits are best served warm.
- In general, keep your biscuits fresh by storing them in an airtight container at room temperature. However, if they contain any perishable ingredients, such as cheese, they should be stored in the refrigerator. Biscuits will be at their best if eaten within 1 to 2 days. Can't eat them that quickly? Put them in the freezer—they'll keep for up to 3 months.

Bacon-Apple Cider Biscuits

Bacon-Apple Cider Biscuits

(Pictured above)

Prep: 20 min. **Bake:** 15 min.

The sweet and salty flavors of apple and bacon make these special biscuits from our Test Kitchen stand out. Be prepared to make more—they're gonna go fast!

2 cups all-purpose flour
2 teaspoons baking powder
2 teaspoons brown sugar
1/2 teaspoon salt
1/4 teaspoon baking soda
1/4 teaspoon apple pie spice
8 tablespoons cold butter, cubed, *divided*
5 bacon strips, cooked and crumbled
3/4 cup apple cider *or* juice
1/8 teaspoon ground cinnamon

In a large bowl, combine the first six ingredients. Cut in 7 tablespoons butter until mixture resembles coarse crumbs. Add bacon. Stir in cider just until combined.

Turn onto a lightly floured surface; knead 8-10 times. Roll into a 10-in. x 6-in. rectangle. Melt remaining butter; brush over dough. Sprinkle with cinnamon.

Cut into eight rectangles. Place 1 in. apart on an ungreased baking sheet. Bake at 450° for 12-15 minutes or until golden brown. Serve warm. **Yield:** 8 biscuits.

Making the Cut

The term "cut in" refers to distributing cold butter, margarine or shortening into a flour mixture, either using a pastry blender or two chilled knives. Pastry blenders (like the one at right) are available at most kitchen supply stores.

If you don't have a pastry blender, cut in cold butter for biscuits by hand. First, cube or cut the butter into smaller pieces. You'll know it's "cut in" when the flour mixture resembles coarse crumbs.

Bacon-Cheddar Stuffed Potatoes

Potatoes Done To Perfection

YOU'RE in the store in front of an array of potatoes. Your recipe calls for "4 small potatoes," but which ones are right...russet, Idaho, new reds, Yukon Gold? The type of potato you choose can affect the outcome of your dish. See the tip box on the next page to find out which spud is best suited to your recipe.

Bacon-Cheddar Stuffed Potatoes

(Pictured above)

Prep: 25 min. **Cook:** 25 min.

My daughters tell their friends that these are the best potatoes in the world! The hearty spuds can make a meal all by themselves. —*Julie Putnam, Lebanon, Ohio*

4 medium baking potatoes
1/3 cup mayonnaise
3/4 cup plus 6 tablespoons shredded cheddar cheese, *divided*
3/4 cup French onion dip
1/2 cup real bacon bits
4 green onions, chopped
1/4 to 1/2 teaspoon pepper

Scrub and pierce potatoes; place on a microwave-safe plate. Microwave, uncovered, on high for 18-22 minutes or until tender, turning once. Let stand for 5 minutes or until cool enough to handle.

Meanwhile, in a small bowl, combine the mayonnaise, 3/4 cup cheese, dip, bacon, onions and pepper. Cut a thin slice off the top of each potato and discard. Scoop out the pulp, leaving a thin shell. Add pulp to the mayonnaise mixture and mash.

Spoon into potato shells. Return to the microwave-safe plate. Sprinkle with remaining cheese. Microwave, uncovered, on high for 5 minutes or until heated through. **Yield:** 4 servings.

Editor's Note: This recipe was tested in a 1,100-watt microwave.

Tangy Asparagus Potato Salad

(Pictured below)

Prep/Total Time: 25 min.

I look forward to preparing this warm, colorful medley whenever asparagus season rolls around. It's been a favorite for years. —*Debbie Konietzki, Neenah, Wisconsin*

4 small red potatoes, cut into 1/4-inch wedges
1 pound fresh asparagus, trimmed
1 tablespoon Dijon mustard
1 tablespoon lemon juice
1/4 cup olive oil
2 tablespoons minced chives
1/8 teaspoon salt
Dash pepper

Place potatoes in a large saucepan; cover with water. Bring to a boil; cook for 6-7 minutes or just until tender.

Meanwhile, in a large skillet, bring 1/2 in. of water to a boil. Add the asparagus; cover and boil for 3 minutes. Drain and immediately place the asparagus in ice water. Drain and pat dry. Cut into 1-in. pieces.

Drain potatoes and place in a large bowl; add asparagus. In a small bowl, combine the mustard and lemon juice; whisk in oil until combined. Add chives, salt and pepper. Pour over vegetables and toss to coat. Serve warm or at room temperature. **Yield:** 4 servings.

Tangy Asparagus Potato Salad

Golden Potato Soup

Golden Potato Soup

(Pictured above and on page 284)

Prep: 25 min. **Cook:** 25 min.

I get many requests to bring this soup to family events. If you're in the mood for some comfort food, this is the recipe for you! —*Shelly Woods, Blissfield, Michigan*

- **6 cups cubed Yukon Gold potatoes**
- **2 cups water**
- **1 cup sliced celery**
- **1 cup sliced carrots**
- **1/2 cup chopped onion**
- **2 teaspoons dried parsley flakes**
- **2 teaspoons chicken bouillon granules**
- **1 teaspoon salt**
- **1/2 teaspoon pepper**
- **1/4 cup all-purpose flour**
- **2 cups milk,** ***divided***
- **1 package (16 ounces) process cheese (Velveeta), cubed**
- **1 cup cubed fully cooked ham**
- **1/3 cup real bacon bits**

In a Dutch oven, combine the first nine ingredients. Bring to a boil over medium heat. Reduce the heat; cover and simmer for 12-14 minutes or until the potatoes are tender.

In a small bowl, combine flour and 1/4 cup milk until smooth; add to soup. Add the cheese and remaining milk. Bring to a boil; cook and stir for 2 minutes or until thickened. Stir in ham and bacon; heat through. **Yield:** 8 servings (2-3/4 quarts).

Uses for Potato Varieties

For Roasting or Boiling and in Salads: Red potatoes are lower in starch but higher in sugar content, so they brown easily. They're just right for roasting, boiling or sauteing.

For Baking and Mashing: High-starch potatoes, like russets and Idahos, are perfect for baking and also make the fluffiest mashed potatoes and best golden fries.

Jack-of-All-Trades: Versatile Yukon Golds and other yellow-fleshed potatoes with a medium starch content are ideal if you prefer creamy to fluffy mashed potatoes; they can stand up to pan frying and also lend a nice, delicate feel to potato salads.

Cheese-Stuffed Jalapenos

Pointers On Peppers

WHEN FARMERS MARKETS, gardens and grocery stores fill up with vibrant peppers, take advantage of the bounty and jazz up your menu with recipes starring this versatile veggie. On the next page, our Test Kitchen cooks offer their best tips on seeding and slicing peppers—so you're sure of success. Why wait any longer? Add some peppers and pep things up!

Cheese-Stuffed Jalapenos

(Pictured above)

Prep/Total Time: 30 min.

We make these popular snacks throughout the summer season. With just four ingredients, the recipe goes together without any fuss. Everyone loves the jalapenos topped with melted Monterey Jack cheese, bacon bits and bread crumbs.
—Bruce Hahne, Acworth, Georgia

✓ This recipe includes Nutrition Facts and Diabetic Exchanges.

8 ounces Monterey Jack cheese, cut into 2-inch x 1/2-inch x 1/4-inch strips
15 jalapeno peppers, halved lengthwise and seeded
1/4 cup dry bread crumbs
1/4 cup real bacon bits

Place a cheese strip in each pepper half; sprinkle with bread crumbs and bacon bits. Grill the peppers, covered, over medium-hot heat for 4-6 minutes or until peppers are tender and cheese is melted. Serve warm. **Yield:** 2-1/2 dozen.

Editor's Note: When cutting hot peppers, disposable gloves are recommended. Avoid touching your face.

Nutrition Facts: 1 stuffed pepper half equals 38 calories, 3 g fat (2 g saturated fat), 7 mg cholesterol, 87 mg sodium, 1 g carbohydrate, trace fiber, 2 g protein. **Diabetic Exchange:** 1/2 fat.

Pretty Pepper Salad

(Pictured below)

Prep/Total Time: 20 min.

This bright medley is terrific with grilled chicken or ribs... and is a great choice when you want a change from the usual coleslaw. *—Colette Gerow, Raytown, Missouri*

2 medium green peppers, cut into rings
1 medium sweet yellow pepper, cut into rings
1 medium sweet red pepper, cut into rings
1 medium red onion, cut into rings
1 jar (6-1/2 ounces) marinated quartered artichoke hearts, drained
1 can (2-1/4 ounces) sliced ripe olives, drained
1/4 cup vegetable oil
3 tablespoons lemon juice
1/2 to 1 teaspoon minced fresh oregano
1/2 teaspoon sugar
1/2 teaspoon salt
1/4 to 1/2 teaspoon paprika

In a large bowl, combine the peppers, onion, artichokes and olives. In a jar with a tight-fitting lid, combine the remaining ingredients; shake well. Pour over pepper mixture; toss to coat. Chill until serving. Serve with a slotted spoon. **Yield:** 9 servings.

Pretty Pepper Salad

Pepper Lover's Pizza

(Pictured below)

Prep/Total Time: 25 min.

For your Friday pizza night, a Super Bowl party or any time you crave a loaded pizza pie, try this recipe. It yields two breads piled high with three types of peppers, plus onion, pesto and mozzarella cheese. If you like, experiment with different toppings. —*Nancy Zimmerman*
Cape May Court House, New Jersey

- **1 *each* small sweet yellow, orange and red pepper, julienned**
- **1 medium onion, halved and sliced**
- **1/2 teaspoon Italian seasoning**
- **2 tablespoons olive oil**
- **1 cup (4 ounces) shredded part-skim mozzarella cheese**
- **1 loaf (1 pound) unsliced Italian bread**
- **1/3 cup prepared pesto**

In a large skillet, saute the peppers, onion and Italian seasoning in oil until tender. Remove from the heat; toss with mozzarella cheese.

Cut the loaf of Italian bread in half lengthwise; place on a baking sheet. Spread the cut sides of bread with the pesto; top with pepper mixture.

Broil the pizzas 4-6 in. from the heat for 5-8 minutes or until the cheese is melted. Cut pizzas into slices. **Yield:** 10 servings.

How to Seed and Slice

Bell peppers. Holding the pepper by the stem, slice from the top of the pepper down, using a chef's knife. Use this technique to slice around the seeds when a recipe calls for julienned or chopped peppers.

Jalapeno peppers. With gloves on, cut the jalapeno in half; remove and discard the seeds with the tip of a spoon or knife.

Make pepper rings. Run a paring knife around the top of the pepper to detach the core and membrane (ribs). Then twist and pull out the stem. With a spoon, scrape out any remaining seeds and membrane. Use a chef's knife to slice the pepper crosswise for rings.

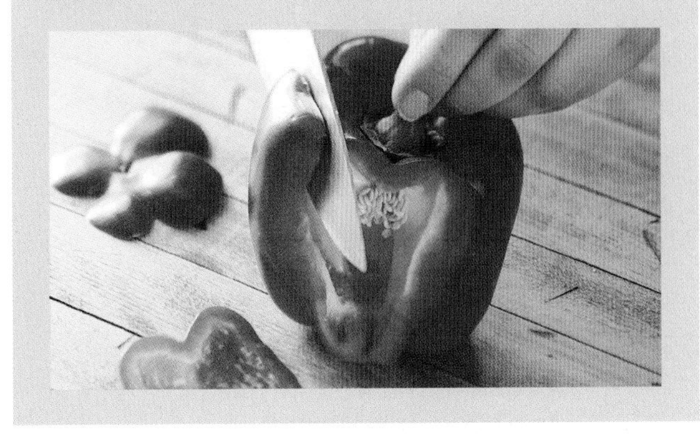

Pepper Lover's Pizza

Thanksgiving Turkey Tips

WHETHER you're a Thanksgiving first-timer or a Turkey Day veteran, these proven recipes and tips are sure to make things easier in the kitchen. Follow the instructions here, and your holiday bird will certainly be the talk of the table!

Lemon-Herb Roasted Turkey

(Pictured at far right)

Prep: 30 min. **Bake:** 2-1/4 hours + standing

Lemon and thyme are the predominant flavors in this golden, tender and moist turkey. It's so easy, you just can't go wrong! —*Felecia Smith, Georgetown, Texas*

1/2 cup butter, melted
3 tablespoons lemon juice
2 teaspoons grated lemon peel
1 teaspoon minced fresh thyme *or* 1/4 teaspoon dried thyme
1 turkey (14 to 16 pounds)
2 teaspoons salt
2 teaspoons pepper
1 medium lemon, halved
1 medium onion, quartered
14 garlic cloves, peeled
24 fresh thyme sprigs
1 tablespoon all-purpose flour
1 turkey-size oven roasting bag

In a small bowl, combine butter, lemon juice, peel and thyme. Pat turkey dry. Sprinkle salt and pepper over skin of turkey and inside cavity; brush with butter mixture. Place lemon, onion, garlic and thyme sprigs inside cavity. Skewer turkey openings; tie drumsticks together.

Place flour in oven bag and shake to coat. Place the bag in a roasting pan; add turkey, breast side up. Cut six 1/2-in. slits in top of bag; close bag with tie provided.

Bake at 350° for 2-1/4 to 2-3/4 hours or until a meat thermometer reads 180°. Remove turkey to a serving platter and keep warm. Let stand for 15 minutes before carving. If desired, thicken the pan drippings for gravy. **Yield:** 14-16 servings.

Easy Turkey Gravy

(Pictured above far right)

Prep/Total Time: 15 min.

With just a few simple ingredients, our Test Kitchen home economists created this flavorful turkey gravy that even beginner cooks will be able to proudly serve guests.

This recipe includes Nutrition Facts and Diabetic Exchanges.

Roasted turkey drippings
Chicken broth *or* water
1/4 cup all-purpose flour
1/8 teaspoon pepper
1/8 teaspoon browning sauce, optional

Pour turkey drippings into a measuring cup. Skim fat, reserving 1/4 cup; set aside. Add enough broth or water to the drippings to measure 2 cups.

In a small saucepan, combine flour and reserved fat until smooth. Gradually stir in drippings mixture. Bring to a boil; cook and stir for 2 minutes or until thickened. Stir in pepper and sauce if desired. **Yield:** 2-1/3 cups.

Nutrition Facts: 2 tablespoons equals 33 calories, 3 g fat (1 g saturated fat), 3 mg cholesterol, 59 mg sodium, 1 g carbohydrate, trace fiber, trace protein. **Diabetic Exchange:** 1/2 fat.

Turkey Techniques

Temping Your Bird
To check the temperature at the end of the roasting time, place a meat thermometer into the thick portion of the inner thigh areas, not touching the bone. The doneness temperature for a whole turkey is 180 degrees.

Skimming the Fat
Remove the turkey from the bag; let it stand. Place the bag drippings in a heat-resistant measuring cup. Skim the fat using a spoon or ladle.

Using a Steel
To carve a turkey safely and easily, make sure that your carving knife is sharp. To sharpen your knife, use a steel. Point the steel's tip on a work surface. Hold your knife at a 20-degree angle on the steel.

Start with the blade's heel against the steel and draw the blade down until you reach the knife's tip. Repeat five times on both sides of the blade.

Easy Turkey Gravy
Lemon-Herb Roasted Turkey

Hints for the Best Holiday Bird

- If your turkey is frozen, allow 24 hours for every 4 pounds when thawing it in the refrigerator. Cold-water thawing is an option that takes less time but requires more attention. The poultry must be in a leak-proof bag, such as its original, tightly sealed wrapper. Submerge the wrapped poultry in cold tap water. Change the water every 30 minutes until the bird is thawed, allowing 30 minutes for every pound.
- Remove the giblets, usually stored in a packet in the bird's neck area. Also remove and discard any large fat pockets present in the neck area. Drain juices, and blot the cavity dry with paper towels.
- Tuck the turkey's wing tips under the body to avoid overbrowning while roasting.
- Roasting a turkey in a roasting bag makes for easy cleanup—a definite plus for cooks who've just prepared a big holiday meal! Choose a roasting pan that's at least 2 inches deep and large enough that the bag can expand during cooking; make sure the bag doesn't touch any racks, heating elements or oven walls.

Peppermint Meltaways

Merry Cookie Decorating

MAKING plain cookies festive for Christmas doesn't have to be time-consuming or difficult. Here, you'll see how you can create eye-catching treats with just a few basic steps. These creative techniques will give you a plateful of holiday spirit in no time!

For example, Peppermint Meltaways (recipe below) get their cheery look from crushed candy canes. See the tip box at right for an easy method of crushing hard candies...and for some additional fun ideas.

Peppermint Meltaways

(Pictured at left)

Prep: 30 min. **Bake:** 10 min./batch + cooling

These goodies are very pretty and cheery on a cookie platter. I like to cover a plate of the meltaways with red or green plastic wrap and top it with a holiday bow.
—Denise Wheeler, Newaygo, Michigan

✓ This recipe includes Nutrition Facts and Diabetic Exchanges.

1 cup butter, softened
1/2 cup confectioners' sugar
1/2 teaspoon peppermint extract
1-1/4 cups all-purpose flour
1/2 cup cornstarch
FROSTING:
2 tablespoons butter, softened
1-1/2 cups confectioners' sugar
2 tablespoons milk
1/4 teaspoon peppermint extract
2 to 3 drops red food coloring, optional
1/2 cup crushed peppermint candies

In a small mixing bowl, cream butter and confectioners' sugar until light and fluffy. Beat in extract. Combine flour and cornstarch; gradually add to creamed mixture and mix well.

Shape dough into 1-in. balls. Place 2 in. apart on ungreased baking sheets. Bake at 350° for 10-12 minutes or until the bottoms are lightly browned. Remove to wire racks to cool.

In a small mixing bowl, beat butter until fluffy. Add the confectioners' sugar, milk, extract and food coloring if desired; beat until smooth. Spread over cooled cookies; sprinkle with crushed candies. Store in an airtight container. **Yield:** 3-1/2 dozen.

Nutrition Facts: 1 cookie equals 90 calories, 5 g fat (3 g saturated fat), 13 mg cholesterol, 36 mg sodium, 11 g carbohydrate, trace fiber, trace protein. **Diabetic Exchanges:** 1 fat, 1/2 starch.

Decorating How-Tos

WANT to make the cookies shown below? It's easy! Simply use your favorite sugar cookie recipe and cookie cutters. Or use one tube (16.5 ounces) of refrigerated sugar cookie dough combined with 2/3 cup all-purpose flour to help the cookies hold their shape. Bake according to the package directions, then decorate the cooled cookies using any of the ideas here.

For example, for the reindeer cutouts below, our Test Kitchen cooks used one tube (16.5 ounces) refrigerated dough and 2/3 cup all-purpose flour to make the cookies, then decorated them using a super-easy technique. The yield was 2-1/2 dozen.

See below for details on how to decorate the reindeer cutouts...as well as how to make glittery, shimmery snowflakes and to create holly designs using just a toothpick and colored gel.

Cheery Reindeer

1. Crush hard candy, such as candy canes, in a large resealable plastic bag.
2. Transfer the candies to a fine-mesh strainer, then shake it over waxed paper to remove fine dust.
3. Dip one edge of each cutout cookie in melted baking chocolate; immediately sprinkle the dipped area with crushed candy. Place cookies on waxed paper to stand until set.

Special Snowflakes

1. Frost each cutout snowflake cookie with canned vanilla frosting.
2. Immediately sprinkle the frosted cookies with coconut and clear edible glitter.

Holiday Holly

1. To make the glaze, combine 3 cups confectioners' sugar and 6 tablespoons milk. Spread the glaze over the cookies.
2. Immediately dot green food gel on each cookie.
3. Gently pull a toothpick through the dots toward the outer edges to form the holly leaves.
4. Place Red Hots candies as desired to make the holly berries.

Chapter 21

On-the-Go Odds & Ends

PLANNING a backyard barbecue and want new recipes for the grill? Need some fast-to-fix stovetop dinners...or ideas for using up leftovers? Maybe you cook for two people and want some smaller-yield recipes for just the pair of you.

You'll find foods that fit all of those categories in this handy chapter. It groups similar dishes together so you can easily locate the types you're searching for—whether skillet suppers or complete meals for two.

Enjoy Chipotle Chicken Fajitas, Garlic Tomato Soup, Zesty Horseradish Meat Loaf, Cinnamon Apple Wraps, Sage Shrimp Skewers, Cranberry Pear Cobblers...and much more!

SKILLET MEAL. Smoked Sausage with Penne and Veggies (p. 311).

Great Grilling

WHEN those long-awaited summer days arrive, it's time to get out and fire up that barbecue! To help you do just that, we've featured sensational main dishes that'll come hot and delicious off the grill.

From Sage Shrimp Skewers and Pineapple Beef Kabobs to Chipotle Chicken Fajitas and Grilled Pork Chops with Cilantro Salsa, you just can't go wrong. The only hard part? Choosing which to try first!

Tomato-Basil Shrimp Skewers

(Pictured below)

Prep: 30 min. + marinating **Grill:** 10 min.

These are the best, most perfectly seasoned shrimp I have ever had. My husband isn't a big fan of shrimp, but he loves these! —Jennifer Fulk, Moreno Valley, California

1/3 cup olive oil
1/4 cup tomato sauce
2 tablespoons minced fresh basil
2 tablespoons red wine vinegar
1-1/2 teaspoons minced garlic
1/4 teaspoon cayenne pepper
2 pounds uncooked jumbo shrimp, peeled and deveined

In a large resealable plastic bag, combine the first six ingredients; add shrimp. Seal bag and turn to coat; refrigerate for up to 30 minutes.

Drain and discard marinade. Thread shrimp onto six metal or soaked wooden skewers. Grill, covered, over medium heat for 3-5 minutes on each side or until shrimp turn pink. **Yield:** 6 servings.

Tomato-Basil Shrimp Skewers

Chipotle Chicken Fajitas

Chipotle Chicken Fajitas

(Pictured above)

Prep: 30 min. + marinating **Grill:** 10 min.

I changed this recipe a bit to suit my husband and me. The chipotle peppers can be very hot—feel free to adjust the amount. —Melissa Thomeczek, Hannibal, Missouri

1 bottle (12 ounces) chili sauce
1/4 cup lime juice
4 chipotle peppers in adobo sauce
1 pound boneless skinless chicken breasts, cut into strips
1/2 cup cider vinegar
1/3 cup packed brown sugar
1/3 cup molasses
4 medium green peppers, cut into 1-inch pieces
1 large onion, cut into 1-inch pieces
1 tablespoon olive oil
1/8 teaspoon salt
1/8 teaspoon pepper
10 flour tortillas (8 inches)
1-1/2 cups chopped tomatoes
1 cup (4 ounces) shredded Mexican cheese blend

Place the chili sauce, lime juice and chipotle peppers in a food processor; cover and process until blended. Transfer 1/2 cup to a large resealable plastic bag; add chicken. Seal bag and turn to coat; refrigerate for 1-4 hours.

Pour remaining marinade into a small bowl; add vinegar, brown sugar and molasses. Cover and refrigerate.

Drain and discard marinade from chicken. On six metal or soaked wooden skewers, alternately thread chicken, green peppers and onion. Brush with oil; sprinkle with salt and pepper. Grill, covered, over medium heat for 10-16 minutes or until chicken juices run clear, turning occasionally.

Unskewer chicken and vegetables into a large bowl; add 1/2 cup chipotle-molasses mixture and toss to coat. Keep warm.

Grill tortillas, uncovered, over medium heat for 45-55 seconds on each side or until warmed. Top with chicken mixture, tomatoes, cheese and remaining chipotle-molasses mixture. **Yield:** 5 servings.

Pineapple Beef Kabobs

(Pictured below)

Prep: 20 min. + marinating **Grill:** 10 min.

These fun, colorful skewers are easy to assemble and impressive for guests. The basting helps keep the kabobs juicy and tender. —Marguerite Shaeffer, Sewell, New Jersey

1 can (6 ounces) unsweetened pineapple juice
1/3 cup honey
1/3 cup soy sauce
3 tablespoons cider vinegar
1-1/2 teaspoons minced garlic
1-1/2 teaspoons ground ginger
1-1/2 pounds boneless beef top sirloin steak, cut into 1-inch pieces
1 fresh pineapple, peeled and cut into 1-inch chunks
12 large fresh mushrooms
1 medium sweet red pepper, cut into 1-inch pieces
1 medium sweet yellow pepper, cut into 1-inch pieces
1 medium red onion, cut into 1-inch pieces
2-1/2 cups uncooked instant rice

In a small bowl, combine the first six ingredients. Pour 3/4 cup into a large resealable plastic bag; add beef. Seal bag and turn to coat; refrigerate for 1-4 hours. Cover and refrigerate remaining marinade for basting.

Coat grill rack with cooking spray before starting the grill. Drain and discard marinade. On 12 metal or soaked wooden skewers, alternately thread the beef, pineapple, mushrooms, peppers and onion. Grill, covered, over medium-hot heat for 8-10 minutes or until meat reaches desired doneness, turning occasionally and basting frequently with reserved marinade.

Cook the rice according to package directions; serve with the kabobs. **Yield:** 6 servings.

Pineapple Beef Kabobs

Grilled Pork Chops with Cilantro Salsa

Grilled Pork Chops with Cilantro Salsa

(Pictured above)

Prep: 15 min. **Cook:** 20 min.

Fresh cilantro can give a fantastic flavor boost to stews, salads and many other recipes. It's great in the fruity salsa for these chops. —Lisa Ruehlow, Blaine, Minnesota

✓ This recipe includes Nutrition Facts and Diabetic Exchanges.

1-1/2 cups cubed cantaloupe
1 cup chopped tomatoes
1/2 cup chopped green pepper
2 tablespoons limeade concentrate
2 tablespoons chopped green onion
2 tablespoons minced fresh cilantro
1/4 teaspoon salt
6 bone-in pork loin chops (7 ounces *each* and 1/2 inch thick)
Pepper to taste

In a large bowl, combine the cantaloupe, tomatoes, green pepper, limeade, onion, cilantro and salt. Cover and refrigerate until serving.

Coat grill rack with cooking spray before starting grill. Season pork with pepper. Grill, covered, over medium heat for 6-7 minutes on each side or until a meat thermometer reads 160°, turning once. Serve with salsa. **Yield:** 6 servings.

Nutrition Facts: 1 pork chop with 1/3 cup salsa equals 240 calories, 9 g fat (3 g saturated fat), 86 mg cholesterol, 168 mg sodium, 9 g carbohydrate, 1 g fiber, 31 g protein. **Diabetic Exchanges:** 5 very lean meat, 1 fat, 1/2 fruit.

Chipotle Pork Tenderloins

Chipotle Pork Tenderloins

(Pictured above)

Prep: 20 min. + marinating **Grill:** 20 min.

This recipe came from a family member and goes over big at cookouts. Berries and avocado help cool the pork's heat. —Priscilla Gilbert, Indian Harbour Beach, Florida

☑ This recipe includes Nutrition Facts and Diabetic Exchanges.

1 cup sliced onion
1/2 cup chipotle peppers in adobo sauce, chopped
1/4 cup lime juice
1-1/2 teaspoons minced garlic
3 pork tenderloins (1 pound *each*)
STRAWBERRY SALSA:
5 cups sliced fresh strawberries
1/4 cup thinly sliced green onions
1/4 cup minced fresh cilantro
1/4 cup lime juice
1/4 teaspoon salt
1 medium ripe avocado, peeled and chopped

In a large resealable plastic bag, combine the onion, chipotle peppers, lime juice and garlic; add pork. Seal bag and turn to coat; refrigerate for at least 1 hour.

Prepare the grill for indirect heat. Drain and discard the marinade. Grill the pork, covered, over indirect medium heat for 10-13 minutes on each side or until a meat thermometer reads 160°. Let stand for 5 minutes before slicing.

For salsa, in a large bowl, combine strawberries, green onions, cilantro, lime juice and salt. Gently stir in avocado. Serve with pork. **Yield:** 9 servings (5 cups salsa).

Nutrition Facts: 4 ounces cooked pork with 1/2 cup salsa equals 246 calories, 9 g fat (2 g saturated fat), 84 mg cholesterol, 173 mg sodium, 11 g carbohydrate, 3 g fiber, 31 g protein. **Diabetic Exchanges:** 4 lean meat, 1/2 fruit, 1/2 fat.

Marinated Grilled Chicken

Prep: 10 min. + marinating **Grill:** 10 min.

This light, tasty main course requires only a few minutes of prep work, and it keeps my kitchen cool by relying on the grill. —Linda Coss, Lake Forest, California

☑ This recipe includes Nutrition Facts and Diabetic Exchanges.

1/4 cup balsamic vinegar
2 tablespoons olive oil
1-1/2 teaspoons lemon juice
1/2 teaspoon lemon-pepper seasoning
4 boneless skinless chicken breast halves (6 ounces *each*)

In a large resealable plastic bag, combine the vinegar, oil, lemon juice and lemon-pepper; add the chicken. Seal bag and turn to coat; refrigerate for 30 minutes.

Drain and discard marinade. Coat grill rack with cooking spray before starting the grill. Grill, covered, over medium heat for 5-7 minutes on each side or until chicken juices run clear. **Yield:** 4 servings.

Nutrition Facts: 1 chicken breast half equals 207 calories, 6 g fat (1 g saturated fat), 94 mg cholesterol, 105 mg sodium, 1 g carbohydrate, trace fiber, 34 g protein. **Diabetic Exchanges:** 5 very lean meat, 1/2 fat.

Sage Shrimp Skewers

(Pictured below)

Prep/Total Time: 20 min.

Sage is not only great for seasoning hearty cuts of meat, but it's also wonderful in these bacon-wrapped shrimp appetizers. —Lacey Kirsch, Vancouver, Washington

Sage Shrimp Skewers

✓ This recipe includes Nutrition Facts and Diabetic Exchanges.

10 bacon strips
10 uncooked jumbo shrimp, peeled and deveined
1 tablespoon olive oil
10 fresh sage leaves

In a large skillet, cook the bacon over medium heat until partially cooked but not crisp. Remove to paper towels to drain.

Coat grill rack with cooking spray before starting the grill. Sprinkle shrimp with oil. Place a sage leaf on each shrimp; wrap with a strip of bacon. Thread shrimp onto two metal or soaked wooden skewers. Grill, covered, over medium heat for 4-6 minutes or until shrimp turn pink, turning once. **Yield:** 10 appetizers.

Nutrition Facts: 1 appetizer equals 68 calories, 4 g fat (1 g saturated fat), 38 mg cholesterol, 176 mg sodium, trace carbohydrate, 0 fiber, 6 g protein. **Diabetic Exchanges:** 1 lean meat, 1/2 fat.

Mayonnaise Lovers' Chicken

(Pictured above)

Prep: 15 min. + marinating **Grill:** 10 min.

My father-in-law was looking for a good chicken marinade when a friend suggested mayonnaise and Italian dressing. With ham and cheese, too, this main course is popular with everyone. —Jennifer Rytting, West Jordan, Utah

1/2 cup Italian salad dressing
1-1/4 cups mayonnaise, *divided*
6 boneless skinless chicken breast halves (4 ounces *each*)
6 slices deli ham
6 slices Swiss cheese
1-1/2 teaspoons prepared mustard
1-1/2 teaspoons honey

In a small bowl, combine salad dressing and 1/2 cup mayonnaise. Pour 3/4 cup into a large resealable plastic bag; add chicken. Seal bag and turn to coat; refrigerate for at least 30 minutes. Cover and refrigerate remaining marinade for basting.

Drain and discard marinade. Grill chicken, covered, over medium heat or broil 4 in. from the heat for 4-6 minutes on each side or until juices run clear, basting frequently with reserved marinade. Top each piece of chicken with a slice of ham and cheese. Grill, covered, 1-2 minutes longer or until cheese is melted.

In a small bowl, combine the mustard, honey and remaining mayonnaise. Serve with the chicken. **Yield:** 6 servings.

Grilling Like a Pro

- Keep your grill stick-free by spraying the unheated grates with cooking spray before placing meat or veggies on them.
- Bring foods to a cool room temperature before grilling. Cold foods may burn on the outside before the interior is fully cooked.
- To turn meat, use tongs instead of a meat fork to avoid piercing and losing the meat's juices.

Zesty Horseradish Meat Loaf

Lively Leftovers

WOULDN'T it be great to get more for your meal? Here, you will! Two of these recipes—Zesty Horseradish Meat Loaf and Oregano Roasting Chicken—will likely make more than you need for dinner, so you'll have leftovers. Use them to fix Second-Chance Reubens and Tortilla-Vegetable Chicken Soup.

Zesty Horseradish Meat Loaf

(Pictured above)

Prep: 15 min. **Bake:** 45 min. + standing

This is a zippy meat loaf...and you can make fantastic sandwiches with any leftovers. —Nancy Zimmerman Cape May Court House, New Jersey

✓ This recipe includes Nutrition Facts and Diabetic Exchanges.

4 slices whole wheat bread, crumbled
1/4 cup milk
1/2 cup finely chopped celery
1/4 cup finely chopped onion
1/4 cup prepared horseradish
2 tablespoons Dijon mustard
2 tablespoons chili sauce
1 egg, beaten
1-1/2 teaspoons Worcestershire sauce
1/2 teaspoon salt
1/4 teaspoon pepper
1-1/2 pounds lean ground beef
1/2 cup ketchup

In a large bowl, soak bread in milk for 5 minutes. Drain and discard milk. Stir in the celery, onion, horseradish, mustard, chili sauce, egg, Worcestershire sauce, salt and pepper. Crumble beef over mixture and mix well.

Shape into a loaf in a greased 11-in. x 7-in. x 2-in. baking dish. Spread top with ketchup. Bake at 350° for 45-55 minutes or until no pink remains and a meat thermometer reads 160°. Let stand for 10 minutes before cutting. **Yield:** 8 servings.

Nutrition Facts: 1 slice equals 207 calories, 8 g fat (3 g saturated fat), 79 mg cholesterol, 640 mg sodium, 14 g carbohydrate, 1 g fiber, 19 g protein. **Diabetic Exchanges:** 2 lean meat, 1 starch, 1/2 fat.

Second-Chance Reubens

(Pictured below)

Prep/Total Time: 20 min.

When you end up with more meat loaf than you can eat for dinner, save the extras for the next day and use them in these simple Reubens. You'll be glad you did! The recipe is a new and delicious take on an old favorite. —Kimberley Johnson, Englewood, Colorado

8 slices rye bread
4 tablespoons Thousand Island salad dressing, ***divided***
4 slices cooked meat loaf, warmed
1 cup sauerkraut, rinsed and well drained
4 slices Swiss cheese
2 tablespoons butter, softened

Spread four bread slices with half of the salad dressing. Layer each with the meat loaf, sauerkraut and cheese. Spread remaining bread with remaining salad dressing; place over cheese. Butter outsides of sandwiches.

In a large skillet over medium heat, toast sandwiches for 2-3 minutes on each side or until bread is lightly browned and cheese is melted. **Yield:** 4 servings.

Second-Chance Reubens

Oregano Roasting Chicken

Oregano Roasting Chicken

(Pictured above)

Prep: 10 min. **Bake:** 2-1/4 hours

This five-ingredient recipe from our Test Kitchen takes almost no time to prep for the oven. Save the drippings and 2 cups of the moist, tender chicken for Tortilla-Vegetable Chicken Soup (recipe above right).

1/4 cup butter, melted
1 envelope Italian salad dressing mix
2 tablespoons lemon juice
1 roasting chicken (6 to 7 pounds)
2 teaspoons dried oregano

Combine butter, salad dressing mix and lemon juice. Place chicken on a rack in an ungreased roasting pan. Spoon butter mixture over chicken.

Cover and bake at 350° for 45 minutes. Uncover; sprinkle with oregano. Bake, uncovered, for 1-1/2 to 1-3/4 hours or until a meat thermometer reads 180°.

Remove the chicken from roasting pan; let stand for 5 minutes. Strain drippings. Cut one chicken breast half into 1-in. cubes. Cover and refrigerate cubed chicken breast and 1/4 cup drippings for Tortilla-Vegetable Chicken Soup (recipe above right) or save for another use. Transfer remaining chicken to serving platter. **Yield:** 4 servings plus 2 cups cubed cooked chicken breast and 1/4 cup drippings.

Tortilla-Vegetable Chicken Soup

(Pictured below)

Prep: 20 min. **Cook:** 15 min.

Most of what you need for this tasty soup is probably already in your pantry. It's a wonderful way to use leftover cooked chicken. —Jan Peri-Wyrick, Fort Worth, Texas

3 flour tortillas (6 inches), cut into 1-inch strips
1/4 cup chicken drippings, optional
1 cup chopped celery
3/4 cup finely chopped carrot
1/2 cup chopped red onion
2 tablespoons olive oil
3 cans (14-1/2 ounces *each*) reduced-sodium chicken broth
1 can (15 ounces) black beans, rinsed and drained
1 can (14-1/2 ounces) beef broth
1 can (10 ounces) diced tomatoes with mild green chilies
2 cups cubed cooked chicken breast
2 cups frozen corn
2 teaspoons dried parsley flakes
1 teaspoon garlic powder
1 teaspoon dried basil
1 teaspoon ground cumin
1 teaspoon ground coriander
Shredded Monterey Jack cheese, optional

Place tortilla strips on a baking sheet coated with cooking spray; bake at 350° for 8-10 minutes or until lightly browned. Set aside.

Meanwhile, skim fat from drippings. In a Dutch oven, saute celery, carrot and onion in oil until tender. Stir in chicken broth, black beans, beef broth, tomatoes, chicken, corn, seasonings and drippings if desired. Bring to a boil. Reduce heat; simmer, uncovered, for 15 minutes.

Serve with cheese if desired and tortilla strips. **Yield:** 6 servings.

Tortilla-Vegetable Chicken Soup

Country Fried Chicken

Stovetop Suppers

WHEN IT COMES to hassle-free dinners the whole family will enjoy, it's hard to beat stovetop cooking. Three of the mealtime recipes here rely on a single skillet to get to the table. And for Smoked Sausage with Penne and Veggies—another skillet dish—the only additional pan you'll need will be one for cooking the pasta. It doesn't get much easier than that!

Country Fried Chicken

(Pictured above)

Prep: 20 min. **Cook:** 40 min.

Why buy restaurant fried chicken when you can quickly make your own version at home? This recipe is sure to please. —Rebekah Miller, Rocky Mountain, Virginia

1 cup all-purpose flour
2 teaspoons garlic salt
2 teaspoons pepper
1 teaspoon paprika
1/2 teaspoon poultry seasoning
1 egg
1/2 cup milk
1 broiler/fryer chicken (3 to 3-1/2 pounds), cut up
Oil for frying

In a large resealable plastic bag, combine the flour and seasonings. In a shallow bowl, beat egg and milk. Dip chicken pieces into egg mixture, then add to bag, a few pieces at a time, and shake to coat.

In a large skillet, heat 1/4 in. of oil; fry chicken in oil until browned on all sides. Cover and simmer for 35-40 minutes or until juices run clear and chicken is tender, turning occasionally. Uncover and cook 5 minutes longer. Drain on paper towels. **Yield:** 4 servings.

Saucy Mushroom Chicken

(Pictured below)

Prep: 15 min. **Cook:** 25 min.

One day when I'd planned to grill out, it ended up raining, so I created this tasty skillet recipe as an indoor alternative. Now I often prepare it for company. —Aline Eyre, Sarnia, Ontario

6 boneless skinless chicken breast halves (5 ounces *each*)
1 teaspoon *each* onion powder, paprika, dried basil, oregano and thyme
1 teaspoon *each* salt and pepper
2 tablespoons olive oil, *divided*
2 cups sliced fresh mushrooms
2 teaspoons minced garlic
3 tablespoons all-purpose flour
2 cups chicken broth
1/2 cup white wine *or* additional chicken broth
1/2 cup heavy whipping cream
Mashed potatoes, optional

Flatten chicken breast halves to 1/2-in. thickness. Combine the seasonings; sprinkle 2 tablespoons over both sides of the chicken.

In a large skillet, cook chicken in 1 tablespoon oil in batches over medium heat for 3-4 minutes on each side or until juices run clear. Remove and keep warm.

In the same skillet, saute the mushrooms, garlic and remaining seasoning mixture in the remaining oil until tender. Stir in the flour. Gradually stir in the chicken broth, wine or additional chicken broth, and cream. Bring to a boil. Reduce heat; cook and stir for 2 minutes or until thickened.

Return chicken to the pan; heat through. Serve with mashed potatoes if desired. **Yield:** 6 servings.

Saucy Mushroom Chicken

Smoked Sausage with Penne and Veggies

Smoked Sausage with Penne and Veggies

(Pictured above and on page 302)

Prep: 20 min. **Cook:** 20 min.

This simple dish was inspired by a different pasta recipe. I didn't have the ingredients for it on hand, so I raided the pantry and came up with this instead. I love it!
—Theresa Moore, Mancelona, Michigan

8 ounces uncooked penne pasta
1 cup chopped green pepper
1/2 cup finely chopped onion
2 tablespoons olive oil
1 pound smoked sausage, cut into 1/2-inch slices
2 cans (14-1/2 ounces *each*) Italian stewed tomatoes
2 to 3 small zucchini, quartered lengthwise and sliced 1/2 inch thick
1/2 cup frozen corn
1/2 cup water
1 teaspoon salt
1 teaspoon dried basil
1 teaspoon minced garlic
1/2 teaspoon pepper
Shredded Parmesan cheese, optional

Cook the pasta according to package directions. Meanwhile, in a large skillet, saute green pepper and onion in oil until crisp-tender.

Add the sausage, tomatoes, zucchini, corn, water, salt, basil, garlic and pepper. Bring to a boil. Reduce heat; simmer, uncovered, for 5 minutes.

Drain pasta; toss with sausage mixture. Garnish with Parmesan cheese if desired. **Yield:** 5 servings.

Swiss Corned Beef Hash

Prep: 20 min. **Cook:** 30 min.

Our Test Kitchen home economists combined Irish favorites to make this easy skillet supper. Enjoy it for a St. Patrick's Day celebration or any time at all.

1/2 cup chopped onion
2 tablespoons butter
3 cups cubed peeled potatoes
1 can (14-1/2 ounces) beef broth
1 cup chopped carrots
1/2 teaspoon salt
1/4 teaspoon pepper
6 ounces cooked corned beef brisket, chopped (about 1-1/2 cups)
2 tablespoons minced fresh parsley
1 cup (4 ounces) shredded Swiss cheese

In a large skillet, saute onion in butter until tender. Stir in the potatoes, broth, carrots, salt and pepper. Bring to a boil. Reduce heat to medium; cover and cook for 20-25 minutes or until vegetables are tender and most of the liquid is absorbed.

Stir in corned beef and parsley; heat through. Sprinkle with cheese. Remove from heat. Cover and let stand for 5 minutes or until cheese is melted. **Yield:** 4 servings.

Cooking for Two

WHEN it's just the two of you at the table, you don't have to prepare crowd-size recipes that result in a week's worth of leftovers. Rely on the conveniently pared-down recipes here!

With mouth-watering dishes such as Mom's Meat Loaf, Garlic Tomato Soup, Dutch Potatoes and Cranberry Pear Cobblers, you'll see that a smaller recipe yield can still mean big taste.

Cinnamon Apple Wraps

(Pictured below)

Prep: 20 min. **Bake:** 30 min. + standing

I love to bake but don't always have reason to prepare a huge batch. I scaled down this apple dessert recipe to serve just the two of us. —Linda Nealley, Newburgh, Maine

3/4 cup all-purpose flour
1/2 teaspoon salt
1/4 cup shortening
2 to 3 tablespoons cold water
2 tablespoons butter, melted, *divided*
2 tablespoons sugar
1/2 teaspoon ground cinnamon
1 large apple, peeled and quartered

In a bowl, combine flour and salt; cut in shortening until crumbly. Gradually add water, tossing with a fork until a ball forms. On a lightly floured surface, roll out pastry into a 10-in. square; brush with 1 tablespoon butter. Fold into thirds. Roll into a 10-in. x 6-in. rectangle; cut lengthwise into four strips. Brush with butter.

Combine sugar and cinnamon; sprinkle half over the strips. Place an apple wedge on each; wrap pastry around apple. Line a baking sheet with foil and coat the foil with cooking spray.

Place wraps on prepared pan. Brush with remaining butter; sprinkle with remaining cinnamon-sugar. Bake at 400° for 28-32 minutes or until golden brown. Serve warm. **Yield:** 2 servings.

Cinnamon Apple Wraps

Raisin Waldorf Salad

Raisin Waldorf Salad

(Pictured above)

Prep: 15 min. + chilling

While experimenting with leftover ingredients, I came up with this refreshing salad. Friends have said it's the best they've eaten! —Diana Stucky, Castle Rock, Colorado

3 tablespoons spreadable cream cheese
3 tablespoons mayonnaise
2 tablespoons confectioners' sugar
2 tablespoons whipped topping
1 large unpeeled red apple, cut into 3/4-inch pieces
1/4 cup raisins
1/4 cup chopped pecans
2 tablespoons sliced celery

In a small mixing bowl, beat the cream cheese, mayonnaise, confectioners' sugar and whipped topping until blended. Stir in apple, raisins, pecans and celery. Transfer to a serving bowl. Chill for 1 hour. **Yield:** 2 servings.

A Spin on Salad

A TRADITIONAL Waldorf Salad recipe calls for raw walnuts. However, this classic dish comes in many variations—including Raisin Waldorf Salad (recipe above), which features pecans. Feel free to experiment with different ingredients when making this salad.

Mom's Meat Loaf

(Pictured below)

Prep: 15 min. **Bake:** 40 min.

This is great when you're craving classic meat loaf but not lots of leftovers. You'll love the sage flavor and scrumptious sauce. —*Michelle Beran, Claflin, Kansas*

✓ This recipe includes Nutrition Facts and Diabetic Exchanges.

1 egg
1/4 cup 2% milk
1/3 cup crushed saltines
3 tablespoons chopped onion
1/4 teaspoon salt
1/8 teaspoon rubbed sage
Dash pepper
1/2 pound lean ground beef
1/4 cup ketchup
2 tablespoons brown sugar
1/4 teaspoon Worcestershire sauce

In a bowl, beat the egg. Add milk, cracker crumbs, onion, salt, sage and pepper. Crumble beef over mixture and mix well. Shape into two loaves; place in a shallow baking dish coated with cooking spray.

Combine ketchup, brown sugar and Worcestershire sauce; spoon over loaves. Bake at 350° for 40-45 minutes or until meat is no longer pink and a meat thermometer reads 160°; drain. **Yield:** 2 mini meat loaves.

Nutrition Facts: 1 meat loaf equals 337 calories, 12 g fat (4 g saturated fat), 162 mg cholesterol, 898 mg sodium, 31 g carbohydrate, 1 g fiber, 27 g protein. **Diabetic Exchanges:** 3 lean meat, 2 starch.

Cheesy Hash Browns

(Pictured below)

Prep: 10 min. **Bake:** 35 min.

Frozen hash brown potatoes and canned cream of chicken soup make it a cinch to fix this hash brown casserole. Enjoy it for brunch or as a side dish for dinner.
—*Christy Mahlum, Grand Junction, Michigan*

1/2 cup sour cream
1/3 cup condensed cream of chicken soup, undiluted
2-1/2 cups frozen shredded hash brown potatoes
1 cup (4 ounces) shredded cheddar cheese, *divided*
2 tablespoons chopped onion
1 tablespoon butter, melted
1/8 teaspoon salt
Dash pepper

In a large bowl, combine sour cream and soup. Stir in the potatoes, 1/2 cup cheese, onion, butter, salt and pepper. Pour into a 1-qt. baking dish coated with cooking spray. Sprinkle with remaining cheese.

Cover and bake at 350° for 30 minutes. Uncover; bake 5-10 minutes longer or until bubbly and heated through. **Yield:** 2 servings.

Cheesy Hash Browns
Mom's Meat Loaf

Alfredo Chicken Lasagna

Alfredo Chicken Lasagna

(Pictured above)

Prep: 25 min. **Bake:** 40 min. + standing

This little lasagna bakes in a loaf pan but tastes just as good as full-size versions. Everyone comments on the rich Alfredo sauce and three kinds of cheese.
—Bridgette Monaghan, Masonville, Iowa

6 ounces boneless skinless chicken breast, cut into bite-size pieces
1 cup sliced fresh mushrooms
2 tablespoons chopped onion
1 garlic clove, minced
1 tablespoon olive oil
1 tablespoon all-purpose flour
1 cup Alfredo sauce
3/4 cup 2% cottage cheese
1/4 cup plus 2 tablespoons shredded Parmesan cheese, ***divided***
1 egg, lightly beaten
1/2 teaspoon Italian seasoning
1/2 teaspoon dried parsley flakes
4 lasagna noodles, cooked and drained
1-1/2 cups (6 ounces) shredded part-skim mozzarella cheese

In a large skillet, saute the chicken, mushrooms, onion and garlic in oil until chicken is no longer pink. Stir in flour until blended; stir in Alfredo sauce. Bring to a boil. Reduce heat; simmer, uncovered, for 5 minutes.

In a small bowl, combine the cottage cheese, 1/4 cup Parmesan cheese, egg, Italian seasoning and parsley.

Spread 1/2 cup Alfredo mixture in an 8-in. x 4-in. x 2-in. loaf pan coated with cooking spray. Layer with two noodles (trimmed to fit pan), half of the cottage cheese mixture, 3/4 cup Alfredo mixture and 3/4 cup mozzarella cheese. Sprinkle with the remaining Parmesan cheese. Repeat layers.

Cover and bake at 350° for 30 minutes. Uncover; bake 10 minutes longer or until bubbly. Let stand for 10 minutes before cutting. **Yield:** 3 servings.

Dutch Potatoes

Prep/Total Time: 30 min.

Give mashed potatoes some color and extra nutrition with carrots. Snipped chives are a nice finishing touch for this side dish. *—Perlene Hoekema, Lynden, Washington*

1/4 cup chopped onion
2 teaspoons butter
2 cups cubed peeled potatoes
1 cup sliced fresh carrots
1/4 cup sour cream
1/4 teaspoon salt
Snipped chives

In a small skillet, saute onion in butter for 8-10 minutes or until golden brown. Meanwhile, place potatoes and carrots in a large saucepan and cover with water. Bring to a boil. Reduce heat; cover and cook for 10-15 minutes or until tender. Drain.

In a small mixing bowl, mash potatoes and carrots. Beat in onion, sour cream and salt. Sprinkle with chives. **Yield:** 2 servings.

Garlic Tomato Soup

Prep: 30 min. **Cook:** 30 min.

You'll detect a mellow background flavor of roasted garlic in this rich, creamy tomato soup. Using canned tomatoes and puree makes it a favorite all year long.
—Marilyn Coomer, Louisville, Kentucky

12 garlic cloves, peeled and sliced
1-1/2 teaspoons olive oil
1 can (14-1/2 ounces) diced tomatoes, undrained
1 cup tomato puree
1 pint heavy whipping cream
1/4 teaspoon dried oregano
1/4 teaspoon minced fresh basil
1/4 teaspoon salt
1/8 teaspoon pepper

In a 3-cup baking dish, combine the garlic and oil. Cover and bake at 300° for 25-30 minutes or until lightly browned.

In a large saucepan, bring the garlic, tomatoes and tomato puree to a boil. Reduce heat; cover and simmer for 30 minutes. Add the cream, oregano, basil, salt and pepper. Cool slightly.

Place half of the soup at a time in a blender; cover and process until pureed. Return to the pan; heat through. **Yield:** about 4 cups.

Broccoli Pork Stir-Fry

(Pictured below)

Prep/Total Time: 25 min.

I downsized this convenient one-pot recipe years ago for my husband and me. The stir-fry is delicious, versatile and so easy to double when we're having company.
—Wendy Nuis, Stokes Bay, Ontario

1 package (3 ounces) pork ramen noodles
1 cup warm water
2 teaspoons cornstarch
1/2 teaspoon garlic powder
1/4 teaspoon crushed red pepper flakes
2/3 cup cold water
1-1/2 teaspoons reduced-sodium soy sauce
1 teaspoon white vinegar
4 teaspoons canola oil
1/2 pound pork tenderloin, thinly sliced
6 large fresh mushrooms, sliced
1 cup fresh broccoli florets
1/2 cup julienned sweet red pepper
3 green onions (white portion only), sliced

Set aside 1 teaspoon of seasoning from seasoning packet (discard remaining seasoning or save for another use). Break noodles into small pieces and place in a microwave-safe dish; add warm water. Microwave, uncovered, on high for 2 minutes. Drain and set aside.

In a small bowl, combine cornstarch, garlic powder, pepper flakes and reserved seasoning. Stir in the cold water, soy sauce and vinegar until smooth; set aside.

In a large skillet or wok, heat oil; stir-fry pork and mushrooms for 5 minutes. Add broccoli and red pepper. Stir-fry for 4-5 minutes or until vegetables are crisp-tender and pork is no longer pink. Stir cornstarch mixture and stir into skillet. Add noodles and onions. Bring to a boil; cook and stir for 2 minutes or until thickened. **Yield:** 2 servings.

Editor's Note: This recipe was tested in a 1,100-watt microwave.

Broccoli Pork Stir-Fry

Cranberry Pear Cobblers

Cranberry Pear Cobblers

(Pictured above)

Prep: 15 min. **Bake:** 45 min.

These individual cranberry-and-pear desserts from our Test Kitchen feature a hint of ginger and cinnamon. Serve them warm with ice cream as an added treat.

2 small pears, peeled and cut into 3/4-inch pieces
1/4 cup dried cranberries
3 tablespoons sugar
1-1/2 teaspoons all-purpose flour
1 teaspoon grated fresh gingerroot
1/4 teaspoon ground cinnamon
1 tablespoon butter

TOPPING:

3 tablespoons sugar
1 teaspoon grated fresh gingerroot
1/2 cup all-purpose flour
1/4 teaspoon baking soda
1/8 teaspoon salt
8 teaspoons cold butter
1/4 cup 1% buttermilk

In a bowl, combine the first six ingredients. Spoon into two 10-oz. custard cups coated with cooking spray. Dot with butter. Bake at 350° for 15-20 minutes or until hot and bubbly.

Combine sugar and ginger in a blender; cover and process until crumbly. Set aside 1-1/2 teaspoons of the mixture. Add flour, baking soda and salt to the blender; cover and process for 20 seconds or until combined. Add butter; process until mixture resembles coarse crumbs. Transfer to a small bowl; stir in buttermilk.

Drop by rounded tablespoonfuls onto hot fruit filling; sprinkle with reserved sugar mixture. Bake for 30-35 minutes or until topping is golden brown. Serve warm. **Yield:** 2 servings.

General Recipe Index

This handy index lists every recipe by food category, major ingredient and/or cooking method, so you can easily locate recipes to suit your needs.

APPETIZERS & SNACKS

Appetizers

✓Asparagus Ham Roll-Ups, 84
✓Bacon-Wrapped Appetizers, 97
Beef-Stuffed Crescents, 283
Beer-Battered Potato Wedges, 266
Beer Cheese in a Bread Bowl, 279
Best Barbecue Wings, 280
Bloodshot Eyeballs, 33
Canadian Bacon-Stuffed Mushrooms, 282
✓Cheese-Stuffed Jalapenos, 296
✓Chunky Herbed Pizza Dip, 274
Crab Cheese Fondue, 267
✓Crab Crescents, 91
✓Cranberry Chili Meatballs, 37
Crunchy Monster Claws, 35
Delightful Deviled Eggs, 274
Dijon-Bacon Dip for Pretzels, 264
Festive Feta Cheese Ball, 280
Fiesta Cream Cheese Spread, 279
Fluffy Apple Dip, 75
✓Fresh Fruit Salsa, 275
Italian Egg Rolls, 276
✓Jalapeno Wontons, 265
✓Lemon Fruit Dip, 100
✓Meatballs in Plum Sauce, 282
Mediterranean Dip with Pita Chips, 276
✓Mexican Salsa Pizza, 87
Parmesan-Coated Brie, 106
Patio Pizza, 267
Pepperoni Pizza Twists, 278
✓Pesto Bruschetta, 94
Pizza Fondue, 264
Pizza Loaf, 275
✓Roasted Red Pepper Hummus, 278
✓Sage Shrimp Skewers, 306
✓Salami Roll-Ups, 87
Sausage-Stuffed Mushrooms, 86
✓Shrimp Appetizers with Seafood Sauce, 281
✓Shrimp Canapes, 93
Sloppy Joe Nachos, 265
✓Smoked Salmon Pinwheels, 266
Spicy Crab Dip, 283
Spinach Artichoke-Stuffed Mushrooms, 274
✓Strawberry Salsa, 29
Stromboli Slices, 276
Super Nacho Appetizer, 282
Sweet 'n' Tangy Chicken Wings, 165
Szechwan Chicken Wings, 280
Taco Dip, 281
Veggie Ham Crescent Wreath, 277
Yummy Mummy with Veggie Dip, 31

Snacks

Caramel Apple Snack Mix, 277
Chili Snack Mix, 279
✓Fruit Juice Pops, 79
✓Garlic Pumpkin Seeds, 271
✓Homemade Fudge Pops, 73
Maple Mocha Pops, 75
Mozzarella Rye Snacks, 96
✓Orange Ice Cream Pops, 74
Pretzel Cereal Crunch, 39
Scooter Snacks, 72
✓Star Pastry Snacks, 29

APPLES

✓Apple Blueberry Crisp, 214
Apple Bread Pudding, 225
✓Apple Butter Mix, 171
✓Apple Cherry Punch, 171
✓Apple Cherry Salad, 82
✓Apple Salad, 101
Apple Spice Waffles, 47
Apple-Spiced Pork, 196
Apple Stuffing, 144
Bacon-Apple Cider Biscuits, 293
Baked Apple French Toast, 174
Cinnamon Apple Wraps, 312
✓Cinnamon Orange Cider, 270
Crescent Apple Dessert, 222
Deep-Dish Apple Pie, 224
Fluffy Apple Dip, 75
Pork Chops with Apple Dressing, 205
Raisin Waldorf Salad, 312

APRICOTS

Apricot Bars, 215
✓Apricot Cheesecake Tarts, 221
Curried Apricot Couscous, 55

ARTICHOKES

Artichoke Chicken Fettuccine, 206
Artichoke Shrimp Bake, 251
Herbed Artichoke Cheese Tortellini, 192
Spinach Artichoke-Stuffed Mushrooms, 274

ASPARAGUS

✓Asparagus Ham Roll-Ups, 84
✓Roasted Asparagus, 8
Salami Asparagus Salad, 137

✓Recipe includes Nutrition Facts and Diabetic Exchanges

Stir-Fried Asparagus, 52
Tangy Asparagus Potato Salad, 294

AVOCADOS
✓Almond-Avocado Tossed Salad, 269
Avocado Chicken Pitas, 195
Avocado Tomato Salad, 57
Taco Avocado Wraps, 189

BACON *(see Ham & Bacon)*

BANANAS
Chocolate Banana Smoothies, 50
Cranberry Banana Bread, 152
Frozen Banana Split Pie, 227
Peanut Butter Banana Oatmeal, 173
✓Toasted PB & Banana Sandwiches, 180

BARS & BROWNIES
Apricot Bars, 215
Black Cat Brownie, 32
✓Buckeye Bars, 96
✓Caramel Cashew Chewies, 74
✓Coconut Brownies, 96
Ghostly Graveyard, 34
Mint Sundae Brownie Squares, 213
Minty Cream Cheese Bars, 211
✓Pecan Shortbread Diamonds, 225

BEANS & LENTILS
Bacon-Almond Green Beans, 138
Baked Beans with Ham, 106
✓Beef and Three-Bean Chili, 161
Black Bean Burritos, 199
✓Black Bean Pineapple Salad, 103
Brisket 'n' Bean Burritos, 164
✓Citrus Green Beans, 121
✓Garbanzo Salad, 258
✓Gingered Green Bean Salad, 259
✓Green Bean Ham Quiche, 174
Green Beans in Beer Sauce, 130
Herbed Green Beans, 67
Hot Dog Bean Soup, 101
In-a-Flash Beans, 12
✓Lemon-Pepper Green Beans, 23
Sausage and Bean Soup, 187
Sausage & Beans with Rice, 247
✓Savory Bean & Tomato Salad, 140
Vegetable Lentil Soup, 163
✓White Chili, 104

BEEF *(also see Ground Beef)*
Main Dishes
Beef Fried Rice, 118
Brisket 'n' Bean Burritos, 164
Burgundy Beef, 160
Glazed Corned Beef Dinner, 162
✓Grilled Asian Flank Steak, 235
Grilled Beef Fajitas, 115
Grilled Sirloin Steaks, 117
Hearty Short Ribs, 164
Marinated Beef Tenderloins, 58
Mushroom 'n' Steak Stroganoff, 167
Mushroom Steak 'n' Linguine, 114
Pineapple Beef Kabobs, 305
Pita Fajitas, 206
Reuben Casserole, 243
Slow Cooker Beef Brisket, 167
Slow Cooker Chuck Roast, 159
Smothered Round Steak, 166
✓Steak with Orange-Thyme Sauce, 195
Swiss Corned Beef Hash, 311
✓Teriyaki Beef Tenderloin, 256
Salads
Grilled Steak Tossed Salad, 135
Spicy Teriyaki Beef Salad, 131
Sandwiches
Flank Steak Sandwiches, 189
Hearty Open-Faced Sandwiches, 180
Portobello Roast Beef Hoagies, 10
Texas Toast Steak Sandwiches, 62
Soups
✓Beef and Three-Bean Chili, 161
Stovetop Beef Stew, 182

BEVERAGES
✓Apple Cherry Punch, 171
Chai Tea Latte, 177
Chocolate Banana Smoothies, 50
✓Cinnamon Orange Cider, 270
Ghoul Punch, 33
Ogre Eyes Hot Cocoa, 30
Pineapple Shakes, 102
✓Rosy Rhubarb Punch, 173
✓Tropical Fruit Smoothies, 104

BLUEBERRIES
✓Apple Blueberry Crisp, 214
✓Berry Yogurt Cups, 78
Blueberry Peach Fool, 227
Blueberry-Poppy Seed Brunch Cake, 172
Turkey Salad with Blueberry Vinaigrette, 136

BREADS & ROLLS
Bacon-Apple Cider Biscuits, 293
Bacon Spinach Muffins, 155
Basil-Garlic Cheese Bread, 65
Caraway Beer Bread, 149
Cinnamon Raisin Bread, 153
Cinnamon Raisin Coffee Cake, 149

✓Recipe includes Nutrition Facts and Diabetic Exchanges

BREADS & ROLLS *(continued)*
Cranberry Banana Bread, 152
Creamy Pumpkin-Filled Biscuits, 148
✓Fresh Herb Flat Bread, 153
Garlic-Cheese Crescent Rolls, 151
Garlic-Sesame Pita Chips, 44
Iced Raisin Biscuits, 292
Mini Toffee Rolls, 149
Onion Cheese Biscuits, 151
Parmesan Walnut Muffins, 111
Peach Cobbler Coffee Cake, 154
✓Pesto Parmesan Bread, 150
✓Pull-Apart Caramel Coffee Cake, 152
Pumpkin Oat Muffins, 150
Rhubarb Lemon Muffins, 155
Savory Parmesan Sticks, 68
✓Sour Cream & Chive Biscuits, 155
✓Squash Corn Bread, 233
Surprise Monkey Bread, 148
Sweet & Savory Breadsticks, 120
Three-Cheese Garlic Bread, 46

BREAKFAST & BRUNCH
Amaretto Peach Oatmeal, 174
Andouille Egg Burritos, 176
✓Apple Butter Mix, 171
✓Apple Cherry Punch, 171
Apple Spice Waffles, 47
Bacon Spinach Strata, 235
Baked Apple French Toast, 174
Blueberry-Poppy Seed Brunch Cake, 172
Breakfast Eggs in Foil Bowls, 27
Breakfast Pizza, 172
Brunch Egg Burritos, 170
Chai Tea Latte, 177
Chicken Taco Quiche, 230
Colorful Bacon & Egg Bake, 176
✓Green Bean Ham Quiche, 174
Hearty Breakfast Egg Bake, 234
Maple Oatmeal with Dried Fruit, 173
Mushroom Quiche Lorraine, 177
Nutmeg Syrup, 175
Overnight Raisin French Toast, 232
Peanut Butter Banana Oatmeal, 173
Pork Sausage Patties, 47
Pumpkin Waffles with Orange Walnut Butter, 175
✓Rosy Rhubarb Punch, 173
✓Silver Dollar Oat Pancakes, 76
✓Strawberry Bruschetta, 176
Walnut Fruit Salad, 170
Weekend Breakfast Bake, 173

BROCCOLI
✓Broccoli Cheese Soup, 261
Broccoli Cheese Tortellini, 204
Broccoli Pork Stir-Fry, 315
✓Broccoli Side Dish, 114
Broccoli with Smoked Almonds, 46
Crouton-Topped Broccoli, 107
Elegant Broccoli, 54
Fresh Broccoli Salad, 62
Saucy Chicken and Florets, 202

BRUSSELS SPROUTS
Crumb-Topped Brussels Sprouts, 64
✓Pimiento Brussels Sprouts, 130

CABBAGE & SAUERKRAUT
Calypso Coleslaw, 104
Fruity Coleslaw, 117
Reuben Casserole, 243
Second-Chance Reubens, 308
Sweet 'n' Sour Coleslaw, 14
Turkey Cabbage Bake, 247

CAKES & CUPCAKES
✓Angel Food Cake with Fruit, 258
Bat Cupcakes, 32
✓Cake with Pineapple Pudding, 16
Chocolate Cake with Coconut Sauce, 10
Chocolate Peanut Butter Cake, 216
Mice Cupcakes, 79
Pecan Pear Torte, 216
Poppy Seed Citrus Cake, 218
Raisin Sauce for Pound Cake, 45
Strawberry Pound Cake Dessert, 12
Surprise Spice Cake, 82
Vanilla Cake with Raspberries, 118

CANDY
✓Chocolate-Mallow Peanut Candy, 223
Hawaiian Turtle Cups, 91
✓Lemon Fudge, 93
✓Peanut Butter Clusters, 79
✓Pecan Chocolate Candies, 214
✓Pecan Toffee Fudge, 217

CARROTS
Carrot Coins with Thyme, 51
Carrot Tortellini Salad, 138
✓Carrots and Snow Peas, 257
✓Mango-Chutney Baby Carrots, 66

CASSEROLES
Alfredo Chicken Lasagna, 314
Artichoke Shrimp Bake, 251
Bacon Spinach Strata, 235
Beef Potato Bake, 237
Bow Tie Ham Bake, 232
Chicken Lasagna, 247
Chicken Penne Casserole, 242
Chicken Tater Bake, 233
Chicken Tortilla Bake, 115
Colorful Bacon & Egg Bake, 176
Crescent Turkey Casserole, 36
Ground Beef Noodle Bake, 251
Ground Beef Spiral Bake, 230
Ham & Cheese Casseroles, 233
Ham Ravioli Bake, 244
Hearty Breakfast Egg Bake, 234

✓Recipe includes Nutrition Facts and Diabetic Exchanges

Marvelous Shells 'n' Cheese, 242
Meatless Spinach Lasagna, 250
Meaty Corn Bread Casserole, 246
Mostaccioli Beef Casserole, 240
Nacho Cheese Beef Bake, 245
Penne Chicken with Sun-Dried Tomatoes, 248
Pizza Noodle Bake, 74
Potluck Ham and Pasta, 249
Reuben Casserole, 243
Sausage & Beans with Rice, 247
Sneaky Lasagna, 246
Southwest Creamy Pasta Bake, 250
Spaghetti Beef Casserole, 234
Sweet Potato Sausage Casserole, 241
Three-Cheese Lasagna, 231
Tortilla Lasagna, 245
Turkey Cabbage Bake, 247
Upside-Down Pizza Bake, 72
✓Veggie Lasagna, 236
Weekend Breakfast Bake, 173

CHEESE

✓Apricot Cheesecake Tarts, 221
Bacon-Cheddar Stuffed Potatoes, 294
Bacon Cheeseburger Salad, 122
Baked Parmesan Roughy, 63
Basil-Garlic Cheese Bread, 65
Beer Cheese in a Bread Bowl, 279
Blue Cheese Pear Salad, 107
Brie Mashed Potatoes, 25
✓Broccoli Cheese Soup, 261
Cheese and Chicken Enchiladas, 60
✓Cheese-Stuffed Jalapenos, 296
Cheesy Hash Browns, 313
Chocolate Cherry Cheesecake, 219
Crab Cheese Fondue, 267
Festive Feta Cheese Ball, 280
Feta Salmon Salad, 139
Fiesta Cream Cheese Spread, 279
Frozen Raspberry Cheesecake, 210
Garlic-Cheese Crescent Rolls, 151
Ham & Cheese Casseroles, 233
Ham and Cheese Loaf, 185
Ham 'n' Cheese Pasta, 117
Lemon Shrimp with Parmesan Rice, 205
Marvelous Shells 'n' Cheese, 242
Minty Cream Cheese Bars, 211
Mom's Blue Cheese Dressing, 53
Mozzarella Chicken with Veggies, 200
Mozzarella Rye Snacks, 96
Mushroom Feta Pasta, 59
Mushroom Swiss Burgers, 186
Nacho Cheese Beef Bake, 245
Onion Cheese Biscuits, 151
Orzo with Parmesan & Basil, 56
Parmesan-Coated Brie, 106
Parmesan Pork Chops, 54
Parmesan Walnut Muffins, 111
Party Time Mini Cheeseburgers, 270
✓Pesto Parmesan Bread, 150
Pizza Fondue, 264
Savory Parmesan Sticks, 68
Skillet Mac & Cheese, 89
Swiss Corned Beef Hash, 311
Taco Dip, 281
Tasty Mozzarella Chicken, 240
Three-Cheese Garlic Bread, 46
Three-Cheese Lasagna, 231
Tomato Cheese Pizza, 201
Zucchini Parmesan, 142

CHERRIES

✓Apple Cherry Punch, 171
✓Apple Cherry Salad, 82
✓Bing Cherry Sherbet, 86
Cherry-Stuffed Pork Chops, 290
Chocolate Cherry Cheesecake, 219
Easy Cherry Strudels, 226

CHICKEN

Appetizers

Best Barbecue Wings, 280
Crunchy Monster Claws, 35
Sweet 'n' Tangy Chicken Wings, 165
Szechwan Chicken Wings, 280

Main Dishes

Alfredo Chicken Lasagna, 314
Artichoke Chicken Fettuccine, 206
Avocado Chicken Pitas, 195
Bacon Chicken Roll-Ups, 88
Breaded Chicken Tenders with Noodles, 78
Cheese and Chicken Enchiladas, 60
Chicken Alfredo Pizza, 243
Chicken & Kielbasa with Curried Rice, 125
Chicken-Bow Tie Primavera, 202
Chicken Lasagna, 247
Chicken Lo Mein, 287
Chicken Marsala with Pasta, 197
Chicken Merlot with Mushrooms, 166
Chicken over Curly Noodles, 114
Chicken Pasta Toss, 51
Chicken Penne Casserole, 242
Chicken Pesto Pasta, 68
Chicken Potpies, 232
Chicken Spinach Manicotti, 249
Chicken Taco Quiche, 230
Chicken Tater Bake, 233
Chicken Tortilla Bake, 115
Chipotle Chicken Fajitas, 304
Colorful Chicken Pizza, 53
Country Fried Chicken, 310
Creamy Spinach Chicken Dinner, 123
Creamy Tarragon Chicken, 110
Crumb-Coated Ranch Chicken, 83

✓Recipe includes Nutrition Facts and Diabetic Exchanges

CHICKEN
Main Dishes *(continued)*
Curry Chicken, 199
Dijon Crumb Chicken, 66
Enchilada Chicken Pizza, 250
✓Garlic Pineapple Chicken, 257
✓Garlic Ranch Chicken, 124
Garlic-Roasted Chicken and Potatoes, 244
Golden Chicken Nuggets, 77
Golden Chicken with Rice, 89
Greek Chicken Dinner, 163
Greek Lemon Chicken, 97
Hearty Chicken Pesto Pizzas, 203
Italian Chicken, 158
Lemon Chicken, 160
Lemon Chicken with Rice, 116
✓Lemon Teriyaki Chicken, 46
Mandarin Chicken Stir-Fry, 288
✓Maple-Glazed Chicken, 52
✓Marinated Grilled Chicken, 306
Mayonnaise Lovers' Chicken, 307
Mexican Chicken Penne, 200
Monterey Barbecued Chicken, 12
Mozzarella Chicken with Veggies, 200
Oregano Roasting Chicken, 309
Peachy Barbecue Chicken, 236
✓Pear Chutney Chicken, 260
Penne Chicken with Sun-Dried Tomatoes, 248
✓Pepper Jack Chicken, 158
Ramen Chicken 'n' Vegetables, 204
Saucy Chicken and Florets, 202
Saucy Mushroom Chicken, 310
Southwest Creamy Pasta Bake, 250
Southwest Smothered Chicken, 192
Spicy Bronzed Chicken, 57
Tasty Mozzarella Chicken, 240
Zippy Paprika Chicken, 8
Salads
Chicken Caesar Salad, 143
Hot Chicken Salad, 142
Layered Italian Chicken Salad, 141
Layered Southwestern Chicken Salad, 144
Sandwiches
Cashew Chicken Salad Sandwiches, 189
Chicken Alfredo Sandwiches, 188
Chicken Pesto Wraps, 182
Easy Chicken Melts, 185
Spicy Chicken Bundles, 183
Soups
Chicken Wild Rice Chowder, 111
Chunky Chicken Soup, 126
Tortilla-Vegetable Chicken Soup, 309
✓White Chili, 104

CHOCOLATE
Bat Cupcakes, 32
Black Cat Brownie, 32
✓Buckeye Bars, 96
Chocolate Berry Freeze, 226
Chocolate Cake with Coconut Sauce, 10
Chocolate Cherry Cheesecake, 219
Chocolate Chip Cookie Delight, 268
Chocolate Chip Strawberry Shortcakes, 211
✓Chocolate-Dipped Cranberry Cookies, 40
Chocolate-Filled Crescents, 222
✓Chocolate-Mallow Peanut Candy, 223
Chocolate Peanut Butter Cake, 216
✓Chocolate-Peanut Butter Cookies, 85
Chocolate Reindeer Cookies, 40
Chocolate Silk Pie, 210
Chocolate Wafer Ice Cream, 90
✓Christmas Mice Cookies, 38
✓Coconut Brownies, 96
Fluffy Chocolate Pie, 24
✓Homemade Fudge Pops, 73
Mint Sundae Brownie Squares, 213
Ogre Eyes Hot Cocoa, 30
Peanut Butter S'Mores, 26
✓Pecan Chocolate Candies, 214
✓Pecan Toffee Fudge, 217
Smooth Chocolate Fondue, 103

COCONUT
Chocolate Banana Smoothies, 50
Chocolate Cake with Coconut Sauce, 10
✓Coconut Brownies, 96
Coconut Pistachio Pie, 212
✓Polka-Dot Macaroons, 24

COOKIES *(also see Bars & Brownies)*
✓Chocolate-Dipped Cranberry Cookies, 40
✓Chocolate-Peanut Butter Cookies, 85
Chocolate Reindeer Cookies, 40
✓Christmas Mice Cookies, 38
✓Cookie Pops, 78
✓Crisp Lemon Tea Cookies, 41
Gruesome Green Toes, 31
✓Oatmeal Cranberry Cookie Mix, 39
✓Peanut Butter Jumbos, 77
Peanut Butter S'Mores, 26
✓Peppermint Meltaways, 301
✓Polka-Dot Macaroons, 24
Strawberry Valentine Cookies, 22
✓Thumbprint Cookies, 41

✓Recipe includes Nutrition Facts and Diabetic Exchanges

CORN
Buttery-Onion Corn on the Cob, 89
Calico Corn Cakes, 135
✓Confetti Corn, 48
Confetti Corn Salad, 60
Corn on the Cob with Lemon-Pepper Butter, 94
Mushroom Corn Chowder, 180

CRANBERRIES
✓Chocolate-Dipped Cranberry Cookies, 40
Cranberry Banana Bread, 152
✓Cranberry Chili Meatballs, 37
Cranberry Pear Cobblers, 315
Cranberry-Pineapple Pork Chops, 61
Cranberry Pork Chops with Rice, 37
✓Oatmeal Cranberry Cookie Mix, 39

CUCUMBERS
Anytime Cucumber Salad, 58
Tomato Cucumber Salad, 95

DESSERTS *(also see Bars & Brownies; Cakes & Cupcakes; Candy; Cookies; Pies)*
✓Apple Blueberry Crisp, 214
Apple Bread Pudding, 225
✓Apricot Cheesecake Tarts, 221
Berry Rhubarb Fool, 92
✓Berry Yogurt Cups, 78
✓Bing Cherry Sherbet, 86
Blueberry Peach Fool, 227
Chocolate Berry Freeze, 226
Chocolate Cherry Cheesecake, 219
Chocolate Chip Cookie Delight, 268
Chocolate Chip Strawberry Shortcakes, 211
Chocolate-Filled Crescents, 222
Chocolate Wafer Ice Cream, 90
Cinnamon Apple Wraps, 312
Citrus Raspberry Shortcakes, 223
Cranberry Pear Cobblers, 315
Crescent Apple Dessert, 222
Dream Clouds, 18
Easy Cherry Strudels, 226
✓Fresh Blackberry Cobbler, 220
Frosty Mallow Fruit Dessert, 221
Frozen Raspberry Cheesecake, 210
Fruit Pizza, 218
✓Gelatin Parfaits, 271
Lime Poppy Seed Shortcakes, 224
Nutty Cookies & Cream Dessert, 215
✓Peaches with Lemon Cream, 226
Peppermint Stick Sauce, 90
Rainbow Sherbet Dessert, 213
Smooth Chocolate Fondue, 103
Strawberry Sundae Sauce, 223
Strawberry Trifle, 214
Sweetened Whipped Cream, 220
Swirled Sherbet Dessert, 217
Vanilla Chip Dessert, 22
Watermelon Bombe, 212

EGGS
Andouille Egg Burritos, 176
Bacon Spinach Strata, 235
Bloodshot Eyeballs, 33
Breakfast Eggs in Foil Bowls, 27
Breakfast Pizza, 172
Brunch Egg Burritos, 170
Chicken Taco Quiche, 230
Colorful Bacon & Egg Bake, 176
Delightful Deviled Eggs, 274
✓Green Bean Ham Quiche, 174
Hearty Breakfast Egg Bake, 234
Mushroom Quiche Lorraine, 177
Weekend Breakfast Bake, 173

FISH *(also see Seafood)*
Appetizers
✓Smoked Salmon Pinwheels, 266
Main Dishes
Almond-Crusted Salmon, 196
Baked Parmesan Roughy, 63
Company Swordfish, 248
✓Creole Baked Tilapia, 255
Lemon Butter Salmon, 55
Lemon Parsley Swordfish, 59
Mustard Fried Catfish, 14
✓Orange Roughy with Rice, 113
Orange Salmon with Rice, 97
Salmon with Curry Chutney Sauce, 48
Tilapia Wraps, 201
Tuna Crescent Ring, 207
✓Tuna Veggie Kabobs, 254
Tuna Veggie Macaroni, 203
✓Vegetable Fish Dinner, 193
Salads
Feta Salmon Salad, 139
Tuna-Stuffed Tomatoes, 193
Sandwiches
Fish Sandwich Loaf, 112
Hot Tuna Sandwiches, 123

FRUIT *(also see specific kinds)*
✓Angel Food Cake with Fruit, 258
✓Fresh Fruit Salsa, 275
Frosty Mallow Fruit Dessert, 221
Fruit Pizza, 218
Fruit-Topped Pork Chops and Rice, 202
Fruity Coleslaw, 117
Maple Oatmeal with Dried Fruit, 173
✓Tropical Fruit Smoothies, 104
Walnut Fruit Salad, 170

GRILLED RECIPES
Appetizers
Best Barbecue Wings, 280
✓Cheese-Stuffed Jalapenos, 296
✓Sage Shrimp Skewers, 306
Desserts
✓Peaches with Lemon Cream, 226
Peanut Butter S'Mores, 26

✓Recipe includes Nutrition Facts and Diabetic Exchanges

GRILLED RECIPES *(continued)*
Main Dishes
Barbecued Pork Chops, 194
Chipotle Chicken Fajitas, 304
✓Chipotle Pork Tenderloins, 306
Greek Lemon Chicken, 97
✓Grilled Asian Flank Steak, 235
Grilled Beef Fajitas, 115
✓Grilled Pork Chops with Cilantro Salsa, 305
✓Grilled Pork Tenderloin, 95
Grilled Sirloin Steaks, 117
Marinated Beef Tenderloins, 58
✓Marinated Grilled Chicken, 306
Mayonnaise Lovers' Chicken, 307
Pineapple Beef Kabobs, 305
Pork Tenderloin Fajitas, 121
Summer Sausage Hobo Packets, 26
Sweet 'n' Spicy Country Ribs, 234
Tomato-Basil Shrimp Skewers, 304
✓Tuna Veggie Kabobs, 254
Salads
Feta Salmon Salad, 139
Grilled Caesar Salad, 27
Sandwiches
Flank Steak Sandwiches, 189
Grilled Bacon Burgers, 181
Guacamole Burgers, 69
Turkey Brats with Slaw, 268
Side Dishes
Corn on the Cob with Lemon-Pepper Butter, 94
✓Dilly Grilled Veggies, 140
Grilled Sweet Onions, 132

GROUND BEEF
Appetizers
Beef-Stuffed Crescents, 283
✓Cranberry Chili Meatballs, 37
✓Meatballs in Plum Sauce, 282
Pizza Loaf, 275
Sloppy Joe Nachos, 265
Super Nacho Appetizer, 282
Main Dishes
Beef Fettuccine Dinner, 197
Beef Potato Bake, 237
Beef-Stuffed Zucchini, 120
✓Beefy Tomato Rice Skillet, 261
Burritos Made Easy, 193
✓Chili Rice Dinner, 260
✓Chunky Pasta Sauce, 161
✓Greek-Style Supper, 44
Ground Beef Noodle Bake, 251
Ground Beef Spiral Bake, 230
Hearty Penne Beef, 124
Jack-o'-Lantern Sloppy Joe Pie, 34
Meaty Corn Bread Casserole, 246
✓Mom's Meat Loaf, 313
Mostaccioli Beef Casserole, 240
Nacho Cheese Beef Bake, 245
Pizza Noodle Bake, 74
Ravioli Skillet, 111
Sloppy Joe Hash Browns, 126
Sneaky Lasagna, 246
South Dakota Meat Loaf Makeover, 291
Spaghetti Beef Casserole, 234
Stuffed Peppers for Four, 112
Taco Macaroni, 75
Three-Cheese Lasagna, 231
Tortilla Lasagna, 245
✓Two-Meat Spaghetti Sauce, 65
✓Zesty Horseradish Meat Loaf, 308
Salads
Bacon Cheeseburger Salad, 122
Taco Salad, 134
Taco Salad Waffles, 76
Sandwiches
Change-of-Pace Burgers, 50
Grilled Bacon Burgers, 181
Guacamole Burgers, 69
Italian Patty Melts, 127
Mushroom Swiss Burgers, 186
Party Time Mini Cheeseburgers, 270
Second-Chance Reubens, 308
Slow Cooker Sloppy Joes, 162
Soup
Veggie Meatball Soup, 159

HAM & BACON
Appetizers
✓Asparagus Ham Roll-Ups, 84
✓Bacon-Wrapped Appetizers, 97
Canadian Bacon-Stuffed Mushrooms, 282
Dijon-Bacon Dip for Pretzels, 264
Veggie Ham Crescent Wreath, 277
Breakfast & Brunch
Bacon Spinach Strata, 235
Colorful Bacon & Egg Bake, 176
✓Green Bean Ham Quiche, 174
Main Dishes
Bacon Chicken Roll-Ups, 88
Baked Beans with Ham, 106
Beer-Glazed Ham, 25
Bow Tie Ham Bake, 232
Cider-Glazed Ham, 159
Ham & Cheese Casseroles, 233
Ham 'n' Cheese Pasta, 117
Ham Fettuccine, 204
Ham Ravioli Bake, 244
Potluck Ham and Pasta, 249
Zucchini Crescent Pie, 241
Salads
Bacon Cheeseburger Salad, 122
Bacon Potato Salad, 230
Sandwiches
Baked Ham Salad Sandwiches, 183
Barbecued Ham Sandwiches, 187
Cobb Salad Sandwiches, 118
Grilled Bacon Burgers, 181
Ham and Cheese Loaf, 185

✓Recipe includes Nutrition Facts and Diabetic Exchanges

Hearty Open-Faced Sandwiches, 180
Meat 'n' Veggie Pockets, 103
Mini Subs, 73
Side Dishes
Bacon-Almond Green Beans, 138
Bacon-Cheddar Stuffed Potatoes, 294
Soups
Farmhouse Ham Chowder, 188
Golden Potato Soup, 295
Mushroom Corn Chowder, 180

HOT DOGS
Hot Dog Bean Soup, 101
Hot Dog Spaghetti Rings, 90
Squirmy Wormy Sandwiches, 30

LEMONS & LIMES
Citrus Raspberry Shortcakes, 223
✓Citrus Spinach Salad, 260
✓Crisp Lemon Tea Cookies, 41
✓Fluffy Lemon Pie, 257
Greek Lemon Chicken, 97
Lemon Butter Salmon, 55
Lemon Chicken, 160
Lemon Chicken with Rice, 116
✓Lemon Fruit Dip, 100
✓Lemon Fudge, 93
Lemon-Herb Roasted Turkey, 298
Lemon Parsley Swordfish, 59
✓Lemon Rice, 49
Lemon Shrimp with Parmesan Rice, 205
✓Lemon Teriyaki Chicken, 46
Lime Poppy Seed Shortcakes, 224
✓Peaches with Lemon Cream, 226
Poppy Seed Citrus Cake, 218
Rhubarb Lemon Muffins, 155

LIMES *(see Lemons)*

MAPLE
✓Maple-Glazed Chicken, 52
Maple Mocha Pops, 75
Maple Oatmeal with Dried Fruit, 173
✓Maple Salad Dressing, 100

MARSHMALLOWS
✓Chocolate-Mallow Peanut Candy, 223
Frosty Mallow Fruit Dessert, 221
Peanut Butter S'Mores, 26

MICROWAVE RECIPES
Appetizers
Beer Cheese in a Bread Bowl, 279
✓Meatballs in Plum Sauce, 282
Spicy Crab Dip, 283
Main Dishes
Baked Beans with Ham, 106
Beef-Stuffed Zucchini, 120
Black Bean Burritos, 199
Cheese and Chicken Enchiladas, 60
Hot Dog Spaghetti Rings, 90
Pork Chops with Apple Dressing, 205
Saucy Chicken and Florets, 202
South Dakota Meat Loaf Makeover, 291
Stuffed Peppers for Four, 112
✓Vegetable Fish Dinner, 193
Side Dishes
Bacon-Cheddar Stuffed Potatoes, 294
✓Broccoli Side Dish, 114
Crouton-Topped Broccoli, 107
Crumb-Topped Brussels Sprouts, 64
Elegant Broccoli, 54
Herbed Green Beans, 67
✓Mango-Chutney Baby Carrots, 66
✓Microwave Acorn Squash, 85
Potato Wedges, 73
Potatoes, Peas & Pearl Onions, 63
Soup
Hot Dog Bean Soup, 101

MINT
Mint Sundae Brownie Squares, 213
Minty Cream Cheese Bars, 211
✓Minty Sugar Snap Peas, 107
✓Peppermint Meltaways, 301
Peppermint Stick Sauce, 90

MUFFINS *(see Breads & Rolls)*

MUSHROOMS
Canadian Bacon-Stuffed Mushrooms, 282
Chicken Merlot with Mushrooms, 166
Mushroom 'n' Steak Stroganoff, 167
Mushroom Corn Chowder, 180
Mushroom Feta Pasta, 59
Mushroom Quiche Lorraine, 177
Mushroom Spinach Salad, 28
Mushroom Steak 'n' Linguine, 114
Mushroom Swiss Burgers, 186
Portobello Roast Beef Hoagies, 10
Saucy Mushroom Chicken, 310
Sausage-Stuffed Mushrooms, 86
Spinach Artichoke-Stuffed Mushrooms, 274

NUTS *(also see Peanut Butter)*
✓Almond-Avocado Tossed Salad, 269

✓Recipe includes Nutrition Facts and Diabetic Exchanges

NUTS *(continued)*
Almond-Crusted Salmon, 196
Almond Rice, 18
Angel Hair with Walnuts, 133
Bacon-Almond Green Beans, 138
Broccoli with Smoked Almonds, 46
✓Caramel Cashew Chewies, 74
Cashew Chicken Salad Sandwiches, 189
✓Chocolate-Mallow Peanut Candy, 223
Coconut Pistachio Pie, 212
Hawaiian Turtle Cups, 91
Nutty Cookies & Cream Dessert, 215
Nutty Pork Fried Rice, 287
Parmesan Walnut Muffins, 111
✓Pecan Chocolate Candies, 214
Pecan Pear Torte, 216
✓Pecan Shortbread Diamonds, 225
✓Pecan Toffee Fudge, 217
✓Pine Nut Salad Dressing, 102
Pumpkin Waffles with Orange Walnut Butter, 175
Walnut Fruit Salad, 170
Walnut Rice, 61

OATS
Amaretto Peach Oatmeal, 174
Maple Oatmeal with Dried Fruit, 173
✓Oatmeal Cranberry Cookie Mix, 39
Peanut Butter Banana Oatmeal, 173
Pumpkin Oat Muffins, 150
✓Silver Dollar Oat Pancakes, 76

ONIONS
Buttery-Onion Corn on the Cob, 89
Grilled Sweet Onions, 132
Onion Cheese Biscuits, 151
✓Pork Chops with Onion Gravy, 49
Potatoes, Peas & Pearl Onions, 63

ORANGES
✓Cinnamon Orange Cider, 270
✓Citrus Green Beans, 121
Citrus Raspberry Shortcakes, 223
✓Citrus Spinach Salad, 260
Dream Clouds, 18
Mandarin Chicken Stir-Fry, 288
Mandarin Romaine Salad, 142
✓Orange Ice Cream Pops, 74
✓Orange-Glazed Beets, 145
Orange Salmon with Rice, 97
Poppy Seed Citrus Cake, 218
✓Pork Roast with Twist of Orange, 165
Pumpkin Waffles with Orange Walnut Butter, 175
✓Steak with Orange-Thyme Sauce, 195

OVEN ENTREES *(also see Casseroles)*
Beef & Ground Beef
Jack-o'-Lantern Sloppy Joe Pie, 34
✓Mom's Meat Loaf, 313
✓Steak with Orange-Thyme Sauce, 195
✓Teriyaki Beef Tenderloin, 256
✓Zesty Horseradish Meat Loaf, 308
Chicken
Avocado Chicken Pitas, 195
Bacon Chicken Roll-Ups, 88
Chicken Alfredo Pizza, 243
Chicken Potpies, 232
Chicken Spinach Manicotti, 249
Colorful Chicken Pizza, 53
Crumb-Coated Ranch Chicken, 83
Enchilada Chicken Pizza, 250
Garlic-Roasted Chicken and Potatoes, 244
Golden Chicken Nuggets, 77
Golden Chicken with Rice, 89
Hearty Chicken Pesto Pizzas, 203
Lemon Chicken with Rice, 116
Oregano Roasting Chicken, 309
Tasty Mozzarella Chicken, 240
Fish & Seafood
Almond-Crusted Salmon, 196
Baked Parmesan Roughy, 63
Company Swordfish, 248
✓Creole Baked Tilapia, 255
Lemon Butter Salmon, 55
Lemon Parsley Swordfish, 59
Seafood Alfredo Baskets, 23
Tuna Crescent Ring, 207
Meatless
Pepper Lover's Pizza, 297
Spinach Pizza, 88
Tomato Cheese Pizza, 201
Pork, Ham & Sausage
Beer-Glazed Ham, 25
Broiled Pork Chops with Mango Sauce, 196
Family-Pleasing Pizza, 16
Pesto Sausage Pizza Makeover, 291
Zucchini Crescent Pie, 241
Turkey
Club-Style Turkey Enchiladas, 36
Lemon-Herb Roasted Turkey, 298

PASTA
Alfredo Chicken Lasagna, 314
Angel Hair with Walnuts, 133
Artichoke Chicken Fettuccine, 206
Beef Fettuccine Dinner, 197
Bow Tie Ham Bake, 232
Breaded Chicken Tenders with Noodles, 78
Broccoli Cheese Tortellini, 204
Carrot Tortellini Salad, 138

✓Recipe includes Nutrition Facts and Diabetic Exchanges

Chicken-Bow Tie Primavera, 202
Chicken Lasagna, 247
Chicken Lo Mein, 287
Chicken Marsala with Pasta, 197
Chicken over Curly Noodles, 114
Chicken Pasta Toss, 51
Chicken Penne Casserole, 242
Chicken Pesto Pasta, 68
Chicken Spinach Manicotti, 249
✓Chunky Pasta Sauce, 161
Creamy Shrimp 'n' Spaghetti, 194
Creamy Spinach Chicken Dinner, 123
Curried Apricot Couscous, 55
Fettuccine with Sausage and Leeks, 82
✓Garden Primavera Fettuccine, 137
Ground Beef Noodle Bake, 251
Ground Beef Spiral Bake, 230
Ham 'n' Cheese Pasta, 117
Ham Fettuccine, 204
Ham Ravioli Bake, 244
Hearty Penne Beef, 124
Hearty Tortellini Salad, 269
Herbed Artichoke Cheese Tortellini, 192
Hot Dog Spaghetti Rings, 90
Kielbasa Bow Tie Skillet, 45
Marvelous Shells 'n' Cheese, 242
Meatless Spinach Lasagna, 250
Mexican Chicken Penne, 200
Mostaccioli Beef Casserole, 240
Mushroom Feta Pasta, 59
Mushroom Steak 'n' Linguine, 114
Orzo with Parmesan & Basil, 56
Penne Chicken with Sun-Dried Tomatoes, 248
Pesto Tortellini Salad, 94
Pizza Noodle Bake, 74
Potluck Ham and Pasta, 249
Ramen Chicken 'n' Vegetables, 204
Ravioli Skillet, 111
Salami Pasta Salad, 143
Seafood Pasta Salad, 137
Skillet Mac & Cheese, 89
Smoked Sausage with Penne and Veggies, 311
Sneaky Lasagna, 246
Southwest Creamy Pasta Bake, 250
Spaghetti Beef Casserole, 234
✓Spinach Pasta Salad, 92
✓Spinach Tortellini Soup, 261
Taco Macaroni, 75
✓Tangy Pasta 'n' Peas, 134
Three-Cheese Lasagna, 231
Tuna Veggie Macaroni, 203
✓Two-Meat Spaghetti Sauce, 65
Vegetable Macaroni Salad, 69
✓Veggie Lasagna, 236

PEACHES

Amaretto Peach Oatmeal, 174
Blueberry Peach Fool, 227
Peach Cobbler Coffee Cake, 154
✓Peaches with Lemon Cream, 226
Peachy Barbecue Chicken, 236

PEANUT BUTTER

Chocolate Peanut Butter Cake, 216
✓Chocolate-Peanut Butter Cookies, 85
Peanut Butter Banana Oatmeal, 173
✓Peanut Butter Clusters, 79
✓Peanut Butter Jumbos, 77
Peanut Butter S'Mores, 26
✓Toasted PB & Banana Sandwiches, 180

PEARS

Blue Cheese Pear Salad, 107
Cranberry Pear Cobblers, 315
Pecan Pear Torte, 216
✓Pear Chutney Chicken, 260

PEAS

✓Carrots and Snow Peas, 257
✓Minty Sugar Snap Peas, 107
Potatoes, Peas & Pearl Onions, 63
✓Tangy Pasta 'n' Peas, 134

PEPPERONI & SALAMI

Appetizers

Pepperoni Pizza Twists, 278
Pizza Fondue, 264
✓Salami Roll-Ups, 87
Stromboli Slices, 276

Main Dishes

Pizza Noodle Bake, 74
✓Two-Meat Spaghetti Sauce, 65

Salads

Antipasto Salad with Basil Dressing, 133
Hearty Tortellini Salad, 269
Salami Asparagus Salad, 137
Salami Pasta Salad, 143

Sandwiches

Zippy Calzones, 67

PEPPERS

✓Cheese-Stuffed Jalapenos, 296
Chipotle Chicken Fajitas, 304
✓Chipotle Pork Tenderloins, 306
Grilled Beef Fajitas, 115
✓Jalapeno Wontons, 265
✓Pepper Jack Chicken, 158
Pepper Lover's Pizza, 297
✓Pepperoncini Arugula Salad, 10
Pita Fajitas, 206
Pork Tenderloin Fajitas, 121
Pretty Pepper Salad, 296
✓Roasted Potatoes and Peppers, 83
✓Roasted Red Pepper Hummus, 278
Stuffed Peppers for Four, 112
Sweet-and-Sour Scallops, 18

PIES

Chocolate Silk Pie, 210
Cinnamon Pumpkin Pie, 219
Coconut Pistachio Pie, 212

✓Recipe includes Nutrition Facts and Diabetic Exchanges

PIES *(continued)*
Coffee Ice Cream Pie, 220
Deep-Dish Apple Pie, 224
Fluffy Chocolate Pie, 24
✓Fluffy Lemon Pie, 257
Frozen Banana Split Pie, 227

PINEAPPLE
✓Black Bean Pineapple Salad, 103
✓Cake with Pineapple Pudding, 16
Cranberry-Pineapple Pork Chops, 61
✓Garlic Pineapple Chicken, 257
Hawaiian Pork Roast, 163
Hawaiian Turtle Cups, 91
✓Honey-Pineapple Sweet Potatoes, 145
Pineapple Beef Kabobs, 305
Pineapple Shakes, 102
Sweet-and-Sour Scallops, 18

PORK *(also see Ham & Bacon; Hot Dogs; Pepperoni & Salami; Sausage)*
Main Dishes
Apple-Spiced Pork, 196
Barbecued Pork Chops, 194
Broccoli Pork Stir-Fry, 315
Broiled Pork Chops with Mango Sauce, 196
Cherry-Stuffed Pork Chops, 290
✓Chipotle Pork Tenderloins, 306
✓Chunky Pasta Sauce, 161
Country Pork Chop Supper, 167
Cranberry-Pineapple Pork Chops, 61
Cranberry Pork Chops with Rice, 37
Creole Pork Chops, 198
Fruit-Topped Pork Chops and Rice, 202
✓Grilled Pork Chops with Cilantro Salsa, 305
✓Grilled Pork Tenderloin, 95
Hawaiian Pork Roast, 163
Nutty Pork Fried Rice, 287
Parmesan Pork Chops, 54
Pizza Pork Chops, 56
Pork Chops with Apple Dressing, 205
✓Pork Chops with Onion Gravy, 49
Pork Chops with Sour Cream Sauce, 206
Pork Medallions with Garlic-Strawberry Sauce, 120
✓Pork Roast with Twist of Orange, 165
Pork Spareribs, 165
Pork Tenderloin Fajitas, 121
Saucy Pork Chops, 200
Slow-Cooked Ribs, 89
Slow Cooker Pork Chops, 166
✓Sweet 'n' Sour Pork Chops, 259
Sweet 'n' Spicy Country Ribs, 234
Sandwiches
✓Pulled Pork Sandwiches, 162
Soup
Hearty Minestrone, 231

POTATOES *(also see Sweet Potatoes)*
Bacon-Cheddar Stuffed Potatoes, 294
Bacon Potato Salad, 230
Beef Potato Bake, 237
Beer-Battered Potato Wedges, 266
Brie Mashed Potatoes, 25
Cheesy Hash Browns, 313
Chicken Tater Bake, 233
Confetti Mashed Potatoes, 136
Creamy Potato Soup, 90
Dijon Scalloped Potatoes, 134
✓Dilled Mashed Potatoes, 84
Dutch Potatoes, 314
Garlic New Potatoes, 14
Garlic-Roasted Chicken and Potatoes, 244
Golden Potato Soup, 295
Loaded Waffle Fries, 50
Mashed Potatoes Supreme, 132
Mashed Potatoes with a Kick, 144
Potato Kielbasa Skillet, 127
Potato Wedges, 73
Potatoes, Peas & Pearl Onions, 63
✓Roasted Potatoes and Peppers, 83
Sausage Pierogi Skillet, 198
Sloppy Joe Hash Browns, 126
Smashed Potatoes, 8
Swiss Corned Beef Hash, 311
Tangy Asparagus Potato Salad, 294

PUMPKIN
Creamy Pumpkin-Filled Biscuits, 148
Pumpkin Oat Muffins, 150
Pumpkin Waffles with Orange Walnut Butter, 175
Cinnamon Pumpkin Pie, 219
✓Garlic Pumpkin Seeds, 271

RAISINS
Cinnamon Raisin Bread, 153
Cinnamon Raisin Coffee Cake, 149
Iced Raisin Biscuits, 292
Overnight Raisin French Toast, 232
Raisin Sauce for Pound Cake, 45
Raisin Waldorf Salad, 312

RASPBERRIES
✓Berry Gelatin Mold, 139
Citrus Raspberry Shortcakes, 223
Frozen Raspberry Cheesecake, 210
✓Raspberry-Turkey Spinach Salad, 141
Vanilla Cake with Raspberries, 118

RHUBARB
Berry Rhubarb Fool, 92

✓Recipe includes Nutrition Facts and Diabetic Exchanges

Rhubarb Lemon Muffins, 155
✓Rosy Rhubarb Punch, 173

RICE
Almond Rice, 18
Beef Fried Rice, 118
✓Beefy Tomato Rice Skillet, 261
✓Cajun Shrimp and Rice, 105
Chicken & Kielbasa with Curried Rice, 125
Chicken Wild Rice Chowder, 111
✓Chili Rice Dinner, 260
Cranberry Pork Chops with Rice, 37
Fruit-Topped Pork Chops and Rice, 202
Golden Chicken with Rice, 89
Jiffy Jambalaya, 121
Lemon Chicken with Rice, 116
✓Lemon Rice, 49
Lemon Shrimp with Parmesan Rice, 205
Mixed Herb Rice, 133
Nutty Pork Fried Rice, 287
✓Orange Roughy with Rice, 113
Orange Salmon with Rice, 97
Sausage & Beans with Rice, 247
Walnut Rice, 61

ROLLS *(see Breads & Rolls)*

SALADS & DRESSINGS
Dressings
✓Maple Salad Dressing, 100
Mom's Blue Cheese Dressing, 53
✓Pine Nut Salad Dressing, 102
Salads
✓Almond-Avocado Tossed Salad, 269
Antipasto Salad with Basil Dressing, 133
Anytime Cucumber Salad, 58
✓Apple Cherry Salad, 82
✓Apple Salad, 101
Avocado Tomato Salad, 57
Bacon Cheeseburger Salad, 122
Bacon Potato Salad, 230
✓Berry Gelatin Mold, 139
✓Black Bean Pineapple Salad, 103
Blue Cheese Pear Salad, 107
Calypso Coleslaw, 104
Carrot Tortellini Salad, 138
Chicken Caesar Salad, 143
✓Citrus Spinach Salad, 260
Confetti Corn Salad, 60
Feta Salmon Salad, 139
Fresh Broccoli Salad, 62
✓Fresh Vegetable Salad, 255
Fruity Coleslaw, 117
✓Garbanzo Salad, 258
✓Gingered Green Bean Salad, 259
Greek Tossed Salad, 138
Grilled Caesar Salad, 27
Grilled Steak Tossed Salad, 135
Hearty Tortellini Salad, 269
Hot Chicken Salad, 142
Italian Side Salad, 112
Italian Spinach Salad, 131
Layered Italian Chicken Salad, 141
Layered Southwestern Chicken Salad, 144
Mandarin Romaine Salad, 142
Mushroom Spinach Salad, 28
✓Pepperoncini Arugula Salad, 10
Pesto Tortellini Salad, 94
Picnic Vegetable Salad, 141
Pretty Pepper Salad, 296
Raisin Waldorf Salad, 312
✓Raspberry-Turkey Spinach Salad, 141
✓Refreshing Shrimp Salad, 119
Salami Asparagus Salad, 137
Salami Pasta Salad, 143
✓Savory Bean & Tomato Salad, 140
Seafood Pasta Salad, 137
Spicy Teriyaki Beef Salad, 131
✓Spinach Pasta Salad, 92
Sweet 'n' Sour Coleslaw, 14
Taco Salad, 134
Taco Salad Waffles, 76
Tangy Asparagus Potato Salad, 294
Tangy Spinach Salad, 16
Tomato Cucumber Salad, 95
Tuna-Stuffed Tomatoes, 193
Turkey Salad with Blueberry Vinaigrette, 136
Vegetable Macaroni Salad, 69
Walnut Fruit Salad, 170
✓Zesty Spinach Salad, 115

SANDWICHES
Baked Ham Salad Sandwiches, 183
Barbecued Ham Sandwiches, 187
Cashew Chicken Salad Sandwiches, 189
Change-of-Pace Burgers, 50
Chicken Alfredo Sandwiches, 188
Chicken Pesto Wraps, 182
Cobb Salad Sandwiches, 118
Easy Chicken Melts, 185
Fish Sandwich Loaf, 112
Flank Steak Sandwiches, 189
Grilled Bacon Burgers, 181
Guacamole Burgers, 69
Ham and Cheese Loaf, 185
Hearty Open-Faced Sandwiches, 180
Hearty Sausage Stromboli, 183
Hot Tuna Sandwiches, 123
Italian Muffuletta, 28
Italian Patty Melts, 127
Meat 'n' Veggie Pockets, 103
Mini Subs, 73
Mushroom Swiss Burgers, 186
Party Time Mini Cheeseburgers, 270
Portobello Roast Beef Hoagies, 10
✓Pulled Pork Sandwiches, 162
Second-Chance Reubens, 308

✓Recipe includes Nutrition Facts and Diabetic Exchanges

SANDWICHES *(continued)*
Slow Cooker Sloppy Joes, 162
Spicy Chicken Bundles, 183
Squirmy Wormy Sandwiches, 30
Taco Avocado Wraps, 189
Tarragon Crab Sandwiches, 186
Texas Toast Steak Sandwiches, 62
✓Toasted PB & Banana Sandwiches, 180
Turkey Brats with Slaw, 268
Turkey Salad Sandwiches, 184
Zippy Calzones, 67

SAUSAGE *(also see Pepperoni & Salami)*
Appetizers
Italian Egg Rolls, 276
Sausage-Stuffed Mushrooms, 86
Super Nacho Appetizer, 282
Breakfast & Brunch
Andouille Egg Burritos, 176
Breakfast Eggs in Foil Bowls, 27
Hearty Breakfast Egg Bake, 234
Pork Sausage Patties, 47
Weekend Breakfast Bake, 173
Main Dishes
Chicken & Kielbasa with Curried Rice, 125
Family-Pleasing Pizza, 16
Fettuccine with Sausage and Leeks, 82
Jiffy Jambalaya, 121
Kielbasa Bow Tie Skillet, 45
Meaty Corn Bread Casserole, 246
Pesto Sausage Pizza Makeover, 291
Potato Kielbasa Skillet, 127
Sausage & Beans with Rice, 247
Summer Sausage Hobo Packets, 26
Sweet Potato Sausage Casserole, 241
Upside-Down Pizza Bake, 72
Sandwiches
Hearty Sausage Stromboli, 183
Italian Muffuletta, 28
Soup
Sausage and Bean Soup, 187

SEAFOOD *(also see Fish)*
Appetizers
Crab Cheese Fondue, 267
✓Crab Crescents, 91
✓Sage Shrimp Skewers, 306
✓Shrimp Appetizers with Seafood Sauce, 281
✓Shrimp Canapes, 93
Spicy Crab Dip, 283
Main Dishes
Artichoke Shrimp Bake, 251
✓Cajun Shrimp and Rice, 105
Creamy Shrimp 'n' Spaghetti, 194
Jiffy Jambalaya, 121
Lemon Shrimp with Parmesan Rice, 205
Scallops with Thai Sauce, 194
Seafood Alfredo Baskets, 23
Simple Shrimp Scampi, 102
Sweet-and-Sour Scallops, 18
Tomato-Basil Shrimp Skewers, 304
Salads
✓Refreshing Shrimp Salad, 119
Seafood Pasta Salad, 137
Sandwiches
Tarragon Crab Sandwiches, 186
Soups
✓Low-Fat Clam Chowder, 255
Tomato Seafood Soup, 181

SIDE DISHES
Pasta
Angel Hair with Walnuts, 133
Curried Apricot Couscous, 55
✓Garden Primavera Fettuccine, 137
Mushroom Feta Pasta, 59
Orzo with Parmesan & Basil, 56
Skillet Mac & Cheese, 89
✓Tangy Pasta 'n' Peas, 134
Rice
Almond Rice, 18
✓Lemon Rice, 49
Mixed Herb Rice, 133
Walnut Rice, 61
Vegetables
Bacon-Almond Green Beans, 138
Bacon-Cheddar Stuffed Potatoes, 294
Brie Mashed Potatoes, 25
✓Broccoli Side Dish, 114
Broccoli with Smoked Almonds, 46
Buttery-Onion Corn on the Cob, 89
Calico Corn Cakes, 135
Carrot Coins with Thyme, 51
✓Carrots and Snow Peas, 257
Cheesy Hash Browns, 313
✓Citrus Green Beans, 121
✓Confetti Corn, 48
Confetti Mashed Potatoes, 136
Corn on the Cob with Lemon-Pepper Butter, 94
Crouton-Topped Broccoli, 107
Crumb-Topped Brussels Sprouts, 64
Dijon Scalloped Potatoes, 134
✓Dilled Mashed Potatoes, 84
✓Dilly Grilled Veggies, 140
Dutch Potatoes, 314
Elegant Broccoli, 54
Garlic New Potatoes, 14
Green Beans in Beer Sauce, 130
Grilled Sweet Onions, 132
Herbed Green Beans, 67
✓Honey-Pineapple Sweet Potatoes, 145
In-a-Flash Beans, 12
✓Lemon-Pepper Green Beans, 23

✓Recipe includes Nutrition Facts and Diabetic Exchanges

Loaded Waffle Fries, 50
✓Mango-Chutney Baby Carrots, 66
Mashed Potatoes Supreme, 132
Mashed Potatoes with a Kick, 144
✓Microwave Acorn Squash, 85
✓Minty Sugar Snap Peas, 107
✓Orange-Glazed Beets, 145
✓Pimiento Brussels Sprouts, 130
Potato Wedges, 73
Potatoes, Peas & Pearl Onions, 63
✓Roasted Asparagus, 8
✓Roasted Potatoes and Peppers, 83
Smashed Potatoes, 8
Stir-Fried Asparagus, 52
Zucchini Parmesan, 142
✓Zucchini Saute, 258

SLOW COOKER RECIPES

Appetizers

Sweet 'n' Tangy Chicken Wings, 165

Main Dishes

Brisket 'n' Bean Burritos, 164
Burgundy Beef, 160
Chicken Merlot with Mushrooms, 166
✓Chunky Pasta Sauce, 161
Cider-Glazed Ham, 159
Country Pork Chop Supper, 167
Creamy Tarragon Chicken, 110
Glazed Corned Beef Dinner, 162
Greek Chicken Dinner, 163
Hawaiian Pork Roast, 163
Hearty Short Ribs, 164
Italian Chicken, 158
Lemon Chicken, 160
Mushroom 'n' Steak Stroganoff, 167
✓Pepper Jack Chicken, 158
✓Pork Roast with Twist of Orange, 165
Pork Spareribs, 165
Slow-Cooked Ribs, 89
Slow Cooker Beef Brisket, 167
Slow Cooker Chuck Roast, 159
Slow Cooker Pork Chops, 166
Smothered Round Steak, 166

Sandwiches

✓Pulled Pork Sandwiches, 162
Slow Cooker Sloppy Joes, 162

Soups

✓Beef and Three-Bean Chili, 161
Vegetable Lentil Soup, 163
Veggie Meatball Soup, 159

SOUPS

✓Beef and Three-Bean Chili, 161
✓Broccoli Cheese Soup, 261
Chicken Wild Rice Chowder, 111
Chili-Filled Coffin, 35
Chunky Chicken Soup, 126
Creamy Potato Soup, 90
Creamy Turkey Vegetable Soup, 186
Farmhouse Ham Chowder, 188
Garlic Tomato Soup, 314
Golden Potato Soup, 295
Hearty Minestrone, 231
Herbed Tomato Soup, 185
Hot Dog Bean Soup, 101
✓Low-Fat Clam Chowder, 255
Mushroom Corn Chowder, 180
Sausage and Bean Soup, 187
✓Spinach Tortellini Soup, 261
✓Terrific Turkey Chili, 256
Tomato Seafood Soup, 181
Tortilla-Vegetable Chicken Soup, 309
Vegetable Lentil Soup, 163
Veggie Meatball Soup, 159
Wedding Soup, 184
✓White Chili, 104

SPINACH

Bacon Spinach Muffins, 155
Bacon Spinach Strata, 235
Chicken Spinach Manicotti, 249
✓Citrus Spinach Salad, 260
Creamy Spinach Chicken Dinner, 123
Italian Spinach Salad, 131
Meatless Spinach Lasagna, 250
Mushroom Spinach Salad, 28
✓Raspberry-Turkey Spinach Salad, 141
Spinach Artichoke-Stuffed Mushrooms, 274
✓Spinach Pasta Salad, 92
Spinach Pizza, 88
✓Spinach Tortellini Soup, 261
Tangy Spinach Salad, 16
Wedding Soup, 184
✓Zesty Spinach Salad, 115

SQUASH *(see Zucchini & Squash)*

STOVETOP ENTREES

Beef & Ground Beef

Beef Fettuccine Dinner, 197
Beef Fried Rice, 118
✓Beefy Tomato Rice Skillet, 261
Burritos Made Easy, 193
✓Chili Rice Dinner, 260
✓Greek-Style Supper, 44
Hearty Penne Beef, 124
Mushroom Steak 'n' Linguine, 114
Pita Fajitas, 206
Ravioli Skillet, 111
Sloppy Joe Hash Browns, 126
Swiss Corned Beef Hash, 311
Taco Macaroni, 75
✓Two-Meat Spaghetti Sauce, 65

Chicken

Artichoke Chicken Fettuccine, 206
Breaded Chicken Tenders with Noodles, 78
Chicken & Kielbasa with Curried Rice, 125
Chicken-Bow Tie Primavera, 202

✓Recipe includes Nutrition Facts and Diabetic Exchanges

STOVETOP ENTREES
Chicken *(continued)*
Chicken Lo Mein, 287
Chicken Marsala with Pasta, 197
Chicken over Curly Noodles, 114
Chicken Pasta Toss, 51
Chicken Pesto Pasta, 68
Creamy Spinach Chicken Dinner, 123
Curry Chicken, 199
Dijon Crumb Chicken, 66
✓Garlic Pineapple Chicken, 257
✓Garlic Ranch Chicken, 124
✓Lemon Teriyaki Chicken, 46
Mandarin Chicken Stir-Fry, 288
✓Maple-Glazed Chicken, 52
Mexican Chicken Penne, 200
Monterey Barbecued Chicken, 12
Mozzarella Chicken with Veggies, 200
Peachy Barbecue Chicken, 236
✓Pear Chutney Chicken, 260
Ramen Chicken 'n' Vegetables, 204
Saucy Mushroom Chicken, 310
Southwest Smothered Chicken, 192
Spicy Bronzed Chicken, 57
Zippy Paprika Chicken, 8
Fish & Seafood
✓Cajun Shrimp and Rice, 105
Creamy Shrimp 'n' Spaghetti, 194
Jiffy Jambalaya, 121
Lemon Shrimp with Parmesan Rice, 205
✓Orange Roughy with Rice, 113
Orange Salmon with Rice, 97
Salmon with Curry Chutney Sauce, 48
Scallops with Thai Sauce, 194
Seafood Alfredo Baskets, 23
Simple Shrimp Scampi, 102
Sweet-and-Sour Scallops, 18
Tilapia Wraps, 201
Tuna Veggie Macaroni, 203
Meatless
Broccoli Cheese Tortellini, 204
Herbed Artichoke Cheese Tortellini, 192
Soft Vegetable Tacos, 207
Pork, Ham & Sausage
Apple-Spiced Pork, 196
Broccoli Pork Stir-Fry, 315
Cherry-Stuffed Pork Chops, 290
Chicken & Kielbasa with Curried Rice, 125
Cranberry-Pineapple Pork Chops, 61
Cranberry Pork Chops with Rice, 37
Creole Pork Chops, 198
Fettuccine with Sausage and Leeks, 82
Fruit-Topped Pork Chops and Rice, 202
Ham 'n' Cheese Pasta, 117
Ham Fettuccine, 204
Jiffy Jambalaya, 121
Kielbasa Bow Tie Skillet, 45
Nutty Pork Fried Rice, 287
Parmesan Pork Chops, 54
Pizza Pork Chops, 56
✓Pork Chops with Onion Gravy, 49
Pork Chops with Sour Cream Sauce, 206
Pork Medallions with Garlic-Strawberry Sauce, 120
Potato Kielbasa Skillet, 127
Saucy Pork Chops, 200
Smoked Sausage with Penne and Veggies, 311
✓Sweet 'n' Sour Pork Chops, 259
Turkey
Sausage Pierogi Skillet, 198
Turkey Stir-Fry, 288
Turkey Sweet Potato Supper, 64

STRAWBERRIES
✓Berry Gelatin Mold, 139
Berry Rhubarb Fool, 92
✓Berry Yogurt Cups, 78
Chocolate Berry Freeze, 226
Chocolate Chip Strawberry Shortcakes, 211
Pork Medallions with Garlic-Strawberry Sauce, 120
✓Strawberry Bruschetta, 176
Strawberry Pound Cake Dessert, 12
✓Strawberry Salsa, 29
Strawberry Sundae Sauce, 223
Strawberry Trifle, 214
Strawberry Valentine Cookies, 22

SWEET POTATOES
✓Honey-Pineapple Sweet Potatoes, 145
Sweet Potato Sausage Casserole, 241
Turkey Sweet Potato Supper, 64

TOMATOES
Avocado Tomato Salad, 57
✓Beefy Tomato Rice Skillet, 261
✓Chunky Herbed Pizza Dip, 274
Garlic Tomato Soup, 314
Herbed Tomato Soup, 185
Penne Chicken with Sun-Dried Tomatoes, 248
✓Pesto Bruschetta, 94
✓Savory Bean & Tomato Salad, 140
Tomato-Basil Shrimp Skewers, 304
Tomato Cheese Pizza, 201
Tomato Cucumber Salad, 95
Tomato Seafood Soup, 181
Tuna-Stuffed Tomatoes, 193

TURKEY
Main Dishes
Club-Style Turkey Enchiladas, 36
Crescent Turkey Casserole, 36

✓Recipe includes Nutrition Facts and Diabetic Exchanges

Lemon-Herb Roasted Turkey, 298
Sausage Pierogi Skillet, 198
Turkey Cabbage Bake, 247
Turkey Stir-Fry, 288
Turkey Sweet Potato Supper, 64

Salads
✓Raspberry-Turkey Spinach Salad, 141
Turkey Salad with Blueberry Vinaigrette, 136

Sandwiches
Italian Muffuletta, 28
Meat 'n' Veggie Pockets, 103
Mini Subs, 73
Turkey Brats with Slaw, 268
Turkey Salad Sandwiches, 184

Soups
Creamy Turkey Vegetable Soup, 186
✓Terrific Turkey Chili, 256
Wedding Soup, 184

VEGETABLES *(also see specific kinds)*
Chicken-Bow Tie Primavera, 202
Creamy Turkey Vegetable Soup, 186
✓Dilly Grilled Veggies, 140
✓Fresh Vegetable Salad, 255
✓Garden Primavera Fettuccine, 137
Garden Vegetable Soup, 237
Meat 'n' Veggie Pockets, 103
Mozzarella Chicken with Veggies, 200
Picnic Vegetable Salad, 141
Ramen Chicken 'n' Vegetables, 204
Smoked Sausage with Penne and Veggies, 311
Soft Vegetable Tacos, 207
Tortilla-Vegetable Chicken Soup, 309
✓Tuna Veggie Kabobs, 254
Tuna Veggie Macaroni, 203
✓Vegetable Fish Dinner, 193
Vegetable Lentil Soup, 163
Vegetable Macaroni Salad, 69
Veggie Ham Crescent Wreath, 277
✓Veggie Lasagna, 236
Veggie Meatball Soup, 159

ZUCCHINI & SQUASH
Beef-Stuffed Zucchini, 120
✓Microwave Acorn Squash, 85
✓Squash Corn Bread, 233
Zucchini Crescent Pie, 241
Zucchini Parmesan, 142
✓Zucchini Saute, 258

✓Recipe includes Nutrition Facts and Diabetic Exchanges

Alphabetical Index

This handy index lists every recipe in alphabetical order, so you can easily find your favorite recipes.

A

Alfredo Chicken Lasagna, 314
✓Almond-Avocado Tossed Salad, 269
Almond-Crusted Salmon, 196
Almond Rice, 18
Amaretto Peach Oatmeal, 174
Andouille Egg Burritos, 176
✓Angel Food Cake with Fruit, 258
Angel Hair with Walnuts, 133
Antipasto Salad with Basil Dressing, 133
Anytime Cucumber Salad, 58
✓Apple Blueberry Crisp, 214
Apple Bread Pudding, 225
✓Apple Butter Mix, 171
✓Apple Cherry Punch, 171
✓Apple Cherry Salad, 82
✓Apple Salad, 101
Apple Spice Waffles, 47
Apple-Spiced Pork, 196
Apple Stuffing, 144
Apricot Bars, 215
✓Apricot Cheesecake Tarts, 221
Artichoke Chicken Fettuccine, 206
Artichoke Shrimp Bake, 251
✓Asparagus Ham Roll-Ups, 84
Avocado Chicken Pitas, 195
Avocado Tomato Salad, 57

B

Bacon-Almond Green Beans, 138
Bacon-Apple Cider Biscuits, 293
Bacon-Cheddar Stuffed Potatoes, 294
Bacon Cheeseburger Salad, 122
Bacon Chicken Roll-Ups, 88
Bacon Potato Salad, 230
Bacon Spinach Muffins, 155
Bacon Spinach Strata, 235
✓Bacon-Wrapped Appetizers, 97
Baked Apple French Toast, 174
Baked Beans with Ham, 106
Baked Ham Salad Sandwiches, 183
Baked Parmesan Roughy, 63
Barbecued Ham Sandwiches, 187
Barbecued Pork Chops, 194
Basil-Garlic Cheese Bread, 65
Bat Cupcakes, 32
✓Beef and Three-Bean Chili, 161
Beef Fettuccine Dinner, 197
Beef Fried Rice, 118
Beef Potato Bake, 237
Beef-Stuffed Crescents, 283
Beef-Stuffed Zucchini, 120
✓Beefy Tomato Rice Skillet, 261
Beer-Battered Potato Wedges, 266
Beer Cheese in a Bread Bowl, 279
Beer-Glazed Ham, 25
✓Berry Gelatin Mold, 139
Berry Rhubarb Fool, 92
✓Berry Yogurt Cups, 78
Best Barbecue Wings, 280
✓Bing Cherry Sherbet, 86
Black Bean Burritos, 199
✓Black Bean Pineapple Salad, 103
Black Cat Brownie, 32
Bloodshot Eyeballs, 33
Blue Cheese Pear Salad, 107
Blueberry Peach Fool, 227
Blueberry-Poppy Seed Brunch Cake, 172
Bow Tie Ham Bake, 232
Breaded Chicken Tenders with Noodles, 78
Breakfast Eggs in Foil Bowls, 27
Breakfast Pizza, 172
Brie Mashed Potatoes, 25
Brisket 'n' Bean Burritos, 164
✓Broccoli Cheese Soup, 261
Broccoli Cheese Tortellini, 204
Broccoli Pork Stir-Fry, 315
✓Broccoli Side Dish, 114
Broccoli with Smoked Almonds, 46
Broiled Pork Chops with Mango Sauce, 196
Brunch Egg Burritos, 170
✓Buckeye Bars, 96
Burgundy Beef, 160
Burritos Made Easy, 193
Buttery-Onion Corn on the Cob, 89

C

✓Cajun Shrimp and Rice, 105
✓Cake with Pineapple Pudding, 16
Calico Corn Cakes, 135
Calypso Coleslaw, 104
Canadian Bacon-Stuffed Mushrooms, 282
Caramel Apple Snack Mix, 277
✓Caramel Cashew Chewies, 74
Caraway Beer Bread, 149
Carrot Coins with Thyme, 51
Carrot Tortellini Salad, 138
✓Carrots and Snow Peas, 257
Cashew Chicken Salad Sandwiches, 189
Chai Tea Latte, 177
Change-of-Pace Burgers, 50
Cheese and Chicken Enchiladas, 60
✓Cheese-Stuffed Jalapenos, 296
Cheesy Hash Browns, 313
Cherry-Stuffed Pork Chops, 290
Chicken Alfredo Pizza, 243
Chicken Alfredo Sandwiches, 188
Chicken & Kielbasa with Curried Rice, 125
Chicken-Bow Tie Primavera, 202
Chicken Caesar Salad, 143
Chicken Lasagna, 247
Chicken Lo Mein, 287
Chicken Marsala with Pasta, 197
Chicken Merlot with Mushrooms, 166

✓Recipe includes Nutrition Facts and Diabetic Exchanges

Chicken over Curly Noodles, 114
Chicken Pasta Toss, 51
Chicken Penne Casserole, 242
Chicken Pesto Pasta, 68
Chicken Pesto Wraps, 182
Chicken Potpies, 232
Chicken Spinach Manicotti, 249
Chicken Taco Quiche, 230
Chicken Tater Bake, 233
Chicken Tortilla Bake, 115
Chicken Wild Rice Chowder, 111
Chili-Filled Coffin, 35
✓Chili Rice Dinner, 260
Chili Seasoning Mix, 38
Chili Snack Mix, 279
Chipotle Chicken Fajitas, 304
✓Chipotle Pork Tenderloins, 306
Chocolate Banana Smoothies, 50
Chocolate Berry Freeze, 226
Chocolate Cake with Coconut Sauce, 10
Chocolate Cherry Cheesecake, 219
Chocolate Chip Cookie Delight, 268
Chocolate Chip Strawberry Shortcakes, 211
✓Chocolate-Dipped Cranberry Cookies, 40
Chocolate-Filled Crescents, 222
✓Chocolate-Mallow Peanut Candy, 223
Chocolate Peanut Butter Cake, 216
✓Chocolate-Peanut Butter Cookies, 85
Chocolate Reindeer Cookies, 40
Chocolate Silk Pie, 210
Chocolate Wafer Ice Cream, 90
✓Christmas Mice Cookies, 38
Chunky Chicken Soup, 126
✓Chunky Herbed Pizza Dip, 274
✓Chunky Pasta Sauce, 161
Cider-Glazed Ham, 159
Cinnamon Apple Wraps, 312
✓Cinnamon Orange Cider, 270
Cinnamon Pumpkin Pie, 219
Cinnamon Raisin Bread, 153
Cinnamon Raisin Coffee Cake, 149
✓Citrus Green Beans, 121
Citrus Raspberry Shortcakes, 223
✓Citrus Spinach Salad, 260
Club-Style Turkey Enchiladas, 36
Cobb Salad Sandwiches, 118
✓Coconut Brownies, 96
Coconut Pistachio Pie, 212
Coffee Ice Cream Pie, 220
Colorful Bacon & Egg Bake, 176
Colorful Chicken Pizza, 53
Company Swordfish, 248
✓Confetti Corn, 48
Confetti Corn Salad, 60
Confetti Mashed Potatoes, 136
✓Cookie Pops, 78
Corn on the Cob with Lemon-Pepper Butter, 94
Country Fried Chicken, 310
Country Pork Chop Supper, 167
Crab Cheese Fondue, 267
✓Crab Crescents, 91
Cranberry Banana Bread, 152
✓Cranberry Chili Meatballs, 37
Cranberry Pear Cobblers, 315
Cranberry-Pineapple Pork Chops, 61
Cranberry Pork Chops with Rice, 37
Creamy Potato Soup, 90
Creamy Pumpkin-Filled Biscuits, 148
Creamy Shrimp 'n' Spaghetti, 194
Creamy Spinach Chicken Dinner, 123
Creamy Tarragon Chicken, 110
Creamy Turkey Vegetable Soup, 186
✓Creole Baked Tilapia, 255
Creole Pork Chops, 198
Crescent Apple Dessert, 222
Crescent Turkey Casserole, 36
✓Crisp Lemon Tea Cookies, 41
Crouton-Topped Broccoli, 107
Crumb-Coated Ranch Chicken, 83
Crumb-Topped Brussels Sprouts, 64
Crunchy Monster Claws, 35
Curried Apricot Couscous, 55
Curry Chicken, 199

D

Deep-Dish Apple Pie, 224
Delightful Deviled Eggs, 274
Dijon-Bacon Dip for Pretzels, 264
Dijon Crumb Chicken, 66
Dijon Scalloped Potatoes, 134
✓Dilled Mashed Potatoes, 84
✓Dilly Grilled Veggies, 140
Dream Clouds, 18
Dutch Potatoes, 314

E

Easy Cherry Strudels, 226
Easy Chicken Melts, 185
✓Easy Turkey Gravy, 298
Elegant Broccoli, 54
Enchilada Chicken Pizza, 250

F

Family-Pleasing Pizza, 16
Farmhouse Ham Chowder, 188
Festive Feta Cheese Ball, 280
Feta Salmon Salad, 139
Fettuccine with Sausage and Leeks, 82
Fiesta Cream Cheese Spread, 279
Fish Sandwich Loaf, 112
Flank Steak Sandwiches, 189
Fluffy Apple Dip, 75
Fluffy Chocolate Pie, 24
✓Fluffy Lemon Pie, 257
✓Fresh Blackberry Cobbler, 220
Fresh Broccoli Salad, 62
✓Fresh Fruit Salsa, 275
✓Fresh Herb Flat Bread, 153
✓Fresh Vegetable Salad, 255
Frosty Mallow Fruit Dessert, 221
Frozen Banana Split Pie, 227
Frozen Raspberry Cheesecake, 210
✓Fruit Juice Pops, 79
Fruit Pizza, 218
Fruit-Topped Pork Chops and Rice, 202
Fruity Coleslaw, 117

✓Recipe includes Nutrition Facts and Diabetic Exchanges

G

✓Garbanzo Salad, 258
✓Garden Primavera Fettuccine, 137
Garden Vegetable Soup, 237
Garlic-Cheese Crescent Rolls, 151
Garlic New Potatoes, 14
✓Garlic Pineapple Chicken, 257
✓Garlic Pumpkin Seeds, 271
✓Garlic Ranch Chicken, 124
Garlic-Roasted Chicken and Potatoes, 244
Garlic-Sesame Pita Chips, 44
Garlic Tomato Soup, 314
✓Gelatin Parfaits, 271
Ghostly Graveyard, 34
Ghoul Punch, 33
✓Gingered Green Bean Salad, 259
Glazed Corned Beef Dinner, 162
Golden Chicken Nuggets, 77
Golden Chicken with Rice, 89
Golden Potato Soup, 295
Greek Chicken Dinner, 163
Greek Lemon Chicken, 97
✓Greek-Style Supper, 44
Greek Tossed Salad, 138
✓Green Bean Ham Quiche, 174
Green Beans in Beer Sauce, 130
✓Grilled Asian Flank Steak, 235
Grilled Bacon Burgers, 181
Grilled Beef Fajitas, 115
Grilled Caesar Salad, 27
✓Grilled Pork Chops with Cilantro Salsa, 305
✓Grilled Pork Tenderloin, 95
Grilled Sirloin Steaks, 117
Grilled Steak Tossed Salad, 135
Grilled Sweet Onions, 132
Ground Beef Noodle Bake, 251
Ground Beef Spiral Bake, 230
Gruesome Green Toes, 31
Guacamole Burgers, 69

H

Ham & Cheese Casseroles, 233
Ham and Cheese Loaf, 185
Ham 'n' Cheese Pasta, 117
Ham Fettuccine, 204
Ham Ravioli Bake, 244
Hawaiian Pork Roast, 163
Hawaiian Turtle Cups, 91
Hearty Breakfast Egg Bake, 234
Hearty Chicken Pesto Pizzas, 203
Hearty Minestrone, 231
Hearty Open-Faced Sandwiches, 180
Hearty Penne Beef, 124
Hearty Sausage Stromboli, 183
Hearty Short Ribs, 164
Hearty Tortellini Salad, 269
Herbed Artichoke Cheese Tortellini, 192
Herbed Green Beans, 67
Herbed Tomato Soup, 185
✓Homemade Fudge Pops, 73
✓Honey-Pineapple Sweet Potatoes, 145
Hot Chicken Salad, 142
Hot Dog Bean Soup, 101
Hot Dog Spaghetti Rings, 90
Hot Tuna Sandwiches, 123

I

Iced Raisin Biscuits, 292
In-a-Flash Beans, 12
Italian Chicken, 158
Italian Egg Rolls, 276
Italian Muffuletta, 28
Italian Patty Melts, 127
Italian Side Salad, 112
Italian Spinach Salad, 131

J

Jack-o'-Lantern Sloppy Joe Pie, 34
✓Jalapeno Wontons, 265
Jiffy Jambalaya, 121

K

Kielbasa Bow Tie Skillet, 45

L

Layered Italian Chicken Salad, 141
Layered Southwestern Chicken Salad, 144
Lemon Butter Salmon, 55
Lemon Chicken, 160
Lemon Chicken with Rice, 116
✓Lemon Fruit Dip, 100
✓Lemon Fudge, 93
Lemon-Herb Roasted Turkey, 298
Lemon Parsley Swordfish, 59
✓Lemon-Pepper Green Beans, 23
✓Lemon Rice, 49
Lemon Shrimp with Parmesan Rice, 205
✓Lemon Teriyaki Chicken, 46
Lime Poppy Seed Shortcakes, 224
Loaded Waffle Fries, 50
✓Low-Fat Clam Chowder, 255

M

Mandarin Chicken Stir-Fry, 288
Mandarin Romaine Salad, 142
✓Mango-Chutney Baby Carrots, 66
✓Maple-Glazed Chicken, 52
Maple Mocha Pops, 75
Maple Oatmeal with Dried Fruit, 173
✓Maple Salad Dressing, 100
Marinated Beef Tenderloins, 58
✓Marinated Grilled Chicken, 306
Marvelous Shells 'n' Cheese, 242
Mashed Potatoes Supreme, 132
Mashed Potatoes with a Kick, 144
Mayonnaise Lovers' Chicken, 307
Meat 'n' Veggie Pockets, 103
✓Meatballs in Plum Sauce, 282
Meatless Spinach Lasagna, 250
Meaty Corn Bread Casserole, 246
Mediterranean Dip with Pita Chips, 276
Mexican Chicken Penne, 200
✓Mexican Salsa Pizza, 87
Mice Cupcakes, 79
✓Microwave Acorn Squash, 85
Mini Subs, 73
Mini Toffee Rolls, 149
Mint Sundae Brownie Squares, 213
Minty Cream Cheese Bars, 211
✓Minty Sugar Snap Peas, 107
Mixed Herb Rice, 133
Mom's Blue Cheese Dressing, 53

✓Recipe includes Nutrition Facts and Diabetic Exchanges

✓Mom's Meat Loaf, 313
Monterey Barbecued Chicken, 12
Mostaccioli Beef Casserole, 240
Mozzarella Chicken with Veggies, 200
Mozzarella Rye Snacks, 96
Mushroom 'n' Steak Stroganoff, 167
Mushroom Corn Chowder, 180
Mushroom Feta Pasta, 59
Mushroom Quiche Lorraine, 177
Mushroom Spinach Salad, 28
Mushroom Steak 'n' Linguine, 114
Mushroom Swiss Burgers, 186
Mustard Fried Catfish, 14

N

Nacho Cheese Beef Bake, 245
Nutmeg Syrup, 175
Nutty Cookies & Cream Dessert, 215
Nutty Pork Fried Rice, 287

O

✓Oatmeal Cranberry Cookie Mix, 39
Ogre Eyes Hot Cocoa, 30
Onion Cheese Biscuits, 151
✓Orange-Glazed Beets, 145
✓Orange Ice Cream Pops, 74
✓Orange Roughy with Rice, 113
Orange Salmon with Rice, 97
Oregano Roasting Chicken, 309
Orzo with Parmesan & Basil, 56
Overnight Raisin French Toast, 232

P

Parmesan-Coated Brie, 106
Parmesan Pork Chops, 54
Parmesan Walnut Muffins, 111
Party Time Mini Cheeseburgers, 270
Patio Pizza, 267
Peach Cobbler Coffee Cake, 154
✓Peaches with Lemon Cream, 226
Peachy Barbecue Chicken, 236
Peanut Butter Banana Oatmeal, 173
✓Peanut Butter Clusters, 79
✓Peanut Butter Jumbos, 77
Peanut Butter S'Mores, 26
✓Pear Chutney Chicken, 260
✓Pecan Chocolate Candies, 214
Pecan Pear Torte, 216
✓Pecan Shortbread Diamonds, 225
✓Pecan Toffee Fudge, 217
Penne Chicken with Sun-Dried Tomatoes, 248
✓Pepper Jack Chicken, 158
Pepper Lover's Pizza, 297
✓Peppermint Meltaways, 301
Peppermint Stick Sauce, 90
✓Pepperoncini Arugula Salad, 10
Pepperoni Pizza Twists, 278
✓Pesto Bruschetta, 94
✓Pesto Parmesan Bread, 150
Pesto Sausage Pizza Makeover, 291
Pesto Tortellini Salad, 94
Picnic Vegetable Salad, 141
✓Pimiento Brussels Sprouts, 130
✓Pine Nut Salad Dressing, 102
Pineapple Beef Kabobs, 305
Pineapple Shakes, 102
Pita Fajitas, 206
Pizza Fondue, 264
Pizza Loaf, 275
Pizza Noodle Bake, 74
Pizza Pork Chops, 56
✓Polka-Dot Macaroons, 24
Poppy Seed Citrus Cake, 218
Pork Chops with Apple Dressing, 205
✓Pork Chops with Onion Gravy, 49
Pork Chops with Sour Cream Sauce, 206
Pork Medallions with Garlic-Strawberry Sauce, 120
✓Pork Roast with Twist of Orange, 165
Pork Sausage Patties, 47
Pork Spareribs, 165
Pork Tenderloin Fajitas, 121
Portobello Roast Beef Hoagies, 10
Potato Kielbasa Skillet, 127
Potato Wedges, 73
Potatoes, Peas & Pearl Onions, 63
Potluck Ham and Pasta, 249
Pretty Pepper Salad, 296
Pretzel Cereal Crunch, 39
✓Pull-Apart Caramel Coffee Cake, 152
✓Pulled Pork Sandwiches, 162
Pumpkin Oat Muffins, 150
Pumpkin Waffles with Orange Walnut Butter, 175

R

Rainbow Sherbet Dessert, 213
Raisin Sauce for Pound Cake, 45
Raisin Waldorf Salad, 312
Ramen Chicken 'n' Vegetables, 204
✓Raspberry-Turkey Spinach Salad, 141
Ravioli Skillet, 111
✓Refreshing Shrimp Salad, 119
Reuben Casserole, 243
Rhubarb Lemon Muffins, 155
✓Roasted Asparagus, 8
✓Roasted Potatoes and Peppers, 83
✓Roasted Red Pepper Hummus, 278
✓Rosy Rhubarb Punch, 173

S

✓Sage Shrimp Skewers, 306
Salami Asparagus Salad, 137
Salami Pasta Salad, 143
✓Salami Roll-Ups, 87
Salmon with Curry Chutney Sauce, 48
Saucy Chicken and Florets, 202
Saucy Mushroom Chicken, 310
Saucy Pork Chops, 200
Sausage and Bean Soup, 187
Sausage & Beans with Rice, 247
Sausage Pierogi Skillet, 198
Sausage-Stuffed Mushrooms, 86
✓Savory Bean & Tomato Salad, 140
Savory Parmesan Sticks, 68
Scallops with Thai Sauce, 194
Scooter Snacks, 72
Seafood Alfredo Baskets, 23
Seafood Pasta Salad, 137

✓Recipe includes Nutrition Facts and Diabetic Exchanges

Second-Chance Reubens, 308
✓Shrimp Appetizers with Seafood Sauce, 281
✓Shrimp Canapes, 93
✓Silver Dollar Oat Pancakes, 76
Simple Shrimp Scampi, 102
Skillet Mac & Cheese, 89
Sloppy Joe Hash Browns, 126
Sloppy Joe Nachos, 265
Slow-Cooked Ribs, 89
Slow Cooker Beef Brisket, 167
Slow Cooker Chuck Roast, 159
Slow Cooker Pork Chops, 166
Slow Cooker Sloppy Joes, 162
Smashed Potatoes, 8
✓Smoked Salmon Pinwheels, 266
Smoked Sausage with Penne and Veggies, 311
Smooth Chocolate Fondue, 103
Smothered Round Steak, 166
Sneaky Lasagna, 246
Soft Vegetable Tacos, 207
✓Sour Cream & Chive Biscuits, 155
South Dakota Meat Loaf Makeover, 291
Southwest Creamy Pasta Bake, 250
Southwest Smothered Chicken, 192
Soy Sauce Substitute, 288
Spaghetti Beef Casserole, 234
Spicy Bronzed Chicken, 57
Spicy Chicken Bundles, 183
Spicy Crab Dip, 283
Spicy Teriyaki Beef Salad, 131
Spinach Artichoke-Stuffed Mushrooms, 274
✓Spinach Pasta Salad, 92
Spinach Pizza, 88
✓Spinach Tortellini Soup, 261
✓Squash Corn Bread, 233
Squirmy Wormy Sandwiches, 30
✓Star Pastry Snacks, 29
✓Steak with Orange-Thyme Sauce, 195
Stir-Fried Asparagus, 52
Stovetop Beef Stew, 182
✓Strawberry Bruschetta, 176
Strawberry Pound Cake Dessert, 12
✓Strawberry Salsa, 29
Strawberry Sundae Sauce, 223
Strawberry Trifle, 214
Strawberry Valentine Cookies, 22
Stromboli Slices, 276
Stuffed Peppers for Four, 112
Summer Sausage Hobo Packets, 26
Super Nacho Appetizer, 282
Surprise Monkey Bread, 148
Surprise Spice Cake, 82
Sweet & Savory Breadsticks, 120
Sweet 'n' Sour Coleslaw, 14
✓Sweet 'n' Sour Pork Chops, 259
Sweet-and-Sour Scallops, 18
Sweet 'n' Spicy Country Ribs, 234
Sweet 'n' Tangy Chicken Wings, 165
Sweet Potato Sausage Casserole, 241
Sweetened Whipped Cream, 220
Swirled Sherbet Dessert, 217
Swiss Corned Beef Hash, 311
Szechwan Chicken Wings, 280

T

Taco Avocado Wraps, 189
Taco Dip, 281
Taco Macaroni, 75
Taco Salad, 134
Taco Salad Waffles, 76
Tangy Asparagus Potato Salad, 294
✓Tangy Pasta 'n' Peas, 134
Tangy Spinach Salad, 16
Tarragon Crab Sandwiches, 186
Tasty Mozzarella Chicken, 240
✓Teriyaki Beef Tenderloin, 256
✓Terrific Turkey Chili, 256
Texas Toast Steak Sandwiches, 62
Three-Cheese Garlic Bread, 46
Three-Cheese Lasagna, 231
✓Thumbprint Cookies, 41
Tilapia Wraps, 201
✓Toasted PB & Banana Sandwiches, 180
Tomato-Basil Shrimp Skewers, 304
Tomato Cheese Pizza, 201
Tomato Cucumber Salad, 95
Tomato Seafood Soup, 181
Tortilla Lasagna, 245
Tortilla-Vegetable Chicken Soup, 309
✓Tropical Fruit Smoothies, 104
Tuna Crescent Ring, 207
Tuna-Stuffed Tomatoes, 193
✓Tuna Veggie Kabobs, 254
Tuna Veggie Macaroni, 203
Turkey Brats with Slaw, 268
Turkey Cabbage Bake, 247
Turkey Salad Sandwiches, 184
Turkey Salad with Blueberry Vinaigrette, 136
Turkey Stir-Fry, 288
Turkey Sweet Potato Supper, 64
✓Two-Meat Spaghetti Sauce, 65

U

Upside-Down Pizza Bake, 72

V

Vanilla Cake with Raspberries, 118
Vanilla Chip Dessert, 22
✓Vegetable Fish Dinner, 193
Vegetable Lentil Soup, 163
Vegetable Macaroni Salad, 69
Veggie Ham Crescent Wreath, 277
✓Veggie Lasagna, 236
Veggie Meatball Soup, 159

W

Walnut Fruit Salad, 170
Walnut Rice, 61
Watermelon Bombe, 212
Wedding Soup, 184
Weekend Breakfast Bake, 173
✓White Chili, 104

Y

Yummy Mummy with Veggie Dip, 31

Z

✓Zesty Horseradish Meat Loaf, 308
✓Zesty Spinach Salad, 115
Zippy Calzones, 67
Zippy Paprika Chicken, 8
Zucchini Crescent Pie, 241
Zucchini Parmesan, 142
✓Zucchini Saute, 258

✓Recipe includes Nutrition Facts and Diabetic Exchanges